The Sacred Act of Reading

New World Studies

J. Michael Dash, Editor

Frank Moya Pons and
Sandra Pouchet Paquet,
Associate Editors

The Sacred Act of Reading

SPIRITUALITY, PERFORMANCE, AND
POWER IN AFRO-DIASPORIC LITERATURE

Anne Margaret Castro

University of Virginia Press
Charlottesville and London

University of Virginia Press
© 2020 by the Rector and Visitors of the University of Virginia
All rights reserved
Printed in the United States of America on acid-free paper

First published 2020

9 8 7 6 5 4 3 2 1

Names: Castro, Anne Margaret, author.
Title: The sacred act of reading : spirituality, performance, and power in Afro-diasporic literature / Anne Margaret Castro.
Description: Charlottesville : University of Virginia Press, 2020. | Series: New World studies | Includes bibliographical references and index.
Identifiers: LCCN 2019030175 (print) | LCCN 2019030176 (ebook) | ISBN 9780813943442 (hardcover) | ISBN 9780813943459 (paperback) | ISBN 9780813943466 (epub)
Subjects: LCSH: American literature—African American authors—History and criticism. | Literature—Black authors—History and criticism. | Literature and anthropology. | Spirituality in literature. | African diaspora.
Classification: LCC PS153.N5 C38 2020 (print) | LCC PS153.N5 (ebook) | DDC 810.9/896073—dc23
LC record available at https://lccn.loc.gov/2019030175
LC ebook record available at https://lccn.loc.gov/2019030176

Cover art: iStock.com/Galyna_P

for my mom, who taught me to love reading

Contents

Personal Prologue	ix
Acknowledgments	xi
Introduction	1
1. "You Preached!": Zora Neale Hurston's and Toni Morrison's Sermonic Performances	23
2. The Hermeneutics of Spirit Possession: Interpreting Mediums in *Changó, The Biggest Badass* and *Louisiana*	66
3. The Spiritual Life of Power: Zombies in *Myal* and *Brown Girl in the Ring*	102
4. Reading the Prophetic Stage: Imagining the Limits of the Possible in *Bedward* and *Dream on Monkey Mountain*	148
Epilogue: Interpretive Communities	191
Notes	201
Works Cited	227
Index	251

Personal Prologue

I HAVE COME to see my gravitation toward religion and spirituality in crafting this book as a playful nod to my own youthful desires to become a preacher as well as to my family history exemplified by my Mexican American grandfather's career as a Protestant missionary-minister in Colombia (where my father grew up). The intersections of race, gender, social power, literacy, and colonialism have always shaped my understandings of spirituality. In the construction of this manuscript, I have been given the opportunity to critically reflect on the truly *spiritual* life of power, along with the powerful life of spirituality.

This project's theoretical investments in the rhetorical and physical mechanisms of institutionalized power were born in the cognitive dissonance of my childhood. I am a white Latina woman who was raised in an affluent, white, and overwhelmingly Protestant suburb of Houston, Texas. Like other individuals growing up in an ethnically mixed household, I recognized at a relatively young age that ethnicity and race were sometimes socially illegible and sometimes contingent experiences of self that could inform social standing. I saw that to some degree, all of our defining categories of community and self were determined through shifting interpretations, and I realized that in a few cases these interpretations could be manipulated in an effort to secure a tenuous sense of social belonging. As an inquisitive, justice-oriented, and at times passionately religious child, I anxiously tried to understand and secure my place in the world by adopting whatever ideological lens seemed to be expected of me at that moment by the nearest authority figure. This was exhausting. Over time, I struggled to reconcile material examples of inequity (inherent in neoliberal capitalist societies such as mine) with the belief systems promoted at school and in church. Though I now realize how much hegemonic privilege I experience as a result of my racial coding and socioeconomic status, I grew up feeling like a poorly veiled nonsubject, a person never quite at home in any place or even in any ideological paradigm.

This internal conflict of belonging is likely why I have always been drawn to narratives of liminality, marginalization, and diasporic consciousness. For example, I was overwhelmed with excitement and gratitude when I first read Judith Butler's *Gender Trouble* as an undergraduate at the University of Texas at Austin. Butler's basic proposition—that (gendered) subjectivity and social structures are manifested through performances rife with contradictions and ideological negotiations—has become a foundational presumption for my current work, which, like Butler's philosophy, explores the interstices of belief and embodiment; unlike Butler, I do so through spiritual paradigms.

While this publication is deeply indebted to Euro-American philosophical discourse, its critical frameworks and hermeneutical methodologies are grounded in the spiritual knowledge systems presented within Afro-diasporic literature. On the one hand, my turn to Afro-diasporic religious content and methods was the result of a practical realization that an adequate analysis of these works required it. That being said, it quickly became obvious that in-depth critical engagement with Afro-diasporic spiritual philosophies and epistemologies could contribute to wider projects of decolonizing the modern academy. Since the US presidential campaign of 2016—itself but one of the many emboldening moments for the global far right—we have seen an increasing normalization of performative racism on the public stage. White supremacist and anti-immigrant groups march through US college campuses shouting "blood and soil" as nativist media and government outlets coordinate violent acts of discrimination. Material iterations of racist violence have always been the cause and effect of the sociopolitical mechanisms of racial hierarchies. As academics, we may ask ourselves: How can we think beyond the parameters of thought that have facilitated colonialism, domination, and our current political environment? I suggest that, among other things, we turn to Afro-diasporic authors' writings and theories. My greatest wish for *The Sacred Act of Reading* is that it will honor the voices of the Afro-diasporic writers, performers, practitioners, and artists represented throughout this volume.

Acknowledgments

THIS BOOK AND I have been supported by a great many people. What is more, this book is a testament to the generations of scholars who sought to create a place for respectful intellectual work on the Afro-diasporic Americas within the academy.

I must begin by thanking my supervisors and mentors at Vanderbilt University. Thanks to Vera Kutzinski's generosity of time and energy, I learned that English scholarship can be both rigorous and joyful when practiced in community. Thanks to Ifeoma Nwankwo's consideration and guidance, as well as to the Vanderbilt Drake Fellowship, I had the career-changing opportunity to conduct oral history interviews with Erna Brodber and Petal Samuel in Woodside, Jamaica. I can only hope that this book demonstrates a small amount of the respect, creativity, and rigor that Erna Brodber displays when writing about and working with her community. Thank you also to my dissertation committee members Hortense Spillers, Marzia Milazzo, and Victor Anderson, whose support and scholarly feedback helped to shape this work. I am deeply grateful for my friend and colleague Tatiana McInnis, whose critical insights and fellowship have transformed my understanding of academic endeavors. A veritable chorus of colleagues at Vanderbilt contributed to the development of my thoughts before and during this project including Kathleen DeGuzman, Stephanie Higgs, Lucy Mensah, Shelby Johnson, R. J. Boutelle, and Jennifer Bagneris. I would also like to express my appreciation for Gretchen Murphy at the University of Texas at Austin and Kathryn Schwarz and Katie Crawford at Vanderbilt University, scholars who always treated my work as valuable (even when I thought I had invented the concept of performative speech).

At Oxford, thanks go to the Andrew Mellon Fellowship, the University of Oxford's Faculty of Medieval and Modern Languages, and The Oxford

Research Centre in the Humanities (TORCH). This project blossomed at Oxford thanks to the kind and sagacious mentorship I received from Lloyd Pratt and María del Pilar Blanco. Special thanks to Elleke Boehmer, whose leadership at TORCH helped me to understand the vital work of decolonial movements within the academy. The collaborative and inquisitive spirit demonstrated by those in the Race and Resistance program and throughout the wider TORCH community encouraged me and my project to blossom. Particular thanks to Claire Savina, whose intellectual perspectives have added nuance and richness to my thinking. I am grateful for the many interdisciplinary conversations I enjoyed with my fellow researchers and friends in the Academic Writing Group. And my sincerest gratitude goes to Hanna Smyth and Jackie Thompson, whose kindness and patience have bettered my work and life.

Having moved to Miami following my postdoctoral fellowship in Oxford, I have been fortunate to join yet another thriving and collegial intellectual community at Florida International University. Thank you to my department chair Heather Russell and fellow faculty members. I am deeply appreciative of the support and help that I have received from so many people. I would like especially to thank Michael Grafals and Cayce Wicks for their friendship and wisdom. And particular thanks to my new colleague and confidante, Mark Kelley, whose generosity of spirit has blown me away.

Thank you to all of those at the University of Virginia Press, without whom this book would not exist. Thank you in particular to Eric Brandt for his enthusiastic and steady support throughout the revision and publishing process, Leslie Tingle for her smart and careful editing, and to the anonymous readers for their considerate and thorough feedback.

While writing and revising this book, I was lucky enough to have Rebecca Wilbanks as my transcontinental and translantic writing partner. Rebecca's kindness, intellect, and scholarly acumen have been invaluable to me. Most importantly, her friendship has been paramount and deeply felt.

Portions of chapter 3 were published in the *Journal of West Indian Literature* 23, no. 1/2 as "Sounding Out Spirit Thievery in Erna Brodber's *Myal*," and a highly truncated version of chapter 1 is currently being revised for resubmission to *Religion and Literature*. The lyrics of Bob Marley's "Redemption Song" are reprinted in chapter 4 thanks to Blue Mountain Music Limited.

There are so many others to thank for holding me up over the course of this project. Thank you to Casey Hurstell, with whom I learned how to imagine as a child and with whom I learned how to be caring and true as an adult. I am grateful for the wisdom, humor, and compassion of so many people, including Nina Barker, Jessi Zazu Wariner, Alexandra Axel, Jones Zimmerman, Christie Bates, Debbie Williams, Jaime Hatch, and Alejandra Rondón. I am regularly overwhelmed with the gratitude I feel for Annette Lancaster, who taught me the steps with gentleness and honesty. Thank you to Autumn Morgan Allen, who walks alongside me and whose friendship makes my life more wonderful.

And finally, I offer my heartful thanks to every person in my family. To the Castro and Vogt families: Elwood Wayne, Nancy, Vicente, Margaret, David, Nancy Margaret, David Jr., Katie, Alicia, and David "Trip," I love you all fiercely.

The Sacred Act of Reading

Introduction

> And my prayer
> is versed with
> what you call obscene language.
> God within is a poet.
> Goddess within is a poet with action.
> Is she a performer?
> Poetic license well employed.
> —Josefina Báez, *Comrade, Bliss Ain't Playing*

JOSEFINA BÁEZ'S PERFORMANCE text *Comrade, Bliss Ain't Playing* (first performed in 2008) invites its readers to actively participate in the reading process, often by both visually and sonically tracing the poem's bilingual wordplay, as "up-down-and center, some kind of Scrabble/is encountered." Originally written for a one-woman performance starring Báez, the work is described on the copyright page of the printed volume as "performance theatre text; performance poetry, non-denominational spiritual practice of urban devotee; Dominican artist inner diary" (the printed text's pages are unnumbered). Here, the author manipulates the cataloguing mechanisms of published texts to frame her work and, in extension, her authorial voice and thematic content in generic and modal multiplicity. Similarly, interpreting *Comrade, Bliss Ain't Playing* becomes an exercise in multiplicity for readers closely following the carefully choreographed rhythms and rhymes embedded within the text's "Dancing Syntax." Such stylistic maneuvers encourage readers to imagine themselves in the roles of narrator, performer, mediator, and audience member, all while engaging with this "Grammatically innocrrect/Holy world ... [and] Testimonal. Poetic Drama." Báez fosters a reading experience marked by dynamic positionality and circuitous linguistic drama. In doing so, her work inspires sustained reflection on the intricate practices of performance and interpretation that constitute the act of reading.

Comrade, Bliss Ain't Playing is only one example of the many Afro-diasporic literary works that blur generic boundaries between literature and performance while simultaneously calling into question conceptual boundaries between material and spiritual topics. The realms of literary creation and performance are never far from those of spirituality and physical action in this piece, where "God within is a poet,/Goddess within is a poet with action." In particular, Báez uses language about creative production and narratives about her own spirituality to reflect on the social, economic, and political power relations that shape and contour the contemporary world. Throughout the work the author/performer invokes a range of metaphysical rhetoric to discursively transform discussions of material topics such as racial representation, disaster capitalism, bodily functions, and climate change into meditations on the "divine," "Holy," "sacred," "cosmic," "Quantum," and "Supreme." Across the Americas, authors of the African diaspora like Báez draw on religious, spiritual, and otherwise supernatural motifs in order to establish spiritual explanations of earthly power structures.

The Sacred Act of Reading builds on two principal contentions introduced in my short reading of Josefina Báez's *Comrade, Bliss Ain't Playing*. The first proposes that authors of the African diaspora use literary depictions of spiritual phenomena as theoretical frameworks for understanding societal structures in the modern and contemporary Americas. The second contends that any sophisticated textual analysis of these theoretical frameworks requires a multisensory and embodiment-focused methodology of reading. I argue that a hermeneutical practice especially attuned to the performance-inflected principles of ritual and experiential knowledge is both a necessary resource for—and a natural consequence of—prolonged intellectual engagement with the sacred formulations of power embedded within this creative archive. To this end, *The Sacred Act of Reading* is guided by a constellation of central interpretive practices which I call "performative textual hermeneutics." In its broadest definition, performative textual hermeneutics uses issues of performance as a means of reading written texts. Moving across genres and modalities, performative textual hermeneutics not only reads embodied performances of spirituality within discursive texts but also studies these performance events as acts of textual discourse and meaning-making. This method of reading is inspired by key tenets in performance studies scholarship and the ritually oriented beliefs and practices of the Afro-diasporic religions portrayed throughout the primary materials.

Connected by this central interpretive practice, *The Sacred Act of Reading* is organized around comparative readings of select spiritual phenomena such as conversion and possession in Afro-diasporic literary works. Each chapter focuses on the communicative and interpretive acts that enable a text's characters and audience members to derive meaning from the depicted spiritual events. In turn, these comparative studies gesture beyond their source materials and present broader methodological and theoretical frameworks. I use these frameworks to analyze the myriad ways in which performances of meaning-making shape societal power relations across the Afro-diasporic Americas. I begin by studying rituals of collective authority within the preaching scenes of Zora Neale Hurston (*Sermon in the Valley,* 1931; "The Sermon," 1934; *Jonah's Gourd Vine,* 1934) and Toni Morrison (*Beloved,* 1987, audiobook, 2007). I then concentrate on individual rituals marked by agential action and capitulation within spiritual possession narratives by Manuel Zapata Olivella (*Changó, The Biggest Badass,* 1999) and Erna Brodber (*Louisiana,* 1997). Chapter 3 extends this study to examine nonagential occupations related to interpretation and performance in Brodber's *Myal* (1989) and Nalo Hopkinson's *Brown Girl in the Ring* (1998). The final chapter studies prophesy as a hermeneutic performance of resistance and potential domination in the works of Louis Marriott (*Bedward,* 1960, rev. 1984) and Derek Walcott (*Dream on Monkey Mountain,* 1967). Featuring prose, poetry, theater, and audiobooks dating from 1931 to 2010 and authors from the United States, St. Lucia, Jamaica, Colombia, and Canada, this book uses its performance-inflected analysis of spiritual tropes to conceive of an Afro-diasporic literary network in the New World that cuts across geography, time, and language.[1]

In each of the studied texts, religious and metaphysical motifs elucidate the ideological presumptions and material conditions that demarcate the restrictive parameters of Afro-diasporic existence in the New World. This is to say that the literature mediates subjects' social and political conditions through spiritual paradigms in both physical and abstract terms.[2] In the Americas, slavery and colonialism continue to mark the lived experiences of African-descended persons, though the mechanisms of abuse may appear more abstract to those less familiar with the physical processes and effects of anti-Black racism and other forms of institutionalized inequity. By adopting a hermeneutical practice focused on performance, *The Sacred Act of Reading* illuminates the embodied practices that physically actualize seemingly abstract systems of sociopolitical oppression. Furthermore, many of the African-descended and diasporic spiritual realms represented in these texts undermine and resist these same political projects. A key insight of this study is that many of these religious rituals and spiritual phenomena invoke philosophical and epistemological paradigms that are incompatible with the underpinning logics of hegemonic power in the Western Hemisphere. In this way, I contend that Afro-diasporic authors use spirituality to think within, against, and beyond existing relations of dominance, dependence, autonomy, and interdependence.

Because these Afro-diasporic texts are always working across disciplines and even epistemologies, so too does this monograph. In addition to theological and anthropological studies of the Afro-diasporic Americas, *The Sacred Act of Reading* considers a variety of twentieth- and twenty-first-century scholarly voices, including those of Édouard Glissant, Erna Brodber, Alessandra Benedicty-Kokken, Maurice Blanchot, Michel Foucault, and Zora Neale Hurston. These authors examine how individuals and groups navigate structural hierarchies from an array of theoretical viewpoints such as critical race studies, Marxism and post-Marxism, performance and dance studies, postcolonialism, comparative sociology, and linguistic deconstruction. Many of the Afro-diasporic creators studied here were well versed in the critical theories of philosophers and social scientists popular around the times of their literary publications. For example, Erna Brodber describes her fiction as an attempt to bring together the language and ideas of the academy with that of popular Jamaican culture ("Me and My Head-Hurting Fiction," 118), and Manuel Zapata Olivella's writing emerged from his schooling as an anthropologist and physician, as well as from a childhood steeped in both the Western philosophy of his father and the "African popular traditions" passed down by his mother (Jiménez). Through the use of Western and non-Western—namely, African-derived—epistemologies, the primary texts studied here question commonly held beliefs rooted in liberal, humanistic tenets such as individualism and freedom. As scholars including Toni Morrison, Alexander Weheliye, and Lisa Lowe have demonstrated, such concepts are indebted to the long-rehearsed denial of nonwhite subjects' humanity, and so ascribing value to these ideas without questioning their historical and contemporary connotations could mean playing the lexical games of white supremacy and colonialism.[3] In turning to the spiritually inspired epistemologies and philosophies in these literary works, we can discover methods for engaging in theoretical debate beyond the limiting parameters of post-Enlightenment philosophy.

Under the guiding assumption that each literary text offers a wealth of theoretical knowledge, *The Sacred Act of Reading* becomes an exegetical exercise, albeit an often confounding one. In the creative works studied throughout this book, disorientation abounds. Time and again the spiritual events described in this project challenge readers' previous understandings of reality, knowledge, and power, not to mention what it means to engage in the sacred act of reading.

Performative Textual Hermeneutics

Born out of a desire to properly attend to the complexities of signification within Afro-diasporic spiritual philosophies and epistemologies, *The Sacred Act of Reading* approaches literary interpretation by focusing on principles of performance and ritual. More specifically, I adopt a hermeneutical methodology that foregrounds issues such as embodied action, linguistic and experiential effectiveness, visual and sonic citation, and audience reception. The term hermeneutics refers to the study of textual interpretation—either specific practices of biblical exegesis or more general issues of literary interpretation. Hermeneutics is the study of how we read and derive meaning from written texts; in the words of Joseph Roach, "It means a way of interpreting interpretations" (353). The adjective "performative," on the other hand, "inflects what it modifies with performance-like qualities" (Schechner, 123). What might we learn by inflecting the process of textual interpretation with the qualities of a performance?[4] Because hermeneutics is most often associated with the interpretation of *texts,* and the term "performative" usually refers to the study of spoken utterances or similarly *nontextual* practices and traditions, my positing of a performative textual hermeneutics asks scholars to embrace and explore a paradoxical approach to reading. Inspired by the epistemological and communicative methods within Afro-diasporic spiritualities, performative textual hermeneutics brings theoretical quandaries from studies in performance, theater, religion, and anthropology to bear on the discipline of English literary criticism. This practice results in a mode of reading attuned to the performative elements that characterize the dynamic tradition of literary creativity of the Afro-diasporic Americas. These elements are various and range from material examples of ritual engagement to sociolinguistic debates about the "performative," or effective, capacities of spoken utterances and gestures.

Performative textual hermeneutics involves several critical moves, all of which incorporate an analytical focus on "performance" in regards to a text's genre, production history, stylistics, linguistic mechanisms, and content. For this study, I define "performances" as aesthetic, communicative acts that occur amongst participating bodies within culturally recognized frameworks of time, space, modality, and mediation. Performance realms explored in *The Sacred Act of Reading* include staged dramas, formal and informal religious rituals, literary recitations, oral folktales, masked carnival movements, and audio productions. Like research by early twentieth-century thinkers such as Hurston, Fernando Ortiz, and Melville Herskovitz, *The Sacred Act of Reading* recognizes the crucial influence of nontextual African religious traditions in Afro-diasporic art and culture in the English, French, and Spanish-speaking Americas.[5] Performative textual hermeneutics asks us not only to consider the performances and performed behaviors of characters or actors, but also to examine the embodied rituals of reading and listening themselves. This book therefore attends to the active, reflective processes—or acts—of textual creation, mediation, and interpretation. Moreover, reading via a performative textual hermeneutics means interpreting discursive renderings of abstract ideologies and belief systems through an action-oriented and material lens.

I use the terms "performance" and "performative" to refer to a constellation of events, effects, concepts, and processes operating in the realms of literary representation, discursive analysis, and—at times—material experience. While Diana Taylor prefers the term "performatic" to "performative" in light of the latter's indebtedness to the academically privileged realm of textual discourse, I employ the vocabulary of the "performative" for this very reason (6). Performative textual hermeneutics is an approach to reading written works with the understanding that knowledge is formulated and meaning is transferred both within and outside the world of the discursive text.[6] While this project is indebted to the insights of performance studies scholarship, it deviates from that field's efforts to substantially decenter the text in favor of performed activities, or in the rhetoric of Taylor, to decenter the "archive" in favor of the "repertoire" (16). As a result of African-derived rituals of orality and performance, along with the systematic destruction and denial of material resources for Afro-diasporic creators in the New World, the study of this literary tradition certainly calls for attention to both the archive and the repertoire.[7] By moving within and between the media and modalities of performance and literature, this book contributes to the interdisciplinary critical enterprises of scholars such as Alessandra Benedicty-Kokken, Guillermina

De Ferrari, Paget Henry, Tuire Valkeakari, Jeannine Murray-Román, and Gerard Aching.[8]

Linguistic and poststructuralist theories allow that to describe a concept (i.e., gender) as "performative" also implies that this concept may not be ontologically stable. Rather, the works of Judith Butler and Jacques Derrida argue that a performative concept comes into meaning (and an illusion of stability) through its capacity for repetition in everyday behaviors and discourse.[9] In every iteration/performance of that concept, there lurks a transformative potential. This construction of reality mirrors the simultaneously real and imaginary lives not only of spiritual phenomena in the literature studied here, but also of the dual existences of ontological categories that have long been used to restrict the agential capacities of Afro-diasporic subjects. What is more, the vexing word "performative" also encourages readers to consider how words themselves become actions, or how, in some cases, "the issuing of the utterance is the performing of an action" (Austin, 7). I use the term "performative" to describe my book's methodology as a direct nod to the philosophical questions regarding interpellation, agency, and sovereignty lurking beneath the surface of J. L. Austin's linguistic arguments, but even more so in order to capitalize on the term's inherent tensions between abstract thought, speech, and action. After all, spirituality always signals a confluence of metaphysical and physical actions.

In the Afro-diasporic works studied throughout this volume, processes of meaning-making develop through fluid collections of "acts," or performed actions. In the words of performance studies scholar Richard Schechner, "performances are actions" (1), and so a hermeneutical practice oriented toward performance is inherently oriented toward representational and physical actions. Furthermore, in the contexts of theater and religious ritual, to perform a particular role, be it a scripted character or an ecclesiastical position, means to corporeally *enact* the expected movements and utterances of that role. These actions both represent and create spiritual experiences and frameworks of thought. Therefore, religious paradigms are acted through some kind of bodily movement ranging from a slight manipulation of the mouth and vocal chords to complex bodily practices such as dance or a set of specialized gestures indicating an experience of spiritual rapture, possession, or both. This book begins by studying Zora Neale Hurston's pioneering methods for archiving such religious choreographies. In *The Sermon in the Valley,* "The Sermon," and *Jonah's Gourd Vine,* Hurston experiments with representing these embodied performance practices in poetry, ethnographic essays, novels, and plays. To interpret a written text like these by means of a performative textual hermeneutics means reading in a way that considers how the work imagines and actualizes forms of embodied action, even when it is not meant to be staged. The same chapter comparatively studies Toni Morrison's written and performed versions of *Beloved* to show how both authors negotiate the parameters of different genres and media in order to represent these codes of performance. *The Sacred Act of Reading* meditates on the methodologies of spiritual performance and the methodologies of reading and interpretation both depicted and invoked throughout this set of scribal novels, audiobooks, poems, and written plays.

The Sacred Act of Reading takes this focus on the actions of interpretation even further as it considers not only the movements of characters or performers (which can be imagined, material, or both) but also the communicative acts performed by each text's readers and listeners. The audience is integral to this project, for just as every performance needs a spectator to witness the event, every text needs a reader. In this way performative textual hermeneutics engages in what Andrew Parker and Eve Sedgwick articulate as an "interrogation of the space of reception" and "interpellation" (7). Antonio Benítez-Rojo adopts similarly performative rhetoric to describe the shifting relationships between audience and literature.

> One might think that literature is a solitary art as private and quiet as prayer. Not true. Literature is one of the most exhibitionistic expressions in the world. This is because it is a stream of texts and there are few things as exhibitionist as a text. It should be remembered that what a performer writes—the word *author* has justifiably fallen into disuse—is not a text, but something previous and qualitatively different: a pre-text. . . . [A] text is born when it is read by the Other: the reader. From this moment on text and reader connect with each other like a machine of reciprocal seductions.

The texts I study in this analysis not only seduce but insistently distance readers with confounding stories of spiritual knowledge that both implicate and yet alienate them. The text's audience becomes a ritual participant in the communicative performance by means of its own embodied acts of interpretation and yet is also routinely alienated from the meaning-making event, enacting a play on avant-garde dramaturge Bertolt Brecht's theater of alienation.[10] In each of these situations, the readers' recognitions of themselves as audience make this a particularly performative mode of interpreting literature. Marvin Carlson writes, "Performance implies not just doing or even re-doing, but a self-consciousness about doing and re-doing on part of both performers and spectators" (ix).

The Sacred Act of Reading shows how epistemological and hermeneutical acts such as those involved in reading, participating in spiritual ceremony, or watching a live drama are at once embodied, discursive, and potentially sacred. In light of this contention, chapters 1 and 2 study sensorial information as intellectual formation in religious ceremonies and spiritual mediation; chapter 3 explores sound and corporeal vulnerability in spirit possession; and chapters 3 and 4 question how temporality and citation structure narrative possibility in play scripts and oral folk rhymes. Scholars in critical dance studies such as Melissa Blanco Borelli, Thomas DeFrantz, and Susan Foster have emphasized the corporeality of performance, teaching us to see "the body as a rich discursive site" in and of itself (Blanco Borelli, 13). With this understanding, corporeality (whether represented in a text or live on the stage) may be understood as more than a simplistic symbol of larger cultural systems. Rather, bodies in motion are, as Borelli explains, a form of "intelligent materiality" (14). In the texts explored throughout this monograph, bodies act as agents of intellectual production and distribution, physical archives of collective memory, hermeneutical frameworks, sites of mediation with divine forces, and epistemological instruments. What is more, in Afro-diasporic theological systems such as Vodou, Kumina, and Myal, theology is itself a function of corporeal experience.[11] As a result, this project's interpretive investment in physical, sensorial, and experiential modes of knowledge creation and understanding serves to integrate the embodied epistemologies of Afro-diasporic religious practices into literary criticism.

A performative textual hermeneutics is a system of interpretation that takes seriously the physical, factual realities of metaphysical phenomena, from colonial indoctrination by way of spirit possession to ancestrally oriented performances that manifest collective decolonization. In advancing this hermeneutical practice, this project argues that literary scholarship can and should consistently engage with both Western- and African-derived cosmologies, philosophies, and epistemologies. The texts studied here repeatedly demonstrate how spiritual phenomena throw into relief the arbitrary nature of dominant, Enlightenment-based epistemologies.[12] By presenting metaphysical phenomena as factual reality, the authors in this book call into question the predominant Western scientific methodologies derivative of the Enlightenment's presumption that an objective, "transcendental verity" can be determined based on measurements of physical evidence.[13] By analyzing processes of communication and reception through a performative lens, we ultimately can see the ways in which the texts implicate their readers in the rituals of interpretation and render readers conscious of their participation in the creation of worlds that transcend the bounds of commonly assumed logic. These authors play on the divisions between art and reality, echoing centuries of debate surrounding the dangerous possibilities of performances that through manipulations of theatrical artifice potentially obscure objective truth. These texts, like theatrical productions, are "imagination made flesh," artistic events that illuminate the tangled relationships between the supposedly factual, physical world and the fantastical realms of metaphysical spirituality (Schechner, 124).

Religion and Spirituality in Literary Scholarship

In many ways *The Sacred Act of Reading*'s intertwined interests in methods of interpretation and spirituality harken back to the very origins of modern literary study in the West by way of hermeneutics. The term is said to have derived from the name of the Greek deity Hermes, who acted as a mediator between the gods and humans. In *Introduction to Philosophical Hermeneutics,* Jean Grondin cites Gerhard Ebeling, who distinguishes three senses of ancient philosophies of hermeneutics, or *hermeneuein* as "expression (utterance, speaking), explication (interpretation, explanation) and translation (acting as an interpreter)," all aspects of meaning-making explored throughout this monograph (4). Grondin explains that each of the senses of "hermeneuin" attempts to encapsulate "similar movements of spirit" through language, exemplified by Plato's discussions of "poets as 'hermeneuts of the divine'" (Grondin 21; Zimmerman 3). In literary studies Henry Louis Gates uses the mythological legacies of West African messenger-deity Yoruban Esu-Elegbara to metaphorically explain his deconstructive engagements with "multiplicity" and "open-endedness" in African American literature (Gates, *Signifying Monkey,* 21). Likewise, Heather Russell promotes the "divine linguist" Legba as a paradigmatic figure for her delineation of Afro-Caribbean narratology (Russell, 9).[14] While it is a fool's errand to construct simplistic narratives about hermeneutics in Western and African-derived intellectual thought—just as it would be for any such capacious and foundational philosophical endeavors—the sacred frameworks that underpin practices of textual interpretation and literary scholarship are difficult to deny.

The Sacred Act of Reading thus builds on interpretive traditions as old as scripture and as contentious as scriptural debates. This book implicitly and explicitly draws on theological precursors in its explorations of textual interpretation and understanding; however, it deviates from standard English scholarship in the United States and Europe by appropriately valuing texts and practices of Afro-diasporic spirituality with the same kind of literary attention usually bestowed upon biblical hermeneutics.[15] Because conventions of worship in African and Afro-diasporic communities have not been recognized historically as legitimate religious practices by Euro-American academic authorities, literary representations of the sacred that align with these metaphysical paradigms are often categorized strictly as "spirituality."[16] While *The Sacred Act of Reading* does focus on the spiritual nature of such representations, it does so with consideration of how these philosophies, rituals, and themes stem from established religions.[17]

Religion, like culture and politics, signifies a wide variety of practices, beliefs, and organizations aimed at the dispersal, consolidation, and maintenance of power. The diasporic religious traditions depicted in these texts include Vodou, Myal, Kumina, Rastafari, and forms of Protestant Christianity such as the Sanctified Church and Revival Zion.[18] Anthropologist Clifford Geertz's definition of religion resonates with the founding contentions of this project. Geertz writes that religion is "a system of symbols which acts to establish powerful, pervasive, and longlasting moods and motivations in men by formulating conceptions of a general order of existence and clothing these conceptions with such an aura of factuality that the moods and motivations seem uniquely realistic" (90).[19] This book delves into the ordering power structures and motivations underlining religious rhetoric, all while reading any spiritual occurrences with the "aura of factuality" appropriate for the world of the text. The intellectual regard that this book devotes to spiritual paradigms in literature of the Black Americas has been enabled by the literary criticism of a robust and growing community of scholars including Tuire Valkeakari, Paul Humphrey, Judylyn S. Ryan, James Coleman, Katherine Clay Bassard, Qiana Whitted, and Chanette Romero.[20] Like these scholars, I consider how Afro-diasporic authors turn to religious and spiritual discourse as a means of explaining and imagining futures outside of the ongoing legacies of racialized oppression and trauma in the Western Hemisphere.[21] *The Sacred Act of Reading* contributes to this kaleidoscopic body of scholarship by approaching Afro-diasporic religious texts with the contention that supernatural events like zombification, possession, and prophetic revelation should not be read as mere analogies for sociopolitical projects. What is more, this performative textual hermeneutics allows critics to consistently recognize and examine both the embodied materialities and discursive techniques that enable spiritual and secular forces to formulate conceptions of a general order of existence.

The denigration and criminalization of African and Afro-diasporic (including Christian) religious practices and the promotion of carefully curated Christian teachings in the New World have been pivotal mechanisms in colonial enterprises of enslavement and domination.[22] Early European writings on African and later African-derived religions operated politically to undermine African humanity and champion the multifaceted violence of white supremacy. Evangelism of "heathen" Africans was a common justification for both Protestant and Catholic European plantation systems. From the fifteenth century onwards, European colonists wielded interpretations of Christian scripture and praxis as weapons for subjugating African peoples, religions, and knowledge, usually promoting obedience to masters as obedience to God (Copeland, 50). Europeans similarly argued that the supposed inferiority of African indigenous religions demonstrated the mental deficiencies of African individuals (Olupona, xx). Disregard for African and African-derived spiritual philosophies served to institutionalize racist ideologies and rationalize the dehumanizing practices of enslaved labor.[23] At the same time, planters across the Americas expressed concern that the enslaved population's participation in Christian rites such as baptism, along with their exposure to certain biblical narratives detailing liberation and spiritual equity, might foment manumission or collective uprisings. This fear was not without reason, considering the crucial role of Christian scripture in the rhetoric of David Walker, Frederick Douglass, Henry "Box" Brown, Jarena Lee, and Gabriel Prosser in the United States.[24] In Jamaica, Protestant Christianity played a key role in the slave rebellion known as the Baptist War of 1831, and Catholic influence abounds in the African-diasporic religion of Vodou, which helped foment the San Domingo Revolution in what is now Haiti. In response, white authority figures in almost every area of the colonial Americas deemed African-descended religious practices illegal, demonic, and punishable.[25] Yet if Afro-diasporic religions' marginalization is as old as European colonialism, so too is its persistence and development.[26]

Contemporary scholarship oftentimes implicitly marginalizes Afro-diasporic religion via disciplinary divisions that are themselves products of this violent colonial past. In *Three Eyes for the Journey,* a theological exploration of Kumina and other Afro-Caribbean religions, Dianne Stewart explains, "To date, studies on the African religious traditions of the Caribbean and the Americas have been conducted primarily under the influence of disciplines such as anthropology, sociology, and history" (xiii).[27] Informed theological discussions regarding the spiritual philosophies and epistemologies of the African diaspora have been hindered in the literary academy thanks to an ongoing understanding of theology as a function of discourse that can be located primarily within written archives.[28] Afro-diasporic religions, as a result of the limited resources during enslavement and continuation of African oral traditions, are not primarily located in sacred texts, but rather in the performances of worshippers. John Mbiti explains that in the African indigenous context, "religion is written not on paper but in people's hearts, minds, oral history, rituals and religious personages" (3). The disciplinary relegation of Afro-diasporic religion to cultural studies or anthropology and other social sciences is a contemporary manifestation of a long history of institutionalized bias. Yet as Kwame Anthony Appiah states, "There are many devices for supporting the transmission of a complex and nuanced body of practice and belief without writing" (132). Over the course of this book, I make a case for literary studies by way of these texts outside of my own discipline, works by scholars who have creatively and doggedly made space for the study of Afro-diasporic spiritualties in the academy.

In *The Sacred Act of Reading,* I adopt performative hermeneutical methods of reading texts as a means of contending with this seeming disjuncture between literary scholarship and nonscribal methods for articulating religious thought. I concentrate on depictions of embodied spiritual practices in order to illuminate methods of "knowing" in Afro-diasporic literature. This book demonstrates how modern and contemporary literary scholars can use textual works to analyze faithful worldviews not found in stated beliefs or scriptural sources. As Charles H. Long writes, "A total hermeneutical discussion cannot overlook the role of signification in the creation of theoretical formulation" (2). I argue that within the context of Afro-diasporic religions, signification functions via a looping and mutually constitutive network of meaning-making activities. These communicative and interpretive acts are themselves always operating within performative and discursive epistemologies.

By way of its performative textual hermeneutics, *The Sacred Act of Reading* studies the conceptual complexities and performative processes of signification occurring within African-derived spiritual discourses alongside their material and cultural contexts. Chapters 1 and 3 examine representations of spirit possession, mediumship, and zombification in four novels by Caribbean, South American, and Caribbean-Canadian authors. In analyzing the works of Erna Brodber, Manuel Zapata Olivella, and Nalo Hopkinson, I draw on sociology, history, and theology focusing on Afro-Caribbean religious practices including Christianity, Myal, Vodou, Obeah, and Kumina, as well as Yoruban African cosmologies. These first and third chapters are informed by anthropological and historical research on Black religious movements from across the New World by academics such as Maureen Warner Lewis, Nathaniel Samuel Murrell, Leonard Barnett, Lizabeth Paravisini-Gebert, and Margarite Fernández Olmos.[29] In chapters 2 and 4, I closely read performances of prophecy and preaching in scripted plays, print novels, and an audiobook by African American and Caribbean authors. In studying the works of Zora Neale Hurston, Toni Morrison, Derek Walcott, and Louis Marriott, I explore spiritual authority and leadership in relation to Afro-diasporic Christianity, Revival Zion, and Rastafari in the Caribbean and the United States. In this work I am particularly indebted to the groundbreaking scholarship on African American Christianity by sociologists such as C. Eric Lincoln and Lawrence Mamiya, theologians like Victor Anderson, and Womanist thinkers including Kelly Brown Douglass and Katie Geneva Cannon.[30] Every instance of literary analysis in *The Sacred Act of Reading* interweaves the foundational literary and theological insights on the Black church with Dianne Stewart's insistence that non-Christian practices also be studied with the rigor of theology. What is more, by analyzing discourses of spirituality and power through a focus on bodily movements in Afro-diasporic Christian contexts, rather than on faith or belief, this project addresses the overwhelming influence of Euro-American Christian traditions and the Enlightenment's intellectual legacies in the Western academy.

This project's approach to reading spiritual thought as embodied practice in Afro-diasporic literature was a response to the theoretical frameworks already operating in these religious epistemologies. By integrating performance practices rooted in religious ritual into their literary works, the authors studied in this book explore the ways in which beliefs about the self and the world can never be disentangled from the physical experiences of the body. Theologian Anthony Pinn writes, "Through the ritual structures and symbolic sources provided in various religions, humans give their thought and actions meaning. Therefore, religion at its core is a process of meaning-making" (xxiv). In the literary works studied here, religious meaning-making operates via embodied performances that combine thought and action to establish, communicate, and interpret understandings of the self in relation to the world. Therefore, meaning derives from a series of communicative performances, which in turn subtend the smooth or disturbed functioning of social and political power. What is more, these processes of individual and collective interpretation help us to understand the very relationship between what we consider to be thought and action. Because I concentrate on *literary* representations of religious performances, I study how authors use symbolic discourses to represent (and sometimes evoke) embodied spiritual practices that maneuver between metaphysical and physical registers, complicating the boundaries between abstract thought and material action. As a result, each chapter of this book thinks through various formulations of performance, textuality, and embodiment in order to show how these conceits are conceptualized and complicated in different literary works. In this vein, *The Sacred Act of Reading* demonstrates several ways in which academic criticism may be conducted so as to better reflect the multifarious literary and cultural traditions of the Afro-diasporic Americas. These traditions, as a result of their origins and conditions of creation, have always transcended the bounds of discipline, genre, medium, and intellectual assumptions.

Situating the Afro-Diasporic Americas

The Sacred Act of Reading is an Afro-diasporic, Black-centric, and hemispheric American project focused on discourses and themes that are both local and transnational. Each author in this project has explicitly recognized the African-derived heritages at play in his or her creative career and has situated those heritages within regional cultural frameworks specific to the Western Hemisphere. I invoke the hyphenated term "Afro-diasporic" throughout this volume to describe such African-influenced but distinctly American spiritual systems, creative archives, and epistemologies present in the studied works. Like the adjectival form of "performative," which is so key to this book's argument and methodology, "diasporic" is a term that allows this project to attend to notions of movement. In referring to the Afro-diasporic Americas, I am citing the forced physical movements of living bodies across space and time, and I am calling on a collection of symbolic movements by which African-descended communities have established collective frameworks of culture and identity.

The term "Afro-diasporic" allows this work to center the myriad historical experiences that constituted the African diaspora and shaped the

New World within ongoing discussions of modern Black artistry, religion, and thought. This book operates under the guiding assumptions of hemispheric American studies—that while varied and distinct, the nations of the Western Hemisphere are connected through "histories of conquest, colonialism, slavery, indigenous rights, imperialism, migration and globalization (to name some of the issues)" (Landers and Robinson, xvii). By the early 1700s Portuguese, Spanish, British, French, and Dutch colonial economies in the so-called New World had come to rely heavily on systems of enslaved labor. The African diaspora in the Americas encapsulates a centuries-long historical period in which an estimated 12.5 to 30 million individuals from the African continent (primarily West and Central African regions) were kidnapped by or traded to European companies and then shipped as living cargo to work in the Americas. While there are differences in the specific histories of colonialism and slavery according to geographic region and political sovereignty, European colonialism and the subsequent African diaspora have indelibly defined what we know as the modern Western Hemisphere. I use the term "the Afro-diasporic Americas" as a citation to these histories of forced migration and labor and as a conceptual framework that references an imagined community symbolically and physically enacted through discursive exchange and debate (Edwards, 63–64). The overarching power structures and individual actors who precipitated and prolonged the African diaspora ubiquitously worked to enforce "abjectifying" parameters of existence for persons of African descent. Contemporary notions of "race" are rooted in this epoch of European empire-making, and current racial categories are inextricably imbricated in a *"vertical* system" of "privilege and subordination" (Mills, 50, emphasis in orig.). *The Sacred Act of Reading* illuminates how the abjectifying parameters used by white European authorities (including religious leaders) to defend race-based slavery continue to mark the lived experiences of Afro-diasporic communities in the New World, particularly via the material and abstract apparatuses that substantiate anti-Black racism.

The African diaspora also greatly influenced the varied contours of religious traditions, including Christianity, Islam, Judaism, Buddhism, African traditional religions, African-derived religions, and folk traditions in the Americas. Religious systems, while often concerned with metaphysical quandaries, are always grounded in the material experiences of worshippers in the world. For African-descended communities across the Americas, these material experiences include the Middle Passage, colonialism, and the many operating conditions propping up white racial hegemony. This book thus uses the capacious term Afro-diasporic to call attention to these shared historical contingencies that inform the varied religious practices represented in texts from North America, the Caribbean, and South America. Joseph Murphy writes, "The religious traditions of the African diaspora are alike in that each shares a social history of enslavement and racial discrimination. Each tradition became the focus for an extraordinary struggle for survival against and triumph over brutal systems of exploitation. They share an elevated sense of solidarity against injustice and a commitment to the protection and advancement of their communities" (2). As a result of their common histories punctuated by trauma and abuse, Afro-diasporic religions often explicitly intertwine questions of the individual's and the community's spiritual and physical wellbeing. J. Lorand Matory notes that "the Atlantic perimeter hosts a range of groups profoundly influenced by Western African conceptions of personhood and the divine" (5). While the selected texts in this project vary widely in their approaches to African-derived religious action and thought, they together demonstrate a common practice within the literary archive of the modern and contemporary Afro-diasporic Americas: the literary depiction of spiritual rituals, which enable metacritical meditations on sociopolitical power and epistemologies in the wake of common historical events.[31] Through comparative literary analyses, *The Sacred Act of Reading* traces a complex web of African-influenced religious thought (whether traditional or substantially altered) and political action across a wide geographic landscape.

"Diaspora" is a term that encompasses the dynamic imaginings and reimaginings of community through cultural, historical, and political frameworks. It is, like religious ritual and literary interpretation, a set of communicative and meaning-making acts manifested through "performance and practice" (Redmond, 64). These communicative choreographies explore ever-proliferating questions about what it means to live and create in an environment suffused with Euro-colonial values and epistemes while also identifying with African ancestry, Black racial identity, or both. The concept of "Afro-diasporic Americas" is not fixed, but rather one way to articulate a complex network of relationships between unique individuals and collectives within the Western Hemisphere. The authors featured in *The Sacred Act of Reading* operate within several communities and realms of discourse simultaneously. These include but are by no means limited to discursive spheres informed by Western academic training and colonial cultures, those informed by African ancestral ideas and practices, and those specific to the contemporaneous culture of

18 *The Sacred Act of Reading*

the text's or the author's locality. In *Comrade, Bliss Ain't Playing,* Josefina Báez decides that she will go "just [her] way" after discovering "in many/sacred books . . . all possible tortures, battles, wars/and human destruction." After encountering references to domination and destruction in "many" religious writings, Báez chooses to forge her own "way" of relating with the world. "Yes, just my way," Báez proclaims, before immediately adding, "But I will meet others' ways. We are entangled, anyways./This island do has bridges." *The Sacred Act of Reading* uses the conceptual framework of the Afro-diasporic Americas alongside its methodology of performative textual hermeneutics to better understand meaning-making processes by which "ways" of knowing are entangled and "islands" may be either forged or bridged.

Chapter Overview

Chapter 1, "'You Preached!': Zora Neale Hurston's and Toni Morrison's Sermonic Performances," studies representations of preaching as a performative art in a collection of prose, plays, poems, and audiobooks by Hurston and Morrison. These printed and performed texts, I contend, can be understood as theoretical explorations of preaching, liturgy, and performance. The chapter focuses on stylistic details to demonstrate how Afro-diasporic authors across the Americas manipulate the mechanisms of their media to depict and manifest relationships of spiritual power, thus establishing the critical practice cultivated throughout this project. I begin by studying a sermon originally recorded by Hurston in Eau Gallie, Florida, in 1929 and re-presented by Hurston as poetry, prose, and theater. By close reading Hurston's ethnographic, theatrical, and novelistic writings on preaching in the Sanctified Church, I show how she uses editorial practices to decenter the spiritual authority of the preacher and portrays the preaching event as a performative liturgical set of acts constituted through embodied collaboration centered on rhythmic breath. I study Toni Morrison's textual and audiobook presentation of a sermon in *Beloved* (1987; 2007) to argue that the novel posits a heart-centered theory of effective preaching through communal embodiment. Both authors take on the task of translating the sounds and gestures of religious performance into print, mediating across media format and semiotic systems. In the case of her audiobook, Morrison even mediates the preaching scene back from print into oral performance. I draw on Hurston's and Morrison's generic mediations to show how their printed publications encourage the performative hermeneutics that guide this book's methodology. In studying the theatrical and audio versions of Hurston's and Morrison's religious works alongside their prose, readers can *hear* their print matter in new ways.

Chapter 2, "The Hermeneutics of Spirit Possession: Interpreting Mediums in *Changó, The Biggest Badass* and *Louisiana*," considers the hermeneutical and epistemological ramifications of spiritual mediation in Manuel Zapata Olivella's *Changó, The Biggest Badass* (1983) and Erna Brodber's *Louisiana* (1997). These two novels demonstrate how engagement with a spiritually transformative text or performance can come about through either involuntary or intentional capitulation with possessing agent/s. Through the critical frameworks of translation and opacity, I demonstrate how both mediums engage in performative hermeneutical practices in order to grapple with the epistemological uncertainty of spiritual possession and revelation. Blurring the boundaries between "text" and "flesh," the character Agne Brown in Zapata Olivella's *Changó* comes to represent the processes and products of literary translation. The spiritual mediations performed by and through Agne in the novel's plot, I contend, are analogous to the translatorial moves executed by *Changó*'s Spanish-English translator, Jonathan Tittler, in 2010. In Brodber's *Louisiana*, a spiritual hermeneutics of opacity allows Ella Townsend to negotiate epistemological confusion while mediating between the spiritual and physical realms. I argue that Brodber presents a mode of interpretation that calls for the active labor of letting go of totalizing interpretations. I call this hermeneutical orientation "engaged surrender." The practice of engaged surrender allows for the novels' protagonists and readers to imagine a performative textual hermeneutics that can continually reimagine the capacities and limitations of individual subjectivity and community knowledge. By reading these novels with a focus on performance practices, "The Hermeneutics of Spirit Possession" takes the themes of mediation and collectivity introduced through texts explicitly tied to performance in chapter 1 and theoretically expands them. Chapter 2 elucidates the corporeal nature of discursive interpretation, casting the sacred act/s of hermeneutics as metaphor and effect within layered diegetical contexts.

Chapter 3, "The Spiritual Life of Power: Zombies in *Myal* and *Brown Girl in the Ring*," revisits the subject of the spiritually occupied body via readings of Erna Brodber's *Myal* (1988) and Nalo Hopkinson's *Brown Girl in the Ring* (1997). These novels of zombification and healing, I argue, demonstrate the embodied foundations and repercussions of abstract ideas and systems of power. In each novel, women's bodies physically manifest the ideological effects of discourse and performance; by extension, they embody the impossibility of disentangling abstract beliefs from material experience. As I argue, Erna Brodber's representations of sound in *Myal* demonstrate how power operates through the embodied performances of abstract ideas. Specifically, she presents concurrently abstract and material experiences of spirit thievery (zombification) and spirit reclamation. One possessed character illustrates the materiality of thought by invoking sound in her narrative, while another young woman signals the parameters for occupied subjects' creative agency through the use and retention of her voice. I then analyze Hopkinson's intensely visceral, visual representations of zombification in her speculative fiction, *Brown Girl in the Ring,* in order to show how spiritual, socioeconomic, and political regimes of power function via the manipulation, categorization, and violation of physical bodies. By layering her novel with references to performance practices such as masking and children's ring games, Hopkinson encourages the reader to adopt a performative hermeneutics focused on the visual registers of embodiment lurking below the ideological discourse of late capitalism. This chapter reads these two novels with a focus on the spiritual rituals of zombification and healing alongside issues of textual interpretation, and in doing so confirms the collective interpretive practices that subtend performative textual hermeneutics.

Chapter 4, "Reading the Prophetic Stage: Imagining the Limits of the Possible in *Bedward* and *Dream on Monkey Mountain,*" analyzes the collective spiritual resistance (introduced in the previous chapter) in light of the prophetic modalities at work in Louis Marriott's 1960 Jamaican history-play and Derek Walcott's avant-garde 1970 drama. By aligning the possibilities and limitations of prophetic time and hermeneutics with the generic parameters of staged drama, I demonstrate how these theatrical works manage to both portray and actualize prophecy as a mode of collective interpretation. This chapter adopts a critical framework rooted in notions of millennial and messianic time and charismatic prophecy. I contend that in Marriott's *Bedward* and Walcott's *Dream on Monkey Mountain,* prophecy challenges hegemonic power structures by usurping traditional methods for legitimating authority and encouraging followers to imagine the world via radical hermeneutics. *Bedward's* theatrical form, I argue, complicates the narrative's emphasis on the impossibility of the historical protagonist's millennialist vision because the genre necessarily transforms the prophet's legacy into a continual messianic event. Walcott's *Dream on Monkey Mountain,* I contend, shows that prophetic claims are always substantiated by audience participation. A radical prophecy can only be efficacious so long as there is an audience to collectively interpret society through the lens of the prophet's cosmology. By taking up two dramatic works explicitly connected with performance, chapter 4 returns to the original construction of performative textual hermeneutics presented in chapter 1. I use this methodological scaffolding to build on this book's overarching theoretical quandaries about the performative capacities of hermeneutics. I specifically question the extent to which a text or a hermeneutical system can not only imagine but also enact alternative readings of—and thus modes of existence in—the world.

The epilogue, "Interpretive Communities," briefly returns to Josefina Báez's *Comrade, Bliss Ain't Playing* and Ntozake Shange's *For Colored Girls Who Have Considered Suicide/When the Rainbow Is Enuf* to reflect on how shifting interpretive communities have been and may be developed. As I show, Shange and Báez dramatize the relational dance between author, audience, message, and medium, a dance whose steps this book constantly retraces. In the process of discursively representing and physically manifesting the spiritual acts of all mediation, Shange and Báez confirm that the collective, embodied acts of interpretation developed throughout this project can be used to better understand interpretive communities within the academy and beyond it. By making real that which seems abstract, and communal that which seems individual, works like those studied here invite us to consciously participate in (and at times surrender to) the collective practice of hermeneutics. A system of performative textual hermeneutics attuned to the spiritual underpinnings of Afro-diasporic texts can help us to embrace the epistemological uncertainty required in any attempt to creatively engage with a text, each other, and ourselves. Ultimately, then, the chapters that follow divine the sacred possibilities inherent in every act of reading.

1 "You Preached!"

Zora Neale Hurston's and Toni Morrison's Sermonic Performances

> That's what the black church means. Our beating heart. The place where our dignity as a people is inviolate.
> —President Barack Obama, eulogy for the Honorable Reverend Clementa Pinckney, June 26, 2015

> The truth is, that the religious service is a conscious art expression. The artist is consciously creating—carefully choosing every syllable and every breath.
> —Zora Neale Hurston, "Spirituals and Neo-Spirituals"

THE FIGURE OF the black folk preacher looms large throughout the African American literary tradition. This is no surprise considering the pivotal cultural, political, and religious roles that the Protestant Christian preacher has performed throughout Afro-diasporic history in the United States.[1] According to W. E. B. Du Bois in *The Souls of Black Folk* (1903), the Negro preacher began as the African priest who on the slave plantation took on additional cultural and social responsibilities. While the African chief's traditional authorities were overwhelmed by the "far greater and more despotic powers" (119) of the white master on the slave plantation, the figure of the priest or medicine man endured, and his services came to carry even more significance for enslaved communities. Du Bois writes that this preacher/medicine man "appeared on the plantation and found his function as the healer of the sick, the interpreter of the Unknown, the comforter of the sorrowing, the supernatural avenger of the wrong, and the one who rudely but picturesquely expressed the longing, disappointment, and resentment of a stolen and oppressed people. Thus, as bard, physician, judge, and priest, within the narrow limits allowed by the slave system, rose the Negro preacher, and under him the first Afro-American institution, the Negro church" (119). In order to illustrate how the preacher figure became integral to African American spiritual life, Du Bois lingers on the interpretive and communicative functions with which these enslaved spiritual leaders were increasingly tasked. Generally construed, preaching is the religious art of interpreting sacred (usually biblical) texts and presenting those interpretations to a congregation. Preaching practices include but are not limited to storytelling, rhetorical argument, and poetics (Floyd-Thomas et al., 203–19). For Du Bois the hermeneutical and performative practices that constitute preaching came to define not only the role of the preacher but the cultural institution that is the Afro-American church.

Du Bois, though often considered the first, is far from the only scholar of African American Christian religion to emphasize the expressive, bard-like aspects of the Protestant black preacher amidst a longer list of pastoral and prophetic roles. For example, the editors of *Black Church Studies* call preachers "interpreters, heralds, conveyors of truth, witnesses, translators, artists and performers" (208), and Eric Lincoln and Lawrence Mamiya go so far as to say that "the Black Church was the first theater in the black community," suggesting that the preacher was the first leading actor (6). In the modern and contemporary United States, the communicative responsibilities of black preachers are best demonstrated in their homiletics, or performances of preaching. Black preaching styles have been so fundamental to studies in the African American Christian church that preacher and scholar Henry H. Mitchell's canonical *Black Preaching* argues for a theological reading of the Black church based on popular homiletic performances (124).

These theological and cultural insights inform this chapter's textual analyses, which focus on the communicative and interpretive elements of homiletic performance in several works by Zora Neale Hurston and Toni Morrison. More specifically, this study of performative preaching focuses on a sermon entitled "The Wounds of Jesus," which Hurston textually presents in three separate publications between 1931 and 1934; this is followed by Toni Morrison's textual and audiobook presentations of a sermon in the novel *Beloved* (1987, 2007). By studying Hurston's coauthored play *The Sermon in the Valley* and Morrison's audiobook reading, this study expands conceptions of both the text and performance archives for each figure. Through performative textual hermeneutics, I reveal that Hurston and Morrison present preaching as a liturgical event by both describing and evoking experiences of collective, embodied collaboration. For these two authors, then, preaching becomes a component of a larger ritual structure legitimated through the encoded actions performed by the congregants in chorus with the preacher.

The performative textual hermeneutics developed throughout this book offer fitting methods of interpretation for these religious works because preaching, particularly in the context of the Black Christian church, is understood as a performative art in terms of both the theatrical mechanisms that shape it and its effective capacities. For decades scholars of African American preaching have employed the term "performative" not only to highlight the dramatic, or even theatrical, stylizations of homiletics but also to indicate that when preachers properly say their sermons, they are expected to do something for the worshipping community.[2] Dolan Hubbard writes that as a result of societal oppression and marginalization, "African Americans attempted to redefine themselves and their history through speech acts. Grounded in the church and based to a large extent on improvisation, these speech acts, keyed to the preacher's speech act, provided the aesthetic underpinnings for black oral expression" (4). The African American preaching event is defined by its performative nature; it is an artistic drama that also, at its best, creates effective change.

The performative, or effective, preaching event is often considered to be one that engenders an experience of catharsis for worshipers. Scholars of African American literature and religion often argue that preachers gain spiritual and social authority according to their ability to deliver a sermon in a way that creates a sense of collective catharsis. Hortense Spillers describes the sermon as a poetic "instrument of collective catharsis, binding once again the isolated members of the community" ("Fabrics of History," 4). Similarly, Henry Mitchell refers to a "healing catharsis" that can result from a successful preaching event (111), and Lincoln and Mamiya explain that "the charisma of church leaders was demonstrated both in appeal of their personalities and especially in their ability to preach and elicit a strong cathartic response" (14). Additionally, what Spillers, Lincoln, and Mamiya call "catharsis," anthropologist Victor Turner would likely consider "spontaneous communitas" (132), a concept that, as Tim Olaveson has noted, also correlates with what Emile Durkheim calls "collective effervescence" (89). Every one of these descriptors implies a kind of communal experience that transcends the limits of language and reason and promotes group cohesion through shared emotions, sensations, and activities.[3]

In the sermonic works of Hurston and Morrison, I contend, these extratextual moments are tied to spiritual practices and ideas connected to the African diaspora in the Americas. Hurston and Morrison combine their capacious knowledge of the religious and secular Euro-American canon with Afro-diasporic references and ways of thinking, particularly regarding the relationship between discourse and action. Hurston's descriptions of religious practices such as "shouting" demonstrate her schooling in ethnography under Franz Boas and her investment in paying academic and aesthetic respect to what she saw as African elements present in the contemporary Black church. Similarly, La Vinia Delois Jennings explains that Morrison's narratives, including *Beloved,* not only "stylistically exemplify . . . an amalgamated West and Central African traditional culture in the diaspora of the Americas" but also "draw upon the Middle Passage survival of traditional cosmologies from these regions" (1). The African-derived themes and aesthetic practices identified in Hurston and Morrison's writings inspired this project's performative textual hermeneutics. The specific works studied in this chapter reference and aesthetically emulate rituals such as drumming, dance, and call-and-response speech patterns, which draw on the underlying beliefs and philosophies of the diverse religions that were brought over and transformed as a result of the Atlantic slave trade. By balancing action and interpretation this methodology integrates the principles of these rituals and diasporic methods of thinking into the discourse-oriented world of academic critical reading.

Both Hurston and Morrison use the mechanisms of their written texts to show how sermons are not simply discursive genres but components of larger ritual structures focused on ultimate experiences of catharsis. Roy A. Rappaport explains, "Ritual not only communicates something but is taken by those performing it to be 'doing something' as well," suggesting that ritual, like performative speech, is both expression and action (77). In order to express the dual nature of this genre and its wider events, Hurston and Morrison must think across modalities. Hurston, whose work is already known for pushing the boundaries of genre, explicitly moves between modalities when she adapts the "Wounds of Jesus" sermon to fit the formats of a theatrical script, a poetic ethnographic transcription, and a novel. Like Hurston's work, Morrison's novel *Beloved* is well known for challenging distinctions between genre and media. And Morrison herself has explained that she wanted the book to be more oral and less print (Morrison, "Talking to Myself"). What is more, when Morrison performed for her audiobook of *Beloved,* she made clear authorial choices about her oral delivery style, and I show how she transformed the character Baby Suggs's sermon for this new media format.

Throughout this chapter I develop a performative textual hermeneutics as a response to the challenges of comparatively reading Hurston's and Morrison's sermonic works across genre and media formats, as well as to the noted theoretical importance of thinking through African-derived rituals and concepts. This method of reading and studying Afro-diasporic works, like the portrayed preaching events by Hurston and Morrison, considers language and discourse with a focus on sensations, embodiment, and action. Hurston's and Morrison's religious work reflects the tradition of African American women's writing described by Katherine Clay Bassard in *Transforming Scriptures*. Like nineteenth-century authors, including Maria W. Stewart, Hurston and Morrison "push the boundaries of written language to create multi-layered, multivocal texts that 'sample' the scriptures, pushing the genre of prayer to cultural performance" (Bassard, 4). For this tradition of African American women's religious writings, including those by Hurston and Morrison, preaching may be rooted in the realm of discourse and language, but it operates outside of those same parameters as it manifests through embodied performances and leads to performative, or effective, phenomena. In both explicit and implicit terms, the two authors here draw on religious practices of the African diaspora, particularly those that see spirit as a function of embodied knowledge, which access meaning on deeply metaphysical, cognitive, and somatic planes. In Hurston's and Morrison's sermonic texts, the body becomes the central site for eliciting, experiencing, and proving the performative capacities of preaching.

Liturgical Preaching in Hurston's Sermonic Texts

Hurston's editorial practices, I argue, present preaching in the Sanctified Church as a liturgical performance. By calling Hurston's theory of preaching liturgical, I mean to emphasize that in her works, spiritual authority is not centralized in the preacher but rather is enacted through embodied, ritual acts performed by the entire congregation. Therefore, the term "liturgical" is used here to signify that Hurston showcases a wider distribution of religious authority during the preaching event. Furthermore, by adopting a performance-focused method of interpreting the written word, this chapter demonstrates how Hurston's literary maneuvers enact the key elements of collaboration, embodiment, and continuation that I identify in her liturgical theory of preaching. The chapter's conclusion places the term "liturgical" in conversation with a theatrical reference invoked by Hurston to show that while her theory of preaching decentralizes power, it still assumes the presence of established hierarchies through encoded traditions.

Hurston heard the Reverend C. C. Lovelace deliver the sermon "The Wounds of Jesus" on May 3, 1929, in Eau Gallie, Florida, and it undoubtedly became one of her favorite works of religious material.[4] In Hurston's oeuvre, versions of "The Wounds of Jesus" appear in the following textual formats: a dramatic monologue in the one-act play *The Sermon in the Valley*, performed by Cleveland's Gilpin players in 1931, 1934, and 1949 (and published in 2008 in *Zora Neale Hurston: Collected Plays*); an ethnographic transcription entitled "The Sermon," in Nancy Cunard's *Negro: An Anthology* (1934; reprinted in *The Sanctified Church*, 1981); and the climactic final sermon delivered by protagonist John Pearson in Hurston's novel *Jonah's Gourd Vine* (1934). Hurston formats the sermon to fit three genres—ethnography, theater, and narrative. The sheer number of this sermon's iterations indicates that she was especially interested in the ways that Lovelace's original text could take on new artistic force through revisions and contextualizations.[5]

Hurston's numerous re-presentations of Lovelace's sermon demonstrate her willingness to artistically reimagine ethnographic material through editorial practices. In a letter dated April 30, 1929, Hurston wrote to her then-friend and collaborator Langston Hughes about this openness to artistic revision: "Oh, I love my religious material. Some of it is priceless. Know what I am attempting? To set an entire Bapt. service word for word and note for note. The prayers are to be done in blank verse for thats what they are, prose poetry. I have four dandy ones. I dont like my sermon as well, but I shall prop it up on every leaning side. I shall cut the dull spots in the service to the minimum and play up the art" (Letter to Hughes, 140). In the letter Hurston makes clear that while she strives to "set" a Baptist church service "word for word," she intends to do so with a focus on the *artistry* of her "religious material" rather than on the ethnographic fidelity of capturing each exact word and note. Hurston's enthusiasm for condensing and reformatting the ethnographic material for artistic purposes, which would be "anathema" to many contemporary anthropologists, reveals her unapologetic enthusiasm for creative invention within the editorial process (Hemenway, 126). Considering that Hurston heard Lovelace's sermon in Eau Gallie less than a week after writing to Hughes from that same location about her desire to "set an entire Bapt. Service" and her dissatisfaction with the current sermon on record, we may assume that the ethnographer listened to "The Wounds of Jesus" with the direct intention of transforming the oral event into a work of textual art for wider publication, and possibly for embodied enactment by way of dramatic performances. Hurston presents "The Wounds of Jesus" in nearly identical formats in Cunard's anthology and *Jonah's Gourd Vine*, suggesting that she found her creative transcription to be a particularly strong piece of material that could perform new aesthetic and narrative functions according to its context. Though the text of the sermon is nearly identical, she recontextualizes the sermon in *Jonah's Gourd Vine*, giving the content new meaning in relation to the novel's plot. While several critics, including Hurston's biographer Robert Hemenway, have considered the Lovelace sermon a clumsy attempt at integrating ethnographic work into literature, I agree with Eric Sundquist, who calls Hurston's textual representation of Lovelace's sermon in *Jonah's Gourd Vine* a "virtuoso performance of fictive creation" (25). "The Wounds of Jesus" so successfully performed as literature in *Jonah's Gourd Vine* that one *New York Times* reviewer infamously declared that Lovelace's sermon in the novel was "too good, too brilliantly splashed with poetic imagery to be the product of any Negro preacher."[6]

In the case of the play *The Sermon in the Valley*, Hurston not only saw herself as a poetic and literary reviser of Lovelace's sermon thanks to her editorial form of authorship, but she also invited others, specifically Rowena Jelliffe, to collaborate on the theatrical representation of the sermon as well. According to the editors of Hurston's collected plays, Jean Lee Cole and Charles Mitchell, the playscript *The Sermon in the Valley* "contains significant additions and revisions made by Jelliffe" (191–92), who along with her husband Russel Jelliffe (both white) founded the Karamu settlement house in Cleveland, which hosted the multiracial acting group the Gilpin Players. While we cannot be sure of the extent to which Jelliffe helped to format the sermon as a one-act play, I consider her a coauthor of the drama just as Hurston becomes a coauthor of Lovelace's "The Wounds of Jesus" each time she re-presents it.[7] Hurston's interest in collaboration did not end with her theatrical works. In the April 30 letter to Hughes, as well as in another of the same year, Hurston either thanks Hughes for helping her to edit her ethnographic material or asks if he would be interested in editing material together.[8] Furthermore, Hurston is well known for weaving choice songs, phrases, and anecdotes from ethnographic research into her fiction and theater. I connect Hurston's editorial proclivity toward ongoing collaborative creation involving Lovelace's sermon to her description of the sermon in what she calls the "Sanctified Church."

Lovelace's sermon "The Wounds of Jesus" begins with a reading of Zechariah 13:6, which prophesies the Messiah being wounded in the house of his friends. The premise of the text is Christ's tragic sacrifice, and it features choice quotes from Matthew, Mark, and John.[9] This focus on crucifixion makes the piece an archetypal point of departure for a cathartic performance. The sermon is rife with further biblical references, including the books of Isaiah and Peter.[10] "The Wounds of Jesus" brings together a messianic telling of the earth's origin with the New Testament story of Jesus calming the sea in Galilee, ultimately insisting that the congregation must get off "de damnation train" and seek redemption in the sacrifice of Jesus Christ. Just as "the sermon is the *text* within the *experience* of the preaching event in the faith community" (Floyd-Thomas et al., 209), the message of Lovelace's sermon becomes the text that Hurston manipulates over and again through formatting to produce an experience of preaching in her literary communities. Because in the one instance Hurston is explicitly formatting her text for a staged enactment, and in the other she is limited to the written text's ability to invoke the imagined experience of embodied action, the differing presentations of "The Wounds of Jesus" challenge us to consider both the potentials and limitations for reading scribal works via a performative textual hermeneutics.

In both *The Sermon in the Valley* and *Jonah's Gourd Vine*, Hurston sets the Lovelace sermon in religious contexts that fit her description of the Sanctified Church. When Hurston discusses the Sanctified Church, she refers to the Holiness-Pentecostal movements of the late nineteenth and early twentieth centuries, particularly the Saints of God in Christ and the Church of God in Christ (Thomas, 35).[11] Hurston and Jelliffe's play *The Sermon in the Valley* depicts itinerant preacher Brother Ezra as he delivers a version of the Lovelace sermon to a group of field-workers. The drama features hallmarks of the Sanctified Church service, namely chanting, bearing up, and singing performed by the eighteen to twenty people who portray the gathered field-workers. The laborers act as Brother Ezra's congregation or "flock" for the duration of the religious event. Sometimes these performances of the Sanctified liturgy appear to erupt spontaneously from the congregants, and at other times the field-workers are led by a young woman from the flock named Caroline. *Jonah's Gourd Vine* tells the story of John Buddy Pearson, an African American man who becomes a successful but philandering Baptist pastor, only to lose everything after his beleaguered wife Lucy dies, leaving him in a tangled web of existential grief. Loosely based on the lives of Hurston's own parents, *Jonah's Gourd Vine* incorporates personal, ethnographic, and theological meditations, and in doing so delves deeply into the complex world of early twentieth-century African American Pentecostal communities.[12]

The sermon in these churches, Hurston explains in an essay unpublished during her lifetime, "is not the set thing that is in the other protestant churches. It is loose and formless and is in reality merely a framework upon which to hang more songs. Every opportunity to introduce a new rhythm is eagerly seized upon. The whole movement of the Sanctified Church is a rebirth of song-making! It has brought in a new era of spiritual-making" ("Sanctified Church," 104). In this essay Hurston still presents the sermon as a work of poetic artistry, but she specifies that the rhetorical artistry of the sermon acts in service of a greater end, making it a performative vehicle for rhythm, song, and spiritual-making. In other words, the sermon here is an impetus to collaborative creation between preacher and congregation. The sermon as an instrument of spiritual-making in the Sanctified Church summons the participatory art of thematic variation. In "Spirituals and Neo-Spirituals," Hurston writes, "The real spirituals are not really just songs. They are unceasing variations around a theme" (79). The Sanctified sermon, then, is a liturgical event, an embodied group ceremony manifested through collective, artistic improvisation around a prescribed ritual format.[13] From the outset, Hurston's desire to "set" and "prop up" the liturgical ritual of "an entire Bapt. service" through the written word necessitated that she find a way to inspire the reader to think about embodied performances while interpreting printed texts.

Throughout her ethnographic and personal nonfiction work on Afro-Caribbean and African American tradition and artistry, Hurston intimates that the curated and informal performance practices evidenced in twentieth-century culture across the Afro-diasporic New World are inspired by the remnants of West and Central African worldviews and rituals. It is no surprise, then, that Hurston describes the Sanctified Church as a "revitalizing element in Negro music and religion" that was "putting back into Negro religion those elements which were brought over from Africa and grafted onto Christianity." Acts such as chanting, "bearing up" the preacher's sermon, and "shouting" Hurston saw as continuations of the "African 'Possession' by the gods" ("Spirituals and Neo-Spirituals," 104–5). Hurston's assertion of African survivals in the Sanctified Church demonstrates her academic alignment with the scholarship of anthropologist Melville Herskovitz in the infamous Herskovitz-Frazier debate regarding the retention of African survivals in the cultural practices of the Afro-diasporic Americas. Her identification of African elements in the Sanctified Church, which served as evidence for Hurston that West and

Central African traditions were key components in twentieth-century African American culture, may help shed light on why this religious context occupied so much of her research and art. The Sanctified Church is an optimal setting for Hurston to explore her scholarly commitments, reflect on her own history of growing up as an itinerant Baptist preacher's daughter, and use her authorial skills to showcase the "life of color of [her] people" in a way that leaves "no loop-holes for the scientific crowd to rend and tear [them]" (Letter to Hughes, 139).

Across her publications that reproduce the Lovelace material, Hurston re-presents the Sanctified sermon according to the guidelines she sets out in her essays—as a collaborative event founded in a prescribed ritual framework—by demonstrating the congregation's liturgical tasks, such as "bearing up" the preacher. In the playscript *The Sermon in the Valley,* Hurston and Jelliffe use stage directions and scripted lines to show the staged congregation, designated by the title "the flock," continually "bearing up" the preacher, Brother Ezra. The flock's members interject into Brother Ezra's sermonic monologue spoken responses in the "tones of fervent prayer," seemingly spontaneous "singing" in chorus, along with "protesting moans and cries" and "chants." In "The Sanctified Church" Hurston explains that "bearing him up," such as that which we see in the play, "is not done just any old way. The chant that breaks out from time to time must grow out of what has been said and done" (104).[14] In other words, bearing up is a collaborative liturgical process because the congregants cannot simply respond to the preacher in any way they feel but must take the preacher's cues in accordance with the encoded set of actions and utterances passed down through memory. In *The Sermon in the Valley* the flock fulfills the religious event's foundational rules by responding to Brother Ezra in ways that augment his tone and demonstrate their responsiveness to both the content and moods of the sermon. When Ezra declares that "Jesus groaned upon the cross/And said: 'It is finished,'" the flock chants back, "And He never said a mumblin' word" (199). In this instance the congregation's chant punctuates the end of the crucifixion story and indicates that Jesus's statements are to be prioritized and treated with spiritual authority in the liturgical event. The churchgoers' performance legitimates the authority of the sermonic event, the preacher, and the biblical Jesus.

It is fitting that Hurston used the Lovelace sermon for a theatrical play that she collaboratively wrote with Rowena Jelliffe and the Gilpin players, considering how Hurston describes bearing up as an example of theatrical creation. In "The Sanctified Church," she writes, "Go into the church and see the priest before the altar chanting his barbaric thunder-poem before the altar with the audience behaving something like a Greek chorus in that they 'pick him up' on every telling point and emphasize it. That is called 'bearing him up'" (103–4). In this play, we actually get to see her stage the religious audience as a theatrical chorus. For example, when Brother Ezra in *The Sermon in the Valley* quotes Jesus as saying, "My heart is exceedingly sorrowful unto death,/For this night one of you shall betray me," the flock responds with "(*Protesting moans and cries*) No, Lord. No—no—," bringing attention to the tragedy of the betrayal and performing their unanimous desire to reject such treachery (196). The flock's utterances of protest at the revelation of betrayal instruct the audience, just as the Greek chorus did in Athenian tragedies, to find catharsis through Jesus's sacrificial demise at the hands of his enemies and former disciple. Because the flock is composed of a group of "some eighteen to twenty people" acting in a drama, it functions as a Greek chorus for two audiences—the audience depicted on the stage and the audience watching the theatrical work.

The Sermon in the Valley's theatrical flock also bears up Brother Ezra by "responding" with repetition to rhetorical questions in the sermon, emphasizing the role of dialogue (an inherently collaborative endeavor) in the Sanctified liturgy as well as in the content of the preaching text. Brother Ezra tells the story of man's creation, saying that first God gathered "water out of the might deep," "a handful o' dirt," and a "thimbleful o' breath," then "ready to make man," asked, "Who shall I make him after? Who?" (195). The flock then *"repeats the chant,"* intoning, "Who shall I make him after?/Who shall I make him after?" (195). The congregants' chant demonstrates that while they are not (nor is anyone else, for that matter) meant to answer God's question, the deity's decision regarding man's creation must be developed in the process of a conversation, just as the Sanctified liturgy is developed through participatory call and response. Again, bearing up serves a necessary legitimating function for the institution of the church and its theology of divine power. Brother Ezra follows the bearing up chant with a story that *"rapid[ly] rise[s] in tempo"* about the ways in which the elements, namely the sun, moon, and stars (all gendered feminine) beg to have man made in their image. God responds to each element with an emphatic "No," before finally declaring, "I'll make man in my own image and I'll put him in the garden" (195). The flock recognizes God's decision here as a positive resolution to the original question with the response, "Hallelujah, hallelujah, Lord have mercy" (195). The "conversation" God has with the elements about making man is only one of the many moments wherein the sermon's message appears through a process of rhetorical dialogue. When God first says that he will make man, "the elders upon the altar cried out that 'Ah, he will sin.'/(*Responses from the flock*)," to which Jesus interjects, "Make man, Oh, make man/And if he sin, I will redeem him/(*Responses from the flock*)" (194). In this celestial conversation born up by congregational utterances, Jesus appears to volunteer for his own crucifixion in order to resolve God and the elders' anxieties about creating man (194). By having Jesus sign up for his own sacrificial role, "The Wounds of Jesus" sermon dramatized in *The Sermon in the Valley* suggests that the Christ figure embraces his participation in the narrative and actively wants for the sermon's audience to achieve cathartic relief at the expense of his life.

In *Jonah's Gourd Vine* Hurston does not insert comments about how the congregation responds to the "Wounds of Jesus" sermon during the text of the sermon, but rather suggests the importance of liturgical collaboration while narrating the scene's beginning and end. She cues the reader to the fact that a Sanctified service is about to begin by having the preacher lead the congregation in singing the Sanctified spiritual derived from the Gospel of John, "Beloved, Beloved, Now We Are the Sons of God," which the author formats in verse to indicate that it should be read as a poetic song. The singing of "Beloved, Beloved" serves to create a sense of community amongst the congregants, just as Toni Morrison's repetition of "we" and "flesh" inspires collectivity in *Beloved,* as I will show in the following section. At the same time, the invocation of "Beloved, Beloved" and the practice of singing in Hurston's prose also demarcate difference between John Pearson and his church members. Furthermore, throughout the text studied in *The Sacred Act of Reading,* the invocation of song prompts readers to read the visual text with a sensitivity to sound, and in extension with an awareness of the text's relationship to embodied performance. On the very next page, Hurston also formats the majority of "The Wounds of Jesus" in poetic verse. By placing the versified song a few paragraphs before the sermon, she encourages readers to make connections between the musical chorus and the role of the same congregational chorus in the performance of preaching. Highlighting the importance of the congregational chorus for the legitimacy of the preacher's liturgical power, Hurston has her protagonist John reflect, "The audience sang with him. They always sang with him well because group singers follow the leader" (174). By having John reflect on the necessary collaboration of his "audience" before opening up the sermonic event, Hurston invites readers to the consider the ways in which the congregational audience must also collaboratively create the Sanctified liturgy he is about to perform, and how that participation maintains John's tenuous position as their leader. At the close of the climactic sermon, Hurston also uses participatory bearing up as an indication of the Sanctified liturgy, writing, "There had been a mighty response to the sermon all thru its length . . . [and] the 'bearing up' had been almost continuous" (181). The fact that the preacher was continually born up tells the reader that he indeed managed to "preach" rather than merely "lecture," successfully inspiring the collaborative participation of his congregation, and, for the time being, preserving John's authority.

While the active participation of the congregants' bodies implicitly undergirds Hurston's theory of bearing up, the formalized actions and utterances of the preacher's body are central to her explanations of Sanctified homiletics. Even when Hurston describes the poetic artistry of a religious sermon, she often does so with a concentration on the embodied performance of that artistry as evidenced in the preacher's oral delivery. As she asserts in "Spirituals and Neo-Spirituals," "The truth is, that the religious service is a conscious art expression. The artist is consciously creating—carefully choosing every syllable and every breath" (81). The preaching event, like the ritual and speech act, is both expression and action, and it must occur within an embodied performance that adheres to existing conventions and regulations. This is because a liturgy can only be said to have successfully occurred so much as all the appropriate people who are present in it have spoken and acted in accordance to tradition.

By comparing the delivery of Lovelace's sermon in the playscript with those given in Cunard's anthology and *Jonah's Gourd Vine,* it becomes apparent how textual mechanisms such as dialect, phonetic spelling, and onomatopoeia especially work to invoke a sense of embodiment in the sermonic scenes not written for live performance. In the case of *The Sermon in the Valley,* Hurston and Jelliffe highlight the importance of recognizing the live embodiment of the Sanctified service by merit of the works' performative genre—or simply by staging the service with the live bodies of actors. The issue of effectively communicating the embodied performance of the sermon comes to the fore, then, in the textual versions of "The Wounds of Jesus," namely in the anthology and *Jonah's Gourd Vine.* In these works not written to be performed on a stage, Hurston uses textual mechanisms such as versification, dialect, and indications of breathing to creatively transform Lovelace's sermon so that readers imaginatively experience the aural preaching event as a live performance through the visual, printed medium of written prose and poetry.[15]

In every iteration of "The Wounds of Jesus," Hurston introduces the sermon's themes and key biblical references in prose, then structures the bulk of the sermonic text as prose poetry, just like the prayers she mentions in her letter to Langston Hughes. In *The Sermon in the Valley* the sermon's versification uses line breaks to instruct the actor playing Brother Ezra in how to deliver the preaching event in a poetic manner. And each of these line breaks instructs the actor in how to create an appropriate rhythm with his breathing. Hurston formulates her religious material as poetry in order to demonstrate how the material *becomes* poetry by way of the liturgical performance, through the act of it being spoken. Like her references to Greek theater, Hurston's decision to write the sermon in verse also allows her to demonstrate the artistry of African American culture to an audience that often strives to demean these religious traditions.

In the case of the anthology and the novel, the poetic format instructs the reader in how to consume the sermon as a poetic text, engendering the experience of embodied sound. Cheryl Wall uses Richard Bauman's definition of performance—"the enactment of the poetic function, the essence of spoken artistry" (3)—when she writes in "Mules and Men and Women" that Hurston anticipated "the work of current-day anthropologists by several decades" when she "both theorized about and put into practice the concept of performance" in her 1930s ethnography (664). I agree with Wall and extend her argument to Hurston's textual representations of Lovelace's sermon. By presenting the sermon in verse, Hurston emphasizes the spoken artistry of the religious event and encourages readers to proceed more slowly with the reading process. The reader is encouraged to pause with each line break and in doing so to mentally mimic the performative choice of "every syllable and every breath," just as the actor playing Brother Ezra would be expected to do in *The Sermon in the Valley*. For the novel *Jonah's Gourd Vine*, the versification of "The Wounds of Jesus" also sets the sermon apart from the rest of the text. With the exception of the Lovelace sermon, a few songs (including "Beloved, Beloved") and chants, *Jonah's Gourd Vine* is primarily written in dialogue-heavy paragraphs with a past-tense, third-person narrator focused on the actions and thoughts of the protagonist, John Pearson. Hurston intensifies the performative nature of the preaching event in *Jonah's Gourd Vine* by noticeably switching from her typical novelistic formal structure to that of poetic verse, aligning the sermon with the spiritual-making evidenced earlier and, thanks to well-placed line breaks, emphasizing the sermon's sonically inspiring partial rhymes such as "I am the teeth of time" and "took de hooks of His power" (175, 179). By styling the sermon as spoken poetry, Hurston orients the reader's attention to the rhyme and rhythm of her language, which in turn bring to light the illusions of silence and sound that play out in readers' minds as they are "delivering" the sermon to themselves.

Hurston's religious scene combines the interpretive force of versification with one of her most well-known stylistic maneuvers, the textual representation of "dialect." Each rendition of "The Wounds of Jesus" features phonetic spellings to indicate specific pronunciations for certain words associated with southern African American Vernacular English. Hurston asserts that a "lack of dialect in the religious expression—particularly in the prayers—will seem irregular" to any Sanctified churchgoer, and in the case of sermons, "dialect breaks through only when the speaker has reached the emotional pitch where he loses all self-consciousness," making it a necessary performative maneuver for promoting the emotional escalation required for a collective experience of spiritual-making and eventual catharsis ("Spirituals and Neo-Spirituals," 81). Hurston writes in a glossary entry for *Jonah's Gourd Vine,* "In his cooler passages the colored preacher attempts to achieve what to him is grammatical correctness, but as he warms up he goes natural" (206), which she evidences in the text of her sermon during a climactic moment when Jesus declares his own betrayal. First Hurston sets up a juxtaposition for the "natural" dialectical grammar by having the preacher almost directly quote the ornate verbiage of Matthew 26:38:

> His eyes flowin' wid tears, ha! He said
> "My soul is exceedingly sorrowful unto death, ha![16]
> For this night, ha!
> One of you shall betray me, ha!"

The preacher's citational use of seventeenth-century English then shifts into a stylized speech pattern that uses similarly antiquated terms but situates them within a grammatical structure that Hurston identifies with the Black southern dialect. The preacher intones,

> "It were not a Roman officer, ha!
> It were not a centurion
> But one of you
> Who I have chosen my bosom friend
> That sops in the dish with me shall betray me." (177)

The preacher's linguistic aesthetic here, I contend, represents the Sanctified sermon as a linguistic work of spiritual-making. Hurston insists that "the jagged harmony is what makes" the spiritual. She adds that "the harmony of the true spiritual is not regular. The dissonances are important and not to be ironed out by the trained musician" ("Spirituals and Neospirituals," 80). "The Wounds of Jesus" performs this "jagged harmony" by emphasizing the compelling linguistic dissonance created when two seemingly competing registers of spoken English are placed in a chorus.[17]

Hurston also writes "The Wounds of Jesus" using phonetic spellings to indicate specific pronunciations for certain words such as "yo'" for "your" and "heben" for "heaven" (*Jonah's Gourd Vine*, 177). Like versification, phonetic representations of dialect force the reader to intentionally imagine the construction of linguistic sound and in turn mimic the performance of orality while consuming visual media. On Hurston's use of dialect to create an aural reading experience in the sermon appearing in *Jonah's Gourd Vine,* Eric Sundquist writes, "Hurston's orthography, her variations in person and tense, and her lack of grammatical markers or punctuating line stops—that is, her unmistakable but also flexible appeal to dialect—support the vividly inventive metaphors of her scene. Here and elsewhere, her use of enjambment, repetition, assonance, and a metrical scheme based on breathing rather than syllabic count drive the verse into a form that is 'readable' only to the degree that is 'heard'" (49). I agree with Sundquist's interpretation of dialect and versification in Hurston's material and build on his reading to argue that Hurston's creation of aurality in the literary text serves to present the religious scene as an embodied liturgical performance. Dialect, again like versification, functions as a means of communicating the embodied performance of the liturgical event more emphatically in Cunard's anthology and *Jonah's Gourd Vine* than it does in the play *The Sermon in the Valley*. In fact, the sermon as written in Hurston and Jelliffe's playscript contains far fewer instances of dialect than do the other two versions. For example, when the anthologized and novelized texts use "de" to indicate the phonetic sound of "the," the drama simply reads, "the." Similarly, the script does not use the dialectical terms "monasters" and "oarus" that appear in the other two versions, opting instead for the "standard" English spellings of "monsters" and "oars."[18] While these changes may have been editorial decisions by Rowena Jelliffe or the Gilpin Players, they still demonstrate how dialect especially serves to evoke a sense of embodied utterance in the versions of the sermon not written for live performance with corporeal actors.

Hurston—one of the first ethnographers to record, transcribe, and then describe the stories, songs, and sermons of the early twentieth-century African American South—extensively considers how dialect highlights the body's role in mediating between visual and aural media throughout her early ethnographic work. In 1935 Hurston assisted Alan Lomax in recording sermons and songs in Florida, but up to this point her fieldwork was accomplished through note-taking and memorization (Sundquist, 59). In the case of "The Wounds of Jesus," Hurston "transformed her acoustic impressions of African American preaching in written form" several times after hearing the original religious performance (Valkeakari, 35).[19] In Hurston's 1935 ethnography *Mules and Men,* a local resident tells a story contending with the aural and oral limitations of written texts. In the story a young woman returns to her father's home after years of schooling and, now fully equipped with alphabetic literacy, attempts to write a letter on his behalf. The father dictates the letter to his daughter: "Now tell him some mo'. 'Our mule is dead but Ah got another mule and when Ah say (clucking sound of tongue and teeth) he moved from de word'" (62). Of course, the daughter tells her father, "Ah can't spell (clucking sound)," to which the father laments, "You mean to tell me you been off to school seben years and can't spell (clucking sound)? Why Ah could spell dat myself and Ah ain't been to school a day in mah life. Well jes' say (clucking sound) he'll know what yo' mean and go on wid de letter" (63). Though not directly related to preaching, this tale beautifully illustrates how one can write out an auditory performance that is defined through the body. The father appears to see literary dictation as an onomatopoeic enterprise, like an anthropologist's tape recorder (an element that will figure prominently in chapter 2), which phonetically documents all sonic variations. We do not know how the daughter notes (clucking sound) in her father's letter, but her difficulties therein demonstrate the incomplete abilities of the written text along with the possibilities of formal manipulations, such as Hurston's notation of "clucking sound of tongue and teeth" that describes sound through bodily action.

The text of "The Wounds of Jesus" also aligns the creation of sound with bodily movement, as when Jesus is said to create music with the sounds of his footsteps on earth. The preacher exclaims and then most likely sings,

> I can hear Him [Jesus] when He walks about the golden streets
> I can hear 'em ring under His footsteps
> Sol me-e-e, Sol do
> Sol me-e-e, Sol do (*Jonah's Gourd Vine*, 178)

Jesus also uses his body to control the powerful sounds of the natural world when he wakes up in the ship during a tremendous storm on the sea of Galilee. As the "storm was in its pitch" and his disciples panicked around him, Jesus stood in the boat

> And placed His foot upon the neck of the storm
> And spoke to the howlin' winds
> And de sea fell at His feet like a marble floor
> And de thunders went back in their vault
> Then He set down on de rim of de ship
> And took de hooks of His power
> And lifted de billows in His lap
> And rocked de winds to sleep on His arm
> And said, "Peace, be still."
> And de Bible says there was calm. (179)

In this scene we see Jesus use the performative power of his utterances to control the seas, thunder, and wind. This formulation of the performative harkens to Austin's theories of effective speech because it appears to actualize the events that it announces. If Jesus's words are powerful enough to calm the environment, it is not clear why he must also use his body to perform his dominating power by putting his foot on the storm's neck and then bodily demonstrating the power of his nurturance by holding the billows like a child on his lap and rocking the wind to sleep in his arms. Perhaps Jesus in this scene is like the embodied preacher, whose words appear to be so powerful as to performatively bring about bodily responses in his congregation, but who in reality must always showcase his body's powerful labor and vulnerability in the liturgical event, usually through theatricalized sweating and beleaguered breathing.

In the case of "The Wounds of Jesus" as it is formatted in Nancy Cunard's anthology and *Jonah's Gourd Vine,* Hurston describes sound through bodily action in onomatopoetic signals of breath, or "ha" expirations.[20] Hurston explains the crucial role of the breathing "ha" in "Spirituals and Neo-Spirituals," writing, "The well-known 'ha!' of the Negro preacher is a breathing device. It is the tail end of the expulsion just before inhalation. Instead of permitting the breath to drain out, when the wind gets too low for words, the remnant is expelled violently. Examine: (inhalation) 'And oh'; (full breath) 'my Father and my wonder-working God'; (explosive exhalation) 'ha!'" (82). In the anthologized sermon and *Jonah's Gourd Vine*, Hurston brings to life the embodied liturgical act of preaching by emphasizing the preacher's live performance of breath through markers of "ha," while, like dialect, these textual cues appear far less frequently in the play version, *The Sermon in the Valley*. For example, the play holds salient differences in the scene I cited earlier during which God considers making man. Rowena and Jelliffe's script reads,

> When God said, "Let us make man."
> The elders upon the altar cried out,
> "If yo' make man . . . if yo' make man . . . Ah, he will sin."
> (*Responses from the flock*)
> Then yo' friend Jesus said, "Father, dear father, Oh, Father." (194)

As already noted, the play version presents this scene with an emphasis on its conversation, placing each line of dialogue on a new verse line and bearing up the importance of each man's fated sin with responses from the staged congregation. *Jonah's Gourd Vine* presents this same scene with more grammatical markers and line breaks defined by indications of breathing:

> When God said, ha!
> Let us make man
> And the elders upon the altar cried, ha!
> If you make man, ha!
> He will sin
> God my master, ha!
> Father!! Ha-aa! (175)

The breath markers are of particular importance for Hurston's textual renderings of the sermonic event, suggesting that they are meant to communicate the embodied performance that is not as evident in literature as in theatrical plays. Breath, in this case, becomes a crucial manner for Hurston to effectively promote a performative hermeneutic for reading the printed text, and in that way communicate the ritual artistry of the "Bapt. service" she discussed with Hughes. Hurston explains, "Negro singing and formal speech are breathy. The audible breathing is part of the performance and various devices are resorted to to adorn the breath taking. Even the lack of breath is embellished with syllables" ("Spirituals and Neo-Spirituals," 81). The lengths to which Hurston goes to demonstrate the preacher's breathing in her textual revisions of the sermon reveal that the preaching event must be actualized through the clearly ritual movements of the preacher in addition to the congregation.

When Hurston uses indications of breath to emphasize the importance of the preacher's breathing body for the actualized liturgy, she manages to decenter the sermonic words in the religious event. In the glossary of *Jonah's Gourd Vine,* Hurston specifies the manner in which signs of breathing indicate the preacher's performative embodiment, saying, "The 'ha' in the sermon marks a breath. The congregation likes to hear the preacher breathing or 'straining'" (206). Hurston demonstrates the importance of a preacher's "straining" voice when the novel's protagonist, John Pearson, so impresses a church congregation with his "good strainin' voice" after a public prayer that a church deacon believes "dat boy is called tuh preach" (89).[21] Like the figure of Jesus in the sermon, John's rhetorical skills appear so powerful as to be performative, effectively transforming his audience members. Hurston narrates, "One night at the altar-call he cried out his barbaric poetry to his 'Wonder-workin' God so effectively that three converts came thru religion under the sound of his voice" (89). Hurston complicates this supposedly performative moment with the preceding line, "He rolled his African drum up to the altar, and called his Congo Gods by Christian names" (89). Her reference to drums and Congo gods is yet another nod to her scholarly belief in African survivals. In addition, it reminds the reader that John's sermonic performance belongs to the Sanctified Church, "putting back into Negro religion those elements which are brought over from Africa and grafted onto Christianity" ("Sanctified Church," 105). Furthermore, John's metaphorical use of African drums aligns his preaching with the collaborative and performative liturgical practice of spiritual-making, specifically the "drum-like rhythm of all Negro spirituals," which Hurston uses as proof that "the Negro has not been Christianized as extensively as it is generally believed" ("Sanctified Church," 103). The reference to African survivals and rhythmic drums also gestures toward the phenomenon of shouting, which Hurston defines as "an emotional explosion, responsive to rhythm" that derives from African possession rituals ("Shouting," 91). In *Jonah's Gourd Vine* she indicates that John Pearson is a Sanctified preacher when his third wife, Sally, hears John preach and comments, "Man, you preached! . . . Only thing Ah heahed so many folks wuz shoutin' Ah couldn't half hear whut you wuz sayin'" (189). Like spirituals, shouting highlights the collaborative gestures and speech that define the liturgical event. Hurston explains, "Shouting is a community thing. It thrives in concert. It is the first shout that is difficult for the preacher to arouse. After that one they are likely to sweep like fire over the church. This is easily understood, for the rhythm is increasing with each shouter who communicated his fervor to someone else" ("Shouting," 91). By connecting John's preaching abilities to spirituals and shouting, Hurston does not fully permit the reader to imagine that John effectively converts church members with only his words. Rather, John Pearson's words become powerful when they are accompanied by his encoded bodily actions and collectively experienced in the bodies of his congregants.

As Hurston ascribes the power of the religious event to the embodied liturgical performance rather than merely to the voice of the preacher or the words of a sermon, she argues that effective preaching depends largely on the ritually recognizable actions and utterances of the congregation that may only be inspired by the capacities of the preacher. The plot of *Jonah's Gourd Vine* and the Sanctified practice of "shouting" exemplify this reality: the preacher cannot be a spiritual leader without a congregation to bear him up. John Pearson is lifted into social and spiritual prominence as a result of his effective preaching abilities, only to meet his ultimate demise when the congregation of Second Zion Baptist church refuses to follow a preacher who has abused his wife and participated in extramarital affairs. When John performs "The Wounds of Jesus," he does so in order to try to convince his dissenting congregation that they should not replace him with a new preacher, Reverend Cozy. Even though John's effective performance of "The Wounds of Jesus" outshines his competitor's ineffective "lecture," he cannot bear to continue leading congregants who have turned their backs on him. Ultimately, John fails to find a new flock and is killed by a train that echoes the "damnation train" described in Lovelace's sermon. In short, John learns that in the Sanctified Church, you cannot be a preacher without a congregation.

The ritualized absorption and participation of the congregation are so key to Hurston's understanding of preaching that a truly effective sermonic event continues to be performed even after the pastor has left the religious stage. Key to Hurston's theory of Sanctified liturgy is the notion that the preaching event continues into futurity under the directions of those who are not the preacher, offering further variations on the theme. *The Sermon in the Valley* does not end when Brother Ezra ceases to speak, but rather continues as Caroline, the only congregant with a name, leads the flock in simultaneous singing. In *Jonah's Gourd Vine* a congregant named Anderson follows up John Pearson's "Wounds of Jesus" sermon by leading the church in chanting. In the case of the novel, the preacher is not even present as the liturgical event continues. John Buddy Pearson's absence shows that while the preacher may have precipitated the ritual event, it is the audience who become the new authorities of spiritual-making. The layered ensembles of performance in the religious event recall Eileen Southern's term, "heterophony," which she uses to describe the "overlapping call-and-response-patterns" of African American spirituals (198, 197). While "the lead singer always began the song" and often improvised "new verses as he sang," other singers would often join in the verses and refrains, allowing for the soloist and other individual singers to build off of each other in patterns of increasingly layered spiritual-making (197). Hurston's reiterative editorial process, then, seems a fitting legacy for "The Wounds of Jesus." Every future liturgical event framed by the sermon is "a new creation" manifested in collaborative, embodied performance ("Spirituals and Neo-Spirituals," 80). In the case of Lovelace's sermon and its many iterations, Hurston and her collaborators riff on the themes of collectivity and corporeality through the metonymic *wounds* of Jesus, Biblical signifiers of both divine and human anatomy. The wounds of Jesus, just like the sermon of the same name, signify stories of suffering and betrayal, all while enabling the manifestation of collective spiritual transcendence for the entire Christian community.

When a Performance Is Not a Performance: Morrison's Reading of Baby Suggs

Perhaps one of the most regularly cited literary examples of transcendent, community-focused preaching is that exhibited by the character Baby Suggs in Toni Morrison's neo-slave narrative *Beloved* (1987). Like Hurston's John Pearson, Morrison's preacher, Baby Suggs, is a powerful spiritual leader who showcases her human materiality in the preaching event. Furthermore, Morrison's preaching event invokes theological ideas from both Western-centric Christianity and diasporic formulations of West and Central African religions, particularly those connected to embodied forms of knowledge and community. Like Hurston, Morrison fuses her capacious knowledge of the Euro-American canon with Afro-diasporic references and ways of thinking throughout *Beloved*. Whereas Hurston's preachers are always men who try to gain their authority by controlling the bodies of others, Baby Suggs is an elderly woman whose preaching takes the form of radical vulnerability. Baby Suggs is an elderly African American woman who begins preaching a message of grace through self-love and spiritual community to free black persons in and outside of churches in mid-nineteenth-century Cincinnati, Ohio. An "unchurched preacher . . . who visited pulpits and opened her great heart to those who could use it" (*Beloved,* 92), Baby Suggs chooses to preach, as Linda Krumholz says, "out of her own heart and imagination" (398) after she achieves social liberation when her son Halle pays for her manumission. Baby Suggs, like John Pearson in *Jonah's Gourd Vine,* is never ordained by an ecclesiastical institution but still guest-preaches to a variety of Black Protestant Christian denominations—"AME's and Baptists, Holiness and Sanctifieds, the Church of the Redeemer and the Redeemed"—when not conducting her own ceremonies in the Clearing (*Beloved,* 92). With most of her body broken and scarred as a result of enslavement, Baby Suggs decides to offer the only organ she has left to give—her heart. Morrison describes Baby Suggs's process of "calling," or preaching, as an exercise of love as she opens her heart in front of others.

In studying the audiobook of *Beloved* alongside the printed version, we can better see how Morrison's prose encourages the reader to adopt performative textual hermeneutics. This method of reading with a focus on embodied action and orality is then turned on its head in the audiobook version, where Morrison thwarts readers' expectations, and in doing so, promotes an active method of listening. By presenting the text in an unexpected mode, Morrison again requires audience engagement by focusing our concentration on embodied performance. My method of reading through embodied performance allows me to build on the work of scholars such as Nancy Jesser and Tuire Valkeakari, who identify the ways in which Baby Suggs's liturgical homiletics explore the complex relationship between corporeality, imagination, and community. Like Jesser, I see Baby Suggs's preaching as both ephemeral and transformative. By shifting into a close reading of Morrison's 2007 recording of *Beloved,* I am able to comparatively analyze Morrison's textual representations with her oral performance and in doing so, to expand this body of criticism. Keeping in mind the impetus for both drama and catharsis in African American preaching, I ask how the concept of performative preaching is challenged by the fact that Morrison refuses to "perform" on her audiobook. Morrison's reading style throughout the recorded novel is breathy, melodic, repetitive, and nontheatrical. She rarely modulates her voice in terms of pitch, inflection, timbre, or register, even when shifting between characters in a dialogue. I argue that Morrison's nontheatrical vocal performance—though uncharacteristically indicative of key elements in

Black preaching contours in the scene within the Clearing—purposefully breaks these expectations. Morrison's reading style is a presentational technique intended to insist that audiobook listeners remain actively invested throughout the interpretation process. A performance-focused hermeneutical method for reading texts allows me to integrate these different modalities within Western and African diasporic spiritual concepts of ritual, embodiment, and collectivity. Morrison's reading style seeks to engage the embodied imagination and thus to participate in the ethics of communal spirituality enacted by her character Baby Suggs.

Throughout *Beloved* the concepts of text and performance are intimately connected and yet distinct, particularly in relation to Baby Suggs. According to Baby Suggs, what distinguishes her from a "real" Black Christian preacher is her lack of literacy and her resulting separation from the written Bible. Baby Suggs is "uncalled, unrobed, [and] unannointed" (92), meaning that she would not be considered a professional preacher by institutional standards. The family friend Stamp Paid recalls "her authority in the pulpit, her dance in the Clearing, her powerful Call (she didn't deliver sermons or preach—insisting she was too ignorant for that—she *called* and the hearing heard)" (185). While Morrison talks about Baby Suggs's "preaching," she herself refers to her speaking in church pulpits and the Clearing as "calling," because according to her, she does not have the knowledge to preach. Later in the novel, Denver clarifies that the reason her grandmother considers herself too "ignorant" to be a preacher is because she cannot read. In Denver's first-person chapter, largely devoted to forms of reading and listening, she remembers that Baby Suggs "said she always wished she could read the Bible like real preachers" and "so it was good for [Denver] to learn how" (218). In Baby Suggs's opinion, what separates her from "real preachers" is her lack of alphabetic literacy, specifically her inability to engage in scriptural hermeneutics with the printed Bible. Indeed, Baby Suggs's sermon, unlike "The Wounds of Jesus," never cites verses from the Bible or mentions biblical characters such as God, Jesus, or the disciples. The assumption that the ability to read establishes personal legitimacy also inspires Denver (who knows that her father became literate for the same reasons) to attend college.[22]

By distinguishing herself from "real" preachers through her ignorance of alphabetic literacy, Baby Suggs also distinguishes herself from the "formal" masculine tradition of Black preaching demonstrated by the male preachers in Hurston's *Mules and Men,* which echoes the "interpretive" duties of the preacher articulated by W. E. B. Du Bois. As Roxanne Reed writes, "The Bible is linked inextricably to a masculinist practice of theology and preaching" (60). Du Bois's Negro preacher derives from the slave era's priest-preacher, who acted as "interpreter of the Unknown" through primarily oral practices and came to do these interpretive tasks by reading and then orally interpreting the Bible to his congregation. This figure gained his leadership position because *he* could claim knowledge of correct textual interpretations and thus was able to "define" terms for the congregation. Similarly, in Hurston's *Mules and Men,* a group of gathered locals distinguish the traveling preacher (accompanied by two women) from a bootlegger by seeing the visual cue of the "dog-eared Bible" and recognizing the key to his sermonizing in his presumed ability to offer the "correct" interpretation of the term "behold" for the audience. What is more, John Buddy Pearson and Brother Ezra end their descriptions of Jesus's sea-changing powers with, "And [the/de] *Bible says* there was calm" (*Sermon in the Valley,* 198; *Jonah's Gourd Vine,* 179). It is the literate preacher's ability to create the definitions of biblical terms that grants him so much social power. Morrison illustrates the power of being the "definer" when the white Schoolteacher beats the enslaved African Sixo "to show him that definitions belonged to the definers—not the defined" (199). While this quote is often referenced to demonstrate Morrison's interest in the linguistic trappings of power, reading it again with this project's focus on the tensions between reading and utterance highlights the ways in which the concurrent physical abuse perpetrated onto Sixo's body is used to both illustrate and make legitimate his cultural authority as a linguistic "definer."[23]

Like Hurston's textual sermon, *Beloved* is well known for pushing the boundaries between media. Therefore, her work also invites a reading via performative textual hermeneutics focused on the multisensory experiences of literary interpretation. Morrison herself states that she intended to create the novel with a "non-book quality," saying, "I wanted the sound to be something I felt was spoken and more oral and less print" (qtd. in C. Hall, 89). A well-known example of Morrison's stylistic maneuvers designed to elicit this aural experience of prose appears in the very first, short line of *Beloved:* "124 was spiteful." The author chooses to use digits because doing so requires the reader to "sound out" the word, predicting Erna Brodber's sonic "solfa-ing" in *Myal* (1983), which I discuss in relation to spirit thievery in chapter 3. This short sentence also brings to mind Hurston's phonetic dialect and breath-based metrical scheme, which

Sundquist notes is "'readable' only to the degree that it is 'heard'" (49). Morrison provides more detail on her use of "124" in an interview about her audiobooks: "*Beloved* opens with a certain rhythm—'124 was spiteful' BOOM dah-du-du-du-du-dah-dah [laughs]—that's the way I hear it" (Morrison, "Talking to Myself"). Cheryl Hall argues, "As critics, we must come to [Morrison's] work with a new set of assumptions" grounded in narratological "forms arising from the oral tradition, in which song and story intertwine and are often inseparable" (90). Hannes Bergthaller similarly identifies the performative nature of Morrison's work when he says that the author creates "simulated orality," adding that studying *Beloved* as an oral story "assumes that the novel itself can function in the same way as the scenes of antiphony and oral instruction which the novel describes—that orality can be successfully simulated, as it were, in a written text" (129).[24] To heed these calls and recognize the orality of Morrison's printed texts, we can consider how the inclusion of orality also invites the acknowledgment of corporeal productions of sound.

Like Hurston's oeuvre, Morrison's novel is distinctly performative and textual. I agree with Tuire Valkeakari that "because several episodes of *Beloved* so emphatically present Baby Suggs as an orator, critics tend to pit her ministry against the written word," and in turn her appreciation for the written word is an "overlooked aspect of her legacy" (166). For Valkeakari, "Baby Suggs . . . embodies the paradox that informs the relationship between the spoken and written words in African American culture, and her legacy points to the possibility of a creative coexistence and dialogue between these two media of expression" (166). Historically, the relationship between formal literate preaching and informal oral preaching is not distinct either. For example, Womanist theologian Karen Baker-Fletcher employs the term "theographia" to explain how materials constituting formal religious literature are often composed of informal sources such as the written and oral expressions of African American women.[25] Theologian Delores Williams calls these sources an "oral text," bringing to mind Bassard's work on the performance of prayer in African American women's literature (*Transforming Scriptures*, 272). Biblical scholar Renita Weems contends that a common lack of literacy during times of enslavement freed practitioners from "allegiance to any official text, translation, or interpretation; hence once they heard biblical passages read and interpreted to them, they in turn were free to remember and repeat in accordance to their own interests and tastes" (61). Baby Suggs's lack of literacy, an absence of knowledge that she believes reduces her legitimacy as an ecclesiastical authority, acts as the key opportunity for her to become an interpreting author of the theology that best suits her community's survival.

Thanks to her messages of Black subjectivity and liberation, literary critics often position Baby Suggs and her ministry in opposition to those Christian traditions that called for obedience and subordination, particularly those practiced by proslavery white ministers using the Hamitic myth as biblical justification for the institution of slavery.[26] But Morrison also distinguishes Baby Suggs's theology from the inspirational messianism evidenced in the Lovelace sermon: "She did not tell them to clean up their lives or to go and sin no more. She did not tell them they were the blessed of the earth, its inheriting meek or its glorybound pure" (93). By not preaching on the African American community's eventual liberation from oppression, Morrison deviates from the frequent theme of Biblical Exodus from slavery preached by black ministers in the nineteenth century.[27] Instead, unlike many African American preachers, Baby Suggs articulates grace as something beyond salvation through Christ, God, or the emancipation of slavery in the United States. Morrison tells the reader, "She told them that the only grace they could have was the grace they could imagine. That if they could not see it, they would not have it" (93). For Baby Suggs, grace exists only as a phenomenon within the believer's creative thoughts, making spiritual transcendence seem to be an experience of personal creation, one that defies the social and political constrictions placed on black bodies within a setting of virulent racism and enslavement. Nancy Jesser connects the experience of "grace" in Suggs's sermon with that of "transcendent change," which is accessible through the "power of the imagination" but which can only be fully manifested in the space of the Clearing, where "connections and emotions are possible that are unendurable beyond it" (333, 332). By studying the novel alongside Morrison's recorded reading of Baby Suggs's sermon, it becomes possible to see how both the scribal and oral versions of this scene evoke experiences of community that imagine a grace that may radically transcend the sacred space of the Clearing. And yet this grace, enacted through relations of love, is always framed within a context of a violent white supremacy that seeks to cut off and destroy the spiritual and physical body of the African American community. In Baby Suggs's preaching, in both message and praxis, this grace, imagination, and love always operate on and through the collective notion of the human body. While the preaching event in *Beloved* indeed inspires moments of "transcendent change" for its audience, even this notion must be nuanced because Baby Suggs eschews a narrative of salvation through the death and resurrection of Christ. As a result, her sermon does not follow a typical arch of spiritual tragedy leading to eventual collective catharsis; nor, I contend, does it promise any form of permanent respite from spiritual or material harm.

Though Baby Suggs's idea of grace through imagination may at first appear to deviate from the themes of collectivity and flesh, moving the conversation to that of individual mental practices, this is far from the case. Like her individual, agential decision to commit her newly freed self to the African American community by sharing her heart with those in the Clearing, Baby Suggs's ministry continually plants personal subjectivity and agency in the community soil of shared embodiment. For example, Morrison carefully uses the pronoun "they" throughout her invocation of imagined grace, suggesting that salvation is not a future experience of individuals but a shared, ongoing practice for the worshippers. Though it is crucial that we not fall into the trap of establishing simplistic dichotomies between theological traditions, Baby Suggs's preaching must be read in the context of the West and Central African theologies that permeate *Beloved,* particularly in regards to how these diasporic traditions are often invoked to challenge the European Enlightenment concept of individualistic autonomy in personal subjectivity. Baby Suggs seeks to honor the humanity and subjectivity of her congregants by way of their flesh. In privileging the flesh in her theology and praxis, she integrates Christian teachings on the sacredness of all persons while eschewing popular teachings in Christianity that warn "against love of the flesh and self" (Jennings, 165) as well as the secular, Cartesian mind-body split often integrated into contemporary Western religious thought.[28]

Though grace exists in a person's imagination, for Baby Suggs the "person" is always interconnected and interdependent with community, which incorporates their living and dead fellows, or what Manuel Zapata Olivella would call *muntu* (see chapter 2).[29] According to K. Zauditu-Selassie, "The African communal psyche is demonstrated by intersubjectivity, mutuality, and interdependence illustrated by the core values expressed in the Bantu expression *umuntu umuntu nagabuntu,* which translates as 'a person is a person because of people'" (7). In this reading, the concept of personhood is always constructed in relation to the recognition of others' subjectivity. For Delois Jennings, the scene of Baby Suggs's calling exemplifies this principle not just of community but also of ancestral community via "the ring shout, a dance that evolved in slave communities as result of African tribes with shared core beliefs absorbing each others' strongest traditions," which focuses on honoring the ancestors and communicating with the living dead (164–65). (I will revisit the performance practice of the ring shout in connection with children's ring games in Nalo Hopkinson's *Brown Girl in the Ring* in the conclusion of chapter 3.) Therefore, in *Beloved* grace can only be imagined for the person so much as it is always already imagined as a collective phenomenon that transcends death. Valerie Smith puts Morrison's emphasis on subjectivity through community in nontheological terms when she writes that Morrison's "characters achieve autonomy and a sense of identity only to the extent that they can understand and name themselves in relation to a social unit" (123). In addition, the imagination itself is not strictly a mental construct in accordance with the West and Central African cosmologies that Morrison integrates throughout her novel, which largely assume "the interconnectedness and interdependence of the conditions of the body and the soul/spirit/mind" (Valkeakari, 61). In light of this, the preaching scene operates through a complex tapestry of subjectivity through interrelation, the strands of which are threaded together in a spiritual understanding that is experientially embodied both within and beyond the individual self.

I argue that Baby Suggs's emphasis on personal imagination and embodied knowledge via communality, along with her own vulnerable physical presentation in the Clearing scene, prohibits her from acting as a single, authoritative mediator between God and the congregation and differentiates her from the masculine Christian preaching portrayed by Hurston. Suggs may be eliciting bodily experiences in her congregants, but she is not relying on her ability to control them or seeking to prove her power by provoking the appropriate liturgical behaviors. Even though *Beloved* is designed as an aural text, Morrison does not focus on Baby Suggs's use of her "straining voice" like Hurston does for the male preachers; rather, she describes Baby Suggs's guest-preaching as "let[ting] her heart beat in their presence" (92). The narrator here equates Baby Suggs's preaching with the beating of a human heart, reminding us of those performative metric punctuations created by Hurston's preachers in the breathing "ha." Baby Suggs and the "Wounds of Jesus" preachers similarly actualize the preaching practice by showcasing their own physiology, emphasizing their bodies' rhythmic capacities. While Baby Suggs's physiologically metered homiletics resemble the male preachers' presentations of bodily rhythm via "strained breath" in "The Wounds of Jesus," her presentation of a steady (and likely unmanipulated) cardiac rhythm starkly contrasts the carefully choreographed straining breath of Hurston's characters. When Baby Suggs "let[s] her heart beat in their presence," she is not aiming to prove her body's performative labor to the congregation but is rather seeking to publicly exist.[30]

The beating heart symbolizes Baby Suggs's homiletics and her foundational impetus to preach at all, an impetus grounded in past pain and present choice. After the bodily destruction suffered during enslavement, Baby Suggs "decided that, because slave life had 'busted her legs, back, head, eyes, hands, kidneys, womb and tongue,' she had nothing left to make a living with but her heart—which she put to work at once" (92). Not only is the heart a metonym for the element of love here, but it represents those physically battered body parts that still survive, such as Sethe's scarred back, a result of Schoolteacher's beating, and her mother's mutilated mouth, a result of the use of the iron bit. Corporeally and metaphorically wrecked as a result of forced labor, Baby Suggs chooses to put her remaining heart to work now, and so the old woman's preaching represents the free choice to perform spiritual labor for her black community. This sacrificial choice is reminiscent of Jesus's in "The Wounds of Jesus," when he volunteers to suffer for the sins of man. When Stamp Paid pleads with Baby Suggs not to quit calling, he exclaims, "You can't quit the Word. It's given to you to speak. You can't quit the Word, I don't care what all happen to you" (186). Here Stamp Paid misunderstands Baby Suggs's relationship to preaching, thinking that her calling to spiritual leadership forces her to sermonize regularly. But the reader knows that Baby Suggs understands her preaching as a use of her heart and sees that she only recognized her capacity to have a heart after being made free through Halle's manumission. Preaching symbolizes choice for Baby Suggs more than anything. In the paradigm Hurston offers, a preacher can only be considered a spiritual authority so long as his or her embodied performance effectively inspires the collaborative liturgical event in the bodies of congregants. In contrast, Baby Suggs's style of preaching, based on the offering of her own heartbeat rather than on the bodies of others, leaves her free to quit preaching without losing her sense of self. What is more, Stamp Paid aligns Baby Suggs's preaching with the "Word"—a term he uses no less than five times in this one dialogue—when she conceptualizes her preaching as nonalphabetic. Finally, Baby Suggs's preaching practice can never be separated from "what happen to [her]" because she chooses to preach as a reckoning with her past, with the things that have happened to her and her community.

Baby Suggs's ceremony in the Clearing is inaugurated through physical performances of community relations. First, like Jesus, Baby Suggs calls the children to her, shouting, "Let the children come!" (audiobook,

3:49:26; print, 92).[31] After Baby Suggs instructs the children to laugh for their parents' ears, she calls the "grown men," instructing them to dance for the eyes of the wives and children. She then calls the women and tells them to cry "for the living and the dead. Just cry" (audiobook, 3:50:12; print, 93). This format of the sermon inverts the usual church structure, which uses rhetorical fervor to prompt the congregants to manifest emotion. Instead, Baby Suggs begins with these displays of emotion, harkening even more closely to West African practices, wherein the affective spiritual experience occurs not as much through one person's moving rhetoric but through the embodied practice of all those present together. In *Dancing Wisdom* Yvonne Daniel explains that in religion, culture, and performance of the African diaspora, spirit functions as embodied knowledge, which accesses meaning on deeply metaphysical, cognitive, and somatic planes. Delois Jennings argues that Baby Suggs's ritual in the Clearing should not be read as a Christian sermon nor as preaching at all, but rather should be interpreted in connection with several African-derived practices and theologies, including the "ring shout," the "Kongo cosmogram," and "the refusal to subordinate flesh to spirit, the exegesis of the inseperability of spirit and flesh found in Vodoun" (164–65). I contend that Baby Suggs's preaching praxis interweaves these traditions with the collaborative liturgical event recognizable in the Sanctified Church. She instructs those present to access spirit—or the imagined grace—through their flesh and in doing so provokes a performative religious event geared toward communal embodied understanding and care.

Just as Baby Suggs invites her audience to use their own imaginations and bodies in order to comprehend her theological ideas, Morrison carefully crafts her writing and reading styles in order to inspire understanding through audience engagement. Morrison herself narrates the audiobook of *Beloved,* just as she does for all of her novels recorded in English. As Matthew Rubery notes, "Hearing Toni Morrison read aloud is a very different experience from that of reading her to oneself." As a result of her unique oral style, audience reception for her recorded editions is far more mixed than that for her printed, literary works. While "some find her speech mesmerizing, even haunting . . . , others struggle with her unique cadences and refusal to perform" (Morrison, "Talking to Myself"). Indeed, a cursory look at the titles of reviews of the audiobook of *Beloved* on Audible reveals polarizing perspectives. Select review titles include those discouraging purchase, such as "Amazing Book—Bad Audio Book," "Morrison is a terrible reader," and "Great novel, poor performance." Others show apparent devotion to Morrison's style: "Magnificent—Toni Morrison's voice will haunt me," and "Perfect!," which claims that "there's nothing like hearing the beautiful Music of Toni Morrison's voice reading her own work." Morrison tells Matthew Rubery in a 2013 interview that she decided to record her own audiobooks beginning with *Tar Baby* in 1983 after listening to productions featuring the "first-rate actresses" Lynne Thigpen and Alfre Woodard.[32] Morrison decided "the rhythm was wrong." She continues, "She didn't put the emphasis where I had heard it in my head. So I thought, well, then I'll read it the way I think it ought to sound" ("Talking to Myself").[33] Morrison has since narrated all of her own books in the style she uses when reading before audiences, with—as she puts it—"the right emphasis, accent, and so on." It should come as no surprise that an author who wrote her novel to "sound" "more oral and less print" also thinks at length about exactly how her novels should "sound" through nonimagined speech. Rachel Kaadzi Ghansah begins her *New York Times* magazine feature on Morrison with the author at the sound studio in 2015 recording the narration for the audiobook of *God Help the Child,* noting that though "many authors use actors . . . that's not how Morrison hears her own sentences, so she does these tedious sessions herself." In what can only be described as reverent tones, Ghansah recounts listening to Morrison's "barely-a-whisper voice," saying that "because of how [Morrison] was positioned, I couldn't see her; I could hear only her voice. Purring and soft. Dulcet. A faint noise coming from within the darkness." While Morrison's reading style elicits polarizing opinions, her distinct aesthetic nevertheless inspires reflection from a wide array of listeners.

I consider Morrison's distinct, "barely-a-whisper" reading style as a purposeful performance choice, and one that invites and challenges listeners to understand themselves as active participants in the hermeneutical process. One Audible review of *Beloved* warns potential consumers that "this novel requires active participation of the reader" and that they may find listening to it "too arduous." Morrison in fact "want[s] the reader to participate" in the interpretive process and so constructs her written and oral prose to achieve that potentially "arduous" end. When asked by Rubery if she has "a different relationship to readers of [her] books than to audiences who are listening to [her] read," Morrison responds, "I always think they read it and hear it the way I do—but that's wrong. I want the reader to help me with the book. I want the relationship to be that intimate" (Morrison, "Talking to Myself"). Morrison's answer does not distinguish print and audio audiences and instead focuses on her overarching desire to inspire hermeneutical collaboration. With this goal of collaborative meaning-making in mind, I suggest that Morrison is using her textual and oral performances as a means of inviting readers and listeners into the liturgical event of her written and spoken texts. What is more, she tries to create an intimate relationship between herself and the reader/listener, demonstrating a commitment to collectivity within interpretive acts. Morrison thus extends Baby Suggs's focus on community and relational hermeneutics to the project of audiobook narration.

In the pursuit of creating an "intimate" relationship with the audiobook listener, Morrison uses particular stylistic speech patterns as a means of incorporating her readers and listeners into the relational, hermeneutical community. Her listeners become like the embodied and active congregation, helping to enact the spiritual liturgy. A majority of Audible reviewers—even those criticizing Morrison's voice and reading style—overwhelmingly argued that they felt "transformed" or "changed" after listening to the entire narrative. The reviewers' proclamations of transformation echo the rhetoric surrounding effective sermonic events and thus further encourage a study of the audiobook in light of its religious content. With its impetus toward experience, relationality, and change, the audiobook of *Beloved* appears to exemplify "a paradigmatic instance of reading as process, encounter, and potential transformation" (Spillers, "Moving On," 253). In this quote, Hortense Spillers describes the reflective practice of reading nineteenth-century African American sermons. But in the case of this audiobook, the "paradigmatic instance of reading" is turned on itself. A visual text—written to evoke the aural imagination—has been made aural by the author's reading of that same visual text. In that reading process, the author elicits "transformation" by means of her supposed *lack* of performance. Yet even Morrison's lack of performance is not as much an absence of presentational style as it is a performance different from what some listeners expect. Namely, Morrison does not offer the paradigmatic "straining voice" associated with Black preaching; nor, for that matter, does she perform any other phonological or inflectional markers often associated with African American Vernacular English in popular media.[34] Instead, Morrison reads in a limited register and pitch with distinctive "lyrical" patterns that reviewers call monotone, providing minimal tonal distinctions between characters' voices and breaking up her syntax by pausing at unconventional moments. Rather than monotone, Morrison's reading voice, thanks to its proximity to limited tonal range coupled with patterned melodic musical structures, may be best compared to the religious practice of the intoned sermon.

The author's invocation of the intoned sermon is driven by her desire to elicit a relational hermeneutical experience for the audiobook audience. She creates an aural performance that is lyrical and music-like thanks to its noticeable inflectional patterns and minimal tonal variations. In fact, when the character Amy begins singing to Sethe, it is difficult to discern that Morrison's narrative text has moved into the song's poetic verse without first checking the corresponding scene in the printed edition (audiobook, 3:33:13; print, 85). While breathy in its whisper-like resonances, Morrison's intoned stylistic creates an effect that is neither theatrically emphatic nor "strained." Morrison tells Rubery that "dramatizing character voices" is "a little too theatrical and staged for [her] because [she doesn't] want to limit the reader's view or imagination about the characters" (Morrison, "Talking to Myself"). Just as Morrison uses formal elements such as shifting points of view and rhythmic phrases to encourage an active, performance-inflected reading method for her printed prose, the author-turned-performer develops a similar interpretive method for the audiobook listener. By narrating her novel with a consistent pitch and style like that of an intoned sermon, Morrison refuses to use her voice as a means of developing her characters' personalities, insisting that the listener perform that creative labor. In this way she encourages her listener to join the hermeneutical network and actively engage in the "reading" process.

In creating an audiotext that requires considerable concentration from listeners, Morrison expands the concept of liturgical community beyond Baby Suggs's sermon; she opens it up to her wider reading and listening audience. In the Clearing, Baby Suggs tells her congregation "that the only grace they could have was the grace they could imagine. That if they could not see it, they would not have it" (audiobook, 3:51:05–10; print, 88). And in the discussion of her audiobook style, Morrison takes a strikingly similar position, citing her investments in not limiting the readers "view" or "imagination" ("Talking to Myself"). Morrison's reading style, then, actually mirrors the theology of Baby Suggs. Both spiritual transformation and literary, hermeneutical transformation can only be attained through embodied, active participation and imaginational labor performed within relationship to a wider community.

The lack of variation Morrison provides throughout the audiobook only highlights the importance of the slight shifts she does articulate through rhythm, tempo, and pronunciation while reading aloud Baby Sugg's sermonic ritual in the Clearing. Like the "The Wounds of Jesus" as presented in Cunard's anthology and the novel *Jonah's Gourd Vine*,

Morrison's performance of Baby Suggs's sermon in the Clearing offers an especially aural reading experience in her already-aural novel. Morrison creates the illusion of sound in the print edition by means of literary devices such as partial rhyme (particularly the fricative consonance within "flesh") and rhythmically evocative syntactical sequences, which are punctuated by the italicized *"you,"* semicolons, full stops, and one exclamation mark. In the audiobook version of the same scene, Morrison subtly alters her speaking style, adopting distinct contours of intonation, rhythm, pronunciation, and tempo that demarcate the religious event within the larger narrative. Some of the features in Morrison's style during this scene prompt connections to culturally recognizable patterns in Black preaching (otherwise absent in the narrative recording), while others appear to minimize the conventional expectations of the homiletic genre.

The reader is taken back in time to one of Baby Suggs's sermonic performances as Sethe, Denver, and Beloved stand on the outskirts of the Clearing where Baby Suggs once held informal ceremonies. Morrison uses a subtle break between paragraphs and the rhetorical movement into present tense to create the sensation of listening to a live sermonic performance in her printed novel, while the audio version augments this linguistic cue with a distinct pause in the audio track (3:51:10–17).[35] Baby Suggs's sermonic monologue is framed by an introductory phrase signaling that the reader is now entering into the continuous present of Afro-diasporic, religious ritual: "'Here,' she said, 'in this here place'" (audiobook, 3:51:17; print, 88). A new audio "chapter" of *Beloved* begins just before Baby Suggs's first "here," which creates a sonic demarcation between the third-person, past-tense point of view used throughout most of the previous chapter and the "live," present-tense event that is Baby Suggs's sermon. The shift to a new audio chapter on the recording means that the track pauses for approximately seven seconds. Considering that all of Baby Suggs's sermon spans only two minutes and forty-two seconds out of a narrative that is twelve hours and six minutes long, the pause makes up almost four percent of the length of the total sermon. In addition, depending on the space between tracks in the CD version, the listener hears silence for even longer as the electronic device transitions. Considering the religious context in which it appears, this mute portion within the recording can be seen as performing the "moment of silence" that is often invoked before religious prayers and sermons in the Protestant Christian church service. Baby Suggs also prays silently before calling the children, women, and men into the Clearing's sacred space, and the novel describes a silence that overtakes the congregants after they have been left "exhausted and riven ... damp and gasping for breath" as a result of the liturgical displays of emotion preceding the spoken sermon (audiobook, 3:50:33–39; print, 93). In other words, the audiobook's pause enacts the distinction between the sermon as *"text"* and "the *experience* of the preaching event in the faith community" (Floyd-Thomas et al., 212, emphasis in orig.). Though likely an accident of timing and digital manufacturing requirements, the moment of recorded silence encourages listeners to hear the prose of Baby Suggs's sermon as a distinct religious monologue, and in keeping with Morrison's hermeneutical intentions, invites them to adopt a congregational position in the preaching event.

In analyzing Morrison's "reading" of Baby Suggs's oral preaching as an interpellated audience member, we are invited to consider how the author's speaking style (rooted in her desire to elicit audience involvement) inflects the messages of community, embodiment, and imagined grace that characterize Baby Suggs's sermon. From the outset, Baby Suggs's sermon maintains her focus on embodiment: "'Here,' she said, 'in this here place, we flesh; flesh that weeps, laughs; flesh that dances on bare feet in grass. Love it. Love it hard'" (3:51:17–29). She instructs the religious audience, participatory followers who have already been using their bodies to cocreate the liturgical event, to love their flesh and recognize its physiological capacities for emotive and creative expression. Morrison pronounces "flesh" by accenting and elongating the fricatives "fl" and "sh." Prefacing the word with the pronoun "we," Baby Suggs calls in her congregation by emphasizing their shared materiality in embodiment. What is more, the noun "flesh," which has no distinction between singular and plural, inspires the listener to imagine the congregation as a kind of contiguous body or "muntu." Baby Suggs connects the metaphorical church body (common in Christian theology) to the congregants' common ontological features as human "flesh." I contend that she is also gesturing to the worshippers' shared historical experiences. Each of these black individuals has been physically and spiritually harmed by a slaveholding nation obsessed with classifying and ranking humans by way of their racial codifications of flesh. Morrison pauses and emphasizes the gravely quality of her voice as she says, "Love it. Love it hard," elongating the first "o" in "love it" and lowering her pitch emphatically as she elongates the "a" in "love it hard." Morrison then contrasts her declination of pitch in "love it hard" with sentences detailing how "they" do not love your flesh. Flesh is the communal site of divine care within the community space, and it is the site of enmity from those outside "this here place."

Morrison creates a sense of continuation and interrogation when she describes "their" brutality in a series of phrases spoken in ascending pitch. "Yonder they do not love your flesh. They despise it. They don't love your eyes; they'd just as soon pick 'em out. No more do they love the skin on your back. Yonder they flay it" (3:51:29–43). Morrison uses this inflectional pattern of repeated upswings in pitch throughout Baby Suggs's sermon, repeatedly creating a sense of uncertainty (interrogatives in English feature the ascending contour) and circularity. When Morrison looked for literary inspirations in creating a more "oral" scribal novel in *Beloved,* she explains, "The closest I came, I think, to finding it was in some books written by Africans, novels that were loose . . . the kind that people could call unstructured because they were circular, and because they sounded like somebody was telling you a story" (qtd. in C. Hall, 89). Zauditu-Selassie ties Morrison's use of circularity in *Beloved* to the invocation of African-derived ancestral presences, writing that "like memory, this circularity serves as structure, theme, narrative device, and ancestral characterization" (150). The oral pattern of pitch ascension throughout the sermon manages to create the circularity and looseness that characterize *Beloved* as a whole and that Morrison admired in African scribal stories. In this particular moment, that circularity points to the seemingly indeterminate question of physical abuse in the lives of black subjects.

In the recorded version Morrison's tempo slows considerably as she says, "And O my people they do not love your hands," signaling her change in anatomical focus (3:51:43–46). Morrison then switches to a rapid staccato as she rattles off the words of bodily abuse toward the hands—"tie, bind, chop off and leave empty"—after which she returns to a slower pace, finally extending the final vowel for the command, "Love your hands!" (3:51:46–53). After hearing the rapid staccato Morrison adopts in the audiobook, the reader who returns to the printed text becomes more acutely aware of the techniques Morrison employs to encourage a performative reading in this scene: sharp, monosyllabic verbs and verb phrases that reference complex structures of exploitation, enslavement, debilitation, and neglect of African Americans (93). On the recording Morrison's vocal registers and rhythms perform the work of body-centric Womanist theology, which seeks to decode "white supremacist constructions of black bodies, especially black women's bodies" in order to reframe the flesh as a site of sacred wisdom and possibility (T. Johnson, 106). In Baby Suggs's rendering, white constructions of the black body are underpinned by a circuitous series of corporeal atomizations and destructions. Even in her slower exhortation that "they do not love your hands," Baby Suggs first intones, "O my people," and in so doing frames the threatening statement in a moment of shared community.

Morrison's pattern of speaking quickly about violence and slowly about self-love allots more time to any words or phrases devoted to caring for the body, meaning that Morrison has Baby Suggs thematically focus on white racist violence while performatively minimizing the very same subject. Delois Jennings contends that Baby Suggs's "theology of flesh . . . rejects European Americans' physical persecution and spiritual rupture of the African other, as well as the spiritual persecution of their material selves" (165). It is as if Morrison's reading sonically manifests what she hopes her literature will also do—devote less attention and airtime to white characters and messages all while confronting African American experiences of racial violence.

> Love them. Raise them up and kiss them. Touch others with them, pat them together, stroke them on your face 'cause they don't love that either. *You* got to love it, *you!* And no, they ain't in love with your mouth. Yonder, out there, they will see it broken and break it again. What you say out of it they will not heed. What you scream from it they do not hear. What you put into it to nourish your body they will snatch away and give you leavins instead. No, they don't love your mouth. *You* got to love it. (audiobook, 3:51:53–52:30; print, 93, emphasis in orig.)

By turning the readers' and listeners' attention to the physical form of the mouth, Morrison explicitly ties together orality, rhetorical performances, and the material needs of the body. The mouth here becomes a synecdoche for the body as a metaphorical and physical site of reception and as an agent of action. The mouth "scream[s]" in order to advocate for its physical and spiritual needs, but the same mouth is abandoned and neglected by the white listener, who does not "hear" and instead doles out the abuse of targeted malnourishment and disdain.

In the above selection we see Morrison meet several of the stylistic expectations for Black preaching. Roxanne Reed argues that in the text version of this passage, which she calls a selection from "one of Baby Suggs's preacherly performances," Morrison's "phrasing suggests a rhythmic pattern typically found in Black preaching . . . namely the triplet figure" (61). Jon Michael Spenser identifies the triplet figure as a common phrasing in preaching by black men. According to Reed, the triplet is created through "emphasis on the initial word in each of the short phrases, [which] suggests an accented beat followed by unaccented beat or beats"

(61). Morrison creates this pattern in the instructional phrases pertaining to physical affection, specifically those beginning with the verbs "raise," "touch," "pat," and "stroke." In the audio version, Morrison increases her volume and pitch steadily throughout these short commands, then quickly drops back to a matter-of-fact tone, again creating a sense of harshness when concluding, "'cause they don't love that either." This drop in pitch signals the mundane cruelties of white feeling, even as its comparatively detached emotional resonance refuses to invest substantial energy in the details of this affective violence.

Morrison sets up and then repeatedly inverts listeners' expectations of the African American sermon in ways that effectively "perform" the message of Baby Suggs's sermon, and in doing so she demands a hermeneutics of receptivity, which balances passivity and agency. As a visual and sonic narrator, Morrison manipulates the delivery of her rhetoric in order to promote the participation of her audience; she encourages the reader and listener to adopt active and responsive methods of interpretation that can consistently engage with the written and spoken text. In both text and audiobook formats, the preaching scene encourages audiences to recognize the "centripetal pull" of African American cultural performances. Bassard uses Lawrence Levine's phrase "centripetal pull" to describe "precisely that aspect of [early African American] spirituals in performance which ... draws the boundaries between participants within the communal performance and those outside the performing collective" (*Spiritual Interrogations*, 134).[36] Morrison's diverse audiences are asked to feel the impetus to collective participation in the religious event thanks to her style of speaking. At the same time, the content of the sermon clearly demarcates the "bar between outsider and insider" by repeatedly describing the ways in which those white Americans "outside" the Clearing harm the African American community within the liturgical circle (134).

Baby Suggs begins her sermonic event through participatory ritual, then rhetorically invokes the collective "flesh" of her listeners. Having interpellated her congregants as an interwoven community, Baby Suggs uses the image of the empty "hands" to chronicle the endless cycles of violence perpetrated in a racist society and uses the "mouth" to demonstrate how the body can be concurrently active and passive, physical and metaphysical. At this point the sermon returns to the communal nature of embodiment through "flesh," then adopts a selective lens to itemize not only the specific physical components of her audience's bodies but also the potential abuse and nurturance those body parts can receive from others and themselves.

This is flesh I'm talking about here. Flesh that needs to be loved. Feet that need to rest and to dance; backs that need support; shoulders that need arms, strong arms I'm telling you. And O my people, out yonder, hear me, they do not love your neck unnoosed and straight. So love your neck; put a hand on it, grace it, stroke it and hold it up. And all your inside parts that they'd just as soon slop for hogs, you got to love them. The dark, dark liver—love it, love it, and the beat and beating heart, love that too. More than eyes or feet. More than lungs that have yet to draw free air. More than your life-holding womb and your life-giving private parts, hear me now, love your heart. For this is the prize. (audiobook, 3:52:31–53:33; print, 93–94)

Baby Suggs closes her sermon by imploring her congregants to fiercely concentrate their enactments of love not to the body parts most often associated with agential action: the feet, hands, arms, and womb that "dance," "stroke," or even "hold" and "give" "life." Rather, Suggs devotes her sermon's climax to the organ that motivates her own preaching praxis, the "beat and beating heart." When Morrison itemizes the "flesh that needs to be loved," she again performs the triplet pattern, accenting each of the first words, all of which happen to be parts of the body: "*Feet* that need to rest and to dance; *backs* that need support; *shoulders* that need arms, *strong arms* I'm telling you" (audiobook, 3:52:36–44; print, 93, emphasis mine). By tonally emphasizing each element of the body needing compassion, Morrison gives each of those body parts the positive attention for which her sermon argues. Morrison uses the literary text to make real her loving focus on the body.

This chapter contends that in focusing on the embodied components of performative preaching, Hurston and Morrison emphasize the ritualistic, liturgical aspects of their written sermons. The preaching event must occur within an embodied performance because a liturgy can only be said to have "successfully" occurred insomuch as everyone, including the congregation members, have engaged with the process, and in doing so, have demonstrated a performative response to the preacher's utterances and gestures. In other words, if the event is successful and has elicited a cathartic response, then that response will be communicated through the embodied rituals of the preacher and wider congregation. The collective liturgical performance of Hurston's Sanctified preaching is based on a framework of tradition that enables the cumulative expression of religious feeling that she calls "spiritual-making." In the case of Morrison's performance, embodied ritual explicitly preempts the body of Baby

Suggs's sermon in a way that lays bare the necessity of audience engagement. This hermeneutical process of embodied relationality characterizes not only the homiletics and theology of Baby Suggs but also the reading and performing styles enacted by Morrison.

While the multiple modalities and generic formatting of Hurston's and Morrison's work explicitly call for the performative textual hermeneutics that I introduce and develop throughout this chapter, I will demonstrate how this practice of interpretation can be taken up in analyses of other spiritually rich Afro-diasporic works, including novels that have only appeared as written publications. In the next chapter I build on the principles of engaged interpretation identified in Hurston's and Morrison's preaching texts in order to tease apart the complex and often confusing relationship between the body, subjectivity, and community in two novels by Manuel Zapata Olivella and Erna Brodber, respectively. The two women mediums in these texts are forced to reckon with their new identities as conduits between the metaphysical world of the ancestors and the physical world of the living. These stories inspire questions about how the spiritual power of communication (for authors, translators, and readers) disrupts the very notion of an understandable and static experience of embodiment and subjectivity. I draw on my analysis of adaptation across genres and modalities in Huston and Morrison to concentrate on the mediating practices of linguistic translation and opacity. As do Hurston and Morrison, Manuel Zapata Olivella and Erna Brodber configure their texts to elicit these reflections on hermeneutical methods that invite larger explorations of spiritual and sociopolitical power.

Both Toni Morrison's and Zora Neale Hurston's depictions of preaching diffuse spiritual power by locating sacred experience in the collective participation of individual bodies in worship. At the same time, both authors do not negate the inherent inequities of power that may exist within or outside of the religious ceremony. By close reading Hurston's ethnographic, theatrical, and novelistic writings on religion (particularly those of preaching in the Sanctified Church), I contend that Hurston uses editorial maneuvers to portray Sanctified preaching events as performative, liturgical events constituted through embodied collaboration. While I have focused on the distribution of power that such a liturgical theory proffers, that is not to suggest that Hurston establishes a homiletics devoid of the trappings of institutionalized authority. A religious liturgy features a prescribed order of acts and utterances, whose conventions and regulations worshipers follow. Hurston points out the encoded nature of the Baptist and Pentecostal church service, saying, "Beneath the seeming informality of religious worship there is a set formality" ("Spirituals and Neo-Spirituals," 83). Because liturgy manifests religious authority through the performance of encoded actions and utterances, the "set formality" of the service also belies a set system of power that circulates in the preaching event. Rappaport writes that to perform a liturgical order means to conform to the sequence of acts and utterances encoded by another person; therefore "authority and directive [are] intrinsic to liturgical order" (192–93). The intrinsic order of the Sanctified sermon is exemplified in Hurston's description of the congregation as a Greek chorus. In theater "the concept of a chorus always contains a fundamental tension between the need for the chorus to act as a unified entity and for the individuals in the chorus to preserve an identity and dramatic function of their own" (Pickering, 86). Huston's choral depiction of liturgical power insists on the very tensions of subjectivity in community that Morrison so beautifully narrates.

In Morrison's *Beloved* the sacred ceremony refuses to ignore, or predict, a triumphant messianic end to the centuries of subjugation against African-descended individuals in the Americas. Rather, Baby Suggs preaches individual and communal love for the subjugated body in the midst of systemic suffering. As Nancy Jesser succinctly puts it, "Baby Suggs sings a litany of loving all the pieces that make up the body" (332). Jesser contends that Suggs promises "transcendent change . . . clear and boundless freedom to love and dance in the world" through the "power of the imagination" (333). I suggest that the performativity of Baby Suggs's preaching, that which allows this scene to become seemingly "transcendent," is not rooted in any vision of futurity or liberation outside of the present, liturgical moment. Rather, I see Suggs's sermon as already admitting that no amount of dance or self-love can force white persons to respect and love black persons' bodies. Her ceremony is not a performative act of domination or protection for the congregants. Instead, Suggs promises that the only "transcendent change" available to her congregants is that inherently transitory experience of self and communal love, the love focused on the "beat and beating heart," which they manifest together in the Clearing through embodied engagement, including dance, emotional expression, and collective hearing. The intense embodiment of Baby Suggs's sermon goes against the strict idea of mental transcendence. The sermon urges listeners to love their physical bodies and not to escape into a disembodied realm of the imagination. As Kwame Gyekye writes (referring to the Akan of Ghana), "The condition of the soul depends upon the condition of the body" (65). Similarly, Carl Paris notes that

"African scholar Babatunde Lawal maintains that it is through the body that this spirit or life force manifests itself, acting as a threshold between the secular and the sacred, enabling the human being to interact directly with the superhuman" (41). Rather than the disembodied concept of spiritual transcendence, Baby Suggs preaches immanence, wherein the divine is manifested in the material world. After all, the material body is loved and thus worshipped as divine through the Clearing ceremony.

Baby Suggs does appear defeated by the reality that no matter what, white people can enter into a black person's yard and destroy the sense of personhood that self and communal love have established. In fact, the community to whom she has offered her heart ultimately turns its back on Baby Suggs when she appears too generous, flaunting her emotional bounty. They then abandon Baby Suggs after Sethe kills the baby Beloved. This rejection of Baby Suggs's ministry brings to mind the plight of John Pearson in Hurston's *Jonah's Gourd Vine*. Both preachers are denied the right to "call" for their previous community as a result of their perceived domestic failures and scandals of violence within the family unit. In contrast to Hurston's novel, *Beloved* shows how a group of neighboring women who had once disavowed the family within 124 do come together years after Baby Suggs passed away in isolation in order to aid in ridding the "spiteful" home of its haunting. This incident demonstrates that Baby Suggs's family system has not been entirely rejected and, more specifically, that the granddaughter Denver can still elicit the gendered community's empathy and spiritual support.

I argue that Baby Suggs's decision to retire from preaching and instead "get in [her] bed and lay down [and] fix on something harmless in this world" (*Beloved*, 188) does not disagree with her sermon's message at all. Instead, she agrees that "the heart that pumped out love, the mouth that spoke the Word, didn't count. They [white people] came in her yard anyway and she could not approve or condemn Sethe's rough choice" (188). As much as this tragic reality may seem to contradict Baby Suggs's uplifting sermon, the conclusion is the same—the practice of treating the heart as beloved is the true "prize." The only point of Baby Suggs's spiritual ceremony is to somatically and spiritually love yourself because no matter what, the oppressor will never do it for you. The act of love is the reason to enact love.

2 The Hermeneutics of Spirit Possession

Interpreting Mediums in *Changó, The Biggest Badass* and *Louisiana*

> So Dad has joined the others up there. I feel that they do watch and guide, and I also feel that they join me in the hope that this story of our people can help alleviate the legacies of the fact that preponderantly the histories have been written by the winners.
> —Alex Haley, *Roots: The Saga of an American Family*

> We think we are at ease in our own language, we feel a coziness, a familiarity, a shelter in the language we call our own, in which we think that we are not alienated. What the translation reveals is that this alienation is at its strongest in our relation to our own original language, that the original language within which we are engaged is disarticulated in a way which imposes upon us a particular alienation, a particular suffering.
> —Walter Benjamin, "The Task of the Translator"

IN A 2014 episode of the American public radio show "On Being," Vodou priest and scholar of Africology Patrick Bellegarde-Smith says that being "ridden" in a possession trance is "the equivalent of handing the keys to your car to a very good friend . . . and then hoping the car will not be mangled, and it will come back to you in one piece at some point" ("Living Vodou"). In this analogy the car is the human medium's body, and the driving friend is the dominant possessing agent. This dominant external force temporarily takes control of the medium's being in order to communicate a message to the gathered worshipping community.[1] Such possession is, as host Krista Tippet reflects, a "real releasing of self" for the medium. This nonrigidity of "self" is integral to what anthropologists call spirit possession or possession trance.[2] In her review of scholarship pertaining to the wide array of "phenomena glossed as possession and/or possession trance," Janice Boddy broadly defines possession as "an integration of spirit and matter, force or power and corporeal reality, in a cosmos where the boundaries between an individual and her environment are acknowledged to be permeable, flexibly drawn, or at least negotiable" (408, 407). This formulation of reality as integrative and fluid thoroughly challenges formative Western philosophical tenets of self-knowledge and individualistic subjectivity.[3] Perhaps this challenge is why mediumship and trance have long fascinated and perplexed Euro-American audiences entrenched in a philosophical tradition that both presupposes and debates those terms, including those who may encounter Bellegarde-Smith's interview on NPR. In practice, the intellectual history of spirit possession in Western discourse evidences centuries of ethnocentrism and racism. As Alessandra Benedicty-Kokken has detailed, the practice of using the word "possession" to define the kinds of experiences described by Bellegarde-Smith derives not from practitioners but from twentieth-century researchers writing about Haiti first in French and later in English (2).[4] Often practitioners of Vodou and Santería describe what we call "possession" as a spirit mounting its horse: *Monte chwa* in Haitian Kreyol and "orichas montando . . . bailando o subiendo la cabeza" in Cuban Spanish (2). I use the phrase "spirit possession" to indicate a variety of phenomena in which an individual submits to an external power through ritual practices. Like Hurston's and Morrison's liturgical rituals, spirit possession invites questions about agency, knowledge, and authorship.

In this chapter and in chapter 3, I study a variety of representations of the occupied body in late twentieth-century Afro-Caribbean literature. Inspired by George Balandier's proposition that "possession is a form of intellectual communication" (qtd. in Stoller, 19), I read two fictional representations of spirit possession as literary meditations on the nature of interpreting and understanding the self and the external world. I begin by studying the character Agne Brown, a spiritual medium, in Afro-Colombian Manuel Zapata Olivella's epic novel *Changó, The Biggest Badass* (1983). In chapter 1 we saw African American preachers' integral roles as mediators, interpreters, and translators of the biblical word. Like these preachers, Agne Brown is called to mediate and communicate spiritual knowledge for her community. I used a performative method of reading to show that Hurston's and Morrison's religious works emphasize embodied participation. Through the trope of spirit possession, Zapata

Olivella amplifies in his written text this connection between spiritual power and embodiment. Agne Brown's physical flesh comes to signify both the religious text and the processes of interpreting such metaphysical discourse. Her interpretive struggles with her own subjectivity guide my own use of performative textual hermeneutics and theories of translation as I analyze the novel's hermeneutics of uncertainty. In this chapter's second section, I follow the story of another fictional spiritual medium, Ella Townsend (later named Ella Kohl, and then Louisiana), in Afro-Jamaican writer Erna Brodber's novel of historical fiction, *Louisiana* (1994). Like Zapata Olivella, Brodber portrays a performative hermeneutical practice founded in a principle that I call "engaged surrender." This paradoxical method of interpretation calls for the active passivity of the reader. What is more, engaged surrender informs this book's broader formulation of a performative textual hermeneutics. These works reveal that spiritually attuned practices of textual mediation are always subtended by disorienting integrations of spirit and matter, past and present, and the individual and her community.

Changó: Translation as Medium, Translation as Message

Changó, The Biggest Badass is undoubtedly a book of translations.[5] When Zapata Olivella originally wrote *Changó, el gran putas* in Spanish, the geographical and chronological breadth of his narrative required a series of translations across language, media, and culture. I use the term "translation" in my study of *Changó* in an expansive light. Specifically, I consider the negotiations that authors, translators, and readers make between languages as well as between "both source and target cultural signs" (Bassnett and Lefevere, 12). Zapata Olivella's expansive epic brings together disparate Afro-diasporic histories into one bound volume. It thematically ties the different customs, cultures, and religions imbedded within each history together with the single thread of one Yoruban god, Changó. In his introduction to the English translation, William Luis writes, "Zapata Olivella immerses himself, and by extension the reader, in the lives, customs, cultures, and religions of the peoples who inhabit the Sub-Saharan African continent, those whose origins can be traced to the Ashanti, Yoruba, Wolof, Kru, Fon, Mandingo, Hausa, Fulani, Congo, Bib, Ganga, Ibos, and Bushmen, among many other tribes" (xvi). The author does not limit himself to the philosophy or mythology of African Religions. Instead, he discusses an array of traditions throughout the lengthy book, including but not limited to Christian Catholicism, North African and US iterations of Islam, and Haitian Vodou. In bringing these disparate religious and cultural paradigms together in one novel, Zapata Olivella performs "cultural translations" as he transmutes images and ideas from one system of thought into another.[6] Zapata Olivella also translated in the traditional, linguistic sense of the term for the 1983 publication, rendering in Spanish written historical and literary documents from languages including English, Portuguese, French, and Dutch. Furthermore, *Changó* is consistently translating across media. In using a written text to depict African and Afro-diasporic oral religious traditions, Zapata Olivella performs religio-cultural translations through what Ramon Jakobson would call "intersemiotic translation" (139). In summary, the plot and material history of *Changó* represent complex networks of translation, which in turn illuminate a "broad intellectual topography" (Apter, 5).

Perhaps the most distinct translatorial action Zapata Olivella demonstrates in *Changó* is his selective *inaction,* or those instances when he chooses to retain a non-Spanish term rather than transpose it. Particularly, Zapata Olivella refuses to translate words that carry spiritual connotations for the novel. For example, the author employs the English form of "soul" (rather than the Spanish *alma*) when the word is embedded within the African American (English-speaking) context. Similarly, Zapata Olivella employs the African designation "Bantú" throughout the novel. While the term "Bantú" generally denotes peoples within the Niger-Congo language families (Yoruba, Igbo, Fula, and Swahili, for example), Zapata Olivella gives it, and its related term "muntu," a particular spiritual connotation. The author writes that Bantú "alludes to the force that joins in a single knot mankind with its forebears and offspring, all immersed in the present, past, and future universe" (449; alude a la fuerza que une un solo nudo al hombre con su ascendencia y descendencia inmersos en el universo presente, pasado, y future, 730). The author's retention of "Bantú" and "muntu," as well as his description of the metaphysical thinking the African words are meant to convey, demonstrates how Zapata Olivella treats both translation and non-translation as a site for "knowledge-production, or insight, somehow beyond the boundaries of equivalence" (Pym, 96). In other words, Zapata Olivella recognizes how translatorial action—the series of decisions and maneuvers undertaken by a translator—can transform others' understandings of the source material.

In building this understanding, Zapata Olivella recognizes translatorial action as a kind of interpretive action and recognizes how translations inevitably direct readers' interpretations of a target text. Zapata Olivella provides a glossary at the end of his novel, for example, and in the process acknowledges that "texts are not immediately meaningful and need to be actively interpreted" (Pym, 99). Subsequently, Zapata Olivella signals an agreement with the foundational tenet of nineteenth-century German hermeneutics—evinced by hermeneutical philosopher, Christian theologian, and translator Friedrich Schleiermacher's own glossaries—which influenced almost all our contemporary theories on translation in the Western academy today.[7] And yet, despite providing a glossary, *Changó* also contains a preface dedicated "to the fellow traveler" that rejects the notion that authors can or should control acts of reading and interpretation. He instructs readers by noting,

> If you come upon a mysterious term, give it your own meaning, reinvent it. Don't consult the glossary at the end of the book, because that serves only to show the landmarks you have already passed; it will not orient you along the paths ahead. (1)

> Si descubres un vocablo misteriosos, dale tu propia connotación, reinvéntala. No acudas al "Cuaderno de bitácora" al final del libro, porque este solo tiene por objeto mostrar los riscos por donde has andado; no es una brújula para descubrir caminos. (35)

What kind of hermeneutical practice is Zapata Olivella encouraging here? Surely, the author is chuckling at his reader's inevitable "failure" to resist taking advantage of the much-needed "navigation" key offered in the back of the book. On the one hand, this recognition leads Zapata Olivella to be didactic in his paratextual guidance. He goes so far as to define the abstract "sense" of words, taking advantage of the knowledge production he can create through translation. For example, he defines "soul" as "the most authentic expression of black feeling" in a "North American text" (461; en referencia al contexto norteamericano, alude a la mayor autenticidad del sentimiento del negro, 665). On the other hand, he tells the reader to ignore the vocabulary instructions altogether and create new meanings for foreign terms. Zapata Olivella dares his readers to embrace the instability of language and read like radical deconstructionists. The structuring glossary notwithstanding, readers are called to constantly question the creation of meaning through interpretation.

These interpretive quandaries within translation are then magnified in the case of the English translation of the novel, published in 2010. Specifically, explorations of translation and interpretation actualized and narrated throughout the English version of *Changó* must likewise privilege a hermeneutical method of uncertainty that extends beyond translational equivalence.

After all, linguistic translation is simply one piece of a more expansive field of questions regarding how we come to interpret and understand any form of communication. As John Biguenet and Rainer Schulte state in *The Craft of Translation,* the translation process affirms the "how" but not the "what" of reading and understanding. If one asks, "What does something mean?" one expects a statement-like answer. If one asks the question, "How does something come to mean?" avenues are opened that lead to the exploration of the complexities inherent in a text (xii). Because the original Spanish-language edition of *Changó, el gran putas* already presents a complex puzzle of translational meaning-making, the English translation is nothing less than a palimpsest of translations and interpretive possibilities. The Spanish-to-English translator, Jonathan Tittler, a white professor of Spanish at Rutgers University, spent fifteen years translating *Changó.* He hoped that the epic would "be known by English-speaking readers," particularly by graduate students in English literary studies ("Rutgers-Camden Spanish Professor Translates").

While Tittler sought to introduce Zapata Olivella's epic to more readers, especially within a pedagogical setting, his methods of translation do not necessarily make it easy for his intended English-speaking audience to "know" the novel *Changó.* The resistant translation, like Zapata Olivella's contradictory directions on interpretation, requires readers to adopt a hermeneutical orientation that foregrounds the inherent instabilities of any linguistic translation. For example, Tittler strove to maintain the novel's "non-Western worldview with regard to time" by alternating between disparate verb tenses in English that attempt to match the disorienting changes Zapata Olivella makes in Spanish (intro. to *Changó,* xi). This technique results in sentences such as "We always contemplate the already known becoming of our children" (423; Siempre contemplamos el devenir ya conocido de nuestros hijos, 611). Tittler explains that his approach to translating *Changó* into English was informed by what he perceived as Zapata Olivella's "resistencia al pensamiento occidental basándose éste en textos escritos" (189; resistance to Western thinking that has stemmed from written texts) ("*Changó en traducción,*" 189, author's trans.). According to Tittler, *Changó's* thematic and formal investments in resistance are evidenced in the novel's challenging content and disorienting narrative techniques "calculado para producir efectos desconcertantes en los lectores del texto fuente" (188; calculated to produce disconcerting effects in the readers of the source text). Referencing the translation theories of Lawrence Venuti, Tittler calls his English-language version of *Changó* "una traducción paralelamente resistente, la que intenta devolver su opacidad al invisble traductor" (189; a likewise resistant translation, which attempts to return opacity to the invisible translator). In returning opacity to the translator, Tittler puts the act of translation on display. By rendering the translation of *Changó* opaque, Tittler eschews the illusion of an easily conquered text and promotes labor-intensive reading practices for his target audience. According to this logic, the visibility of translation in Tittler's rendering of *Changó* leads to the subsequent visibility of hermeneutics. Tittler's insistence on visibility for translation, I later demonstrate, reveals a unique take on textual opacity.

Tittler expressly links his translation to a reinterpretation of the novel's place in Afro-diasporic literature. He says that he performs resistant translation through the use of "archaisms, *foreignisms,* or neologisms" that remind the reader that the text is a translation and not "*just the same as* North American or first-world writing" (intro. to *Changó,* xii).[8] For example, Tittler adopts what Phillip E. Lewis terms "abusive fidelity" (56) by following the source text so closely that it seems strange to target readers. Tittler employs abusive fidelity when he chooses to literally translate Zapata Olivella's Spanish translation of lines from Claude McKay's English-language poem "If We Must Die" rather than render it in its original English form.[9]

McKay's original:

If we must die—let it not be like hogs

. . . .

Pressed to the wall, dying, but fighting back!

Zapata Olivella's Spanish translation:

Si hemos de morir
que no sea como cerdos . . .

. . . .

y frente al muro
morir matando:
¡Disparad hacia atrás!

Tittler's translation:

If we must die,
Let it not be like swine . . .
But with our backs to the wall
Die killing:
Fire back!

This literary rendition via "back-translation" from McKay's original English to Tittler's translated English highlights the extensive mediations and interpretations that underpin all of *Changó, The Biggest Badass*. In the process, Tittler implicates the reader in an ongoing process of knowledge creation. His use of back-translation for this poem ultimately reminds his audience of trained English scholars, who will likely be familiar with McKay's canonical poem, that they cannot simply rely on traditional literary knowledge when reading this novel. Rather, the target graduate student readers must constantly interrogate their assumptions about what counts as a source text and about how we determine a source text's meaning. Tittler's back-translation, like Zapata Olivella's paradoxical paratext, embraces the ways that translation creates new meaning and methods of meaning-making.

The hermeneutical performances of translation in particular and communication in general that permeate Tittler's version of *Changó* are made exaggeratedly manifest through Agne Brown's experiences as a spiritual medium in the novel's US-set final section. In "Ancestral Combatants," Brown (a character likely inspired by Angela Davis) becomes a medium as a result of spirit possession.[10] Specifically, she is mentally and bodily overwhelmed by the power of external metaphysical forces, namely the god Changó. Her experiences of spirit possession are reminiscent of trance experiences in several Afro-diasporic traditions, including Vodou, Candomblé, Santería, and Myal. It is unsurprising that the depiction of spirit possession in Zapata Olivella's novel does not fit squarely into any one Afro-diasporic religious tradition, considering that the epic also brings together diverse languages, cultures, religions, and communities. The phrase "spirit possession" is itself a concept that emerged "as translation and comparative class" amongst Western anthropologists, who predominantly studied what were considered cultural "others." In his study of the genealogy of spirit possession, Paul Christopher Johnson notes that in early colonial trading between European and African communities, "possession, the spirit speaking through the sorcerer . . . presented crises of transparency, *translation,* and confidence" (394, 408, emphasis mine). How can the reader ever come to fully understand Agne's meaning or that of the novel she represents, if, as a result of spirit possession, she is always an embodiment of multiple, conflicting voices? To put this in terms of translation: How can we ever reconcile the inherent uncertainty of all communication that translation makes discomfortingly apparent?

Agne Brown physically and metaphorically embodies the translatorial actions of mediation and in doing so promotes all of the hermeneutical anxieties such actions engender. As Douglas Robinson explains in his

(Eurocentric) text on spirit-channeling and translation theory, "In many significant ways translating resembles, or has been commonly thought of in terms that resemble, spirit-channeling—communicating with and/or mediating for others the spirits of dead people, or, as spiritualist writers like to put it, 'discarante spirits'" (21).[11] As a spiritual medium, Agne translates messages and herself as she crosses time and space. In turn, she brings divine knowledge from the gods and ancestors to the living Bantú. Marked with the sign of the "divine linguist" Elegba, Agne is tasked with communicating supernatural messages in a semiotic code that her fellow humans can understand (Russell, 9). Thought another way, she represents the processes of translation. Just as scholars of translation still deliberate over the extent to which a translator's own authorship should be considered a "faithful" rendering of a text, Agne's claims to authorship and agency oscillate throughout her experiences with mediumship. In one encounter with her white (and implicitly racist) professor of African anthropology, Dr. Harrington, Agne explains, "I pronounce the words, dictated by another" (307). Via this appeal to dictation, Agne attests to her position as the medium through which another's words are expressed. In Tittler's translation Agne claims to have no authorship over the words she pronounces. Instead, she acts simply as a "consecrated object," or the instrument of expression. In Zapata Olivella's Spanish-language version, however, Agne's authorial position is far less clear. She says that she is "moduladas por otro, pronunciaré las palabras" (450). Unlike Tittler's turn to mediumship as dictation, here Agne is the translator who allows the "spirit" of the source author to calibrate her transmission of meaning. This shift in connotation also transforms the reader's understanding of Agne's agency. In Tittler's rendering, Agne's mediumship takes a more simplistic form of embodied transmission without change. In Zapata Olivella's writing, Agne's engaged acts of interpretation are implicated, though still subtle.

In a novel overflowing with complex human and beyond-human subjectivities, the source authors Zapata Olivella cites include the living and the dead, who are either spirits themselves or who belong to a wider spiritual community. For example, Zapata Olivella uses the term *ekobio* in his writings, including his personal correspondence with Tittler, to denote a "'fellow member' or 'brother' among the Ñáñigos or Afro-Cuban priests" (452; Sinónimo de cófrade entre los ñáñigos de Cuba, 653).[12] Olivella uses "ekobio" in a distinctly democratic and politically motivated fashion throughout his novel. Rather than merely referencing "male . . . best friends" amongst "Afro-Cubans" (Montero, 198), Olivella names all men *and* women who struggle for Afro-diasporic freedoms throughout history as ekobios. Through this naming, he creates the sense of an expansive liberationist fellowship that exemplifies the "polyfaceted rapport between socialism and spiritualism" that Tittler recognizes in Olivella's writings ("Catching the Spirit," 109). The medium Agne is chosen by this spiritual community, is incorporated into its ranks, *and* is used by the group for their larger political goals.

Agne is not merely a translator in this novel; she herself becomes a textual medium that, like the novel *Changó,* manifests a culmination of many translations. Agne is similar to the ekobio's correlate, a *nganga,* as described by Lydia Cabrera. Namely, she is "both a priest and consecrated *object*" in this situation (222, emphasis mine). Changó's messenger Ngafúa (a fellow translator of sorts), tells Agne Brown,

> Among all the ekobios, Changó has chosen you—woman, daughter, sister, and lover—so you may gather the broken, persecuted, murdered family of the Muntu [singular of Bantu] in the great crucible of all bloodlines. (301)

> Changó, entre todos los ekobios, te ha escogido a ti: mujer, hija, hermana y amante para que reúnas la rota, perseguida, asesinada familia del muntu en la gran caldera de todas las sangres. (443)

Agne, like the novel *Changó,* acts as a site for collecting, translating, and communicating the memories of the Afro-diasporic persons who had come before. She is the substance that contains and carries on ancestral wisdom; she embodies the process of translatorial "afterlife" *(fortleben,* or "prolonged life") that Walter Benjamin identifies in "The Task of the Translator" (76). Like the book *Changó,* Agne holds together and passes on generations of translation and communication. Throughout "Ancestral Combatants" Agne is visited by famous figures such as Nat Turner (343) and Sojourner Truth (371), as well as lesser-known African Americans like Osborn Perry Anderson (381), the only surviving black combatant in the raid on Harper's Ferry. Agne then collects each visiting ekobio's story. She is the "crucible of all bloodlines" by way of storylines.[13]

If Agne becomes like a translated text, she is also analogous to Tittler's resistant English translation of *Changó.* The multiplicity of voices that Agne comes to embody is reflected in the style of her mediumship, just as the dynamic complexity of Zapata Olivella's Afro-diasporic novel is reflected in Tittler's style of translation. The character of Malcolm X comments on the layers of voices he recognizes in Agne's mediumship. He describes her style of communication:

76   *The Sacred Act of Reading*

> It was your voice, Agne Brown. You spoke with the old accents of ekobios I have heard speak only here in the House of the Dead. Benkos Biojo, Gunga Zumbi, The Aleijadinho, L'Ouverture, José María Morelos, Bolívar, Nat Turner. (375–76)

> Era tu voz, Agne Brown. Tenías viejos acentos de ekobios a quienes solo he oído hablar aquí en la Casa de los Muertos. Benkos Biohó, Gunga Zumbi, el Aleijaidinho, L'Ouverture, José María Morelos, Bolívar, Nat Turner. (545).

Agne embodies all of these ancestors, and so her voice expresses this long lineage. The medium's voice is a bridge between the physical and abstract. It enlivens the timbres and tones of the dead. Agne's mediumship acknowledges the previous translators and authors that came before her, mirroring Tittler's dedication to including the symphony of voices and transpositions that characterize Zapata Olivella's epic undertaking. As the medium Agne physically embodies the textual afterlives of translation, and in her performances of mediumship, she repeatedly actualizes those sonic resurrections.

Debates within the novel about this mediumship's relative meaning and value are themselves restagings of competing Christian and Afro-diasporic hermeneutical practices. One paradigmatic illustration of Agne's contested mediumship occurs after she witnesses the lynching of her African American father. Though only a child, Agne delivers an impassioned speech about Changó's prophecy of racial justice from the pulpit of her white stepfather's Christian church while under a possession trance. Agne's heterodox utterances in this scene beg Douglas Robinson's question: "What forces are active within [the translator's subjectivity], and to what extent are those forces channeled into it from without?" (3). Changó's messenger Ngafúa tells Agne that as she climbs the pulpit, "Changó's fire has already set your tongue aflame" (305; Calladamente subes al púlpito pero ya el fuego de Changó encendía tu lengua, 448). Zapata Olivella uses the past imperfect "has already" here to distinguish that the action of Changó's fire happened long before Agne walks up to speak. The act of pronouncement to follow is not exclusively her own but is to a certain extent Changó's words channeled through her. Agne's speech is also seen as the translation of an external entity's message, though a nefarious one, by her reverend stepfather. Horrified at Agne's violent speech, Reverend Robert begs her to "pronounce the word God" and to "let the force of light overcome the dark shadows that invade" her (305; pronuncia la palabra Dios . . . Agnes, por última vez te ruego sobrepongas la fuerza de la luz las oscuras tinieblas que te invaden, 448). Reverend Robert's view of possession here evokes "Christian discourses of demonology" (P. Johnson, 396), in which the possessing force is assumed to be satanic. In this view, evil can only be exorcised by a speech act that calls on the dominant metaphysical force of the Christian god.[14] Both Ngafúa and Reverend Robert see Agne as the embodied translator of another entity's message; her submission to the overpowering force also grants her some kind of moral neutrality in the situation.

Agne's experience of embodied mediumship both overwhelms her and imbues her with spiritual force amidst a white-dominant setting where her racial embodiment does not easily grant her self-possession. The power dynamics at play in this scene resonate with Alessandra Benedicty-Kokken's argument that during the possession ritual, the medium's body becomes one of the only landscapes over which the often politically disempowered medium finds self-possession through ownership of the body's symbolic "place." Yet young Agne does not choose to become a medium for Changó and thus cannot be said to be making any choices here, even though she may later embrace her own possession. Indeed, her role as medium or translator appears particularly divested of personal agency and subjectivity thanks to the juxtaposition of Agne's childish innocence and the vehement hostility of the message she speaks. This seeming displacement of the medium's agency in favor of the possessing deity is reminiscent of Orisha possession trance in the southern Caribbean (Murrell, 219) as well as of Vodou trances in Haiti (Deren, 16). Benedicty-Kokken shows how in modernist Haitian and Francophone Caribbean literature, the experience of seeming displacement during a possessive trance can instead be read as "a representational form that helps the individual to negotiate 'displacement and desubjectification'" (34). Just as translation reveals the *process* of meaning-making through language, Agne's experiences with spirit possession and mediumship reveal the methods of interpretation through which we come to know ourselves as subjects. For Agne this interpretive framework is bound in Afro-diasporic spiritual practices from which she herself had been displaced.

In practice, then, Agne's journey in coming to know herself as a newly formed subject operates according to a hermeneutics of uncertainty. If Agne's possession illuminates for the reader the "path to self-possession" that Benedicty-Kokken identifies, she does so with a focus on confusion. Agne's experiences of mediumship through possession create constant uncertainty for the reader about her subjectivity, which comes to represent the identity of the translator and the translated text.[15] Zapata

Olivella develops this self-directed hermeneutics of uncertainty for Agne by toggling between narrative perspective and voice. At the beginning of "Ancestral Combatants," readers bounce between Ngafúa's seemingly omniscient narration, which addresses Agne in the second person, and Agne's limited first-person perspective. "Everything I remember," Agne tells the reader, "is just a borrowed memory" (312; Todo cuanto recuerdo no es más que la memoria prestada, 457). Here Agne is pressed to navigate the layers of distance between herself and her story, which is only "prestada" (rendered, borrowed). Ngafúa addresses Agne with the imperative, "You have to remember everything" (312; Tienes que recordar todo, 457). Agne, like the novel *Changó*, must attempt to "recordar" (remember, record) all the translated histories of her people—histories which can never be fully captured in translation.

Even when Agne appears to be speaking for herself in the first person, the unpredictable transitions between narrative voices create more confusion than clarity about Agne's subjectivity. Erika Bourguignon writes, "A belief in *possession* exists when the people in question hold that a given person is changed in some way through the presence in or on him of a spirit entity or power, other than his own personality, soul, self, or the like.... *Possession trance* exists in a given society when we find that there is such a belief in possession and that it is used to account for alterations or discontinuity in consciousness, awareness, personality, or other aspects of psychological functioning" (Bourguignon, 7–8, emphasis in orig.). Because Agne appears to undergo a series of possession trances throughout her story—involving alterations and discontinuity in her consciousness, awareness, and personality—her identity can never be considered ontologically static and understandable. For example, when Agne's new "Aunt" Harriet (a racist white woman) hears her reverend brother call Agne his "daughter," the text enigmatically begins in first person and ends in the second. "Aunt Harriet casts her eyes over my insignificant presence," Agnes notes. "She had seen me. But it was as if you did not exist" (314). This turn of grammar is even more difficult to comprehend in Spanish: "La tía Harriet vuelve la vista sobre mi insignificante presencia. Me había visto. Pero eras algo así como si no existieras" (460). It is up for interpretation whether the second person here is Agne speaking to herself, which would illustrate her sense of split identity. Alternately, the second person could be Ngafúa, the messenger, giving Agne back her own buried memories to translate into a narrative of self. When Agne's subjectivity becomes tangled like this in the narrative, it questions the solidity of the "I" and "you" completely, "as if *you* did not exist."

By analyzing "the *idea* of the occupied body and spoken-through person," that is, in considering Agne's mediumship through "possession as an episteme" (P. Johnson, 395), we can also recognize how the formulation of static subjectivity is itself an interpretive construct.[16] The concept of solid subjectivity is actually the result of a hermeneutical process. We create the idea of a stable self by interpreting our experiences, our stories, into a cohesive whole. Spirit possession, which involves the integration (or possibly total domination) of external forces within the boundaries of the human, necessarily undermines the belief in perfectly sustained personhood. Agne's hermeneutical crisis of personal subjectivity as a result of spirit possession sheds light on the extent to which concepts of identity are founded on narratives of individualistic autonomy tied to Western philosophies.

In the case of *Changó,* Agne's individualistic autonomy is rendered obsolete when she realizes that she cannot control the boundaries of her own body and mind. The sense of being constituted by possibly conflicting agents is exemplified in the scene during which Agne recognizes while in the shower that her body is marked with a "stain between [her] breasts" that represents Elegba's snakes (302; la macula en mitad de los senos, 444). At first Agne is frightened by the uninvited marking on her skin and responds by trying to "brush it away" (trataste de sacudirla). She attempts to regain control of her physical body's stable and individual boundary. After the physical marking is revealed, certain mental objects—knowledge and memories—begin to trespass into her mind. At this point Agne loses control of her own mental states. Ngafúa narrates Agne's experiences to her:

> You turn on the light. The living and fleshy root persisted there between your breast. A vague feeling stirs the memory of past anguish, the smell of burning flesh. You intuit the stain's shape: two snakes biting each other's tail. You try to relieve your unease with the pious idea that you are drowning in a nightmare. (302)

> Enciendes la luz. Allí persistía entre tus senos el vivo y encarnado cuajarón. Un vago sentimiento revive el olvido de pasadas angustias, el olor a carne quemada. Intuirás la forma de la mancha: dos serpientes mordiéndose las colas. Tratas de aliviar tu desazón con la piadosa idea de que te ahogas en una pesadilla. (444)

For Agne, this disintegration of external boundaries and personal control is rife with the terror of losing her mind and sense of self. Agne's role as medium is made manifest here in several respects. The stain of Elegba's serpents makes her body the means and material by which something is communicated and renders it a host substance to alien life. The serpents also graphically connect the frightened protagonist to the medium-like oricha Elegba, who is "the link between the living and the dead" (308; la ligazón entre los vivos y los muertos, 452). In this moment Agne becomes a physical avatar for what Benedicty-Kokken calls "embodied knowledge systems," in which phenomena that exceed the capacities of language such as "extreme pain" are communicated through ritual forms of embodiment like Vodou possession (15). As Agne's body physically changes as it receives spiritual and ancestral knowledge, she emulates Elegba. The oricha, Heather Russell notes, not only "shifts his own shape" but, more importantly, "shifts the *shape* of received knowledge" (9). Agne's own embodied shifts are ones of shape and knowledge.

The image of the oricha signals the death of any illusion Agne had of a bounded, knowable self; namely it declares that "to be reborn you have to die" (308; para renacer hay que morir, 452). Joseph Murphy has analyzed this death of self in several "diasporan" traditions in the Americas including Vodou, Candomblé, Santería, Revival Zion, and ecstatic African American churches in the United States. He writes: "To be mounted, crowned, or converted by the spirit is to die to a former life and be reborn in to a new one 'in the spirit.' When an individual receives the spirit, a part of his or her inner nature is also transformed to partake of the spirit's divinity" (185). For our protagonist, resurrection into new life as the medium working for her community's liberation requires the death of her former sense of self in internal and external ways. That is, she must abandon her previous methods of interpreting her own subjectivity. This prior interpretation includes the internalization of predominant beliefs and discourses defining Agne's personhood through racial hierarchies. While rooted in her body and described in "fleshy" terms, the new spiritual relation forming between Agne and the deity Elegba demonstrates that while the body seems to be "irreducibly material," it is, at the same time, what Guillermina De Ferrari calls, a "phantasmatic presence," something that is conceived through language and culture as well as "inevitably caught in one or more systems of value" (9). As an African American woman who watched her father's lynching and who experienced rejection from adopted white relatives at first prejudicial sight, Agne is well aware of the ways in which racial and gendered discourses can define and regulate bodily experiences. Moving through the world within a body that is constantly read through the lens of a subjugating social discourse inevitably affects an individual's self-perceptions. I will elaborate on these external and internal processes of subject-formation in my discussion of Brodber's *Myal* in chapter 3. In Zapata Olivella's novel, spiritual forces etch and ink themselves onto Agne to mark her body as both text and flesh, or as an object and subject belonging to the realms of symbolic discourse and material life. When Agne's flesh is made word, her previous understandings of human life must perish. In their place an alternative spiritual formulation of subjectivity can be born.

Agne undergoes a radical unfamiliarity of self that is integral in the practice of mediumship through spirit possession. Agne both experiences epistemological uncertainty of the self here and becomes a signifier of that hermeneutical process. If the concept of the self only materializes through a subject's embodied relationship with the world, Agne must redefine herself. After all, she has been awakened to a new kind of relationship between her subject and the world—both physically and metaphysically.[17] Agne's experience of self-alienation as a result of her newfound embodiment allows us to recognize how Zapata Olivella's representations of flesh and subjectivity in *Changó* resonate with theories of translation and interpretation. Agne's confusing struggle specifically brings to mind Benjamin's theorizations about the disorienting repercussions of linguistic translation cited in this chapter's epigraph. Benjamin's premise that translation brings to light our preexisting alienation from the original language we supposedly knew reminds us of Tittler's unfamiliar rendering of McKay's poem within the familiar semiotic landscape of English. Tittler's back-translation ultimately alienates the academic English audience while inviting them to join Agne's struggles (and "particular suffering") of hermeneutical reimagining. Surely there is no better demonstration of the particular suffering experienced in a process of self-alienation than the terrified Agne in the shower. The stains on Agne's breasts make visible the hermeneutical disorientation of translation and mediumship.

Similarly, there could be no better symbol for Agne's destabilized subjectivity as a gendered translator and translation than the "ambiguous messenger trickster deity" Elegba. After all, Elegba is an oricha whose cross-dressing in Santería and androgyny in Vodou illustrate the fluidity of identity via gender (Murrell, 35, 78, 110). I caution against overly championing Elegba's gendered fluidity in as masculinist a text as *Changó*. As Sylvia Wynter notes, challenging dominant discourses of "gender" is one, and only one, method of working to disassemble the many "genres" of the human. Appeals to these genres, Wynter confirms, have served to reify the dominance of Western "Man," and simply deconstructing discourses of gender is not enough ("Unsettling the Coloniality"). Rather, any radical and liberating discourse must abolish the notion of "Man once and for all," and in doing so, destroy that notion's implicit hierarchies of humanity and subjectivity (Weheliye, 22). Keeping in mind Wynter's capacious approach to emancipatory discourse, we can acknowledge Elegba's liminality between *genres* of the human. In the process we may recognize how Zapata Olivella deconstructs the notion of "Man" and, so doing, makes explicitly emancipatory discursive moves. Indeed, Elegba's possession of Agne represents what Russell calls Elegba's "strategic duality—his mastery of discourse and attendant recognition of its gross limitation" (9). To abolish an idea as central as "individual [human] self" in Agne's body in favor of a dualistic spirit possession not only affirms discursive processes such as translation and interpretation *but also* confirms the power of that which exceeds the bounds of language.

And while Agne's death and resurrection in the shower may appear horrifying, Zapata Olivella challenges a simplistic reading of Agne's journey into mediumship through suffering. When Agne discovers the stain of Elegba's snakes, the stain that marks her as belonging to Changó's mission for the muntu, she paradoxically "slowly take[s] possession of [her] body" (302). Tittler's translation retains the keyword "possession" here from the Spanish (lentamente entras en posesión de tu cuerpo, 444). In the process Tittler highlights Agne's newfound self-possession through the seeming surrender of herself and indicates her movement into an active relationship with self-surrender. In a logical contradiction, Agne begins to truly possess her own body just as she recognizes the signs of Changó having already staked possession of her. And when the reader meets Agne in a Harlem jail for another moment of mediumship at the end of the novel, she is no longer the frightened child and young adult to whom the reader was first introduced. This woman describes herself in the first person as "certain that I am not a stranger to myself" (420–21; segura de que no soy una extraña a mí misma, 608). She is no longer a woman afraid of losing her sense of identity and agency. Somehow, Agne's self-alienation through spirit possession also becomes her gateway into heightened self-connection.

Ultimately, Agne engages in an interpretive act I call "engaged surrender." Engaged surrender is the conscious decision to let go of a totalizing sense of personal willpower. Agne becomes the active participant in her own possession narrative in order to serve her community as a physical and metaphorical text of translations. The seeming paradox of spirit possession in *Changó* is that Agne becomes most fully herself only after allowing herself to be objectified by the spirits. In order to explain Agne's shift from frightened disorientation to engaged surrender, I turn to Erna Brodber's novel *Louisiana,* in which she will also invite academics to question their preconceived methods of certainty. In each novel, flesh and text are intimately tied to parallel processes of interpretation and translation.

Engaged Surrender in *Louisiana*

Like *Changó,* Erna Brodber's *Louisiana* (1994) is a disorienting novel. It challenges readers to consider their own interpretive practices and to reconsider how those practices relate to questions about the formulation of personal subjectivity and collective belonging. *Louisiana* takes readers across geographies, time periods, and metaphysical realms as it gradually illuminates the interconnected fragments of various personal stories. Whereas *Changó* voices the convergent narratives of "Ancestral Combatants" together through the articulated mediumship of Agne Brown, *Louisiana* uses the sensorial perceptions of the medium Ella Townsend/Louisiana to reveal the expansive narrative mosaic that encompasses several Afro-diasporic biographies.

Set in the mid-twentieth century, *Louisiana* narrates the metaphysical journey of Ella Townsend, a Jamaican-born woman raised in the United States, who is "ridden," or possessed, by metaphysical powers while she conducts anthropological research for the Works Project Administration. Ella begins the novel as a data-oriented graduate student of anthropology in Chicago. She is soon forced to question her scientific assumptions about reality after a supernatural oral history interview in Louisiana with an elderly African American woman, Anna "Mammy" King. Upon reviewing the recording, Ella discovers that she has become a reluctant spiritual medium. Specifically, she has been a subject of ancestral possession by Louise "Lowly," a deceased Afro-Jamaican woman, and Anna, an African American woman from the United States who dies shortly after her interview. Ella, as well as the novel's readers, spend the majority of the text attempting to understand her incredible experiences; in the process both protagonists and readers are ultimately encouraged to struggle to reconcile seemingly contradictory epistemologies. Ella, much like Agne Brown, must question her presumptions about personal subjectivity following spirit possession. At first this disorientation of self frustrates Ella because it upends her existing hermeneutical approach to "reality." Yet she, like Agne, eventually becomes an active participant in her own capitulation to the power of spirit possession. Ella ultimately consents to the "hegemony of the spirit" and becomes a conjure woman and spiritual memory-keeper in New Orleans (98). At the end of the novel, Ella grows too frail to continue recording her personal memoirs about mediating in a world of opacity. At this point, her husband Reuben (who has also left his career as a social scientist) takes over for her.

Like *Changó*, Brodber's *Louisiana* is marketed to a US academic audience dominated by readers who are most likely unfamiliar with the Afro-Caribbean religious concept of spirit possession that foregrounds the novel's cosmological events. *Louisiana* can be considered a vehicle of cultural translation just like *Changó*. *Louisiana* is Brodber's first novel set predominately in the United States (rather than in her home country of Jamaica) and published by an academic press (the University of Mississippi Press). *Changó, The Biggest Badass* is also set in the United States and its English-language edition was published in 2010 by Texas Tech University Press.[18] Like the "disconcerting" and "resistant" *Changó*, *Louisiana* does not pander to passive readers hoping to learn about foreign events in a domesticated fashion. On the contrary, Brodber emulates Morrison's oral performance of *Beloved* by calling for an engaged practice of reading. This invitation to readers' participation also requires a paradoxical hermeneutical orientation of engaged surrender. In other words, *Louisiana* sets the reader up to work very hard at letting go of interpretation.

Similar to the authors and translators of the immense and tortuous *Changó*, Brodber narrates this enigmatic story using appropriately complex literary devices such as nonchronological plot structures, dialogic formatting without indication of the speaker, and shifting narrative perspectives. She also obliquely references music, politics, folktales, Eurocentric academic discourse, and, of course, religions from across the globe in mixtures of *patois* and "standard" written English. Because *Louisiana*, like *Changó*, does not attempt to "domesticate" unfamiliar ideas and concepts for the Western academic audience, the reader embarks on a journey of interpretive frustration. Brodber frames her intentionally disorienting writing style (in both *Louisiana* and elsewhere) as an invitation for active reading. She states, "I put the words on the page in unusual ways in the hope that people would ask why and in the process pay attention and get to my meaning" ("Me and My Head-Hurting," 121). Brodber's desire for active engagement recalls Morrison's stylistic choices that worked to call upon readers' and listeners' "help" in interpreting *Beloved*. What might "meaning" signify in a novel like *Louisiana*, which is deeply dedicated to accepting that which is not easily known? At the heart of the question of meaning in *Louisiana* is an exploration of epistemological uncertainty. The overwhelming disorientation of epistemological uncertainty in *Louisiana* is reminiscent of Zapata Olivella's "disconcerting" narrative techniques and Jonathon Tittler's "resistant" translatorial actions. Each encourages English-speaking academic readers to see their own epistemological assumptions as unstable.

In creating sustained epistemological uncertainty for her readers and characters, Brodber's novel advocates for a hermeneutical practice that welcomes what Martinican scholar Édouard Glissant terms "opacity." In order to engage Glissant's concept of opacity with regards to Brodber's *Louisiana,* it is first crucial that I elucidate his philosophical tenet of "Relation," which is foregrounded in "respect for the Other as *different* from oneself" (Britton, 11). In *Edouard Glissant and Postcolonial Theory,* Celia Britton explains that Glissant conceptualizes Relation as "a fluid and unsystematic system whose elements are engaged in a radically nonhierarchical free play of interrelatedness" (11). Brodber's reader finds that in *Louisiana,* characters, cultures, and plotlines exist in a similarly fluid dance. Narrative structure slowly arises out of a seemingly unsystematic choreography of moving bodies and voices. According to Édouard Glissant, in order to respect our interconnection with *and* separation from the Other (be that an individual human or unfamiliar religious tradition), we must protect the Other's right to opacity, or their right to exist outside of our totalizing understanding. Like Brodber's readers, the protagonist Ella must learn to embrace "the welcome opaqueness, through which the other escapes" her (*Caribbean Discourse,* 162). Spirit possession is an apt theme for creating narrative opacity in a US-published text. After all, spirit possession signified for early modern Western colonizers "the problem of interpreting and controlling interior lives of peoples encountered in newly occupied lands" (P. Johnson, 396). Spirit possession becomes a ready tool for literary opacity due to its negation of clearly identifiable subjectivities through stable identity or clear agency. After all, how can you easily interpret the interior life of a person who is not always the same person? Brodber shares with Zapata Olivella and Tittler a commitment to creating new interpretive and epistemological formulations via the trope of spirit possession as well as via forms of narrative and linguistic confusion.

Ultimately, Ella accepts that while she must actively participate in the discovery and transmission of knowledge through her own work as a medium, much of that work is done by purposefully waiting for the revelation of knowledge "in the fullness of time" (*Louisiana,* 115). This formulation creates the hermeneutical paradigm of engaged surrender, which encompasses not only a deep respect for the Other's right to opacity but also the realization of our own personal opacity *to ourselves*. In a deeply ironic twist, Ella's journey into undoing her need to categorize others leads her to also reject her previous assumptions about her own subjectivity. Ella becomes like the individual who learns to "accept that there are places where [her] identity is obscure to [her]" (Glissant, *Caribbean Discourse*, 192). Ella accepts that she must work to understand the "community tale" as well as strive to see herself as integral to that narrative. In the process she must also recognize the instability of her own identity, an identity which she cannot render fully legible even to herself (161). The spiritual force Anna and Louise's interview holds over Ella's internal states reflects Brodber's own career in what she calls "psychic anthropology." In a personal interview, Brodber explains that she found herself thoroughly "sucked in by the feel" of oral history interviews when she began her career as an anthropologist. "Who will turn me off?" she began to ask herself (Brodber interview with the author, March 18, 2013). While Brodber explains that she has since learned to psychically recalibrate after particularly transformative interviews, Ella Townsend never "turns off." Instead, she cultivates an entirely new identity and career path. The protagonist ritualizes this shift in self-understanding when she renames herself "Louisiana" and devotes her life to what she calls the "hegemony of the spirit" (*Louisiana*, 98). This devotion is defined by her active consent to being dominated by metaphysical forces that she cannot understand (98). In the following pages, I illustrate the ways in which Brodber creates disorientation for her readers and characters through conflicting epistemologies. I then explore the implications of welcoming opacity. After this, I extend an anecdote Ella tells about deciphering a religious picture in a church's stained glass window. This anecdote, I argue, is a trope for engaged surrender, or the active waiting required in spiritual investigation through possession.

Louisiana establishes the prominence of the unknown before the plot even begins. An editorial letter from the office of E. R. Anderson at the Black World Press frames the body of the novel, namely by presenting the text's origins, plot, and protagonists as enigmas. This editorial framing technique ironically draws on the eighteenth- and nineteenth-century practice of using authenticating paratextual devices such as introductory letters by white editors to legitimize slave narratives. Befitting this legacy, the editor offers Ella's academic and publishing credentials. This connection will only deepen and complicate when the protagonist pieces together the forgotten stories of enslaved persons in the United States and Jamaica. Unlike traditional authentications by white editors for narratives by Afro-diasporic authors, *Louisiana's* introductory letter makes it clear that this novel's fragmented personal stories will not be so easily assembled. According to the editor's prologue, the manuscript simply "appeared" on the editor's desk from unknown origins. The manuscript's primary author, Ella Townsend, seems to have "disappeared" into unknown territories, or spaces not systematized in the realms of the public record (3). Ella somehow came "under the influence of psychic forces," after which time she was no longer identifiable in the academic records of rational epistemologies (4). Anderson's letter therefore flips the genre expectations of such an "authenticating" paratext on its head by only authenticating the text's disorienting narrative style and underlining the difficulties of "knowing" the opaque focal character.

In addition to foreshadowing Ella's enigmatic identity throughout the novel, E. R. Anderson's paratext demonstrates the pitfalls of imposing one, straightforward narrative meaning to Brodber's historical novel. Anderson proffers a conjectured chronological structure for the manuscript by cobbling together the text's sections into one storyline. Anderson explains that the anonymous manuscript was "divided into six parts" and speculates that each section's title possibly contributes to a coherent message, albeit one that requires the addition of his or her own words in parentheses. That message reads: "I heard the voice from Heaven say, 'first the goat must be killed (and you get) out of Eden and get over (to be) Louisiana.' Den a who sey Sammy dead, (if this can happen)" (5).[19] Alas, even this confounding editorial suggestion is only "a hypothesis," one informed guess among many (5). The guess itself ends with the conditional of "if this can happen," thereby presenting the narrative's events as contingent. In addition, the term "hypothesis" introduces an Enlightenment-derived rationalist method of examining the nonrationalist theme of spiritual possession. This epistemological disjuncture presages Ella's early attempts to understand her situation scientifically and predictively undermines the expected methods of investigation for many of Brodber's academic readers in the United States. At the same time, the editorial frame mocks the publisher's inability to impress logical transparency on the story through an impetus to narrative closure. After all, the hypothesis ends in conjecture and so doing fails to clarify the plot. This fictionalized framing structure is akin to Zapata Olivella's contradictory advice to readers in the prologue of *Changó*. As a result, both paratexts present a hermeneutics of uncertainty.

While the framing narrative glimpses a world where the scientific method falters and "there are more ways of knowing than are accessible to the five senses," the first scene in the body of the text engulfs the reader in that world with all its inevitable confusion.[20] The first section of *Louisiana*, "I heard a voice from Heaven say," is a transcript from Ella's mystical recording machine. In this scene a deceased Afro-Jamaican woman—known by several names including Louise and Lowly—tells her still-living friend, whom I refer to as Anna (the intended subject of Ella's WPA interview) about being "translated" into the next realm after death. By referring to death as translation, *Louisiana* privileges an Afro-centric concept of the afterlife in which death is primarily a transition into a new, ancestral realm where the deceased can still communicate to some extent with the living.[21] Likewise, the concept of translation into a form of life after death also aligns well with Christian discourse on eternal life through salvation.[22] Furthermore, Benjamin's work on the "after lives" of source texts through translation resonates with the active role Louise will take throughout the novel. Ella is the medium through which Louise may attain her "latest, continually renewed, and most complete unfolding" in the afterlife (255). Brodber's use of the literary term "translation" in this moment encourages readers to connect hermeneutics with the syncretic Afro-Christian spiritual experiences of mediumship, resurrection, possession, and revelation. Louise's "translation" into the afterlife illustrates the ways in which (as Friedrich Nietzsche and J. Habermas would contend) hermeneutics can be applied not only to literature but also to the horizons of our "interpretations of reality" (Grondin, 14). The reader joins the story *in medias res*, while the deceased Louise is speaking telepathically to Anna. Louise fittingly begins with questions about memories that the reader cannot yet access: "Anna, do you remember? Can you still hear me singing it?" (9). From the outset Brodber turns the reader's attention toward the yet-inaccessible knowledge that resides within present perceptions (hearing) of the ongoing ancestral past.[23]

This orientation toward non-Western concepts of time echoes the nonchronological narrative techniques of Zapata Olivella's epic novel of Afro-diasporic spirituality. In fact, much of the novel's plot is dedicated to the anthropologist protagonist's attempts to culturally translate the spiritual events she witnesses and experiences into a secular, scholarly idiom. As Vera Kutzinski explains, the character of Ella is linked to early twentieth-century African American ethnographer Zora Neale Hurston, who studied under Franz Boas at Columbia University and whose religious work I discussed in chapter 1.[24] For a social anthropologist like

Ella or Hurston, the research process is inherently a translational exercise.[25] Namely, research is an act "where the task of the ethnographer is to describe the foreign culture," usually considered a non-Western Other, in such a way that Western academic audiences can analyze their traditions and customs (Pym, 138). The concept of spirit possession, as I have noted, emerged "as translation and comparative class" among Western anthropologists studying what were considered cultural "others" (P. Johnson, 394).[26] Spirit possession is therefore an optimal subject for a social anthropologist like Ella to attempt to culturally translate for "the white people" she reports to back in Chicago (*Louisiana,* 21). But Ella's unexpected personal experiences with mediumship and spirit possession ultimately render her observations opaque. These experiences thwart all of her attempts to culturally translate the "important data" she witnesses while performing her field work in the southern United States (21).

Louisiana's readers join Ella in her anthropological research and indirectly experience the difficulties she encounters when applying the interpretive techniques of Western social science to a reality whose horizons are structured by African-derived religious philosophies. By beginning the novel's plot with a dialogue between the living and the dead, Brodber invokes "an African, ancestrally oriented hermeneutics" pivotal to African-derived Jamaican religious practices (Stewart, 227). Practitioners may perform devotional rituals designed to facilitate the "critical interpretation of messages from the Divine Community," a "community of venerated deities and invisible beings" that sometimes includes ancestors like Louise (227, 24).[27] These communicative, spiritual acts' literary representations in *Louisiana* thus wed textual and performative hermeneutics. After the opening questions about memory and sonic performance, the text jumps to a verse of the song that Louise hears at her own funeral, a Nine-Nights ceremony:

> It is the voice I hear
> the gentle voice I hear
> that calls me home? (9)

Again, the reader is confronted with a question beyond rational logic or previous knowledge, this time in the form of a song.[28] Generally speaking, Nine-Nights are community-wide funerals characteristic of syncretic Jamaican-Christian religions such as Pukumina, Jamaican Baptist, and Revivial Zion (Simpson, 329). Nine-Nights, of course, last nine nights and ultimately serve to usher the deceased's spirit into the next world (their translation). This translation occurs through practices such as singing, vigil-keeping, ritual cleaning, and the offering of foods and items special to the recently deceased (Murrell, 264–65; Simpson, 329). By having Louise discuss the events of her own Nine-Nights, Brodber sets *Louisiana* within a novelistic reality structured by syncretic Afro-Christian religious paradigms that resist rationalist, Western, scientific conceptions of finite death and chronological time.[29] Furthermore, because Louise (Lowly) hails from St. Mary Parish in both Lousiana and Jamaica, and Anna (Mammy) King is from St. Mary Parish, Louisiana, in the United States, the topic of "home" is inherently disorienting as well.[30]

Even for those readers well versed in religious concepts such as ancestral orientation and resurrection, *Louisiana*'s plot, much like those of *Brown Girl in the Ring, Changó, Myal,* and *Dream on Monkey Mountain,* exceeds any singular interpretive framework. Brodber points her readers to Haitian Vodou rituals of spirit possession by having Louise refer to Ella as the "horse" that Anna can ride into the next life (17).[31] However, the idea of Ella's incorporation of multiple others would not coincide with that context (Montilus, 3; Deren, 16; Herskovitz, *Life in a Haitian Valley,* 66).[32] On the transcript, we see Anna ask Louise, "Who is this gal with some bits of me and some bits of you?" (17). Unlike a trance subject in Vodou spirit possession, Ella is described not as the woman embodied in another form but rather somehow as a particularly unique possession created by the two women. Brodber repeatedly describes Ella as a product of both Anna and Louise; a queer, spiritual child generated when "two women sire another" (17). Brodber refuses to allow one single paradigm to guide the interpretive world of *Louisiana*.

Because readers cannot categorize the spiritual practices in *Louisiana* according to existing anthropological paradigms, the metaphysical events cannot be rendered "knowable" and therefore objectifiable through Western academic narratives. During a particularly difficult interview with the stubborn Anna King, Ella reminds herself that Anna both "has important data" and "is important data" for the "history of the struggle of the lower class negro they want to write" (21). Ella notes Anna's value as academic data in order to remind herself that the assignment, both facilitated and frustrated by her and Anna's racial similarities, is an "honour" (21). What is more, the aggregated results of Anna's interview will serve as a barometer for Ella's continued value in her field; in sum, the interview is "put[ting] [her] name and job at stake" (22). Anna and Louise, as evidenced in their telepathic conversations, refuse to cooperate with the purely scholarly pursuit. In so doing they trouble Ella's preexisting sense of title and "name." They probe Ella about her own past and her present values, making the interview "personal and certainly unscholastic" (22). In making the interview unscholastic, they are implicitly also making it less "transparent" and "legitimate" for the intended white audiences. In *Poetics of Relation,* Glissant explains that "understanding" in Western society is often "founded on an insistence on . . . transparency," which reduces the "density" of the Other in order to give the Western observer "a basis for comparisons and perhaps for judgment" (204). Here, Anna and Louise resist the propensity of the social sciences to turn Anna's human experiences into abstracted "data" for white scholars to analyze. With this, *Louisiana* suggests that unlike the engaged surrender that Ella enacts by choosing to become an objectified medium, academic scholars often force "othered" subjects into objectified roles without their consent.

By having Ella's anthropological techniques fail to culturally translate Anna and Louise, *Louisiana* insists on a hermeneutical practice that acknowledges the opacity of fictional subjects. When Glissant "demand[s] for all the right to opacity" (209), he is resisting the imperial prerogative to "understand" the colonial Other and in doing so, to render that person "transparent" to the colonial regime. Ella's commitment to the interpretive tools of the Euro-American academy implicate her as a complicit agent of the humanistic intellectual regimes that fuel imperialist projects. This complicity brings to mind Antonio Benítez-Rojo's claim that Western interpretations of the Caribbean project onto it "dogmas and methods" only relevant to Western societies. As a result, researchers "get into the habit of defining the Caribbean in terms of its resistance to the different methodologies summoned to investigate it" (2). Jonathan Tittler also references this opacity along with Venuti's resistant translation when discussing his translational techniques for *Changó;* namely, he intends to "return opacity to the invisible translator" ("*Changó* en traducción," 189, author's trans.). Tittler's use of opacity is paradoxical. He employs the mechanisms of nontransparency in his translation in order to make the workings of literary translation more visible. The opacity of Brodber's novel likewise disallows readers who may attempt to render characters like Anna King or Ella Townsend transparent to themselves or to each other. Such transparency could diminish the dynamic complexity of their identities and their ways of transmitting ancestral knowledge.

In order to not commit what Gayatri Spivak calls the "epistemic violence" (209) of imposing colonial paradigms of understanding on herself and her subjects, Ella must learn to adopt new hermeneutical epistemological paradigms that allow for the opacity of the Other, and even of herself. In other words, Ella's journey into engaged surrender—her giving up of self in the service of mediumship—begins with sacred acts of (re)interpretation. To adopt a hermeneutical method that embraces opacity means also learning to let go of an overwhelming commitment to any one epistemology. Glissant writes that accepting the Other's opacity "distracts me from the absolute truths whose guardian I might believe myself to be. Far from cornering me within futility and inactivity, by making me sensitive to the limits of every method, [opacity] relativizes every possibility of every action within me" (*Poetics of Relation*, 192). Opacity reveals that all epistemological methods are restrictive. In *Louisiana*, Ella must repeatedly abandon or modify the methods of knowledge-gathering she has acquired in social scientific study. At the beginning of the novel, Ella is a strong adherent to the paradigms of the white academy. For example, when she first hears her own possessed voice singing back to her on the interview tape, "she cannot think 'ghost'" thanks to "so many years of formal schooling" (28). Her professional training has forced such supernatural and therefore "nonscientific" concepts from her cognitive repertoire. This moment makes literal Derrida's loaded statement about the epistemological boundaries of the academy: "A traditional scholar," he notes in *Specters of Marx*, "does not believe in ghosts" (12). Indeed, Janice Boddy writes that recent studies on spirit possession suggest that these experiences require "epistemic premises quite different from the infinitely differentiating, rationalizing, and reifying thrust of global materialism and its attendant scholarly traditions" (407). One such scholarly tradition is the burgeoning field of social science in which Ella participates. In the introductory letter, editor E. R. Anderson assures readers that Ella began her anthropological project with "some evidence of scientific intent and action" (4). Indeed, Ella first attempts to banish personal reflection about her own spiritual possession by telling herself to "let discipline prevail" (4, 62). Of course, discipline does not prevail. Instead, Ella gives into the metaphysical force of the unknown.

In one particularly ironic twist, Ella's use of sociological methodologies to understand the unfamiliar setting of the southern United States ultimately precipitates her move beyond the paradigms of that method. Namely, she returns to the "hungry black box" that initiated this confounding story in the first place. Still living in St. Mary with her sociologist husband after Anna's death, Ella realizes that she knows "so little of thesociology of the place" (48). The lack of a word space between the article "the" and "sociology" suggests that at this time, Ella considers sociology to be a distinct epistemological lens that can be applied to any particular "place" such as St. Mary, Louisiana. At first Ella and Reuben are drawn "into the sociology" by way of other people's houses. This focus allows them to avoid their "odd roommate": the black recording machine in their own temporary residence. Upon noting the villagers' discomfort with her and not her husband, Ella mobilizes her sociological methodologies and alters her own behaviors according to the society's gendered social structures. In particular, she spends more time inside the cottage performing domestic chores.

Thus Ella's sociological conclusions lead her back inside with the recording machine, which she talks to and treats as an antagonist, daughter, and lover at different moments in the narrative (49, 50). By anthropomorphizing the recording machine, Ella begins to let go of her commitment to scientific objectivity and so begins to experiment with an interpretive hermeneutics that attends to nonrationalist formulations of human subjectivity and the performed embodiments that facilitate knowledge transmission. Furthermore, Ella inaugurates a conceptual dialogue with her own spiritual domination. She actively avoids and then tenderly cleans the mysterious machine, which leads Ella to "let go" of her preconceived epistemological assumptions and become "all ears" to the supernatural recording (61). Ella benefits from her decision to submit to the spiritual forces: namely, she discovers new words and voices on the tape's reel with each listen. Going through the new information provided by the machine reel, Ella asks herself what field she has stepped into: "Anthropology of the dead? Celestial ethnography? Crazy. I turned myself back with that break to thinking about the subject I had been paid to come to Louisiana to study. Mammy" (61). Ella's response confirms her growing interpretive flexibility as well as her continued academic rigidity in the face of opacity. She begins by attempting to categorize this new way of knowing and reading required to understand the machine but appears struck by such categories' inadequacy. In short, she is on a path to accepting opacity. In response she cuts herself off from creatively engaging with her shifting epistemologies by calling herself and her new ways of thinking "crazy." Tellingly, she distinguishes between the "break" of engaging the reel—it is ostensibly an incidental exercise that nevertheless threatens to break her prior way of knowing—and her paid academic study. The Western academy does not reward or sanction these alternative spiritual practices, as both she and readers well know.

Ella's journey into knowing beyond academically sanctioned epistemologies requires a psychological death similar to the one Agne Brown experiences in *Changó*. Just like Agne, Ella's transition into her role as a medium requires her to newly "remember" her own childhood episodes of pain and isolation. Ella's transformation of identity begins in earnest only after she undergoes a traumatic flashback that links her to a past self. This flashback begins when she hears West Indian sailors singing the same spiritual Ella had unknowingly sung in the WPA interview: "Sammy dead, Sammy dead, Sammy dead oh" (88). At hearing this, Ella loses control of her body, which "slid from [her] chair to the floor, fluttering like a decapitated fowl" (88). She then spoke while "seeing things as if on a rolling screen, a movie screen," including her Jamaican childhood home. Finally, Ella sees herself as "a baby no more than nine months." She has literally become both observer and observed, anthropological historian and subject. Via performed gestures and utterances, Ella then witnesses her own traumatic memory of watching her granny (then her primary caretaker) collapse and lie incapacitated for hours before dying in front of the grandchild standing in her crib. At this point Ella again watches herself, but this time it is her adult person reliving the infantile trauma, speaking in the voice of a nine-month-old to the gathered crowd. In this moment Ella is possessed by her past self and actualizes that possession in public performance. This possession challenges the narrative of static identity over time. Moreover, Ella appears to act as the witness of her own death and rebirth as previously described by Joseph Murphy in *Working the Spirit*. In other words, Ella is the interpreting reader, performer, and anthropological researcher of her own journey into knowing.

Ella's experience of relived pain from her own life story, paired with her newly acquired medium's abilities for telling others' stories, demonstrates the ways that our identities are implicated in the attainment of knowledge about others. Having experienced psychological death and rebirth, Ella immediately begins "prophesying" to the traveling men. She explains, "I looked at the faces of the men sitting around me and I saw stories. I saw long deep stories, stretching back and back on stacked, ruled, six by eight cards. The first cards said 'name', 'place of birth', 'date of birth' I read that off for nearly all of the men gathered in that room" (91). In this scene Ella clearly acts as a medium much like Agne, except that she is not articulating one god's prophecy. Rather, she interprets and retells the spiritual stories of different, living men. The strength of Ella's remembered childhood suffering continues to overwhelm her. Bouts of sobbing mark her personal history's voyage into her consciousness. Ella believes that "only now it was safe to know the loneliness and the despair, and to react" (92). Knowledge (and the recognition of how much cannot be known) possesses Ella in a sacred act of acquisition, understanding, and communication. The embodied connections between Ella and the sailors' psychologies echo the communal "flesh" and grace through imagination that Toni Morrison details in Baby Suggs's sermon. Ella's surrender to opacity is not simply an "integration of spirit and matter," which Janice Boddy describes in her study of spirit possession. Instead, surrender occurs through what Ella calls "hegemony of the spirit," or "getting over" (98). During possession Ella's body is "depressed into physical collapse" and her mental boundaries are trespassed. In this moment, Ella notes, "something is activated, rather like an injection needle is pushed forward"; the "shell" of subjectivity has broken (98). In response, Ella will adopt the name Louisiana. This name signals the place of her resurrection and marks the death of her past interpretation of self.

In order to understand Ella's acquisition of knowledge through capitulation to the hegemony of spirit, I look closely at a scene prior to Ella's psychic and spiritual "break." I call Ella's experience here a *capitulation* to spirit rather than a strict submission in order to differentiate her story from that of *Changó's* Agne. Ella's tone when describing the practice of losing her individualistic sense of self has resonances with the overwhelming disorientation evident throughout young Agne's possessions. Yet Ella evinces a more meditative and agential understanding of her relationship to the spiritual community. The novel's third chapter, "Out of Eden," begins as Ella remembers the stained glass window in her mother's Anglican church, which she attended as a child in Brooklyn. Ella describes the window with the impressionistic specificity of childhood memories. She recalls, "My mother's church had a stained glass window with a thorn-headed picture of Jesus the Christ, his head slightly leaned to one side, his arms open and his fingers delicately cocked reminding me somehow of the proper way of drinking tea. You could see his heart—it was heart shaped and had, I think, a dart going through it. At his feet in halos were women, the Marys I presumed" (57). The image of the haloed Marys immediately calls to mind the "venerable sisters" (22) of Anna and Louise. These women, like the Marys in the window, are connected through the sacrificed body of another person. The tableaux's "Jesus the Christ," then, may symbolize the "proper" tea-drinking and academically credentialed Ella. Like Jesus, the venerable sisters' medium is positioned between the celestial and material worlds when performing her ancestrally oriented hermeneutics. Most importantly, the novel's reader may recall Anna's command to Ella on the first recording transcript, "Don't say it child. Don't say you are not the Christ" (22). Furthermore, the dart through Christ's heart in this picture foreshadows Ella's description of divine clarity as "a silver spear that goes slowly from one side of the head and through to the other, leaving silver dust in its path" (105–6). If Christ's crucified body precipitates resurrection, then Ella's punctured psyche and flesh prime her eventual reconstitution of self within this spiritual community.

In this moment Ella learns to accept herself as the passive, mediating object who joins persons and realms as well as the active interpreter who perceives and rearticulates new formulations of knowledge. The stained glass picture she views tellingly exists as separate pieces welded together; this union-through-fracture echoes *Louisiana*'s fragmented narrative structure and reflects the stories of Ella, Anna, and Louise. As Ella recalls, "The picture was a mosaic, like a jigsaw puzzle. Someone must have painted it on glass, broken it into pieces of uneven sizes then stuck the parts together in that large window sited over the altar. How did they do this and why?" (57). Clearly, Ella is an analytical thinker who is interested in process and human motivations, or as Brodber once put it, she is one who seeks "awareness of the insides of people's heads" (qtd. in O'Callaghan, "Cultural Penetration," 70).[33] Ella wonders (as have my graduate students who read this novel) why the artist/ author would choose to fragment his or her own work. In light of the ties between the novel's female subjects and those depicted in the stained glass, we are invited to consider how young Ella's epistemological process of "understanding" this picture confirms the way older, anthropologist-Ella goes about understanding the stories of herself, Anna, and Louise. Remembering the stained glass, Ella continues, "The picture responded to light, so that bits of it or the whole were only visible as it was directed towards them. There was no street lamp or beacon close by, revelation had to depend on God's natural light. In winter therefore, there was hardly more of this picture to be seen than the raised lines of the mosaic where the parts were joined. With the coming of the sun and the summer, the whole picture was there and for a considerable time" (57). Like Ella with the recording machine, those Episcopalian worshipers who wish to witness and understand the full meaning of an event must first show up and be present to see the picture. Once in attendance and attuned to the shadowy piece of media, they must wait for a supernatural power to illuminate the separate pieces. In other words, the congregants must make the agential choice to passively receive the image that God's light may transmit. At first the churchgoers see only the "raised lines of the mosaic where the parts are joined." These lines could symbolize the lines of tape from the recording machine, where the voices are brought into conversation together. They could also symbolize Ella's own body, which acts as a joining of places and people. Indeed, it is no coincidence that Ella remembers this stained glass window at the top of a chapter that contains several new revelations from the mystical recording machine. Ella "scour[s] the reel again for any escaped gems," an appropriately prismatic image for knowledge acquisition (64).[34]

Ella's stained glass metaphor for her hermeneutics of engaged surrender predicts the uncertainty of visual truth in Nalo Hopkinson's *Brown Girl in the Ring,* discussed in the following chapter. This metaphor also brings to mind the theories of language (tied to sacred hermeneutics) presented by fourth- and fifth-century Christian theologian Augustine of Hippo (Aurelius Augustinus). Augustine recognizes the indeterminacy of linguistic meaning by referring to ideas as light and to language as simply a trace of that light. For the theologian, communication must still be ventured because our words may provide sense for another person who has also experienced that light, or, in Ella's case, that *divine* light. Ella's prophetic cards, like Augustine's texts, are instruments that "help receivers to recall the illuminations that they have previously found for themselves" (Pym, 97). Ella's illuminations are part of this Christian tradition, but they also recall the revelatory possession rituals and ancestrally oriented hermeneutics found in Afro-diasporic spiritual traditions. In Brodber's novel, each of these disparate traditions constitute sacred acts of "reading."

After Ella and Reuben move to New Orleans, Ella takes up conjure work with Madam Marie; during this time she comes to see her work with Anna and Louise as an active process of waiting, or as an act of "engaged surrender." In New Orleans Ella searches the Christian Bible for relatable stories to her own experiences. She finds many possible companions in the stories of prophets such as Jonah, the Witch of Endor, and Elijah/Elisha. In connecting herself to these figures, Ella realizes that "prophets wait for God" (101). When Ella shares this realization with Madam Marie, the conjure woman responds, "That's why we are so fat. . . . We eat while we wait" (102). Following that observation, Ella further transforms herself through diet, "vow[ing] then and there to be a vegetarian seer" (102). Ultimately, she does not align herself entirely with the biblical precedents for prophets, just as she cannot align her experience or identity with any one episteme. Ella comes to conclusions about her own identity and spiritual role while reflecting on her interactions with a troubled Jamaican sailor, Ben. Ella had spoken Ben's sad life story back to him so that he could work through his past wounds. Ella comments, "I know now, that my practice had defined itself and with divine blessing. The silver sparkles are about my head at their most powerful as I write and I know that I am not Elisha; I am not the unfortunate lady of Endor. I am a soothsayer, yes, but one who looks behind, sees and will see the past. I see that clearly" (106). Ella now clearly sees her own mediumship as a process of actively allowing herself to be possessed by visual knowledge. Paradoxically, Ella may only receive that knowledge so long as she accepts the opacity of the Other and admits her lack of control over the time she must wait to receive her visions. She must be blessed with divine revelation of Others' prophetic pasts. She cannot force their legible transparency. Ella demonstrates that proper interpretation requires the agential willingness to be possessed by the other. She must let herself be carried not away but home. Just as Agne somehow feels herself no longer a stranger after reinterpreting her personal narrative, Ella discovers that she can experience a liberating form of subjectivity by choosing to surrender to the opacity of herself and others.

Both *Changó* and *Louisiana* imagine new formulations of Afro-diasporic community built on the communal struggle for liberation through spiritual forces and ancestral knowledge. The ancestrally oriented formulations of liberation in *Changó* exist in the space of tension between inevitability and free will, a tension that Jonathon Tittler calls "este delicado equilibrio entre el determinismo, el libro albedrío, y el mesianismo" (this delicate balance among determinism, free will, and messianism) ("*Changó* en traducción," 186, author's trans.). The living are called to liberate themselves and fulfill Changó's prophecy, but they are also defined by and confined to the powerful fates of the metaphysical realm. Agne's position as medium—one which she is forced into, often violently, as a young girl and then later as a young woman—likewise symbolizes a form of inherited submission. Hers is not the agential capitulation we see in Louisiana's engaged surrender. Instead, greater spiritual powers force Agne into a generational fellowship and struggle. And yet, later on, she does emulate Louisiana by embracing her role and its requisite paradoxical implications of empowerment through the dispossession of her individual subjectivity. In short, she actively participates in the processes that I call engaged surrender. Still, the question remains: What is the point of Agne and all the other living ekobios rising up if they are circumscribed by the fates and prophesy?

Zapata Olivella answers this question in a few different ways throughout "Ancestral Combatants." First, Osborn Perry Anderson tells Agne that the conspirators of the Harpers Ferry raid choose to gather every night to discuss the events that have already been determined. They do so because "to take past events and fuse them with the present is not only something that brings us comfort but is a necessity if we are not to die altogether" (401–2; Retomar los hechos pasados y volverlos a refundir en el presente, no solo es algo que nos reconforta, sino que es una necesidad para no morirnos, 581). The gathering is motivated by an impetus toward generational communion and temporal negotiation, much like Anna and Louise's determined communions with each other and Ella. A few pages later, as the spirit group tries to shoot at the White Wolf (a white oppressor) who is gunning down members of their spiritual brotherhood, they find that

> the hammer and the guns does not detonate the old gunpowder. Disillusioned, we realize that death only permits us to influence events to the extent that the living are willing to learn from our experience. (406)

> Desilusionados comprendimos que la muerte solo nos permitía regresar a la acción en la medida en que los vivos quieran o no aprovecharse de nuestra experiencia. (588)

Here we see the relationship between author and reader paralleled in the relationship between the living and the dead. That is, the power of the author and messages of the dead can only be made manifest so long as the reader labors to understand. In order to bring that message to future readers and ekobios, there must be a medium who can translate the message into a new context. Agne's mediumship involves production, reproduction, and transformation and so represents the conditions of diaspora as described by Stuart Hall. Her mediations of the spiritual messages, like Zapata Olivella's polyphonic and capacious renderings of the hemispheric Black experience, are, as Hall describes, "defined, not by essence or purity, but by the recognition of a necessary heterogencity, diversity; by a conception of identity which lives with and through, not despite difference, hybridity. Diaspora identities are those which are constantly producing and reproducing themselves anew, through transformation and difference" (75–76). For the diasporic book *Changó*, this "transformation and difference" develops through the processes of linguistic, cultural, and spiritual translation analogized in the character of Agne. We are invited to recognize the merit in a fight that may already be predetermined for the muntu. Likewise, we must see the merit in the engaged act of translation, even though we can recognize the instability of all meaning and the necessary heterogeneity of any Afro-diasporic epic. In chapter 4 I will revisit this tension between destiny and agency by addressing two dramas that transform this tension in the context of prophecy and staged performances. As we can see in both the plot of *Changó* and its print history, it is not the source meaning that matters most. Instead, the impetus to continued interpretation is paramount. Acts of print and interpretation are circumscribed by the author's original message, and yet both acts are necessary for those who came before to be able to impact the present. Agne's journey into engaged surrender begins with the troubling demands of an already-marginalized subject's complete submission to external forces. Her story then develops into a nuanced exploration of diasporic subjectivity. Agne's transition into a state of engaged surrender occurs as she navigates new forms of relationality, forms that recognize a kind of subjectivity that is rooted in greater human and superhuman communities. In turn, the ancestral knowledge that this community bestows on Agne allows her to discover fluid epistemologies of the self. Specifically, forms of possession enable her to continually reimagine belonging through processes of relational interpretation.

Brodber explains that *Louisiana* was designed to "invite the reader to participate in the research process" by aligning the reader with the book's researcher-protagonist, Ella. Whereas Agne represents the literary and cultural translator in *Changó*, Ella personifies the US academic reader of *Louisiana*. In resisting the dominance of any one epistemology and instead assigning hegemony to the spirit, *Louisiana* encourages readers to reflect on their own experiences as both active and passive interpreters of the text. Brodber encourages her readers to, like Ella, consider their own positions as spiritual mediums. They too are crucial pieces of a collective story that no one person completely controls. Just as *Louisiana* reveals the personal empowerment of active inquiry, it also builds on the multifarious representations of subjectivity symbolized through Agne in *Changó*. Each narrative shows the illusion of individualistic knowledge-possession.

At the end of *Louisiana*, Ella uses the word "pentecost" to describe joining Anna and Louise in the ancestral world of the dead, also known as her translation across the "rainbow's mist" (161). A pentecost is an explosive spiritual event that releases divine energy to all in its presence, thereby creating a blessed community that transcends the bounds of language (161). The liberation illustrated here is one grounded in the freedom to belong, or in the hard-won capacity to find meaning as one voice in the "community song" (161). And yet the reader who has traveled alongside Ella through seas of opacity cannot easily forget the pain that mediums like her inevitably endure for the sake of community liberation. Ella's resurrection into belonging is predicated by sacred acts of suffering and sacrifice. On the one hand, Glissant writes, "It does not disturb me to accept that there are places where my identity is obscure to me, and the fact that it amazes me does not mean I relinquish it" (*Poetics of Relation*, 192). In contrast, both Ella and Agne continually try to relinquish the burden of new-found amazements brought on by physically and spiritually disturbing experiences. The novel *Louisiana* culminates in community and paradigm-shattering revelation, but Ella's personal story is neither pleasant nor easy. By extension, she embodies the vulnerability inherent to acts of abandoning those individualistic interpretations of self that both protect and isolate all of us. To act as a medium between the metaphysical and physical worlds means abandoning these preconceived paradigms. It means submitting to the overwhelming power of the community song. In the case of Brodber's readers, this mediumship may begin by letting the novel "ride" you.

The stories of Agne and Ella/Louisiana inspire a hermeneutical system that can continually reimagine the capacities and limitations of individual subjectivity and community knowledge. This method of reading plays with the concept of liminality, particularly that liminality between the body and text, flesh and discourse. In the next chapter I expand this interpretive approach by concentrating extensively on physical processes of zombification and healing. As I show, these processes demonstrate the difficulty in establishing divisions between the realm of ideas and discourse and that of the flesh. Brodber's earlier novel *Myal* (1983) (which features yet another Ella character) and Nalo Hopkinson's debut *Brown Girl in the Ring* (1997) explore the porous boundaries between flesh and discourse through several women's ideologically charged zombie narratives. I approach these women's stories of embodied spirituality with the understanding that, as Hortense Spillers has explained in "Mama's Baby, Papa's Maybe," the flesh "offers a praxis and a theory, a text for living and for dying, and a method for reading both through their diverse mediations" (207).

3 The Spiritual Life of Power
Zombies in *Myal* and *Brown Girl in the Ring*

How to care for the injured body,

the kind of body that can't hold
the content it is living?
    —Claudia Rankine, *Citizen: An American Lyric*

Have you heard the term "zombification" before? The thing's been going around in my head. You know how some words can stay with you?
    —Erna Brodber, *Myal*

THIS CHAPTER, LIKE the one before it, focuses on two novelistic representations of the "occupied body" via experiences of spiritual possession. Unlike my focus in the previous chapter, I concentrate here on the zombie, a horrifying and extreme variant of physical and metaphysical violation. In Erna Brodber's *Myal* (1988) and Nalo Hopkinson's *Brown Girl in the Ring* (1997), the zombified body acts as the "ultimate sign of loss and dispossession," epitomizing the human suffering and deprivation endured by those exploited in sociopolitical systems including slavery, colonialism, and late capitalism (Dayan, 37). Unlike the painful yet spiritually rich epistemological uncertainty that Agne Brown and Ella/Louisiana experience in *Changó, The Biggest Badass* and *Louisiana*, the dispossession of personal subjectivity in these zombie narratives leaves victims bereft of any individual agency or spirit. Engaged surrender, therefore, is not an option for the zombie.

The prominence of spiritual and folk performances in these novels calls for a mode of hermeneutics that is attuned to the integral role of performances and performative practices within the Afro-diasporic worlds of the written texts. Like the liturgies and rituals described in chapters 1 and 2, the zombie's loss of self is constituted through embodied, ceremonial practices that are then textually rendered in the literature. Unlike Hurston's and Morrison's liturgies and Zapata Olivella's and Brodber's rituals of mediumship, the embodied rituals that create zombification are strictly linked to abusive ideological discourses and concepts. Both *Myal* and *Brown Girl in the Ring* contrast these nefarious spiritual performances by depicting a variety of embodied, ritualized practices that can heal victims and undo their zombification. These healing performances again require a negation of the individual self and in turn promote an ethics of physical and metaphysical interconnectedness. The formulations of collective belonging in Brodber's and Hopkinson's novels are reminiscent of *Beloved*'s love-filled sermon in the Clearing, and *Louisiana*'s description of the "community song" (161). In both *Myal* and *Brown Girl in the Ring,* the injured bodies of feminine characters serve as physical sites for systemic cultural traumas *and* as sites for collective healing from such traumas.[1] By studying the performed and performative rituals that initiate and put an end to zombification in these two novels, we can continue to ask questions about embodiment, agency, and subjectivity in light of the African-derived epistemologies introduced in the previous chapters. What is more, a mode of textual interpretation that is rooted in the performative epistemologies of such religious traditions opens key avenues of inquiry about the boundaries of possession and self-possession in these two novels.

This chapter's focus on zombification both corresponds with and deviates from the overall project's approach to *religious* practices in the Afrodiasporic Americas. In contrast to mediums, prophets, and preachers, zombies are discussed almost exclusively as mythological symbols and folk archetypes by contemporary Afro-Caribbean religious scholars and theologians.[2] While zombification is generally considered a mythological construction of the Vodou spirit world, the narrative trajectory of these zombified women—from individualized spiritual suffering toward wellness in community—typifies the principles of liberation, fellowship, and healing that characterize the Afro-Caribbean religions discussed throughout this project.[3]

In *Myal* and *Brown Girl in the Ring,* zombification and spirit-reclamation—like performative textual hermeneutics—operate simultaneously within the realms of abstract discourse and material performance. Both novels demonstrate the embodied foundations and effective, corporeal repercussions of abstract ideas and systems of power. I begin this chapter by focusing on Brodber's depictions of sound in *Myal*. Sound works in the novel, I contend, to demonstrate the concurrently abstract and material experiences of spirit thievery and reclamation. One woman's possession narrative uses sound to illustrate the materiality of thought, while another's use of and retention of voice show how power operates through the embodied performances of abstract ideas. I then analyze Hopkinson's intensely visceral, visual representations of zombification in her speculative fiction *Brown Girl in the Ring*. References to performance practices including folk masks and ring games appear alongside gruesome depictions of zombified flesh in the dystopian novel. Together, these registers of performance and embodiment invoke a performative textual hermeneutics that illuminates the integral role of human corporeality in political and economic processes. These processes, like zombification, require the discursive and material subjugation of select populations. In the remainder of the chapter, I analyze "recovery" scenes in both *Myal* and *Brown Girl in the Ring*. These scenes detail processes of dispossession that take up performative epistemologies of the African diaspora, specifically that of community-based Myalism, or religious healing.[4]

Sounding Out Spirit Thievery in Erna Brodber's *Myal*

Jamaican novelist and sociologist Erna Brodber defines spirit thievery, a form of zombification, as the process in which "somebody takes away your essence . . . and you are left empty" (Brodber interview with the author, July 14, 2013). In Brodber's novel *Myal*, two young women from Grove Town (an early twentieth-century rural Jamaican community) become victims and survivors of spirit thievery. Ella, a light-skinned native of Grove Town, is emptied of her spirit by her new husband from the United States, Selwyn, when he produces a minstrel show that grossly manipulates Ella's Grove Town memories. Darker-skinned, fifteen-year-old Anita has her spirit stolen by Mass Levi, a local Obeah-man who exploits his social and spiritual powers to regain his lost sexual potency. Myalists, or spiritual healers, lead Ella and Anita back to re-possession of their spirits through sonically rich ceremonies.

Like other zombie narratives set in the Caribbean, *Myal* invokes Dahomean legends of the living dead to explain historical experiences of enslavement and oppression for Africans and African-descended individuals in the Caribbean.[5] The majority of existing scholarship on Brodber's *Myal* focuses on spirit thievery through a sociohistorical lens. For example, Shalini Puri describes spirit possession as a "controlling concept-metaphor for cultural imperialism" (101), while Neil Ten Kortenaar counters that

Brodber "posits a literal spirit possession for which cultural imperialism is a metaphor" (51).[6] While scholars have studied the colonial and spiritual themes of zombification in *Myal,* they have often asked that one theme allegorize the other. I read colonialism *and* spirituality as metaphorical conceits and literal events in the text. Not only are spiritual events "factual reality" in *Myal,* but the novel itself explores the "real" physicality of abstract concepts.[7]

Myal complicates the commonly assumed distinction between abstraction and physicality through explorations of sound. In one crucial scene, two key figures of the spiritual community, Willie (also known as Ole African or the pig) and Dan (also known as Reverend Simpson or the dog), explain spirit thievery as the collection of physical and conceptual phenomena initiated through sound. In this discussion integrating Judeo/Christian narrative with African-derived religions of the Caribbean, Willie and Dan set up a theoretical logic of spirit thievery to explain the historical exigencies of Jamaican disenfranchisement. First Willie asks Dan the rhetorical question, "How come we've never won?" then immediately answers, "They stole our sound" (66). This inception of spirit thievery through sound frames my analysis of this oft-cited dialogue via a performative textual hermeneutics and my subsequent readings of Anita's and Ella's zombifications. By using the stealing of sound as an analytical guide, I show the extent to which sound acts as a "material" of language in a physical and theoretical sense throughout the novel (Saussure, 36). I reveal that when sound waves physically materialize abstract concepts communicated through language such as spirituality and ideology, they also transform the bodies and daily lives of these young women.

Sonic metaphors permeate Willie and Dan's conversation. First, Willie tells Dan that the "conjure men, voodoo men, wizards, and priests, [who] didn't like us . . . gave them our voice" (*Myal,* 66). These conjure men—who were likely of African ancestry considering that they knew African-derived religious practices such as Vodou and hoodoo and considered themselves paradigmatic victims of European supremacies—gave the colonial oppressors their Afro-Caribbean fellows' "voices" and "sound," and in the process "sold their own souls" (66). Willie and Dan compare the conjure men, their "brethren" from whom the British "learnt our tune," to Joseph's half-brothers as told in the book of Genesis.[8] Just as the brothers sold Joseph into slavery in Egypt, the conjure men sold their African brethren into slavery in Jamaica. Catching on to Willie's lecture, Dan adds that the British "sent in their message using our voice" (66–67). Therefore, conjure men enabled the British rulers to push their own story of white superiority onto the enslaved Africans and later the Grove Town community by performing the spirit-thieving message in the voice of the oppressed.

Unlike the conjure men who gave away sound, Willie says, "men should keep and learn to use their power," indicating that one's sound is one's power. When Dan quotes the King James version of Second Timothy 1:7 ("For God has not given us the spirit of fear but of power and love and of sound mind"), he paves the way for the text's logic of zombification by aligning "sound" and "mind," and repeating the link Willie already had established between sound and power.[9] Interestingly, throughout this conversation about spirit thievery, the term "spirit" only appears in the Bible verse and as a modifier for the word "thieves." Rather than saying that the conjure men stole the enslaved Africans' "spirits" or even "essence," as Brodber later defined it during my interview, Willie and Dan refer to "sound," "voice," "tune," and finally "power." In Willie and Dan's conversation, sound is revealed to be a sensory medium that communicates ideological messages in addition to being a spiritual power that can be stolen, retrieved, or maintained.

My focus on sound deviates from existing scholarship on *Myal*, which largely responds to the novel's noticeable interest in another medium of ideological communication—books. When *Myal* ends with the enthusiastic call to change the primary school textbooks for the sake of community spirit re-possession, Brodber identifies the British education system as an ideological state apparatus, as Louis Althusser would term it. This regional apparatus maintains the larger abstract ideology of the state through material means, in this case deriding Afro-Caribbean persons and culture through the material of printed texts (695). Brodber explains that her novel was inspired by Lloyd Best's notion that "thought is action for us," with "us" indicating primarily Caribbean readers of the academic *New World Quarterly*, where Best published his 1967 essay "Independent Thought and Caribbean Freedom." And so Brodber describes *Myal* as a "lecture," urging "intellectuals to see their purpose and to use their skill and their position to rewrite works offensive to us [Jamaicans]" ("Me and My Head-Hurting," 122).[10] According to Brodber, *Myal* is deeply invested in the print medium, as it is a book designed to promote the writing and rewriting of more books. This political lecture, like the prophetic dramas I study in the following chapter, assumes that reconstructing a community's dominant narratives by producing printed texts like *Myal* can construct a new "social and spiritual life" that benefits that community (122).

The novel's plot also presents the printed word as a key factor in a community's wellbeing as articulated through the concepts of spirit thievery and spirit reclamation. After all, Willie and Dan's conversation is usually noted for its identification of books as integral to colonial ideology. What is more, Brodber herself uses textual inventions such as nonchronological plot structures, dialogic formatting, and shifting narrative perspectives in her notably scribal fiction to explore the ways in which "the printed word and the ideas it carries" (109) can help commit or resist spirit thievery. Evelyn O'Callaghan remarks that working through Brodber's difficult novels is "an experience that can, if we let it, profoundly change us" (71). I agree with O'Callaghan and add that Brodber, like the similarly transformative author Toni Morrison discussed in chapter 1, often creates these transformative reading experiences by textually manipulating a reader's imagined experience of performance, namely sound. For example, Brodber chooses to leave out Willie and Dan's names for ten lines of their key dialogue, and in doing so both speeds up the pace of their conversation and tangles the two men's voices together in a perplexing exchange of call-and-response. Therefore, Brodber uses the formatting of the printed page to create a sense of collaborative sonic momentum that seems to exceed the capacities of each individual speaker and, I argue, the page itself. This theoretical intersection of text and enacted sound demonstrates how noting the aesthetic aspects of performance in a written text can reveal that work's theoretical formulations of power. Keeping in mind Brodber's use of textual formatting to represent such sonic complexity, I analyze the ways in which *Myal* portrays the ideological power of reading through sound, not scribal text.

Anita's zombification scene interweaves sound and print as it details her process of reading music. In addition to combining reading and aurality/orality, Anita's sight-singing illustrates how abstract ideas become physical sound waves as a result of embodied action. While literary critics often discuss Ella's zombification at the hands of her husband Selwyn, Anita's spirit thievery is rarely explored at length. This discrepancy in scholarly attention may be due to the fact that Ella's more detailed narrative begins and ends the novel, or it may be thanks to the more overt connections Brodber provides between Ella's story and the book's larger arguments about slavery and colonialism. Unlike Ella, Anita's spirit is stolen not by a representative of the British or US empire, but by her subtly manipulative Afro-Jamaican neighbor Mass Levi Clarke, whom Brodber describes as "a strong man. And spiritually too" (63). After suffering a stroke Mass Levi uses his spiritual strength for nefarious purposes—to steal Anita's essence and regain his own sexual potency. Mass Levi exploits his Obeah to send a duppy, or a kind of ghost, to harass Anita and slowly empty her of her spirit, believing that "he could use the young girl's spirit to get him back his own powers" (76).[11]

Later in the novel the Kumina queen Agatha Paisley, or Miss Gatha, performs a possession ceremony with her tabernacle members and successfully saves Anita and leaves Mass Levi deceased on the privy floor.[12] Therefore Anita's spirit is stolen from her *and* restored to her through Afro-Jamaican religious practices, which are historically associated with anticolonial liberation.[13] Thus Anita's storyline is more difficult to read as an allegory of colonialism. June Roberts considers Anita's narrative an "attempt to expose the dirty folk secrets of pedophilia, incest, and rape, as well as the practice of obeah" (156). Roberts's reading helps illuminate the trickiness of writing on Mass Levi's character without either glossing over the sexual violation or reifying colonial prejudices toward Afro-Caribbean men and Obeah, but it does not take into consideration the care with which Brodber details Anita's experiences at the hands of the thieving Mass Levi and the heroic Miss Gatha.[14]

Mass Levi begins his pursuit of the beautiful and intelligent Anita while she is deeply absorbed in her musical education. Brodber writes, "Anita was studying. The kind that splits the mind from the body and both from the soul and leaves each open to infiltration" (28). Here we see Brodber speak of the immaterial mind's distinction from the material flesh in a manner consistent with Eurocentric philosophical traditions that rely on the idea of a mind/body split attributed in popular discourse to Cartesian dualism. And yet Anita's experience troubles the chasm between abstract consciousness and embodied experience. Puri argues that thanks to the "concept metaphors of spirit thievery . . . *Myal* brilliantly overcomes the spirit/matter, mind/body dichotomy, rending it impossible to separate bodily and mental violence" (102). I agree with Puri and note that by repeatedly invoking African diasporic religions such as Myal/Obeah, Kumina, and Revival Zion, the novel also connects the bodily and mental practices of knowing discussed throughout this volume.[15] Dianne Stewart notes that "within the context of African-derived religions," in contrast to Eurocentric Christian theology (and I would add predominant epistemological inheritances from European Enlightenment philosophy), "theological ideas emerge from concretized practice, ritual, and embodied spirituality" (198). Therefore, knowing itself is a bodily experience—a play on Lloyd Best's aforementioned idea that "thought is action." The African theological concept of embodied knowledge, I argue in this chapter's conclusion, also aligns with Althusser's contention that while ideology is understood through imaginary concepts, the "imaginary relation is itself endowed with a material existence" because it is constituted and maintained through the physical action of embodied subjects (695). Brodber's novel, like the work of Édouard Glissant, rejects the idea of "discarnate discourse" and adopts "a language steeped in the oral and the corporeal" (Dash, 611). This Glissantian connection between discourse and embodiment will play an integral role in my reading of the oral exposé during Ella's and Anita's healing ceremonies. In Anita's story we see these theological and philosophical ideas play out in the physical practice of reading music.

Anita's mind, body, and soul are open to Mass Levi's infiltration as she studies printed music by "solfa-ing," a general term for English forms of solmization, or "the use of syllables in association with pitches as a mnemonic device for indicating melodic intervals" (Rainbow and McGuire; Hughes and Gerson-Kiwi). Because "a solmization system is not a notation" but rather "a method of aural rather than visual recognition," what Brodber calls solfa-ing is actually a process of intersemiotic translation from the visual notation to the aural system of solmization (Hughes and Gerson-Kiwi). It should be noted that for Anita, this process of symbolic translation also requires embodied vocalization. In order to read through translation, Anita must use her body and create physical sound waves. The narrator exhaustingly takes the reader through Anita's process of musical interpretation. I quote this passage at length to demonstrate the labor required for interpreting Anita's interpretation.

> [Anita] had to read the notes—first note on the line is "e"—and she had to remember the sounds. "Do re mi fa so la ti do." So if that was "e", it was really "mi" and she sounded it. Now that next one is the first space so it has to be "f" and if it is "f" coming after "e" then it must be "fa" and she sounded that. Then she went back: "Do re mi fa." So what she really wanted was "mi, fa" and she sounded those two. "Mi fa." The other one was a little bit more difficult. It was all the way to the end: the last note on the line so it had to be "f". Now to get at that sound. "Do re mi fa so la ti do." So that was "do". So the three first notes in the piece were "mi fa do". Now to sing them. And she got it. "Mi fa do." Now the words: "Thee I love." She had got it. Now to press on a little further. Teacher had said it was easy. Other sounds joined hers. She heard a slight "ping" but she continued to the fourth note. (28)

Without even the hint of a musical score, *Myal's* methodical prose submerges the reader in the process of sight-singing. Anita's method makes clear that the musical notes are what Glissant may call "Relational"—only legible when considered through "intervals" or in relation to other musical notes. Anita's system of musical interpretation, like Glissant's Relation (which I discussed in chapter 2), is a process of "knowledge in motion," a process that does not derive from nor act upon "prime elements that are separable or reducible" (*Poetics of Relation*, 186, 172). Anita "reads" the written musical score by recognizing visual symbols, then remembering the relationship between abstract sounds in her mind, and finally physically embodying each sound through her voice. Anita's process of reading music is a process of physically performing relationships between abstract concepts.

Anita's sight-singing method is made manifest by Brodber's textual formatting, which asks the reader to "sound out" her printed text in order to better understand. *Myal* walks the reader through this process of interpretation with such detail that it is hard to not join Anita in her sight-singing. If readers are not familiar with solfa-ing, they are likely to get lost in the process of reconciling the written symbols on the page with the symbols' assumed tonal relationships to each other, emulating the vexed representations of translation by Agne Brown in *Changó, The Biggest Badass*. For Anita these symbols take the form of circles and lines on sheet music; for the reader the symbols are English letters and words. With the addition of the lyrics "Thee I love," *Myal* provides yet another layer of symbolic abstraction for Anita to contend with through the material of sound, and it brings Anita's and the reader's experiences of interpretation even more closely together. Just as studying solfa-ing "took a lot of concentration" for Anita, studying Anita's interpretive process requires a performative textual hermeneutics and considerable concentration on the part of Brodber's readers (29).

The sound of Mass Levi's duppy throwing rocks against the zinc roof interrupts Anita as she works with the words "Thee I love."[16] The duppy's sonic disturbance signals the beginning of Anita's spiritual invasion. The pings of the rocks, like the sounds of the written notes Anita voices, are the result of an abstract concept (in this case spiritual malevolence) made physically manifest—they are thought turned into action. Making the physicality of abstraction even more explicit is the fact that a rock ultimately hits Anita on her head, creating a "visible coco," or raised sore (30). The visible coco on Anita's head reinforces the impossibility of separating bodily and mental violence in *Myal*.

I see Anita's reading process as a theoretical work on the part of the novel that allows us to interpret Ella's story through these same methods of abstract knowledge rendered bodily in sound. Scholars may be overlooking the sonic connections between the two characters thanks to Ella's realizations about the spirit-thieving power of books. It is Ella who tells the Christian Methodist Reverend Brassington about the degrading message of the British schoolbooks. She says that this educational system turns young Jamaicans into "duppies, zombies, living deads capable only of receiving orders from someone else and carrying them out" (107). Indeed, Ella's resistance to the spirit thievery of children's readers offers a triumphant vision of Brodber's textual hopes for Jamaican intellectuals. Unsurprisingly, literary critics tend to focus on this plot point, which privileges the medium of their own study and craft.[17] But even when Ella is protesting the schoolbooks, she emphasizes the role of her voice in the learning process, asking, "Must my voice tell that to children who trust me?" (107). Brodber describes *Myal* as a lecture (a primarily oral pedagogical technique) promoting books. The prominence of sound in the novel fits with her intellectual history, which, beginning with early historical and sociological work, has consistently explored nonscribal forms of cultural knowledge that are communicated through voice and other embodied practices in the Caribbean.[18] Ella's story suggests that not only Jamaican cultural wisdom but also harmful colonial beliefs are "known" through embodied practices. By keeping in mind Anita's laborious, physical practices of reading, we can see how the messages imbedded within literary works also become known through rituals. More specifically, Ella's story demonstrates the ways in which ideological subjects perform oppression through embodied rituals, in particular voiced sound.

Brodber begins the chapter on Ella's childhood with four decontextualized stanzas of Rudyard Kipling's colonialist poem "White Man's Burden." The narrator follows the unexplained quotation by reporting, "The words were the words of Kipling but the voice was that of Ella O'Grady aged 13" (5). Kipling's poem represents the ideological state apparatus, or spirit-thieving enterprise of colonial interpellation through British literature. By repeating the term "words" twice in the act of attributing them to the well-known British author, Brodber points out how Ella's cultural performance embodies what the postcolonial scholar Homi Bhabha might refer to as the "semiotic . . . disjuncture between the subject of a proposition" and "the subject of enunciation" (35). In other words, Brodber takes note of the supposed separation between abstract words and physical voice. Kipling's words and Ella's voice exist in Glissantian

"Relation" to each other. Thinking about Ella and the poem in terms of Relation allows the reader to consider how the two are pointedly differentiated from each other during the recitation and, at the same time, to see how both are transformed as a result of the interaction, since the work of Relation "always changes all the elements composing it" (Glissant, *Poetics of Relation,* 172). Brodber makes it clear that Ella is not Kipling's poem, and yet Ella's performance of the textual poem performatively transforms her as well as the written words. According to Glissant, "Relation relinks, (relays), relates," and "domination and resistance, osmosis and withdrawal, the consent to dominating language (*langage*) of dominated languages (*langues*)" can only be understood through a sensorial understanding of Relation (173). As with Anita's musical reading through Relation, the sensorial mechanism of Relation in Ella's recitation is sound. In this case, sound is the vehicle through which the abstract concepts of colonial message and colonized subject position become culturally legible.

As if playing on Glissant's use of "osmosis" to describe colonial domination through ideology, Brodber writes about Ella's school experience, detailing that "in a science class, teacher would talk about OSMOSIS, 'the process by which a thin substance pulls a thick substance through a thin cell wall'" (11). The teacher refused to call on Ella, and "once more unrecognized, Ella would stare through the windows and guess what? She would see the thin liquid struggling to pull the thick one and all of this within the membrane of a leaf" (11). Ella identifies the physical "object lesson" of osmosis outside, while inside the classroom she herself experiences the ideological and spiritual osmosis of the colonial education system, even as she recognizes her lack of legible identity within that space. Brodber uses Ella's recitation of Kipling to illustrate how these seemingly abstract experiences of ideological "osmosis and withdrawal" initiate the physical violence of such ideology. In short, both instances of osmosis are physical.

Myal alludes to the violence of Ella's Kipling recitation when Reverend Simpson compliments the poem's "execution" (5).[19] When the reverend calls Ella "the little lady executionist," he invokes an odd image in which Ella is part executioner, as the oral performer of the colonial poem, and part victim of the poem's spirit-thieving message. The educators cast Ella as a mouthpiece for the colonizers, using her voice to tell the imperial message. Kipling's poem is full of those "Big Steamers" later referenced in Willie and Dan's conversation. Helen Tiffin uses appropriately corporeal metaphors as she discusses recitation as a colonial practice, saying,

"Through recitation . . . the colonized absorbed into their bodies ('hearts') the 'tongue' of the colonizer" ("Cold Hearts," 913).

Here, Ella is set up to be one of the "conjure men" who sell the Afro-Jamaicans' sound to the British and in doing so, sell their own souls. In contrast to the legacy of the conjure men, Ella's recitation is not founded in her dislike for nor lack of faith in the Afro-Jamaican community. Ella is chosen to voice the colonial message thanks to her "sensitivity," a sensitivity that Brodber links to Ella's illegible identity in the colonial paradigm. After Ella (part victim and part oppressor) finishes Kipling's poem with the line describing British colonial subjects as "half devil and half child," Reverend Simpson asks himself, "Whose burden is this half black half white child?" (6). Reverend Simpson thus confirms the split subjectivity that Ella has already "named" through oral performance. Thanks to her "ginger" hair and "strange" parentage, Ella's ancestral relation to Grove Town is considered only partial, bringing to mind the partial familial ties between Joseph and his half-brothers in the Genesis story allegorized by Willie and Dan. Ella's recitation sonically performs her ideological interpellation. Maydene Brassington reflects that while reciting the poem, Ella appears "totally separated from the platform and from the people around her," emphasizing the girl's growing distance from her community (17). While the recitation performs an already-existing ideological position, the act of voicing that imaginary Relation seems to create a physical manifestation on Ella's body. What is more, Maydene extends that separation to the girl's internal life when she recalls Ella's ethereal stage presence as rooted "in a passion so innocent and strong that it could separate body from soul" (17).[20] Ella's self-separating passion brings to mind Anita's self-splitting studying, particularly when Maydene adds that in watching Ella recite, she "saw the abstract," or the spiritual relations of ideology (17). After all, the young girl is chosen for the recitation thanks to the abstract "sensitivity" she has gained through her liminal position between communities, a position *Myal* stages yet again in the ideological state apparatus of the school by having the young girl make "the door to the class room her recess spot," since no one in her class will play with her during the break (10). By thinking about Ella's recitation and classroom experiences through the lens of embodied thought, we can see how the ideological manipulation of colonial subjects' consciousness is ritually performed through physical actions. For example, Ella teaches her young students to read the word "master" by miming her hands and voice in an act of ritual learning: "The whole class would follow, their pointer fingers of their right hands sliding under the words and their voices trying to catch up with Miss Ella. 'M-a-s-t-e-r, Master'" (97). Brodber explicitly combines fingers, words, and voices, bringing together the key elements of performative textual hermeneutics—texts, flesh, and action. Thought is action and taking particular actions (such as reciting a Kipling poem or parroting an instructor) alters a person's mental and spiritual state. Thanks to colonial education, the theft of Ella's spirit begins when she is only a child.

When Ella travels to live with her new husband, Selwyn Langley, in the United States, this theme of metaphysical dispossession through embodied performance reaches a climax. Selwyn takes Ella's childhood stories of growing up in rural Jamaica and turns them into a derisive "coon show" entitled *Caribbean Days and Nights*. The play violates Ella even further by having her role acted by a blonde white woman and grotesquely parodying those she loves in Jamaica with racist tropes of early twentieth-century black-face drama. Selwyn's theft and distortion of Ella's Jamaican memories are a logical extension of the legal conceptions of property and personhood that allowed for enslaved subjects' dispossession and commodification on the market. In *The Fugitive's Properties* Stephen Best traces the legal discourses of enslavement and early twentieth-century intellectual property rights, showing a "historical continuity in the life of the United States in which the idea of personhood is increasingly subject to the domain of property" (270). Because Selwyn's minstrel show "steals" Ella's spirit, it demonstrates how "property [becomes] a version of personhood"; the "objectification of [Ella and Grove Town's] personality" reifies the original objectifications of enslaved individuals under the law (53, 60). By creating *Caribbean Days and Nights,* Selwyn, like the colonialists on their steamships, has manipulated Ella into playing the part of Willie and Dan's "conjure man," taking her sound to transmit his own message of racial inferiority. Selwyn's cruel message betrays Ella by mocking her and her home. Ella sees Selwyn as an "architect" who opened up a "passage" in her, from whence "substance had been drained," that substance being her community's sound, its voices and personalities, and according to Willie and Dan's logic, its spirit and power.[21] Fixated by her husband's directorial choice in his derogatory drama to show every Caribbean fruit in full bloom at the same time of year, all Ella's "obsessed soul could register was: 'Everything is a fruit except me.'" (83). Witnessing this ceremony of mocking subjugation, Ella's senses bombard her with the truth of her Relation to the ideologies physically performed before her—her zombification.[22] Confronted with the fecundity of ideology's material apparatuses on the minstrel stage, Ella finds herself barren in comparison.

Now that Ella has seen the truth of her lifelong ideological and spiritual emptying manifested in oral performances on the musical stage, she attempts to practice bodily resistance against further osmosis and withdrawal. Ella physically resists the sense of having been drained of her own sound by Selwyn, first by retaining what is left of her voice by withholding it from him, and then from all other people. Finally, she physically retains what is left of her bodily fluids: "She stopped speaking to him the night of her visit to the play. A couple months more and her belly was over-sized. She was carrying the baby Jesus. Then she stopped uttering completely. Stopped doing anything. Even stopped going to the lavatory" (83). In this unusual act of self-preservation, Ella intuits the corporeal foundations of her metaphysical violation by Selwyn. By retaining her physical fluids while refraining from speaking, Ella acknowledges the embodied physicality of sound, particularly voice and utterance. Furthermore, she aligns both of these physical elements (utterance and excrement) with the abstract spirit and power. Ella's process of resistant retention follows the same logic of Anita's zombification—abstract concepts are known through physical performance, and this process of knowledge acquisition can effect physical and spiritual violence. Ella's hysterical pregnancy is, like the visible coco on Anita's head, the physical, external manifestation of abstract harm on a woman's body. Unlike Anita's raised sore, Ella's pregnancy represents both the physicality of spiritual violence and the physical gestation of spiritual hope. Before returning to the embodied scene of Anita and Ella's zombifications and potential recoveries in this chapter's conclusion, I turn to the overwhelmingly corporeal, grisly, and stimulating world of Nalo Hopkinson's *Brown Girl in the Ring*.

Economies of Flesh in *Brown Girl in the Ring*

Brown Girl in the Ring's protagonist is Ti-Jeanne, a young Afro-Caribbean mother who lives with her folk healer grandmother, Mami Gros-Jeanne, amongst impoverished immigrant communities of color in the derelict ghetto of central Toronto called The Burn.[23] While Joan Dayan argues that "the zombie tells the story of colonization," in the case of *Brown Girl in the Ring*, it also tells the story of colonialism's racist and classist legacies of capitalistic exploitation. I argue that Hopkinson's speculative fiction details the bodily process of spiritual zombification in horrific detail in ways that extend Brodber's depictions of physical sores to represent ideological damage. Hopkinson's flesh-filled novel demonstrates the bodily violations that underpin political and social subjugation in the contemporary Americas. By studying the zombie and healthcare economies present throughout the novel with a focus on visual rather than oral performance practices, I am building upon my analysis of *Myal* and presenting an additional sensorial method for performatively reading spirit thievery in Afro-diasporic literature. The novel demonstrates that, while all humans are subject to mortality, those systematically dispossessed through histories of colonialism, patriarchy, economic dispossession, and racial hierarchies are overwhelmingly neglected and instrumentalized to ease the physical, psychological, and spiritual suffering of others.

Mami Gros-Jeanne, a practitioner of the healing spiritual practice Myal, faithfully honors a distinctly pan-Caribbean pantheon of spirits as she tries to teach her skeptical granddaughter the benefits of doing the same. Monica Coleman notes that in *Brown Girl in the Ring,* "Hopkinson combine[s] traditional African-derived religious imagery from Haiti, Jamaica, Guadeloupe, Martinique, and Brazil into one pan-Caribbean religious system" (11). Hopkinson's religious and mythical references and phenomena sit alongside plausible yet difficult to comprehend technologies, inviting the reader to imagine the workings of the spirit world as similar to the workings of the scientific world, particularly that of biomedical engineering. Gerald Jonas of the *New York Times* reviewed Hopkinson's science-fiction brand of religion, saying, "She treats spirit-calling the way other science fiction writers treat nanotechnology or virtual reality; like the spirits themselves, the spirit-callers follow rules as clear to them . . . as the equations of motion or thermodynamics are to scientists and engineers" (April 30, 1998). Jonas identifies the ways in which *Brown Girl in the Ring* presents spiritual and scientific knowledge as powerful instruments of "biopower," or the ability to control the bodies and lives of human populations. Hopkinson's narrative shows that these tools can be used for exploitation or liberation in the material world. Jonas may not be aware, however, that Hopkinson's treatment of "spirit-calling" is not remarkable for recognizing a set of distinct rules, since any attempt to synthesize the intricate cosmologies and liturgies of syncretic religious traditions proves immensely difficult thanks to the complex rituals that practitioners have developed, adapted, and passed on over many generations. Rather, Hopkinson's spiritual landscape in *Brown Girl in the Ring* is remarkable because it imagines a world in which *everything* supernatural is made materially real. Gordon Collier describes the novel as a survival narrative, "a racy generic amalgam of dystopia, futuristic technology, supernatural horror and witchcraft, generational romance, mythic quest story, and trickster tale" (444). In the novel there are malevolent spirits associated with Vodou folk mythology (usually de-emphasized by the religion's practitioners), a version of graft-versus-host disease in which the graft organ successfully alters the consciousness of the host, and a divine community of spirits and ancestors who battle against evil on earth.

The novel's plot takes off when Tony, Ti-Jeanne's drug-addicted ex-beau and the (unbeknownst to him) father of her newborn baby, begs Ti-Jeanne and Gros-Jeanne to help him escape The Burn with the aid of their physical and metaphysical herbal knowledge.[24] Tony is desperate to extricate himself from a posse of violent drug dealers. The posse leader, Rudy, has threatened to kill Tony if he does not murder another human being so that Rudy can then harvest and sell that victim's heart for an organ transplant. Rudy, who we later discover is also Ti-Jeanne's grandfather, has secured authority over the residents of The Burn. He also has attained prolonged physical youth by using his Obeah to zombify and otherwise violate those around him. Like Mas Levi and the other conjure men in *Myal*, Rudy is a "shadow-catcher"; he manipulates the neutral powers of the sacred for his own personal gain and in the process sells out his own already-subjugated community (121).[25] Rudy combines his evil version of Jamaican Obeah, or the "the 'putting on' and 'taking off' of 'duppies' or 'jumbees' (ghosts or spirits of the dead)," with a practice of zombification reminiscent of Haitian mythology (Olmos and Paravisini-Gebert, *Healing Cultures*, xix). Ti-Jeanne, like her mother Mi-Jeanne, can "see with more than sight" (9). Gifted with this "second sight" from her Papa loa, Legba/Legbara, Ti-Jeanne experiences "waking dreams" during which she envisions the deaths of others in her community (59, 20, 9). At the beginning of the novel, Ti-Jeanne "hate[s] the visions" and worries that they are symptoms of the postpartum "madness" her mother developed before abandoning the family (20). Ti-Jeanne's ability to see into the grisly futures of those around her endows her with a form of social knowledge that, though disturbing for the young woman, ultimately gives her the power to fight against Rudy's regime of terror and zombification.

In *Brown Girl in the Ring*, soul-stealing occurs at the intersections of physical violation, capitalism, and spirituality. Usually Rudy creates zombies, which I categorize as "flesh objects," by murdering his victims in order to then force their reanimated flesh to labor on his behalf. Rudy's old secretary, Melba, exemplifies the flesh-object zombie, a de-souled individual whose empty "living dead" body is used for another's personal gain.[26] Melba demonstrates her zombification through unflinching obedience to her former employer, even pressing her own neck into the blade of Rudy's knife so that he can flay her skin and feed her to his hungry duppy. Rudy zombifies Melba in order to "teach [her] a lesson" for "holding back some of she earnings" from him, demonstrating how this process of spiritual dispossession dramatizes ideologies of exchange value and power (212). Those like Melba who are doomed to indefinitely perform manual labor for another person represent the extreme manifestation of capitalist oppression, historically rooted in the enslavement inflicted on kidnapped Africans in the Western Hemisphere by European colonists. On the other hand, Melba does not read perfectly as a symbol for the commodification of enslaved Africans because Rudy has no intention to use Melba as a commodity—that is to say, he has objectified Melba and is claiming her labor power as his own but is not exchanging her on a market. Rather, Melba's zombification as a flesh object personifies a collapse between what Marx calls "labor power" and "use value" ("Wage Labor and Capital," 660). In a few special cases, Rudy paralyzes his victims and convinces them to let him control their disembodied souls—also referred to as duppies—creating a particularly dangerous form of zombie, which I call the "disembodied docile body." Rudy turns his daughter, Mi-Jeanne (Ti-Jeanne's mother), into this "living" zombie form by enslaving her soul in a calabash bowl and then using her metaphysical capabilities for spiritual sight in order to accomplish feats that are impossible under the constraints of a human body. The enslaved, duppy zombie resembles the docile body according to Michel Foucault's concept of "'docility,' which joins the analyzable body to the manipulable body" (*Discipline and Punish*, 136). As the disembodied docile body, Mi-Jeanne is able and obligated to swiftly destroy any other living creature that Rudy desires. She becomes an enslaved nonsubject or, in the words of Orlando Patterson, "the ideal human tool . . . perfectly flexible, unattached, and deracinated" (337). Always the capitalist innovator, Rudy unleashes his evil Obeah to enormously increase the use value of his daughter-zombie by anatomizing her flesh and exploiting the component parts.

Rudy's zombie economy operates concurrently with a state-sanctioned physical economy that exchanges flesh objects, namely viable donor organs from pigs and humans. In the novel's prologue, Douglas Baines from the Toronto transplant hospital (ironically named "Angel of Mercy") meets with Rudy to offer him a monetary award if Rudy can procure a human heart for the ailing Canadian premier. Baines believes that his hospital will benefit if it performs Uttley's life-saving surgery, so he initiates a deal with Rudy, knowing that the organ donor will be murdered by the posse. By weaving together the zombie and organ economies in the larger narrative arc, *Brown Girl in the Ring* shows how both economies of flesh share common investments in objectifying the bodies of the socioeconomically dispossessed for the sake of those with capital. As Baines and Rudy negotiate a payment for the heart, they hyperbolically demonstrate Marx's description of "labor power" as "this peculiar commodity which has no other repository than human flesh and blood" ("Wage Labor and Capital," 660). In the case of this deal, not only is Rudy's price of labor reckoned in his own work through human flesh and blood, but the commodity Rudy is producing is in fact human and flesh and blood.

Sarah Wood claims that "*Brown Girl* dramatizes the battle between a mythical and mystical Caribbean culture and the demands of a postindustrial, postcolonial, and here posturban society" (317). I argue that rather than presenting a battle between the mystical and the postindustrial, Hopkinson uses the mystical and mythological trope of zombification to reveal the corporeal underpinnings of this near-future society. I read the gruesome and visually detailed descriptions of bodily harm and spiritual subjugation within the scenes of zombification in the novel as hyperbolic reflections of the broader economic practices and biopolitical regimes present throughout *Brown Girl in the Ring*. While the harrowing and fantastic nature of Rudy's zombification techniques may seem over the top for many North American readers of science fiction, I suggest that they should also be interpreted within the same registers of commonplaceness and interactive performativity as the ring games, traditional sayings, and folktales that punctuate the publication's structure.

Hopkinson draws on a breadth of popular Caribbean performance practices, including myth, religion, and folklore, throughout her novel. For example, the title *Brown Girl in the Ring* references a popular children's ring game, and the book features a series of epigraphs that quote chants, traditional sayings, lullabies, songs, poetry, and folk plays. More than any other source text, Hopkinson repeatedly cites lines from Derek Walcott's play based on a Trinidadian folktale, *Ti-Jean and His Brothers* (1953). Like Walcott's play, *Brown Girl in the Ring* is a story of intergenerational trauma and survival rich with allegory, trickster figures, folklore, and layers of masking. Hopkinson's insistence on repeatedly breaking up the flow of her prose with quotes from songs, scripts, lullabies, and proverbs indicates that these epigraphs offer more than cultural context. Rather, they repeatedly bring the reader's attention back to the methods of meaning-making imbedded within these popular and quotidian performance practices. In a 2005 interview with Hyacinth Simpson, Hopkinson describes how she developed her literary tastes and practices, saying,

> My first encounters with the literature of the fantastic as a child were through folk-tales, fairy-tales, and epic tales. That meant the books on my parents' shelves, the stuff that my father was teaching, such as Homer's *Iliad* and *Gulliver's Travels,* and the work by artists he admired, such as Miss Lou (Louise Bennett Coverly). So I was already steeped in old-style tales and oral tradition (all that Shakespeare and Derek Walcott and Samuel Selvon and Dem Two I saw acted out in Christmas theatres) by the time I started writing science fiction and fantasy. ("Fantastic Alternatives," 102)

Hopkinson's highly citational writing style reflects her personal and literary investments in exploring the liminal spaces between text and performance which exist in both the European and Caribbean canons.[27]

Like Anita's intricate process of reading music in *Myal,* I use Hopkinson's epigraphical scaffolding as a methodological and theoretical guide for interpreting the novel. In contrast to my analysis highlighting oral and sonic performances represented in Brodber's *Myal,* I concentrate on the ways in which the plot and epigraphs of *Brown Girl in the Ring* privilege the visual components of certain performance practices. My focus on the visual rather than sonic aspects of performance in Hopkinson's work may at first appear at odds with the author's understanding of her writing style. In her interview with Simpson, Hopkinson connects her performance-driven foundation with "the love of orality," saying that as a child of poet Slade Hopkinson, who "regularly spoke in iambic pentameter and wrote sonnets," rhythm is important to her, along with "language use, word choice, register, the vernacular, etc." ("Fantastic Alternatives," 102). As critics such as Gregory Rutledge, Alondra Nelson, Ifeoma Nwankwo, and Monica Coleman have noted, Hopkinson uses these elements of orality in her prose, such as when she writes dialogue in Jamaican and Trinidadian Creole. What is more, the epigraphs that punctuate Hopkinson's literary text reflect what Carolyn Cooper calls the "broad repertoire of themes and cultural practices" that constitute what critics often call the "oral tradition" (2). In her study of gender, orality, and performance in Jamaican popular culture, she writes, "The thematic repertoire includes diverse cultural beliefs/practices such as religion—obeah, myal, ettu, revival, kumina, spirit-possession; entertainment/socialisation practices—children's games, story-telling rituals, tea-meetings, and social dance, for examples. The verbal techniques include the compressed allusiveness of proverb, the enigmatic indirection of riddle and the antiphonal repetitions of oral narration which recur as set linguistic formulations in folk-tale, legend, song-text and performance poetry" (2). It is remarkable how many of these elements of the oral tradition—including religion, children's games, social dance, proverb, poetry, and folktale—Hopkinson integrates into her novel. While the presence of oral culture is undeniable in *Brown Girl in the Ring,* I note that the particular elements of this oral repertoire that Hopkinson chooses to weave throughout her novel overwhelmingly point to visual rather than sonic cues of embodied performance. From the injunction to "show me your motion" in the eponymous ring game to the chant "Barkodey . . . And if you laugh me go cut you" to the chorus of Walcott's *Ti-Jean and His Brothers,* "give the Devil a child for dinner," Hopkinson selects epigraphs that put bodies on display through dance, emotion, and devilish consumption (183, 135, 1).

In this study I connect the stories of the Canadian organ economy, Rudy's zombification techniques, and Ti-Jeanne's survival narrative to two particular aspects of visual performance–masking and social dance. While *Brown Girl in the Ring* consistently references a wide array of performances and performance practices that are contextually and narratively defined by the visually recognizable movements of human bodies, I contend that Hopkinson takes particular inspiration from the use of masks in Walcott's folk drama and from the choreographies of children's ring games. I concentrate on the theoretical implications of masking to discuss the novel's depictions of the zombie and organ economies, after which I turn to the methods of social dance within the tradition of ring games in order to explore how community and spiritual belonging are constructed in the book's final scenes.

In addition to the corresponding names and repeated epigraphical citations, Hopkinson alludes to Walcott's *Ti-Jean and His Brothers* in several ways. Both stories tell of three family members battling a devilish figure who wishes to "consume" them and who takes on different forms representing larger social ills of inequitable consumption. Ti-Jeanne is clearly an archetypal hero, who, like the youngest brother in Walcott's play, embodies both the wits and innocence of "Jean" or "High John de Conqueror" and trickster animals such as Anancy, Brer Rabbit, or Compére Lapin. In these folk stories, which Zora Neale Hurston elucidated in her early ethnographic work, the disadvantaged protagonist defeats the bigger and stronger animals (or in the case of John, the plantation master) thanks to his or her capacity to see beyond the masks and deceptions of the antagonists. Through the trickster hero's own performances of savvy deception, she is able to distort the stories' key presumptions.[28] For example, Ti-Jeanne's spiritual visions and conversations with the Jab-Jab are akin to Ti-Jean's communications with anthropomorphized animals in Walcott's play. These extrahuman perceptions and relationships enable the protagonists to recognize their masked oppressors' true identities and, in turn, to exploit their ultimate weaknesses. In addition to alluding to the folktale, Hopkinson challenges that genre's limitations by casting an emotionally complex, unwed, adolescent mother as the hero of her trickster narrative.[29] In addition, the whole of this speculative fiction novel reflects the tradition of folktales that express a political narrative of resistance and oppression in the deceptively simplistic structure of a children's story, or in this case, a science-fiction novel marketed to young adults. Hopkinson tells Simpson, "I am also in love with archetype and metaphor," adding that "those old tales re-enact archetypal dilemmas, and it's possible to turn the tales into metaphors that one weaves through one's work" ("Fantastic Alternatives," 102). *Brown Girl in the Ring* combines the classic trickster and John folktales with futuristic biotechnologies in order to create a world in which the game of life has already been constructed to favor the colonizers and their opportunistic conjure men.

The plot of *Brown Girl in the Ring* twists and turns through a series of disguises and revelations and in so doing draws on the trope of physical and metaphorical masking present in the storytelling techniques of the folk drama. Masks (like reading and sound in *Myal*) are simultaneously abstract and material. In *Masking and Power* Gerard Aching explains that Caribbean literature and popular culture uses masking, unmasking, and demasking to reflect on "the engagement between subjects in uneven or hierarchical social positions" (6). In Walcott's *Ti-Jean and His Brothers,* the audience sees the Devil character don disguises as the Planter and the Old Man/Papa Bois in order to deceive the brothers he hopes to humiliate and consume. In accordance with the folktale format, the play's audience is already familiar with the typical devices of the genre if not the entire plot. Suspense is created by means of dramatic irony as the audience watches each character realize or fatefully fail to realize the reality of the Devil's true identity and schemes lurking below his mask. In fact, the term "mask" or "masquerade" is most often used in *Brown Girl in the Ring* to describe deceitful or untruthful interactions. In accordance with the folktale drama, Hopkinson foments narrative tension by following a hero who, despite her gift of prophetic sight, often knows less than the reader does about the disguised intentions of certain characters. Like Walcott's folk drama, *Brown Girl in the Ring* uses visual disguises and discoveries to explore the relationship between "seeing, knowledge, and power" (Aching, 5). Fittingly, Hopkinson presents climatic moments of collective demasking, such as the moment when Rudy's body rapidly ages before the eyes of the reader and our hero, Ti-Jeanne. Despite this emphasis on "seeing" hidden truths, vision in the world of Hopkinson's novel, like in Walcott's *Dream on Monkey Mountain* (discussed in chapter 4), does not always equate to knowledge or certainty.

In the world of *Brown Girl in the Ring* everything supernatural is made materially real; thus masks often take the form of physical flesh rather than the artificial materials often used for the theatre and public ritual. For example, when Ti-Jeanne envisions the popular costumed Mas character—the Jab-Jab—appearing before her on the street, he is described as having a *"face like a grinning African mask. Only is not a mask; the lips-them moving, and it have real teeth behind them lips, attached to real gums"* (18, italics in orig.). Hopkinson draws upon these recognizable characters from masking traditions, then subverts readers' expectations by presenting them as embodied figures. What is more, the actions and utterances of the Jab-Jab become increasingly more reliable than those of the humans in Ti-Jeanne's life. Over the course of the novel, the reader learns that characters such as Melba, Crazy Betty, Tony, and Rudy are not what they seem, and in the process begins questioning the visual presentations and statements of everyone. These varied scenes of physical and metaphorical masking and demasking ultimately point to the ideological masquerades that enable the smooth functioning of flesh-economies reliant on unequal, racist hierarchies.

By crowding the novel with visual depictions of living, dead, dissected, and reanimated flesh, Hopkinson ensures that readers keep sight of the selective bodily suffering required for the smooth functioning of the diegetic Canadian economies. Detailed descriptions of corporeality are key to Nalo Hopkinson's writing, which Michelle Reid describes as a "challenging patchwork rooted in the body, sexuality, and race" (106). Almost every scene in *Brown Girl in the Ring* includes optic details of bodily functions, from the protagonist Ti-Jeanne's lactating nipples that remind her to feed her baby to Tony's "buff slashes" documenting his intravenous drug use to the "telemetry readout" of the Canadian politician's cardiac arrhythmia, which intensifies as she worries over an upcoming election (81, 93, 37). These visual metrics of embodiment, like masking practices, point to "socioeconomic and ethical concerns" imbedded within "visual regimes (structural ways of seeing) and visual politics (the enforcement or rejection of specific visual regimes)" (Aching, *Masking and Power*, 5).

In *Brown Girl in the Ring* surveillance techniques underpin a set of visual regimes that enable the sociopolitical subjugation of our protagonist and her neighbors in The Burn. For example, the Canadian government has purposefully built walls around the inner city of Toronto in order to segregate and disenfranchise this community by rendering them invisible to the those living in the affluent "satellite suburbs." The effectiveness of this targeted invisibility is exemplified later in the novel, when suburban revelers visiting the urban center fail to notice the protagonist and a glowing duppy walking on the street. Conveniently blind to the plight of those living in destitution, the Canadian economy uses visual regimes and visual politics to shore up institutional "biopower," or "the power to both guarantee and destroy the lives of certain human populations," as Foucault explains in *"Society Must Be Defended"* (247, 253–54). Hopkinson uses the Caribbean proverb "When horse dead, cow get fat" as an epigraphical break between a scene detailing the lack of commercial medicine in The Burn with another scene depicting Premier Uttley in her hospital suite waiting for the heart transplant. The contrasting images of medical care show how the market both creates and depends upon a biological inequity maintained by its visual politics (*Brown Girl*, 37). The residents of The Burn die from what Foucault calls "indirect murder: the fact of exposing someone to death, increasing the risk of death for some people, or, quite simply, political death, expulsion, rejection, and so on" (256).

Structural conventions of seeing and ignoring particular bodies are key to the "biopolitics" of Hopkinson's Toronto. Drawing again on the work of Michel Foucault, biopolitics refers to the mechanisms of late capitalist power in which violence is consistently committed against certain disempowered bodies not through direct abuse but rather by the unquestioned (and unquestioning) passivity of those who are protected by the state.[30] Premier Uttley and her representatives use a combination of biopolitical mechanisms (inspired by both science fiction and spiritual practices) to make those living in The Burn either biologically invisible or visible according to the protected class's own bodily needs and desires. When Uttley needs a new human heart, biometric tools (like those used to inhibit access to certain buildings within the city limits) are distributed to Rudy's henchmen so that they can identify a viable candidate for the illicit organ donation. Uttley and Baines neglect the lives of those in The Burn until they need to use one of their hearts. In other words, not only does the "cow get fat" with more resources when the "horse" is left to die, but the cow may even eat the horse for dinner, much like Walcott's Devil in *Ti-Jean and His Brothers*. The biometric tools allow for those serving the government to "know" the bodies of others through biotechnological forms of documentation, and in doing so, to make their own neglected citizens usable in the organ economy. In *Vulnerable States* Guillermina De Ferrari traces the history of "the vulnerability of the body to the symbolic colonization" of the Caribbean, noting that the ability to make the bodies of the colonized legible through documentation "has constituted an apparatus of domination in the New World, since it was deemed 'New' for the first time in ways that anticipate modern practices of surveillance" (3, 39). Thanks to the "numerous and diverse techniques for achieving the subjugations of bodies and the control of populations" in Hopkinson's biopolitical dystopia, bodily visibility becomes a constant danger for Ti-Jeanne and her grandmother (Foucault, *History of Sexuality*, 1:140).

Like her descriptions of medical biopolitcs, Hopkinson's portrayal of zombification in *Brown Girl in the Ring* centers squarely on graphic descriptions of human flesh, even when the dispossessed are seemingly disembodied duppies, or souls. Rudy secures knowledge and power over his victims' souls first by physically violating them and then by atomizing their bodies to suit his desires. In one particularly gory scene, Rudy shackles Tony to a chair, forcing him to watch as the sadistic Obeah-man "methodically flay[s]" the zombie form of Melba "alive" on a dining table while she can still feel the somatic pain but cannot express it (135). Melba's—and to a lesser degree Tony's—inabilities to communicate their sensorial and emotional experiences here recall the Devil's bargain to eat any brother who shows "rage and human weakness" in *Ti-Jean and His Brothers* (99). Hopkinson foreshadows this cruel game with the ironically playful call-and-response chant "Barkodey, me buddy . . . Them send me to shave you . . . With me ten pound razor. And if you laugh me go cut you," which Hopkinson uses as an epigraph preceding this scene (135). Unable to look away from "the ritual that Rudy was performing in front of him," Tony, who had been a medic before succumbing to buff addiction, "stare[s] transfixed at the anatomy lesson that Melba had become . . . insanely" remembering "a lecturer at college informing them, 'The average human has about twenty square feet of skin weighing about six pounds'" (136). Rudy emphasizes Melba's subjection by turning her torture into an anatomical spectacle. As if unable to stop himself, "Tony's medically trained mind persisted in identifying the structures that Rudy had exposed with his knife: anterior tibialis of the lower leg; the long bulge of the rectus femoris muscle of the thigh; external obliques covering the stomach region; flap of the platysma myoides muscle layered over chin and clavicle; sterno-cledo mastoid just visible behind the ear. The fat pads and gland tissue that had been her breasts had come off with the skin covering her torso" (136). Tony's rote itemization of Melba's exposed body brings to mind the long history of medical experimentation in the United States, which has relied on the (often unethical) use of black subjects and cadavers for the purpose of knowledge acquisition. Hopkinson also uses a graphic list of corporeal detritus to show that this bodily atomization is also a requisite component when creating a duppy zombie, or the disembodied docile body. When Ti-Jeanne finally breaks her grandfather's evil calabash bowl, she frees the imprisoned soul of her mother from eternal enslavement. When the bowl breaks, it first releases the remnants of Rudy's subjugated flesh objects: "Reeking clumps of dirt; a twist of hair; white knuckle bones; the black mummified body of what looked like a dead cat" and then frees Mi-Jeanne's tortured soul along with (in a surprising twist) the soul of Gros-Jeanne's lover, Dunston (204). When Rudy attempts to turn his granddaughter Ti-Jeanne into his next disembodied docile body, he begins by paralyzing and wounding her, demonstrating that in *Brown Girl in the Ring*, soul-stealing is always accomplished through the violation of the human body.

The visceral images that characterize Hopkinson's writing become even more unsettling in two particular zombification scenes that call upon the rape metaphors central to zombie lore (also a thematic of *Myal*).[31] To gain this dominance over another's soul requires "balls" in Rudy's opinion. In his typically masculinist rhetoric, Rudy assumes that the ability to possess others' bodies and spirits requires adequate courage symbolized by male genitalia, making "balls" an ironically base and corporeal synecdoche for masculine dominance over a disembodied soul. In her survey of zombie texts, Lizabeth Paravisini-Gebert connects violent sexual symbolism with "the invocation of black/white sexuality as the repository of the erotic" and the fetishization of white virginity (*Sacred Possessions*, 46), neither of which are playing out in *Brown Girl in the Ring*'s notably troubling erotics. Here a demonstratively aged black man violates his black granddaughter, who is herself a new mother. Rudy's erotic association with power extends beyond his ownership of female bodies in a scene in which he paralyzes and torments Tony. When Tony's "eyes seemed to beg," Rudy recognizes that it is his "power alone to answer that plea," and as a result, he "felt the familiar tightening in his crotch that that sense of power always brought him" (134). In the Ti-Jeanne zombification scene,

Rudy expresses similar sensual pleasure as he repeatedly thrusts his fingers into his granddaughter's thigh. When Rudy tells Ti-Jeanne that her other father figure—her father-god Legbara—told him the secrets to these grotesque rituals, Ti-Jeanne attempts to shout, *"Not Legbara!"* but "all that came from her flaccid mouth was a vague, grunting noise" (213). The flaccid (code: impotent) description of Ti-Jeanne's face emphasizes Rudy's incestuous sexual domination over her.

Considering the graphic violence that structures this novel's aesthetic and plot structure, it comes as no surprise that in the world of *Brown Girl in the Ring*, safety is accessed through a process of masking oneself. Successful masking techniques can render the individual invisible and therefore unknowable to those in power. When Ti-Jeanne asks Mami Gros-Jeanne to help Tony escape Toronto, the grandmother sees that Tony is being surveilled with the "evil eye" upon him, and so she initiates a possession ceremony to request spiritual guidance (20). Through the ritually possessed body of Ti-Jeanne, Legbara tells them that if Tony holds a rose he had previously given to Ti-Jeanne, both he and his lover can become invisible and "safe from eyes" as she travels halfway to Guinea Land for one night (104, 95). Ti-Jeanne's access to temporary invisibility aligns with Robert Farris Thompson's work on the Yoruba philosophy of masking as "the ritual wearing of thresholds" (26), because Ti-Jeanne hides within the liminal space between life and death. But invisibility in *Brown Girl in the Ring* is not just about becoming impossible to visually recognize; at the heart of this spiritual deception is the capacity to make others unable to "hold the thought of [the invisible person] in them heads for long" (115). Hopkinson introduces a method of spiritual masking that disrupts the chain between seeing, knowledge, and power.

In Hopkinson's novel the ultimate goal of invisibility is to make others unable to remember and know you so that they can no longer dominate your body and soul. In that same vein, the zombie must be dispossessed of his or her own visual capacities in order to be rendered fully disempowered. Whereas the conjure men of *Myal* steal their community's spirits through embodied sound, the Afro-Caribbean conjure man Rudy has perfected his own methods of zombification by stealing—and in select cases weaponizing—his victims' embodied vision. Vision becomes yet another mechanism for the visual regimes structuring biopower. In several scenes set in Rudy's office, Melba stands "deathly still" in the corner, "looking at nothing" until Rudy instructs her to assist him (usually by cleaning), after which she moves slowly, "eyes irising in and out of focus" and labors at the assigned task until Rudy orders her to stop (5, 28, 130). Melba's lack of visual focus signifies her hollow, dispossessed state. Anthropologist Alfred Métraux says zombies can be recognized by "their vague look, their dull almost glazed eyes" (250). In *Myal* acoustic elements signal the reader to consider the relationship between the abstract spirit and physical body, and visual cues perform a similar function in *Brown Girl in the Ring*.

After Ti-Jeanne uses her Legbara-given capacity to make herself invisible in order to sneak into Rudy's headquarters, she successfully destroys her mother's duppy-prison before being seized by two of Rudy's henchmen. Ti-Jeanne is strapped to the table used for devilish gastronomic and spiritual consumption and then injected with a paralyzing zombie poison. Bringing to mind Wade Davis's work on zombie drugs, the zombie poison Rudy utilizes is a mixture of the purified street drug called "buff" throughout the novel with "some other Haiti medicine mix in" (211).[32] Still in possession of her own soul and vision, Ti-Jeanne "glare[s] defiantly" at Rudy as he explains his zombie process: "I come to find out something [Legbara] nah tell me. A duppy from a dead somebody not too smart. Smarter than a zombie, but you still can't give it nothing too complicated to do, see? But if you split off the duppy from it body while the body still alive! Well, then you have a servant for true. One that could teach you everything it did know in life" (313). It is this kind of disembodied docile zombie that Rudy turned his daughter into, and it is what he intends to create from his captive granddaughter now. Rudy tells Ti-Jeanne that because her mother was a "seer woman" just like her, she gouged out her eyes for him and placed them in a calabash bowl along with her soul. As for the rest of Mi-Jeanne's corporeal form, it was neglected and left to wander around The Burn as "Crazy Betty," a seemingly insane, and of course blind, homeless woman. By separating the trapped duppy soul and only key component parts of the body (the eyes, in the case of these two women), Rudy's method of possession over another hyperbolically exemplifies Foucault's explanation of discipline. Foucault writes in *Discipline and Punish*: "Discipline increases the forces of the body (in economic terms of utility) and diminishes these same forces (in political terms of obedience). In short, it dissociates power from the body; on the one hand, it turns it into an 'aptitude', a 'capacity,' which it seeks to increase; on the other hand, it reverses the course of the energy, the power that might result from it, and turns it into a relation of strict subjection" (138). By targeting his daughter and granddaughter for their spiritual gift of "sight" and including the eyeballs in the calabash, Rudy shows that their metaphysical "aptitude" and "capacity" for prophetic vision is constrained through physical discipline to the body as a means of soul subjection and ultimate obedience. Rudy's Obeah appears to be informed by the methods of capitalist exploitation he has already perfected with flesh objects. As Foucault explains, "If economic exploitation separates the force and the product of labour, ... disciplinary coercion establishes in the body the constricting link between an increased aptitude and an increased domination" (138).

In order to fully steal Ti-Jeanne's vision and her resulting knowledge, Rudy must first convince her "spirit" to "accept [his] bond" through a bodily spectacle. He places four mounds of gunpowder on a knife, explaining that if Ti-Jeanne's spirit consents to be Rudy's zombie four separate times, making the four mounds explode, then she will become his disembodied duppy forever. Integral to this particular zombie process is the necessity that the zombified person believe in the Obeah-man's symbolic power—believe in the legitimacy of his words and he who utters them (Bourdieu, 170). "Yes," Rudy narrates while the poison spreads through his new victim, "the first stage of making a zombie. Combine the paralysis and the suggestibility with the right kind of um, *indoctrination,* and the zombie go do anything me tell it" (212, emphasis in orig.). In order to control Ti-Jeanne's vision and her subsequent embodied knowledge, he must convince her to believe in the lies he tells her about what it means to be a human. In this chapter's conclusion, I will return to Rudy's definition of human existence in order to elucidate how Hopkinson counters his discourse with the concept of "serving the spirits."

Just as Ella's and Anita's experiences of spirit thievery in *Myal* physically manifest the practices that substantiate colonial ideologies, Rudy's zombification techniques in *Brown Girl in the Ring* allegorize the sociopolitical processes of dehumanization that subtend the racialized biopolitics of Hopkinson's destitute Toronto. Like Brodber's hollowed-out victims of spirit thievery, The Burn has been emptied as a result of European colonialism's continual legacies of racialized disenfranchisement. In her review of the novel Ifeoma Nwankwo states, "Racism and classism are the reasons why the novel's setting even exists" (307). As Sylvia Wynter explains, the mechanisms of capitalistic inequity are coconstitutive with racial inequities. In "No Humans Involved" she writes, "Both W. E. B. Du Bois and Elsa Goveia have emphasized the way in which the code of 'Race' of the Color Line, functions to systematically *pre-determine* the sharply unequal re-distribution of the collectively produced global resources; and therefore, the correlation of the racial ranking rule with the Rich/Poor rule" (52). Hopkinson uses old newspaper headlines to explain that after the indigenous Temagami won their land rights back in a legal case against Ontario, Toronto experienced economic collapse and white flight.[33] She writes that citywide riots over joblessness and fatal infrastructure collapses led to a failed military occupation of the urban center, after which "the satellite cities quickly raised roadblocks at their borders to keep Toronto out" (4). In other words, the Canadian government effectively criminalizes citizens for being dispossessed at the hands of the market and government and then imprisons them in the location of their acute destitution. Though Hopkinson does not explicitly say that these events were racially motivated, it is clear that the majority of those living in The Burn are people of color, namely of Afro-Caribbean and South Asian descent. What is more, the series of events—criminalizing citizens and then imprisoning large swaths of a systemically disenfranchised population—is unmistakably reminiscent of the modern African American experience in the United States. Simon Orpana uses the idea of the "zombie imaginary" (deriving his term from the Americanized rather than Vodou zombie myth) to explain the process by which "problems that are properly structural, political, and economic are personalized and projected onto the devalued, often racialized, and gendered bodies of people" (298). Because addressing the structural problems that led to the collapse of Toronto could risk acknowledging the inequities that undergird the functioning of the state and market, the political and economic leaders of Ontario strive to confine the bodies of the destitute through biopolitical mechanisms of containment and control. In his March 17, 1976, lecture, "Society Must Be Defended," Foucault explains that racism (like that which structures Hopkinson's Toronto) is actually a "precondition for exercising the right to kill," or biopower, through the direct and indirect murder of populations considered threats to the regulated populations of the State (256).

These methods of biopower work through visual regimes enabling an economy that protects one categorical population at the expense of others. *Brown Girl in the Ring*'s capitalist dystopia illustrates how modern markets rely on the continued violation of marginalized human bodies for the biological benefit of humans in power. In the world of Ti-Jeanne these politics are laid bare through images of the legal and extralegal biological economies. In Canada's biological transplant economy, people attempt to buy flesh objects, which in this case become commodities, in order to procure more embodied "time" for their purchasers. In a play on Marx's concept of laborers selling their time for wages, Tony, the key laborer for procuring Uttley's new heart, is indeed selling his labor time to the capitalist, but the flesh objects on the market are also intended the prolong the purchaser's time of life. Tony is told that if he fails to locate and murder someone with a functioning heart for Uttley, he will be flayed alive just like Melba. Tony's situation is possible because life within The Burn has been strategically quarantined from the legal world of Canada, rendering those within it invisible to state protections, while proxy actors of the state (exemplified by Rudy) surveil, control, and use the imprisoned population to suit the bodily needs of those outside the city's walls. The layers of abuse and manipulation in this moment remind the reader of Du Bois's writings on the burgeoning global market in the nineteenth century: "Out of the exploitation of the dark proletariat comes the Surplus Value filched from human beasts" (*Black Reconstruction*, 15). Though not a physical zombie, Tony talks about having sold his "soul" to Rudy because he is now required to devote his time laboring for the posse boss in morally abhorrent ways. With my analysis of *Brown Girl in the Ring*, I am extending Mimi Sheller's work in *Consuming the Caribbean* by studying how the symbolic forms of zombies in this novel illuminate "the actual material relations through which bodies in one place unethically touch bodies in another place" (147–48). Though Hopkinson's novel does not take place within the Caribbean archipelago, the geographic segregation of The Burn allows for similar physical and symbolic regimes of consumption, which are themselves mobilized through visual regimes that structure beliefs about humanity.

The biopolitics of Hopkinson's Toronto inevitably set up (and are rooted in) dichotomies between groups of human creatures. Throughout the novel, Hopkinson's Toronto exemplifies Sylvia Wynter's contentions that the mechanisms of capitalistic inequity are coconstitutive with not only the physical practice of institutionalized inequities but also the creation of cognitive hierarchies that allow for certain humans to be considered "*more* or *less* human, even totally lacking in humanness" at the "level of *race, culture, religion, class, ethnicity, sexuality and sex*" ("No Humans Involved," 54, emphasis in orig.). In *Masking and Power*, Gerard Aching quotes Slavoj Žižek's *Sublime Object of Ideology* to explain that because "the mask does not conceal the 'truth' but embodies the 'ideological distortion,'" masking practices "negotiate degrees of recognition, misrecognition, and nonrecognition between *masked subjects* and *viewing subjects*" (Aching, 4–5). In the novel's first scene, the hospital representative, Baines, encounters the "haggard, blank-eyed" zombie in Rudy's office while initiating the transplant deal (5). While Baines is intimidated by Rudy's obvious power over Melba, he fails to recognize her as a flesh-object zombie, instead accurately recognizing her blind obedience to Rudy as indicative of the proletariat laborer's exploitation under capitalism. Melba's race is not explicit in the novel, and her skin is exclusively described in nonhuman blue and grey tones. And yet her seemingly nonhuman skin tone epitomizes the ideological distortion of racism. Just as racist discourse worked (and continues to work) to justify the inhuman treatment of indigenous and African-descended populations during the European colonial project, Melba's apparently inhuman external body has been "made to yield the symbolic reasons for [her] . . . own political and social domination" (De Ferrari, 2). The misrecognition of Melba's humanity via her skin represents the consequences and foundational premise of racist logic. Furthermore, like the body of the enslaved person Saidiya Hartman analyzes in *Scenes of Subjection,* the power that Rudy displays over his secretary's "captive body" turns her into a "sign and surrogate of the master's body" (120). Without knowing about his Obeah, those who live in The Burn or who negotiate with its inhabitants fear Rudy when they see Melba because it is clear that he possesses powers beyond drug-dealing in order to have so mysteriously taken ownership of this woman's body. Melba's skin is a mask that reveals the structures of power in The Burn, because just as "black subjection" came to frame "questions of sovereignty, right and power" thanks to slavery in the Americas, Melba's subjugated body testifies to Rudy's sovereignty and power among his fellow capitalists (Hartman, 115).

In *Brown Girl in the Ring* processes of demasking through physical transformations often reveal the simplistic "truth" of a character's identity, and in doing so guide readers to question the pervasive ideological masks throughout the novel that enable the selective visual regimes of "social (in)visibility" (Aching, 4). For example, when Ti-Jeanne finally destroys the calabash bowl holding both her mother's and Dunston's souls, Rudy's body is dispossessed of the youth he extracted from those in his community. When Rudy ages, Hopkinson reveals that he is attempting to maintain sovereignty over all flesh objects, including the flesh of his own body. Like the Obeah practitioner in *Myal,* Rudy cannot defy the eventualities of biological degeneration on his own and so must consume the bodies of others. Hopkinson describes Rudy's rapid aging in grotesque detail, emphasizing the experience of living putrefaction integral for all embodied creaturely life: "A network of wrinkles was stitching itself over his face. Swollen veins wormed their way over the backs of his hands, while the knuckles bunched like the knobs of ancient roots; he put his arthritic hands to his mouth, spat his teeth in them. His lips sank in on themselves; a ray of fine lines etched themselves around his pursed, trembling mouth; his hair blanched to grey; his shoulders rounded as his spine curled" (204–5). In this moment of demasking, instead of human and nonhuman body parts acting as servants to the powerful, Rudy's material body appears to mutiny against him; his veins, which carry the blood that for the majority of this novel has represented biological vitality, now take on parasitical connotations as they act as foreign worms spreading and burrowing into his once-youthful skin. Throughout this description Hopkinson writes Rudy's veins, knuckles, lips, hair, shoulders, and spine into the subject position, repeatedly subjugating Rudy to his component parts. Exposed to be nothing more than a desperate, human conjure man, Rudy brings to mind Michael Dash's reading of Glissant's post-Sartrean take on consciousness, which is rooted in embodiment. Rudy, who has desperately ascribed to "the Sartrean sense of the body as utilitarian vessel," is painfully confronted with an alternate reality in which "individual consciousness remains tyrannically in the grips of the body" (611). The human subject Rudy can only move his hands in order to spit and catch defunct teeth, demonstrating the "inextricable bonds between psychic and physical self-assertion" (610). Defanged, Rudy's body, like the persons he has dominated and manipulated for so long in poverty-stricken Toronto, turns against him. By revealing Rudy's true identity and weakness in this moment, Hopkinson explains why, when the hospital representative Bain shook Rudy's hand in the novel's prologue it was "as though he were palping rotting carrion" (8). Furthermore, Rudy's aging process shows that the zombie and organ economies of *Brown Girl in the Ring* are rooted in a desire to overcome the emotional and physical vulnerabilities of all biological life, particularly mortality.

The biological economies in the spiritual-scientific realms of *Brown Girl in the Ring* are inextricably tied to the inevitability of death for all creaturely flesh, and yet the mechanisms by which they operate require the explicit and implicit dehumanization of certain populations at the level of race, class, and sex. What is more, the very concepts of human mortality and ethics are tied to social understandings of who is and who is not fully human and therefore deserving of life. Alexander Weheliye argues that the danger of discussing political violence via supposedly universal discourses such as Foucault's biopolitics or the fear of human mortality is that it can "misconstrue how profoundly race and racism shape the modern idea of the human" (4). Weheliye draws on the theories of Hortense Spillers and Sylvia Wynter to argue that "race be placed front and center in considerations of political violence, albeit not as a biological or cultural classification but as a set of sociopolitical processes of differentiation and hierarchization, which are projected onto the putatively biological human body" (5). In the world of Hopkinson's *Brown Girl in the Ring,* explicit and implicit acts of political violence and dehumanization clearly grow out of the same sociopolitical processes of racial hierarchization identified in the work of Weheliye, Wynter, and Spillers. By making the lives of those living in The Burn socially invisible to residents outside its borders, those in power are able to dehumanize this population in ways that exclude them from a wider ethical community of care. When Ti-Jeanne interacts with Crazy Betty with the knowledge that this eyeless woman is actually her mother, Mi-Jeanne, she thinks to herself, "Funny how eyes defined a face" (151). Ti-Jeanne's meditation on the visual marks of personal identity also speaks to the visual regimes by which persons can be defined as more or less human according to the visual perspectives that project ideologies of white supremacy onto others' racialized, biological bodies.

The political rhetoric surrounding the human organ economy attempts to use a seemingly universal ethics of creaturely life to mask the economy's dependence on maintaining the socioeconomic inequity rooted in selective dehumanizations. Underlining Baines's desire for a human heart for the Canadian premier is Uttley's calculated decision that in order to swing votes in her favor in the next election, she will take an "ethical" stance against an existing industrial husbandry for porcine organ transplants, insisting on finding a human heart for her urgent transplant. Uttley is up for reelection on a "God's Creatures" campaign, which "says the porcine organ farms are immoral," hoping to appeal to those voters who ascribe to a valuation of all creaturely life (3).[34] However, it appears that the moral indignation over porcine organ farms has grown in tandem with a new disease dubbed "Virus Epsilon" "that had jumped from pigs to humans through the an-antigenic porcine organ farms" (39). Instead of condemning potentially diseased nonhuman organ farms, Uttley and her campaign advisor (or her "spin doctor" and "bookie," Constantine) attempt to bring her to power by manipulating Canadian voters into admiring her "moral courage" (40, 239). The mask of the "God's Creatures" campaign, and the necessary lack of recognition for human existence that this rhetoric requires, exemplifies the ideological distortion of a system rooted in the dehumanization of people based primarily on race and class. Constantine tells Uttley, "Make a statement to the press that you're convinced that this is the safe, moral way to go: 'People Helping People,' you're going to call it. Tell them you're so determined that you'll back your words with your life; you've demanded the medical system find you a compatible human heart, and you're imploring the public to sign the voluntary organ donor cards you're going to distribute in the local papers. Tell them you'll refuse the operation unless it's a human heart. Voters'll eat it up" (40). Implicit in this appropriately consumptive (having voters "eat" ideology) attempt to appear ethically responsible toward nonhuman creatures is a continuing disregard for the human life of the racially denigrated and economically dispossessed community in The Burn. While the "God's Creatures" campaign may appear to promote the valuation of all beings, it is actually an ideological distortion of existing economic practices involving, to return to Du Bois, the filching of surplus value from the labor and bodies of human beasts. Constantine's calculated slogan, "People Helping People," mocks the "pseudo-humanism" Aimé Césaire identifies throughout bourgeois ideology in his 1955 manifesto *Discourse on Colonialism* (37). And considering that her voters are likely to be the same citizens who fled urban Toronto and quarantined those in The Burn, this insistence on "God's Creatures" creates a parallel between diseased organs and diseased persons. By locating this crisis in Uttley's diseased body, Hopkinson makes corporeal the metaphor of the "stricken" and "dying" civilization Césaire rails against (31). Later in the novel Uttley, whose parliamentary power is an extension of the British government, will prove "morally and spiritually indefensible," like Césaire's postwar Europe, but in ways that the reader may not expect (32). Both the zombie and transplant plotlines in *Brown Girl in the Ring* reveal the inherent bodily and spiritual violence that undergirds and results from seemingly humanist systems like the "God's Creatures" campaign.

René Depestre argues that "the history of colonization is the process of man's general zombification. It is also the quest for a revitalizing salt capable of restoring to man the use of his imagination and his culture" (20). Both *Brown Girl in the Ring* and *Myal* demonstrate this revitalizing salt through embodied, community practices of spiritual healing, which involve bodily disintegration and re-possession. In the case of Hopkinson's novel, the community healing is enacted through ritual performances that draw on the movements and visual cues found in ring games and dances, while the spiritual healing described in *Myal* is manifested in religious ceremonies featuring embodied sound. Hopkinson's and Brodber's insistence on foregrounding embodiment in scenes of spiritual dispossession and reclamation are indicative of how "the body's literal and figurative vulnerability" can be used by authors as a "strategy toward affective decolonization" (De Ferrari, 3).

When Rudy attempts to indoctrinate his granddaughter, he relies on a fantasy of absolute control through physical and spiritual disconnection. In addition to sowing seeds of doubt about Mami Gros-Jeanne in order to bring Ti-Jeanne to his side, Rudy extols the virtues of existing as a disembodied duppy by focusing on the necessary pains of mortal embodiment. Rudy says his daughter Mi-Jeanne begged him to "help she live only in she spirit, for she didn't want the pains of the body no more" (215). Suggesting that bodily pain is antithetical to the pursuit of power, Rudy coos in his granddaughter's ear, "You nah see the power I did give Mi-Jeanne? Knife couldn't cut she, blows couldn't lick she, love couldn't leave she, heart couldn't hurt she. She coulda go wherever she want, nobody to stop she" (215). Feeling guilty that she has killed her own mother's attempt at infinite life, Ti-Jeanne is swayed by the prospect of "living" without the pain that accompanies existence with others; she imagines how much easier her life would be if she had never felt the need to "tear herself in three to satisfy Tony, and Baby and Mami" (215).

Gretchen Michlitsch describes Rudy's offer to Ti-Jeanne thus: "In his effort to capture and imprison her spirit, Rudy tempts his granddaughter with descriptions of an imagined autonomous independence, with tales of freedom from responsibility and from the heartaches of life" (20). Though the reader has already seen that Mi-Jeanne experiences continual emotional pain despite her disembodied form, the drug-compromised Ti-Jeanne begins to believe that upon abandoning her physical form, she will also be able to abandon her cares for those around her. Rudy's ideology, like the Devil's bargain in Walcott's *Ti-Jean and His Brothers,* relies on seeing human beings as conquerable because they are susceptible to physical and emotional suffering. Rudy's insistence that to be without a body means to transcend suffering makes great sense considering his own obsessive struggle against inevitable degeneration through aging. As the suddenly decrepit Rudy would well know, to have a mortal human body means to have bodily pains. Yet implicit in this textual moment is the irony that Rudy intends to take control of his granddaughter's soul by convincing Ti-Jeanne to fantasize about having extreme self-power without a body or embodied relationships with others.

And yet it is Ti-Jeanne's recognition of the shared vulnerability in flesh that convinces her to resist Rudy's seductive promises. Even while her grandfather slaps her across the face, Ti-Jeanne weeps for "her mother and for the man who had trapped his own daughter's soul in a container so that he would never have to die" (213). Ti-Jeanne's ability to express sentiment for the mother who abandoned her and the grandfather who plans to trap her soul shows the importance of compassion and love portrayed in both *Brown Girl in the Ring* and *Myal*. This chapter in *Brown Girl in the Ring* begins with an epigraph of the traditional saying, "Egg don't have no right at rock-stone dance" (219), suggesting that Ti-Jeanne, like the egg, is doomed to break apart when inserting herself into the violent games of Rudy and his posse. Instead, it becomes clear that Ti-Jeanne's ability to affectively "crack" open—and in doing so, to empathize with the experiences of others—ultimately allows her to transcend her individual experiences in order to call on a wider community of support. After Rudy begins "mumbling the words of a ritual in a language she didn't recognize," Ti-Jeanne's spirit begins to perceive her body as a burden, "nothing but an aching weight dragging her back to the pain of her life" (216–17). But before Ti-Jeanne can fully sign herself over to Rudy, the Jab-Jab, a manifestation of her papa-god Legbara, appears before her to challenge her decision through leading questions and visions of Melba's and Mi-Jeanne's gory deaths at Rudy's hands. The Jab-Jab's horrifying visions of Mi-Jeanne's and Melba's past suffering act as a divine, visual revelation for Ti-Jeanne, who is converted away from Rudy's doctrine to her grandmother's philosophy of spiritual community. The Jab-Jab explains, "Yes, it have plenty names for what Gros-Jeanne was. Myalist, bush doctor, iyalorisha, curandera, four-eye, even obeah woman for them who don't understand. But you what woulda call it, if you had ask she. . . . Gros-Jeanne woulda tell you that all she doing is serving the spirits" (219). He adds that Gros-Jeanne would have said "that anybody who try to live good, who try to help people who need it, who try to have respect for life, and age, and those who go before, them all doing the same thing: serving the spirits" (219). To serve the spirits, then, means individually living in accordance with the universal collective, respecting the mortality of biological flesh as well as the immortality of the soul by acknowledging the ancestors, "those who go before."[35]

In Ti-Jeanne's moment of need, she turns to her spiritual community, and the gods and ancestors respond, materially assisting her in the "effort to preserve wellness" and "pursue liberationist transformative action" (Stewart, 239). During this final scene of spiritual triumph, I turn to Hopkinson's epigraphical and titular point of reference—the ring game—in order to understand how serving the spirits functions through shifting understandings of community and belonging. The three children's ring games referenced throughout this book are Brown Girl in the Ring, Punchinella, and Bluebird Bluebird. In all three of these games, children form a dancing circle and sing a well-known song, whose lyrics to some extent inform the actions and movements of the dancing children. For example, in both Brown Girl in the Ring and Punchinella, children take turns showing off their dancing abilities while being encouraged to "show me your motion" or display "what [they] can do." After this short dance in the middle of the circle, the outer ring responds by having either one selected child or every single spectator in the circle mimic or build on the movements of the featured dancer. All three games feature a balance of pre-scripted and improvised movements in which, as Thomas DeFrantz explains for social dance, "the dancing bodies and their audiences merge" (197). In Brown Girl in the Ring the middle dancer can choose a partner to join her in the ring, who then remains as the individual central performer. Punchinella is often played by having the featured dancer select a new child to improvise and challenge the outer circle before returning to the wider community of spectators/dancers themselves. While the game Bluebird Bluebird is less focused on exchanging dances, it also requires invitations to move within the wider circle. In Bluebird the first child weaves between the arms (representing windows) of the children in the outside circle and then, as in the other two games, selects particular children in the outer circle to become a part of the human train.

Unlike the oppressive visual regimes that predominate *Brown Girl in the Ring,* seeing others and being seen are multidirectional practices that serve to create shifting formulations of community in the social dance. Murray-Román describes how in the performance of the dance circle, "'looking' is not passive spectatorship but a dynamic form of support that is absolutely necessary for those who are, in that particular instant, dancing and moving" (9).[36] Rather than visibility rendering the body vulnerable to domination and atomization, the visible presence becomes a marker of communal meaning-making. In the ring games Brown Girl in the Ring and Punchinella, children practice these methods by demonstrating their embodied agency through dance abilities that then visually prompt the group and individual movements of their fellows. To be seen, then, is to be known as an individual actor and as a guiding member of a community. When Melba returns to fight Rudy as a ghoul, she walks in with a "determined" stride as she "[holds] her own skin draped over one arm" (225). Melba's skin and exposed inner body, which had illustrated her extreme violation and zombification, now signify the trauma she shares with her fellow victims as well as her capacity to be invited into a sacred space of community belonging and self-directed determination within the circle. As Murray-Román explains, "Not only do audience members at social performances have the potential to act as performers, but in both ritual and secular forms of the circle, the audience takes on the task of holding the circle's energy. In this sense, audience and performer together create the circle's meaning" (9). Just as all meaning is only possible so long as all spectators and dancers in the ring game contribute, the spiritual community in *Brown Girl in the Ring* is only accessible so long as every member "play she part" in a wider community of care (98). In the novel Mami Gros-Jeanne teaches Ti-Jeanne how to play her part in the spiritual community by providing medical help to the living community in The Burn, speaking with individual loas during possession trances, paying tribute to the ancestors and gods with tailored offerings, and refusing to eat any animals until they communicate a readiness for death. After Tony kills Gros-Jeanne for her heart, it is the Jab-Jab who tells Ti-Jeanne that it is time for to play her part of a *"Duppy Conqueror"* with the *"cunning and instinct"* of a true trickster hero (192, italics in orig.). Like the ring game, serving the spirits incorporates both adherence to ritual performance practices and improvisation, all of which build on embodied archives of knowledge. While still under the sway of bufo poison (a concentrated form of the street-drug buff), Ti-Jeanne struggles to acknowledge that she can follow the spiritual path of her grandmother while also refusing to perpetuate the cycle of intergenerational domestic violence that she experienced growing up in her grandmother's home. Hopkinson predicts this reckoning with tradition and individuality in an epigraphical lullaby that goes, "I'm sorry to whip you my darling, but true,/My Mama whipped me, so I'm bound to whip you" (31). Overwhelmed by visions of both Mami Gros-Jeanne's and Rudy's past actions, Ti-Jeanne exclaims to the Jab-Jab, "I can't keep giving my will into other people hands no more, ain't? I have to decide what I want to do for myself" (220).

The final spiritual battle in *Brown Girl in the Ring* provides a "quasi-utopian space" like those created in the ring dance and *Beloved*'s Clearing ceremony, where the previously oppressed characters can "practice social transformations and alternative formations of community that would otherwise seem impossible" (Murray-Román, 3). In this final scene the interactive community analogized in the ring game's dances includes the living, the dead, and a pantheon of spiritual figures. Halfway to Guinea Land already, Ti-Jeanne does not have to shout hard as she rattles off the list of names Mami Gros-Jeanne taught her earlier. She calls on the lord of thunder, Shango (Changó in Zapata Olivella's novel); the warrior and spirit of metal-work, Ogun; water goddesses Emanjah and Oshun; the healer, Osain; the lord of disease, Shakpana; the spirit "of the storm," Oya; and her own Eshu, Papa Legbara (221–23). Then, in another "flash of instinct," Ti-Jeanne invites all those Rudy killed, calling "all you children; every one Rudy kill to feed he duppy bowl—come and let we stop he from making another!" (221). As the Old Ones and the recently deceased descend on the skyscraper where Rudy torments his zombies, the reader cannot help but experience a sense of empowerment through spiritual community, a power that only grows as Rudy is defeated by the gods he tried to outwit and the humans he tortured for capital.

Serving the spirits in the novel allows for the dispossessed members of The Burn to "envision spiritually inspired 'relations'" and formulate communities that "collectively resist injustice" (Romero, 1). The spiritual circle created in the climactic battle scene allows the dispossessed to access their own physical and spiritual "vision" and agency again, but it does not negate the physical and metaphysical scars of their pasts.[37] For example, while the afterlife allows Melba to be reunited with her own agency and "determination" that Rudy had previously stolen, she is still seen with her wounds of objectification, her skin. Just as Stewart notes in African-derived Caribbean theology, for Melba "the afterlife is a hostel for relational existence and reconnection" to her own capacity for self-direction and community belonging, but "it does not offer compensation for unmerited earthly suffering" because her trauma is not simply eradicated thanks to the salvation of death (239). Similarly, the circle dance allows for performers to imagine "expansive conceptions of personhood" within the permissive space of the circle, while acknowledging the conscripted formulations of humanity that structure existence outside of that sacred space (Murray-Román, 3). In spite of the overwhelmingly positive aspects of spiritual community for most of the characters in this scene, Rudy is still violated and atomized. When Rudy realizes his impending doom, his face becomes a "mask of terror," and after "the weight of every murder he had done fell on him," Rudy's body turns to "chunks of flesh lying there look[ing] like something that should have been on a butcher's block" (226).

Hopkinson's *Brown Girl in the Ring* and Brodber's *Myal* present a world in which ancestors and the recently deceased can be accessed by the living, drawing on the Central and West African concept of death as only a passage into an alternative state of being. Scholar of theology and ethnography E. Bolaji Idowu explains this concept in terms of the Yoruban religion: "Death is not the end of man, those who departed from this earth in consequence of the phenomenon called death have only gone to live in another 'world,' the 'after-life.'" Idowu adds, "There is a spiritual link between the deceased and those who are still on earth. This conception is linked to a belief in the immortality of the soul," and the dead are considered divine, even to be worshipped (186–87). Afro-Caribbean religious practices such as Vodou and Myal integrated these African-derived concepts of the afterlife with the Christian belief in the continuous life of the soul through resurrection. In Hopkinson's narrative, these religious philosophies are made material and supernatural.

Hopkinson uses the concept of reincarnation to sabotage the corporeal dominance that Uttley and Rudy enjoy in their abusive economies of flesh. In *Brown Girl in the Ring,* the loa of the cemetery, Legbara, and the loa of healing, Osain, undermine Rudy and Uttley's machinations for earthly power by transferring their children's souls, namely those of Gros-Jeanne's lover Dunston and Gros-Jeanne herself, into other human forms. When Ti-Jeanne shoots the calabash bowl, Hopkinson describes how, *"as the duppy bowl cracked, another soul than Mi-Jeanne's flew free of it"* (206). Rudy had also chained and tortured Dunston's soul in *"the microcosmic hell that was the world of the duppy bowl"* until this moment of freedom that Hopkinson describes as *"a world exploding, a heart breaking twice"* (207). In a direct connection to the story of the Bolom in Walcott's *Ti-Jeanne and His Brothers,* the soul of Dunston flies to join the *"bodily housing"* Legbara prepared for him for this exact moment (207). Dunston's soul is then reincarnated in the waiting corporeal house of Ti-Jeanne's own child, referred to interchangeably as Baby and Bolom, meaning fetus. As Legbara's son, then, it appears that Dunston (unlike Mi-Jeanne, who fully dies at her release) can be mortally alive again, "no longer Gros-Jeanne's doomed second husband. Nothing but a baby now" (207).

Predicting the conclusion of *Brown Girl in the Ring,* the transplant doctor transferring Gros-Jeanne's heart into Uttley's body describes Gros-Jeanne as "healthy as a horse" despite her age, punning on two key aspects of the grandmother—her role as a spiritual horse, ridden by Papa god Osain, and her socioeconomic position as one of the horses who had to die in order to help the cow (Uttley) get fat. When Premier Uttley wakes up from the surgery, she too becomes ridden by Gros-Jeanne (who is in turn ridden by Osain) as she fundamentally alters her approach to politics in The Burn. In this scene, it is the materiality of Gros-Jeanne's heart that brings her soul and her worldview into Premier Uttley. In contrast to her previous position that The Burn should either continue to be exploited for cheap labor and seedy tourism or be "revitalized" through a capitalist overhaul with incoming "big business," she now, after being invaded by Gros-Jeanne's soul, promotes a community-oriented approach. Uttley tells her advisor Constantine that they will encourage small business growth within the currently marginalized communities in The Burn. Hopkinson combines the narratives of spiritual possession and organ donation to extend the boundaries of the circle dance, suggesting that the embodied forms of knowledge accessed through performative ceremonies can be harnessed within one transformative heart.

Like *Brown Girl in the Ring*, Brodber's *Myal* focuses on communal practices of sound, spirit, and power. Ella's recitation at the beginning of *Myal* demonstrates Althusser's theory that ideologies of power may be understood as a "spiritual ideal" through our consciousness, but in fact these imaginary ideologies are only constituted when interpellated subjects like Ella execute them through ritualized practices, such as her sonic colonial performance of Kipling's poem (696). Althusser's insistence on ritual as integral to the operation of ideology finds parallels in scholarship on African diasporic religions, which recognize how "spiritual power is internalized and mobilized in human beings" through embodied ceremonies (Paravisini and Olmos, *Creole Religions of the Caribbean*, 13). Anthropologist Joseph Murphy coined the phrase "diasporan liturgies" to describe these religious practices in the Caribbean wherein the abstract "spirit" is both constituted by and constitutes physical ceremonies.

Brodber invokes the concept of spiritual community as a necessary component in any process of physical and metaphysical resistance to abusive power structures, much like Hopkinson's formulation of "serving the spirits." Joseph Murphy explains the critical role of community in "diasporan liturgies" when he writes, "The reciprocity between community and spirit is expressed in physical work as the community works through word, music, and movement to make the spirit present. The spirit in turn works through the physical work of the congregation, filling human actions with its power" (7). Abstract spiritual power is accessed through the physical movements of a group of people. The sonic nature of these diasporan liturgies provides an acoustic, spiritual gloss on Hannah Arendt's formulation of power as "the human ability not just to act but to act in *concert*" (44, emphasis mine). The collective nature of spiritual re-possession is not a surprise in *Myal* considering the ways in which the novel uses ritual performance to illustrate how subjugated persons must also actively participate in a regime of power. The groups of living and deceased persons who band together to seek spiritual healing "fight" oppression with what can only be described as spiritual aggression. Because these revolutionary characters have come to understand the material nature of abstract belief, they can wage battle against seemingly imaginary relations within a liminal space between the material and abstract worlds.[38] Brodber's characters choose sound as their primary vehicle for traveling between the conceptual and the physical in their works of Myal.

In each instance of spirit reclamation, sound again permeates the female character's body in an intense process of "osmosis and withdrawal," this time intended to heal her body and mind/spirit. Each sonic boundary-crossing brings to light the complex Relation of metaphysical and physical worlds, as well as that of the young woman's vulnerability to both "domination and resistance" rituals. The opening scene of Brodber's text depicts Myal-man Mass Cyrus preparing to perform a Myal ritual on Ella's hysterical pregnancy, a ritual that is narrated through musical metaphors and that results in a distinctly physical and sonic explosion of spirit from Ella's infection, with a "whole lot of shaking going on! And the noise" (2).[39] This scene emphasizes the sonic valences of spiritual knowledge through bodily Myal healing practices. The practitioner, whose face is described as a musical score, must listen to the "still small voice" in order to eradicate the "stinkiest, dirtiest ball to come out of a body since creation" (3). Puncturing Ella's skin results in such "banging and ringing and splitting and weeping" that the rural landscape "thought it was another Good Friday many many years ago when the Saviour of the world was lynched" (3). Here Brodber reminds us of the death of Agne Brown's father in *Changó, The Biggest Badass,* as she alludes to a racialized (e.g., lynched) crucifixion of Christ as a comparatively explosive sonic event after bodily violation. Mass Cyrus is either comparing Ella to Christ, or perhaps he is referring to her "stinkiest, dirtiest ball"—her hysterical pregnancy that she herself considered Jesus Christ. By invoking the Christian story of the sacrifice of the embodied God, Brodber invites readers to see the puncturing of the young woman's body as a kind of redemptive violence, an intrusion that somehow serves to heal not only Ella but also the entire Grove Town community. Though redemptive, the sound of Ella's healing is violent, creating such a disturbance in the landscape that it ultimately kills thousands of animals and several hundred humans.

Brodber also describes the physically violent nature of sound in the re-possession ceremony for Anita as sound actually bombards the spirits and bodies of Mass Levi, Anita, and those present in Grove Town.[40] In the case of Anita, *Myal* shows that all bodies, not just that of the zombified woman, are susceptible to the physical osmosis and withdrawal of abstract concepts communicated through sound. The story of Anita's release from Mass Levi's soul-sucking grip begins when "silent Miss Gatha started to talk," inaugurating the noise-filled chapter (70). The Kumina queen, Miss Gatha, performs a re-possession ceremony with singing, drumming, and dancing. The sound that Miss Gatha and her congregation makes in the "programme of music and recitation" is a physically violent one, a bodily aggressive power (71). Made "captive in their own homes," the people of Grove Town listen through closed windows to the "bum-batti-bum-batti-bum-batti-bum" of the drums (71). The singing grows "a hundred times louder," only to be accompanied by the sounds of groaning and dancing feet, all "tramping on the listener's mind" (71). In this moment, human bodies become the audience, musician, and instrument of sound. The physical power of Miss Gatha's ceremonial sound reveals that everybody exists in Relation to communal spirituality. It is fitting that "it was with the ears and the head that people [neighboring residents] saw" the spiritual "concert" (71); fitting because Brodber's use of sonic imagery, onomatopoeia and rhythmic syntax encourages her readers to adopt a similar method of observation. Like the scene of Anita's solfaing, Miss Gatha's ceremony is written in such a way that readers cannot imagine the scene's plot without following the acoustical movements of performance.

Anita's healing ceremony explicitly presents sound as a physical phenomenon when Miss Gatha's musical performance acts as a weapon against Mass Levi. Through the vehicle of sound, Miss Gatha reverses Mass Levi's sexual domination of Anita by emasculating him, enacting a reactionary spirit thievery. Miss Gatha's "slippery" sonic movements and aggressive drumbeats force Mass Levi to drop the doll he was using to possess Anita and terminate his own Obeah practices as he attempts to physically "push the sound from his ears" (72). In Afro-Caribbean religious theology, it is generally understood that "sound has the power to transmit action" (Olmos and Paravisini-Gebert, *Creole Religions,* 12). Here sound transmits Miss Gatha's spiritual action as it violates Mass Levi's body and mind. Just as Mass Levi's pings against the house cross Anita's sonic and then bodily boundaries, so does Miss Gatha's Kumina drum rhythm and song. "On came the groaning and the stomping, like a hundred men stepping on his chest to cut off his breath and to force him into an asthmatic attack" (72). The sound leaves Mass Levi's body like "a baby in the fetal position . . . his bottom in the circle of the latrine seat, his privates hanging down like a wet rat" (72). Mass Levi becomes even more impotent than before, with his masculine organs as limp as the magical doll of a woman in his arms.

Like Ella, Anita must endure further physical violation in order to undo the zombification she has already suffered. Brodber turns her attention to Anita after Mass Levi's death, when the adolescent is finally experiencing relief from Mass Levi's duppy. But Anita, like Mass Levi, evidences pain from Miss Gatha's sound as she begins "putting her hands up to her ears, complaining that the noise from the tabernacle was 'suffocating' her" (73). It is not only Mass Levi who physically suffers from the aggressive sounds Miss Gatha makes during the ceremony. Anita faints at the suffocating noise and then undergoes the body-shifting possession of Miss Gatha's ceremony. Touched by nothing but the sound, the young woman moans on the floor as her face transforms into Miss Gatha's (73). Meanwhile, Miss Gatha herself thrashes on the ground as her face several times transforms between "that of a beautiful fifteen-year-old" and that of a sixty-year-old woman (73). The violence that Miss Gatha and Anita experience as they shift bodies exemplifies celebrated Kumina queen (leading practitioner) Imogene Kennedy's description of Myal as "a somatic experience of aggressive intercourse with a possessing agent" (Stewart, 155).

These embodied, ritualized practices that undo zombification require a negation of the individual self—for the zombified and their healers. In the place of such individualism, *Myal* here promotes an ethical paradigm grounded in physical and metaphysical interconnectedness and even exchange that reminds readers of the layered possessions in *Brown Girl in the Ring*. Surrounded by her religious community in the tabernacle, the changes in Miss Gatha's physical form and her clear duress at the experience are met with exclamations of "joy" such as "'Amen', 'Thank the Lord', 'Telephone from earth to heaven, telephone'" (73). The telephone is a fitting metaphor for Miss Gatha's embodied spiritual mediation. The Kumina leader herself becomes a telephone, a physical conduit of sound between the world of the ancestors and spirits and the world of the living.[41] In the possession trance Miss Gatha and Anita cross each other's bodily and abstract boundaries as they are physically and spiritually connected through sound. Together the two women are the collective physicality of spirit and knowledge, occupying the shared space of the embodied voice.

The space of embodied voice allows subjects to safely, if still somewhat painfully, release their sound and create community in the mutual acts of listening. To illustrate the importance of listening in community revitalization, I return to Willie and Dan's conversation. When Willie begins to teach Dan about colonial zombification, he laments that when "they stole our sound . . . we got no support, man. No one could hear us" (66). Before the Grove Town community can change the mechanisms of power that split them from themselves, they must first hear each other's sound. Anita's and Ella's ceremonies of spirit reclamation suggest that this listening will likely be as upsetting as it is liberating. The "clear clean sound" of listening and telling the half that has never been told prefigures Willie and Dan's plans to revise books and finally turn around ships. Brodber's *Myal*, like Willie and Dan's telepathic conversation, operates in the realm of imagined sound, textually making heard what has for so long been ignored. Brodber's "lecture" challenges readers to "listen" to these imaginary relations, to also become telephones between thought and action.

When readers take the time to pay attention to sound in Brodber's story, they, like Anita and Ella, inhabit a dangerous space between the abstract and material. This space of spiritual vulnerability echoes what Glissant calls the "oral exposé," where the individual is and is not community and where the physical and spiritual interact. Glissant explains the oral exposé thus: "When the oral is confronted with the written, accumulated hurts suddenly find expression; the individual finds a way out of the confined circle. He makes contact, beyond every lived humiliation, a collective meaning, a universal poetics, in which each voice is important, in which each lived moment *finds an explanation*" (*Caribbean Discourse*, 4). For Brodber there are many layers of collective meaning that can be accessed in that embodied space between sound and text, from the spiritual communities that allow her characters to transcend the "lived humiliation[s]" of ritual oppression to the collectivity of active readers her texts hope to inspire. The oral exposé asks us to see how thought is indeed already action. Reading the sounds of *Myal* with an understanding of the fluid boundaries between text and performance (and discourse and embodiment) has very real ideological, spiritual, and material implications for all of us.

While *Brown Girl in the Ring* uses visual performance cues to emphasize the inextricable connections between discourse, racial ideologies, and corporeality, *Myal* deepens these links to reflect on the corporeal and spiritual ramifications of communication and interpretation. In the following chapter, two prophet figures demonstrate the revolutionary possibilities that are made possible when socially and politically dispossessed communities imagine and then enact alternative interpretations of spiritual power. These performances of prophetic enunciation and proliferation align textual hermeneutics with ritual performance. Hopkinson's longest epigraph in *Brown Girl in the Ring*—a selection from her father, Slade Hopkinson—depicts the conflation of materiality and spirituality that guides ritual performances like liturgical preaching, mediumship, spirit possession, healing, and prophecy. His poem reads,

> Ritualist, she tried to reduce the world,
> sketching her violent diagrams
> against a wall of mountains which her stare made totter.
> Her rhythmic ideas detonated into gestures.
> She would jab her knee into the groin of the air,
> fling her sharp instep at the fluttering sky,
> revise perspectives with the hooks of her fingers,
> and butt blood from the teeth of God. (155)

This poetic selection beautifully illustrates the theoretical connections between performance, embodiment, abstract concepts, and movement in *Myal* and *Brown Girl in the Ring*, and it predicts the organizational structure of this monograph. In the poem thoughts are made manifest; vision controls the landscape; and rhythmic ideas become bodily gestures that are themselves inextricably intertwined with a spirituality that is at once violent and liberating. In chapter 4, I expand on this complex dance between agency, violence, narrative revision, and God by studying the plays of Louis Marriott and Derek Walcott.

4 Reading the Prophetic Stage

Imagining the Limits of the Possible in *Bedward* and *Dream on Monkey Mountain*

> Theatrical performance and the social performances that resemble it consist of struggle, the simultaneous experience of mutually exclusive possibilities—truth and illusion, presence and absence, face and mask.
> —Joseph Roach, *It*, 2007

> A prophetic person tells the truth, exposes lies, bears witness and then, usually, is pushed to the margins or shot dead.
> —Cornel West, NPR interview, November 1, 2014

As scholars of religion in the Afro-diasporic Americas have well noted, the "prophetic tradition," which focuses on issues of "justice," has always been a key component to Christian and Afro-Christian religion. The unjust historical contingencies of enslavement that shaped these racially coded religious sects also set the stage for their robust legacies of prophetic discourse in texts and performances (West, *Keeping the Faith*, xi; Floyd-Thomas et al., 204).[1] In the Caribbean context, prophetic figures often ground their concurrently political and religious rhetoric in Afro-Christian paradigms that bring together biblical prophetic practices with African traditions of oral divination, mediumship, and revelation.[2] In most Christian theologies, the signifier "prophet" is used as "a general term for the human agent involved in the giving of a revelation," though most recognition of such prophecy is restricted to early Christianity (Evans, 327). Prophecy most often occurs in the Old Testament, the Hebrew texts of the Christian Bible set in ancient Israel, in which prophets were generally said to be "men or women believed to be recipients through audition, vision or dream of divine messages that they passed on to others by means of speech or symbolic action" (Hill and Whybray, n.p.). In many West and Central African religious practices, the priest (often also a social or political authority such as chief or clan leader) embodies the role of prophet as well as diviner, medium, sorcerer, magician, and healer (Murrell, 41). In every one of these paradigms, we see prophets as persons who assume for themselves considerable social, religious, and political power by merit of having been "chosen" (via charisma) to speak and perform on behalf of some authority greater than those on Earth. Prophetic acts are performances of and about power, substantiated through hermeneutical maneuvers. What is more, prophetic performances bring together key elements from each of the religious rituals discussed throughout *The Sacred Act of Reading:* homiletics, spiritual possession, auditory and visual revelations, translation, ritual healing ceremonies, mediation, and interpretation.

This chapter follows two vastly different prophetic careers: those of Alexander Bedward in Louis Marriott's Jamaican play *Bedward: A Play in Two Acts* (1960) and of Felix Hobain, who is referred to as Makak in Derek Walcott's avant-garde drama *Dream on Monkey Mountain* (1967).[3] In both *Bedward* and *Dream on Monkey Mountain,* the prophetic protagonists adopt messianic belief systems that imagine alternative realities, and in pronouncing their beliefs, they inspire and threaten those around them. This chapter brings *The Sacred Act of Reading*'s spiritually informed practice—performative textual hermeneutics—full circle by returning to two literary works that, like Zora Neale Hurston's *The Sermon in the Valley,* describe performative moments of enunciation and reception *and* were explicitly written for the purpose of staging those religious events. While *Brown Girl in the Ring* and *Myal* show how ideologies of sociopolitical oppression require physical performances to actualize their discursive paradigms, *Bedward* and *Dream on Monkey Mountain* focus on the physical performances of *interpretation* that subtend spiritual movements seeking to combat dispossession. In these two plays, the practice of articulating and thus publicly performing new "readings" of physical texts such as the Christian Bible and abstract political discourse (like the racist ideologies of empire) allows prophets and their followers to establish alternative narratives of power in the modern and contemporary New World. Prophecy, I contend, aligns imagination with interpretation. By using a performative textual hermeneutics to study this theatricalized prophetic speech, I contend that these Caribbean dramas allow audiences to imagine and possibly enact alternative hermeneutics for understanding the world at large.

In order to explain the phenomenon of thinking through prophecy in the postwar Caribbean, this chapter begins with a popular site of discourse rooted in late twentieth-century Jamaica, then moves to a highly theoretical site embedded within continental philosophy. Prophetic speech is not limited to the annals of recognized (often male-centric) scholarship.[4] The more politically powerful the spiritual figure becomes, however, the more likely that voice is to be regarded posthumously as a "prophet" by scholars.[5] I first consider a song by reggae legend Nesta Robert Marley, better known as Bob Marley, then turn to the writings of twentieth-century French philosopher Maurice Blanchot. The topics and formal aesthetics of Marriott's and Walcott's dramas, along with the conceptual questions I am asking about prophecy, authority, epistemology, and time, necessarily produce this kind of multimodality.

Far more than a musician, Bob Marley is often considered a prophet of the Rastafari religion, and much of his music reflects key elements of the Afro-Caribbean prophetic tradition that plays out in both *Bedward* and *Dream on Monkey Mountain*. In "Redemption Song," (released with the Wailers in 1980), Marley first tells the story of enslavement. He sings,

> Old pirates, yes, they rob I
> Sold I to the merchant ships
> Minutes after they took I
> From the bottomonless pit

Here Marley sounds like Erna Brodber's Ol' African in *Myal* as he cites the "pirates" and "merchant ships" that inaugurate the harrowing historical narratives for African-descended communities in the New World. Like Brodber's telepathic characters, Marley's lyrics often reference the "half" that "has never been told," decry institutionalized subjugation, and use spiritual language to imagine forms of collective resistance.[6] Marley's song continues with a justice-oriented note of defiance and pride:

> But my hand was made strong
> By the hand of the Almighty
> We forward this generation
> Triumphantly
>
> Won't you help to sing
> These songs of freedom
> 'Cause all I ever have
> Redemption songs
> Redemption songs

The impetus to remember and reframe the "half that has never been told" is a critical component in the prophetic tradition of Christian and Afro-Christian religions such as Rastafari in Jamaica or Black Pentecostalism in the United States. Prophets like the historical figure Alexander Bedward and Walcott's fictional prophet Makak must not only expose this unjust history symbolized by merchant ships and bottomless pits; they must also provide new ways of interpreting the dominant historical and contemporary narratives that perpetuate such injustices. This new mode of interpretation, or hermeneutics, resists prevailing discourses of colonialism and white supremacy by portraying disenfranchised communities as triumphant survivors.

In the second verse, Marley continues to show that listeners must change their interpretive frameworks and, as Ol' African would say, "fight the spirits thieves" by decolonizing their own minds. He sings, "Emancipate yourselves from mental slavery/None but ourselves can free our minds!" At this point, Marley's now familiar message of politically and spiritually motivated Black liberation takes a turn for the catastrophic as he intones,

> Whoa! Have no fear of the atomic energy
> Cause none of them can stop the time.
> How long shall they kill our prophets?
> While we stand aside and look?
> Yes, some say it's just part of it
> We've got to fulfill the book.

In the space of only twenty seconds of the 1980 recording, Marley references atomic bombs, the assassination of Rasta leaders (possibly implicating his own near assassination in 1976), and the notion of a pre-scripted path to the ultimate destruction of the "existing social order, metaphorically expressed in Rastafarian/New Testament apocalyptic iconography as Babylon" (Cooper, 121). It is safe to assume that "none of them" signifies the Western imperial powers symbolized by Babylon, and "atomic energy" is a way of connoting the atomic bomb, the ultimate symbol of Babylon's destructive practices. Produced five years after the death of Rastafari Haile Selassie I, the proclaimed Lion of Judah and returned messiah, this second stanza of "Redemption Song" points to the more complex issues of seemingly failed messianism, violence against (and as a result of) postcolonial political and millennialist movements, and the artistic practices that, like prophecy itself, combine both book and action, textual hermeneutics and performance.

The act of collectively articulating the radical possibility of a seemingly impossible future is a long-held religious and political tradition for African-descended communities in the Americas. Both *Bedward* and *Dream on Monkey Mountain* illustrate the impossibility of their protagonists' prophetic futures, which challenge existing power structures and methods of substantiating authority and knowledge. According to each drama's narrative, the prophetic futures espoused by protagonists Alexander Bedward and Makak are either doomed to fail or have already been proven defunct by history. At the same time, both Marriott and Walcott choose to use the generic conventions of the theatrical stage in order to promote a mode of performative and literary interpretation that keeps open the door for the seemingly impossible. In order to illuminate this aspect of my argument, I turn to the reclusive French philosopher and novelist Maurice Blanchot. In his 1957 essay "Prophetic Speech," Blanchot writes, "Prophetic speech announces an impossible future, or makes the future it announces, because it announces it, something impossible, a future one would not know how to live and that must upset all the sure givens of existence. When speech becomes prophetic, it is not the future that is given, it is the present that is taken away, and with it any possibility of a firm, stable, lasting presence" (79).[7] In the very moment of its performance, the prophetic speech act precludes the very future it makes known. This prophetic future is one that could never occur, because to live within it would require disassembling the foundational assumptions by which we order our lives. According to Blanchot, even a glimpse into this impossible future so profoundly disorients us that we can no longer rely on the firm belief in a permanent, static state of affairs. And yet, later in the same text, Blanchot complicates his theorization of prophetic impossibility by adding, "When everything is impossible . . . then prophetic speech, which tells of the impossible future, also tells of the 'nonetheless' [that] . . . breaks the impossible and restores time" (81). In a seeming contradiction, prophetic speech also introduces the "nonetheless" that expression of radical possibility that punctures a totalizing vision of reality's structuring truths.

This chapter argues that because Marriott and Walcott choose to physically stage their protagonist's prophetic visions, they invite audiences to recognize the "nonetheless" that accompanies all moments of seeming impossibility. Marriott's *Bedward* presents a narrative of impossible futurity, as the protagonist adopts an increasingly millennialist messianic vision that, thanks to its historical setting, audiences know never came to pass. Considered a precursor to the Rastafari religion, the religious movement known as Bedwardism has often been viewed in parallel with

Rastafari adoration of Haille Selassie—an unfortunate and uncomfortable stain on an otherwise powerful political phenomenon. By considering how the mechanisms of the theatrical stage continually enact, or perform, Bedward's prophetic speech, we can complicate this reading and in doing so portray Bedward's legacy as a messianic event within an African-oriented temporal framework.

In the context of *Dream on Monkey Mountain*, it is clear that even the idea of Makak's revelations being true seems impossible in the context of the colonial and racist Caribbean. After all, Makak begins already disempowered and in jail: he closes the play by recanting his prophecies. Furthermore, the drama's epilogue suggests that the entire story of Makak's divine experiences may have been nothing more than a prolonged fever-dream. But again, an analysis grounded in performance-focused approach to textual hermeneutics reveals how Walcott's use of what I call the "dream structure" not only allows Makak's prophetic realities to be physically manifested on the stage but also encourages audiences to imagine alternative worldviews that counter colonial oppression. Walcott's drama pushes at the boundaries of the prophetic impossible and invites audiences to consider the possibility that Makak's prophetic hermeneutics can be employed to imagine a future "nonetheless" that even the original cannot foresee.

Prophecy in these two plays acts as a radical mode of collective interpretation, one that threatens the existing hierarchies of colonial power and that can even surpass the authority of the original prophet. It is this potential proliferation and dispersal of prophetic power that is so distinct in the late twentieth-century Caribbean. Walcott's and Marriott's dramas become most confounding and theoretically generative in the spaces between prophetic annunciation, performances of explication, and potential proliferation. These two plays, written in visual script with the intention of repeated live performances, call for the performative reading method developed throughout this book, and the topic of prophecy pushes this methodology even further. *Bedward* and *Dream on Monkey Mountain* are best read with consideration of these dual states. They are both pieces of literature published to be read in visual collections, *and* they were written as scripts bound for the theater, where the "dramatic text is fashioned into an event, something existing in space and time" (Worthen, 1). Not only do these texts call on performative textual hermeneutics as a result of their generic form, they also call for this method of interpretation thanks to their narrative, theoretical and aesthetic investments. Both plays draw on a constellation of Caribbean performance practices rooted in African-derived and syncretic religious rituals. Marriott's and Walcott's dramas can be read in the tradition of "the tricky Anansi-like mutability of the oral/scribal literary continuum" that Carolyn Cooper uses to study Bob Marley's songs (117).[8]

Bedward's Impossible Narrative of Theatrical Possibility

Louis Marriott, like most Jamaicans, had only heard of Alexander Bedward as a "figure of ridicule" until he stumbled across conflicting narratives of the Revivalist preacher in archived newspapers at the Kingston West Indian Reference Library (138). To this day Bedward is often remembered as the lunatic preacher who broke his leg when he tried to fly to heaven, a legacy created in great thanks to popular myths and songs.[9] Recently this cultural tide may be turning thanks to Kei Miller's 2016 novel about Bedwardism and Rastafari, *Augustown,* which has inspired reading audiences both within and beyond the Caribbean to approach this spiritual history with a generous imagination and sharp sociopolitical critique. Even Miller, however, recognizes the paucity of nuanced materials on this charismatic figure, stating that he was inspired to write *Augustown* when he heard Kamau Brathwaite pause a "distinguished lecture" to instruct the audience, "It's time to write about Bedward" (238).[10] Half a century before Miller's novel and Brathwaite's comments, Marriott defied the practice of either ignoring or heaping ridicule on the story of Alexander Bedward in his radio drama *The Shepherd*. This radio play produced with the BBC in 1960 would become a stage play later that same year, and after several rewrites it was renamed *Bedward* in 1984. Marriott drew on myriad sources for his scripts, including the blatantly prejudiced written archive, interviews with a small group of surviving Bedwardites in August Town in 1957, and his own fictional machinations. Marriott's playscript presents the prophet's legacy as a story of religious zealotry, anti-African prejudice, and overwhelming charismatic authority.[11] The dramatized Bedward is a complex character; he is a rigidly principled, idealistic, and egomaniacal prophet who eventually prophesies to his dispossessed followers that there will be an imminent and catastrophic eschatological event. The protagonist repeatedly claims he is a black messiah destined to initiate the eschatological event that will destroy the white oppressors (and the Afro-Jamaicans who support them) and ultimately lead to his faithful followers' collective salvation.

While much is still to be learned about the enigmatic Alexander Bedward, historians typically describe his spiritual movement as a precursor to Marcus Garvey's social politics; Rastafarians such as Bongo Jerry considered him a "prophet" (Hutton and Murrell, 45). The son of emancipated Africans, Alexander Bedward (1859–1930) labored as a cooper on the Mona Estate until an illness forced him to migrate to Colón, Panama, where he is said to have received two visions. In these dreams Bedward was supposedly instructed to return to August Town in Jamaica in order to receive baptism and begin fasting.[12] These dreams initiated Bedward's subsequent religious trajectory marked by divine revelations, including those regarding the healing properties of the Mona River and earthquake tremors that hit Jamaica in the early twentieth century (Beckwith, 167; Brooks, 6–8; Murrell, 285).[13] In 1889 Harrison "Shakespeare" Woods, an African American prophet from the United States and founder of the Jamaica Native Baptist Free Church, ordained Bedward as a Native Baptist minister and in 1891 chose Bedward as his successor (Satchell, 80; R. Watson, 232). Bedward was arrested for sedition in 1895 on the grounds that his speech advocated overthrowing the white government by force (R. Watson, 231; Chevannes, 421), but he was acquitted after he was diagnosed as insane. Over the next decade the teachings of the Jamaica Native Baptist Free Church came to be known as Bedwardism as the church grew exponentially, becoming a nationwide phenomenon for proletariat and agro-proletariat Afro-Jamaicans (Satchell, 83; P. Taylor, 423). Bedward began to claim that he was Jesus and prophesied the millenarian end of the world on December 31, 1920. On that date he and his followers were meant to ascend to heaven while the remaining white residents of Jamaica were destroyed (Beckwith, 178; Chevannes, 421). Bedward never did make his flight to heaven, postponing the date at least twice. In 1921 he was arrested for leading a protest march from Union Camp in August Town to Kingston, after which he spent the remainder of his life in an asylum. He ultimately died while institutionalized in 1930 (Burton, 118; R. Watson, 246). It would make sense that, in order to challenge the predominant cultural narratives that mock the "failed" prophecies of Alexander Bedward and Bedwardism, historians like those cited here would choose to deemphasize Bedward's religious legacy in favor of his political influences.[14] That being said, historians in the Caribbean do note that Bedward's religious movements did manage to influence society by means of those he inspired, namely Rastafarian leader (and former Bedwardite) Robert Hinds. In contrast to most works on the "flying preacher," Marriott's play emphasizes Bedward's controversial messianism and his radical politics throughout.

In hearing Bedward's story, we are invited to consider what the past can tell us about an impossible future. Marriott's decision to dramatize this story—to present a time-bending narrative within the temporal parameters of live theater—amplifies the paradoxical nature of prophetic temporalities. What would it mean to stage a historical account of an impossible future? *Bedward*, like Glissant's play *Monsieur Toussaint* (1961), offers contemporary readers and audiences a "prophetic vision of the past"; it is also a "poetic endeavour" into the obscured annals of Afro-diasporic history in the New World (Glissant, 15–16). In the analysis that follows, I demonstrate how the text's narrative insists on the impossibility of Bedward's prophetic future by illustrating the necessary "failure" of Bedward's millennialist project and the state's impetus to contain and delegitimize Bedward's charismatic authority when it becomes threatening. I then argue that the dramatic form of the text re-presents that same narrative of failure as a continuous messianic event, repeatedly performing Blanchot's "nonetheless."[15] This ongoing theatrical enactment of messianic prophecy, I conclude, allows us to reimagine Bedward's prophecy through an African-derived temporal framework that challenges the notion of chronological finitude upon which any failure narrative must rely.

Marriott represents Bedward's prophetic trajectory as a swift march toward impossible futurity and inevitable failure as his rhetoric takes on increasingly insurgent and eschatological qualities. Like most plays, *Bedward* must condense historical time so as to create a narrative that can be enacted on a stage in approximately two hours. Within the first act of Marriott's play, the audience sees the Jamaican prophet Bedward transition from a reticent pastor experiencing promotion in the Jamaica Native Baptist Free Church to a besieged, self-proclaimed black messiah and creator of the millenarian religion Bedwardism, which boasts a following of thousands within and beyond Jamaica. Bedward's claims to being the "Son [of God] and the Holy Ghost . . . sent to redeem the sins of the world" are met with religious fervor by his largely impoverished Afro-Caribbean followers and accusations of sedition and lunacy by colonial Jamaican authorities (*Bedward*, 175). The whirlwind pace of Marriott's drama reflects Bedward's meteoric rise to power through charisma and the accompanying struggle to maintain that charismatic authority. Marriott cites news stories and court documents to show how such a quick ascension to power threatens legal authorities, driving them to orchestrate the prophet's demise.

Marriott's Bedward exemplifies prophetic leadership through charisma. Sociologist Max Weber writes, "The concept of charisma ('the gift of grace') is taken from the vocabulary of early Christianity" ("Pure Types," 47). In the wider fields of anthropology of religion, the development of charisma as a theory begins with Weber, who detached the concept from its Christian roots (via the historical work of Rudolph Sohmn) and applied it more broadly to social systems and political life, making his writings a touchstone for contemporary theologians and scholars studying Western and non-Western religious practices and social customs, including those that grew out of the African diaspora. Divinely gifted, Bedward's charisma bypasses traditional methods of legitimating power and is instead sustained by the reverence of his followers. Weber writes, "It is characteristic of prophets that they do not receive their mission from any human agency, but seize it, as it were" ("The Prophet," 258). As Bedward attests, "For I have the love of my people and therefore no force on earth can stop Alexander Bedward" (*Bedward,* 161). So long as enough people interpret Bedward's words and actions as those of a venerable prophet, he can exercise power without institutional sanctions.[16] The downside of such charisma is that it "can exist only in the process of originating," and so the charismatic prophet must somehow continually reinvent the character of his own charismatic authority (Weber, "Nature of Charismatic Authority," 54). For Bedward, whose rise to power among the socially and economically dispossessed occurs as a result of his healing abilities and antiestablishment politics, this means that he must convince his followers that he can provide ever more healing through salvation and more antagonism to the oppressive government. This trajectory will finally lead him to apocalyptic predictions that, paradoxically, must be interminably deferred for his church to continue operating on earth.

Marriott signals Bedward's growing insurgency toward the colonial regime by quoting portions of an 1895 sermon, transcribed at the time by *Gleaner* reporter John Lanigan, that led to Bedward's arrest for sedition. In the sermon Bedward exclaims in front of a crowd of government representatives and officers, "There is a black wall and a white wall, and the white wall has been closing round the black wall. But now the black wall is growing, and it shall crush the white wall" (*Bedward,* 156). When Bedward performs this infamous prediction in Marriott's drama, he has already connected religion with politics. Bedward identifies the entanglement of class, race, and religion when he tells his bishop Dawson, "In this Church, the needs of the body and the spirit are one. In the white man's church they can separate these things.... We have to be concerned about the condition of the poor" (152). The unification of "body" and "spirit" in the social institution of Bedward's church also reflects the African-derived theological philosophies of spiritual and physical integration common in the Afro-Caribbean religious practices discussed throughout this volume. Bedward's political consciousness becomes threatening to the government when it takes on a tone of prophetic imminence. His proclamation predicts the radical dualism (us-versus-them mentality) that will characterize his millennialism and that the representatives of state power will perceive as potentially militant (Wessinger, 721).

In the play, every time that Bedward's political radicalism grows, he also raises the stakes of his religious rhetoric, reinventing his charismatic authority through both avenues of his popularity (Weber, "Nature of Charismatic Authority," 54). Directly after the rebellious sermon, he tells his exuberant flock, "Your reward is great in heaven. But we may not have to wait for death to get to heaven, for if a man have enough faith he will be able to fly like the birds. Fly away over the heads of our enemies. They better stop troubling me or I will fly" (*Bedward*, 156). This moment marks a turning point in Bedward's religious message: it promises a terrestrial (because he and his followers do not have to die in order to experience it) and imminent resolution to oppression. Bedward promises a "rescue from evil ... for a small community of believers," one of the key components to any millennial theology (T. Daniels, 4).[17] At this point Bedward has not yet fully coupled the two components of his millennial prophecy: the destruction of white political rule and the physical and spiritual liberation of his followers through flight. These two ideas come together once Bedward has envisioned and prophesied the final component to his millennialism, that is, his own messianic identity.

Marriott showcases Bedward's particular form of messianic millennialism during the climax of the sermon in which the prophet calls his church Bedwardism and reveals his newly envisioned divinity as Son and Holy Ghost, the "black man to save the black race" (*Bedward*, 174–75).[18] Patrick E. Bryan writes that "Bedwardian theology accepted the Trinity" and that Marriott presents a Trinity that squarely includes the prophet himself (42). Introduced by a congregation singing the appropriately militaristic spiritual "Onward Christian Soldiers," Bedward begins by prophesying an imminent eschatological battle between good and evil, which he compares with the historical Morant Bay Rebellion and Marcus Garvey's contemporary movement. Bedward ends by calling his followers to prepare to fly into heaven with him before God "send[s] down fire to rain upon the earth" (*Bedward*, 175). The prophet ensures his own failure when he sets a date for his millennial prophecy: "On Christmas Eve, 1920, I shall ascend to my Father. . . . Three days later, I shall return for such of my people as are found in Union Camp; and we shall all soar into the blue beyond together. . . . But on the 30th day of December, 1920, the Lord will send down his fire to scorch the earth, to destroy cities, countries, continents and all mankind. So woe unto any sinner who is found wanting" (175–76). Here Bedward becomes explicitly eschatological, apocalyptical, and therefore doomed to fail so long as the world continues to exist. The audience and readers know that the world did not end on December 30, 1920, and so Bedward has fallen prey "to the peril of all messianisms: the belief in the chosen people and the finality of 'history'" (Fritsch, 80). Marriott's *Bedward* illustrates the inevitable paradox of failure-through-survival that Bedward must experience thanks to his eschatological millennialism, which itself results from his need to substantiate his charismatic authority.

In addition to the impossible futurity Bedward creates for himself, Marriott reveals that the preacher's messianic claims so deeply upset what Blanchot calls the "sure givens of existence" in Jamaica that the ruling classes must ensure his prophetic impossibility. Even before Bedward claims to be the reincarnated Christ, he poses a threat to traditional hierarchies of power because he receives his mission from God rather than any human agency.[19] For example, when the governor tells Bedward that the church must "obey the authority of the state," Bedward retorts, "The only authority we obey is the authority of God" (*Bedward*, 171). The governor interprets Bedward's refusal to recognize state authority as an attempt to create an "empire" that will rival the British crown via the Revivalist religious movement. Bedward grows even more dangerous to existing authority as he swiftly transitions from the more general category of charismatic prophet to that of messianic prophet because this shift attempts to grant Bedward the divine agency from which he claims to receive his messages. After Bedward recognizes himself as an incarnation of Jesus and the Holy Spirit, he implies that not only does he speak for a God that transcends recognized hierarchies of power, but he also is now himself two parts of the three-part God, personally transcending those hierarchies of power. While the governor, magistrate, and other colonial officials mock

Bedward's self-proclaimed messianism, his assertions still place them in a tricky legal bind; they want to erase this radical's popular power while not crediting his agential authority.

The court's decisions to rule Bedward insane and institutionalize him become evidence of the necessary illegibility of Bedward's political agency according to the ideological paradigms of British rule. If the magistrate Burke were to claim that Bedward had consciously chosen to undermine governmental authority figures and imprisoned him for sedition, then he also would be implicitly admitting that Bedward manifests charismatic power as a prophet, be that in a religious sense or not. To recognize Bedward's illegitimate authority would be subversive for the maintenance of existing power structures; it would question the "possibility of a firm, stable, lasting presence" for colonial rule (Blanchot, 79). In Marriott's fictionalization of the Bedward legal cases, Burke acquits the prophet on account of his insanity, then has him almost immediately *"bundle[d] . . . back into court"* on the charge that "being a person of unsound mind, you were found wandering at large" (195).[20] Blanchot writes, "Prophetic speech is a wandering speech that returns to the original demand of movement by opposing all stillness, all settling, any taking root that would be rest" (79). Marriott's portrayal of the colonial court implies that those in power hope to contain Bedward as a means of containing the opposition to stillness that his prophetic speech reveals.

On the one hand, millennial narratives like Bedward's are based on a novelistic hermeneutics of closure, an attempt to create meaning of the past and present by knowing how the story finally ends (Gutierrez, 47). The apocalypse is the ultimate narrative resolution, a plot-point by which all previous events can be ordered and made logical. Of course, Bedward's millennial prophecy is neither confirmed nor denied because he deferred his flight date until he was incarcerated in Kingston. Thus, the colonially sponsored media outlets had to craft narrative closure for Bedward's legacy by claiming that he flew and broke his leg in order to bind up the end of that story. In *Augustown* Kei Miller does create a novelistic climax in a scene of spiritual flight, but he pivots readers' expectations by featuring the miraculous ascension of his modern-day female protagonist, Gina, after she is gunned down by the police. While this poignant scene provides readers with the full expression of the miracle they have been promised (and have already witnessed in a more limited extent) by the preacher Bedward, Miller manages to somewhat evade the hermeneutical closure in his prose by revealing that the now-disembodied, floating Gina has narrated the novel all along from her place in the sky. Miller uses a circular chronology to create a sense of the dead's continued presence, which I will show is key to Marriott's dramatization of *Bedward*.

Marriott's story refuses to offer the closure that Bedward's millennial prophecies might suggest. Roxanne Watson notes the ambivalence of Marriott's play, writing that the author "painted a more sympathetic image of Bedward's movement" but still "portrayed Bedward as eccentric due to his alleged attempt to ascend into heaven and as having a big ego" (235). On the one hand, the drama *Bedward* mythologizes its protagonist in ways that present him as a possible prophet and even messiah through layers of biblical references.[21] On the other hand, Marriott's enigmatic psychological rendering of Bedward nuances polemical readings of the prophet, particularly when he questions followers' loyalty and when he betrays doubt about his supernatural abilities to his confidant Bishop Henry just before his scheduled flight in front of six thousand followers. Marriott endows the drama with a tone of ambivalence that disallows dualistic readings. Despite Bedward's clear psychological weaknesses—and the increasingly fantastical nature of his prophetic claims—Marriott portrays his protagonist as a character worth supporting during his legal conflicts with the colonial elite. While Marriott's Bedward may not be the millennialist black messiah of his visions, his prophetic speech still manages to interrupt the illusion of a still and static present. Bedward's final speech in the play exemplifies his desires to disrupt imperial narratives of stability:

> All of you in high places sought to destroy me because of the love they have for me. Well, you have succeeded to a point, because now you are using the brute force of the law to separate the Shepherd from him flock. But that separation is only temporary. There will come a time, Judge, when the brute force of the law will not be enough to stop the march of the people. . . . You can put space between me and my people for the time being, Your Honour, but you will never win the battle for their souls. Brothers and Sisters, keep on singing. Sing until that day when we are ready to bring the Judge to his final judgment. (203)

In Marriott's play it looks as though the only way that colonial authorities could ensure that the subversive potential of Bedward's prophetic teachings and charismatic storyline could be put to rest was to declare him insane and censure him from the public stage through the legal theater; they could then rewrite his narrative in the public media, namely the *Daily Gleaner*.[22] The extent to which Jamaican oral culture maligned Bedward in Marriott's memory evidences how successfully cultural authorities diffused any dangerous, interpretive openings in Jamaican history that his legacy may leave. Marriott portrays the government's accusation of lunacy as an excuse to erase the prophet's powerful voice and story from the public realm and in doing so to ensure that his future is indeed impossible to even imagine.[23] When Bedward protests at his second trial, "What kind of justice is this where I cannot even speak in my own defense?" the magistrate Burke retorts, "You heard the doctor's evidence. You are a person of unsound mind. A man of unsound mind is not responsible for his actions, his thoughts or his utterances. How can I therefore listen to you? You are a lunatic, Sir, and I cannot listen to any incoherent story" (*Bedward*, 202). Burke's tautological argument here not only empties Bedward of legal responsibility but also strips his legal rights and agency through mental control. As in Erna Brodber's *Myal* (chapter 2), the phrase "unsound mind" (which references Second Timothy 1:7 in the King James Bible), plays on the connection between sound and recognizable subjectivity. According to Burke's argument, Bedward's diagnosis by state representatives as being without a sound mind also denies him the right to have his voiced sound received and heard by others. Considering that a prophet is defined by the performance of prophetic speech acts, then Burke's refusal to allow Bedward an audience also refuses his continued prophecy. In her synthesis of the historical drama, Melissa Dana Gibson writes that "one of the primary issues addressed in sophisticated drama was that of historical agency" (593), and *Bedward* explicitly addresses the ways in which the courts and press worked to strip any sense of agency from this spiritual and political leader. In continually re-presenting Bedward's revolutionary speeches throughout the drama, Marriott makes heard and seen what the colonial government deemed "obscene" in the legal theater of the courtroom and on the public stage.

By presenting Bedward's revised history as a theatrical play, Marriott ensures that Bedward's prophecies for social revolution are spoken, enacted, and witnessed repeatedly in staged performances, giving Bedward's legacy the audience that the courts had denied.[24] As Daniel Keegan recognizes in his analysis of prophecy on the early modern stage, to understand prophetic activity in its original meaning of "speaking out" or "speaking before [an audience]" (citing Edward L. Risden) is to consider the phenomenon "in theatrical terms" (422). In other words, there can be no prophetic speech without an audience to witness it. Bedward belies this prophetic dependence on audience reception when he announces his "greatest vision of all" to his elder, Henry.

> *Bedward:* In this vision, Henry, I came face to face with God, and God said to me, 'Who do you say that you are?' And I answered, 'Why? I am Alexander Bedward.' And God the Father said unto me. 'You are Alexander Bedward to men. But you are my messenger on earth. And they that follow you will know that you are a part of the Holy Trinity. You are Jesus come again to redeem the sins of the world. And you are the Holy Ghost the Comforter.'
> *Henry:* Yes, Shepherd.
> *Bedward:* You hear me, Henry? In the vision God told me I am Jesus Christ and the Holy Ghost . . . Redeemer and Comforter . . .
> *Bedward:* . . . Call the people. Let me tell them about the wonderful visitation of the Father unto the Son and the Holy Ghost. (172–73)

In a potentially comedic moment, Bedward cannot accept Henry's mild affirmative response to his most heterodoxical assertion yet, that of his incarnation as Jesus Christ. According to Paul in his letters to the early Christian church (First Corinthians 14:29), prophetic utterances always required "'testing' or 'evaluation' by other prophets," which makes Bedward's anxious appeal to his next highest authority in the church a logical step (Hill and Whybray, n.p.). Without the tested confirmation of another prophet, Bedward must at least confirm that his disciple aurally witnessed the prophetic speech act ("You hear me, Henry?"), after which he needs to repeat the pronouncement to his disciple and then the larger audience, substantiating the prophetic speech act through repetition and re-presentation. In the chorus of Bob Marley's "Redemption Song," the reggae prophet repeatedly calls for group-singing of freedom and redemption songs:

> Won't you help to sing
> These songs of freedom
> 'Cause all I ever have
> Redemption songs
> Redemption songs.

His pleas demonstrate this idea that for a prophetic movement to be successful (like the preaching events in Zora Neale Hurston's works), there must be a critical mass of people willing to physically enact or collectively perform their belief in the prophet's visions.

While all performances "consist of twice-behaved, coded, transmittable behaviors" (Schechner, 52), theatrical performances consist of a network of twice-behaved behaviors that have been scripted, choreographed, then repeatedly rehearsed and enacted before shifting audiences.[25] Theater is a genre of repetition. Yvonne Brewster, the director for the most recent production of *Bedward* in Jamaica (2012), insisted on adhering to such repetition, telling the *Gleaner*, "The actors must remain true to the words of the playwright. I say people you cannot change this line. You cannot write it so you cannot change it. You must find a way of making it work" (Rowe, n.p.). While Marriott himself states that Brewster "brought a new approach to *Bedward*," that approach did not incorporate alterations to the printed script. In the case of Marriott's *Bedward*, this generic imperative of repetition for the theatrical playscript reframes the August Town prophet's cultural narrative by turning his story of "failed millennialism" into an ongoing prophetic event. Rather than a terminable history of prophetic failure, Bedward's dramatized story becomes a continual performance of messianism localized on the stage.

Every performance reintroduces Blanchot's "nonetheless," not only referring but also enacting "a time of interruption, that *other* time that is always present in all time" (81). In regards to the history play, Gibson explains, "the dramaturgy of the nineteenth- and twentieth-century history play has largely rested on Hegelian notions of history as stable historical epochs punctuated by moments of crisis that bring forth great men" (593). Marriott's drama features one of history's "great men," but it resists the Hegelian concept of stable time thanks to the protagonist's prophetic pronouncements and the genre's reenactments of his seemingly impossible messianism. Throughout his work Glissant argues that a break from "Western" conceptions of temporal history is critical in formulating Caribbean philosophy and literary forms. In the preface to her translation of *Poetics of Relation*, Betsy Wing explains that Glissant displays a "determined refusal to accept the logic of linear sequences as the only productive logic. For a country whose history is composed of ruptures, to accept this linearity would imply a continued blindness to its own crazy history, its *temps éperdu*, and acceptance of the Western European epistemological principles that claim this history as its destiny" (xii). By refusing to accept a linear formulation of history, Glissant resists similar historical narratives of closure, which often reify a mythos of the inevitable dominance of Western powers. Heather Russell explains this, saying a historiography based in "such linearity coupled with its dichotomizing imperatives attends as well the discourses of slavery, white supremacy and colonialism" (2). Before turning to the African-derived theological constructions of temporality present in *Bedward*, I consider how Marriott's work also speaks to the Western tradition of what we might call post-Hegelian philosophy. Caribbean and Afro-diasporic theorists such as Glissant and Russell participate in these philosophical debates all while working to distinguish their own artistic and intellectual traditions, those of the Caribbean and African Atlantic, from the assumed Eurocentric and American-centric canon. In turning Bedward's story into a drama, Marriott opens Walter Benjamin's metaphorical gate "through which the Messiah might enter," if for only a set amount of time during rehearsals and performances ("Philosophy of History," 264).[26] Giorgio Agamben, greatly influenced by Benjamin's writings on Jewish messianism, uses the apostle Paul's writings in the New Testament to define messianic time as "a condensed present, an urgent 'now'" (62).[27] For Agamben, messianic time is not about the end of time but rather "the time that contracts itself and begins to end," that is, the suspended climax of the ever-approaching impossible future (62). *Bedward*'s audience, knowing that their protagonist's doom is swiftly approaching as he amplifies his messianic claims, collectively dwells in a state similar to that experienced by Bedward's followers awaiting the apocalypse. They increasingly anticipate the time during which time may begin to end. Theater scholar Yair Lipschitz notes that in the Western theatrical tradition, "dramatic time bears a resemblance to Benjamin and Agamben's messianic 'now-time,' contracted through action" (240).[28] The parameters of staged performances, particularly for the historically sweeping *Bedward,* engender this temporal sensation of distilled action.

Marriott uses the contracted "now-time" of the live theater to reintroduce Bedward's now-forgotten voice from the past. I suggest that this temporal reconfiguration results in a form of messianic "now-time" that incorporates a key element of African-derived religious philosophy: the ever-presence of the past. Just as "the beliefs and structure of Revival Zion are steeped in classical African ideas" (Stewart, 107), Marriott's dramatization of the Revival Zion prophet couples Christian terminology with the practice of the African-derived Myal religion. Dianne Stewart explains that the most significant characteristics "uniting traditional Myalism, Native Baptist Christian Myalism, and Revival traditions" are "divination, visions, prophecy, and healing" (108), all of which feature prominently in Marriott's *Bedward*.[29] Marriott portrays Bedward as a typical Native Baptist or Revival Zion preacher of the late nineteenth century in that his roles as spiritual healer and diviner are of equal if not greater importance to his pastoral and homiletic performances.[30] In fact, Marriott repeatedly quotes *Gleaner* articles throughout the play that attempt to disparage Bedwardism because of its connection with African traditions, calling the worship services "scenes rivaling those of darkest superstition in any part of the Old World" (i.e., Africa, 161). One running joke throughout the drama is the colonial officials' frustrated attempts to discover incidents of "orgiastic" activity in Bedward's church. While Marriott's Bedward does not play into the anti-African tropes that he satirizes throughout the drama, actual practices and beliefs of the African-derived religion Myal, which permeates Revivalist Christian religions in Jamaica, are present throughout the text.

Bedward also uses biblical interpretive practices as a means of affirming African religiosity, another cornerstone of Revivalist churches in the late nineteenth-century Caribbean. This hermeneutical maneuvering occurs throughout the drama and figures prominently in Bedward's "black and white wall" sermon described earlier. Referencing Matthew 16:1–8, Bedward compares the white dissenters who have interrupted worship to chemically test the Mona River to the "Pharisees and Sadducees" who asked Jesus for a sign (156). By likening the dubious colonial officials to the dubious Jewish officials, Bedward uses Christian scripture to criticize disbelief in "African ideas of the spiritual properties of water" (Murrell, 285). The protagonist additionally demonstrates the Myal-inspired "anti-establishment preaching" of Christian Baptists when he criticizes the government for stealing from the poor and demands the white interlopers leave his balmyard by quoting Matthew 7:23: "Depart from me, ye that work iniquity" (156). After a *"great emotional reaction from the Congregation,"* the white officials disperse, making Bedward appear like a victorious incarnation of Jesus with the ability to clear the stage for his message only. Bedward's exercise in biblical hermeneutics on the public stage allows him to also perform the message of his words.

Crudely stated, African-derived temporal frameworks are cyclical and oriented toward the past, while Western frameworks are linear and oriented toward the future. Jacob Olupona points out that while linear time is privileged in the West and cyclical time is privileged in Africa, both are found everywhere. In fact, philosophical writings on time in Western scholarship (particularly those I invoke in this chapter) usually focus on the ways in which a totalizing view of linear time experiences rupture. Fittingly, these scholars, including Agamben and Derrida, often invoke supernatural and theatrical references to explore these questions—namely, the moment in Shakespeare's *Hamlet* in which time is "out of joint" and Hamlet becomes oriented to his dead father, his "ancestor." Similarly, scholars of African religion nuance John S. Mbiti's canonical assertion in *African Religions and Philosophy* that in African religion the future does not exist, and time is conceived as only a continual accumulation of the past in an ongoing present moment. It is not that there is no future in African religious thought, but rather that the general orientation of the present is not toward the future, as it would be in progressive concepts of linear time in the West. African religious time is attuned to the past, constantly cycling back to the events and the people who have come before. Olupona explains that this cyclical structure relies on the "cosmic renewal of time" (8). Dominique Zahan refigures this temporal framework as an orientation toward the ancestors. He writes,

> For the African, time is inconceivable without generations as its framework. The succession of human beings issuing one from another offers to African thought the ideal basis for establishing the three fundamental correlative stages of duration: past, present, and future. However, contrary to what we might expect, a succession of individuals linked by ties of birth appears on the ideal axis of time facing not the future but the past. The human being goes backward in time: [the human being] is oriented toward the world of the ancestors, towards those who no longer belong to the world of the living. (45)

Marriott's staging of Bedward's future-oriented messianism actually enables the audience and reader to orient themselves toward the past, toward the ancestors. Thus, we can see *Bedward* as form of what Derrida calls "revolutionary memory," a "mourning work in the course of which the living maintain the dead" (*Specters of Marx,* 113, 185). Marriott mourns, honors, and maintains the prophetic past by reanimating the legacy of Bedward on the stage. Fittingly, the 2011 *Gleaner* article announcing a revival of the play for the upcoming year commented that the play's venue at a Jamaica college auditorium was ideal because the historical Alexander Bedward was known for traveling around that very location and "perhaps he may have stopped in the very area" where "aspects of his life will unfold" onstage. Here, journalist Marcia Rowe uses the physical location of this drama's production as a means of heightening the audience's relationship with Alexander Bedward's memory and prophetic legacy.

Just as Revival Zion enacted African-derived religious philosophies and customs by way of adopting tropes and thoughts from Christianity, Marriott's play features the terminology of Judeo-Christian messianism and yet presents that vocabulary in a format that materially rehearses African religious orientation toward the ancestors. The belief in ancestral participation in the present necessarily negates a narrative of temporal finitude and closure. By emphasizing both the political radicalness of Bedward's history and the ancestral valences of the script and dramatic productions of the play, I am suggesting that this performative text resonates with several Caribbean religious traditions. These include "Myalism, the Native Baptist movement, Bedwardism, and Rastafarianism," which "all belong in one set of Afro-Jamaican religions which consciously aim to demolish the politico-economic evils of their age" and practices attributed to "the ancestor cults," which usually deemphasize "socio-economic conditions" in favor of "communal history" (Warner-Lewis, "Ancestral Factor," 74). This communal and ancestrally oriented history "is relived in possessions, dreams, shared communions of food, and the immortalization of individuals and groups through song" (74). The play may be theatrically resurrecting Bedward by refusing his own historical emphasis on apocalypse. Instead, the repeated performances of Bedward's prophetic speech situate his story in an African temporal universe, thus successfully incorporating him into the Divine Community as an ancestor rather than as two parts of the Christian Trinity he had once claimed.[31] In this configuration, Bedward's legacy characterized on the stage serves as an ancestral reminder of the prophetic "nonetheless" that Blanchot reminds us "is always present in all time" (81).

Prophecy as Hermeneutics in *Dream on Monkey Mountain*

Like Marriott's Bedward, Derek Walcott's prophetic protagonist Felix Hobain/Makak must confront the legal ramifications of his spiritually inspired actions while being imprisoned by representatives of a colonial Caribbean government. Both men are considered insane and dangerous. In his literary analysis of Makak's seeming "lunacy," Patrick Colm Hogan cites the historical biography of Alexander Bedward to illustrate how Afro-Caribbean religious leaders' "resistance to unjust authority is often characterized by those in authority as madness" (46). In Marriott's play, I contend, the Jamaican state deems Bedward insane so as to dilute the popular figure's claims to agential subjectivity and thus to make him and his messianic prophecy appear impotent. In *Dream on Monkey Mountain*, however, it is the possible prophet Makak who attempts to convince his jailer that because he suffers from madness resulting from divine possession, he cannot be held responsible for his own actions under the court of law. What is more, unlike Bedward, Makak claims to be mad as he begs to be *released* from jail, seeking refuge from punishment in the very diagnosis used to imprison Bedward. Makak intones, "I am an old man. Send me home, Corporal. I suffer from madness. I does see things. Spirits does talk to me. All I have is my dreams and they don't trouble your soul" (225). And yet through an extended dream sequence, Walcott stages Makak's dreams, which in turn trouble his fellow characters' souls greatly. I contend that *Dream on Monkey Mountain*'s use of what I call the theatrical "dream structure" demonstrates how prophecy operates through a process of collaborative interpretation. While *Bedward* also illustrated the necessary participation of others to create a "successful" prophetic movement, *Dream on Monkey Mountain* takes this idea further by implicating the theatrical audience in the prophet's cosmology. Furthermore, Walcott's drama imagines how Makak's prophetic hermeneutics can be employed to imagine a future of "nonetheless" that exceeds the original prophet's own discourse.

Like so many of the spiritually rich texts studied throughout this book, Walcott's *Dream on Monkey Mountain* aggregates different conceptual methods and modalities, creating interpretive challenges suited for a performance-focused approach to textual hermeneutics. *Dream on Monkey Mountain* is particularly invested in playing with issues of embeddedness and boundary-blurring. For example, there are plays within plays, dreams that may or may not be dreams, ghosts, and even an epigraph that references another epigraph. The epigraph, which I will discuss later in the chapter, is not clearly intended to be integrated in a theatrical production and so demonstrates Walcott's understanding of the play-text as both performance and literature. *Dream on Monkey Mountain* creates porous conceptual boundaries between performance and text, religion and the secular, liberation and oppression, and embodiment and apparition. In a review of a 2003 production by the Classical Theater of Harlem, Bruce Weber writes, "Mr. Walcott has employed both mythic and hallucinatory elements in positing Makak as visionary and lunatic, messiah and pathetic old man. Over all, it is difficult to parse, for audiences as well as directors and performers, a likely reason it is rarely produced even while being considered by some to be Mr. Walcott's masterpiece" ("Theatre Review"). While audiences are left questioning the truth of Makak's prophetic message and story line throughout the drama, there is no question that its message and tone permeate the text and production or, as Zohreh Ramin and Monireh Arvin claim, that "the dream in this play belongs both to Makak and to [the] collective atmosphere of the whole plot" (1162).

Before analyzing the drama's tricky use of generic form, it is important to understand the basic contours of this avant-garde play's confounding plot. *Dream on Monkey Mountain* is a surreal text whose plot is structured around a dream of prophetic charisma. This dream acts much like a play-within-a-play and adds ambiguity about the reality of the metatheatrical event. While in a local Caribbean jail, the protagonist Makak (monkey) is pressured to tell his story of messianic divinity as a "deposition" to Corporal Lestrade, a man of mixed race who is an enforcer of white laws, along with fellow prisoners Tigre (tiger) and Souris (rat). All of these men, who constitute Makak's immediate audience, taunt the impoverished dream-prophet. In his dream Makak is visited by a white feminine Apparition, who declares his royal African genealogy and says he should return to Africa; Makak's prophetic speech act occurs as he pronounces his vision in the juridical theater. This back-to-Africa plot recalls the previously discussed texts *Changó, The Biggest Badass* and *Louisiana* (chapter 2), and *Myal* and *Brown Girl in the Ring* (chapter 3), the latter of which represents Africa as a metaphysical "Guinea Land." In addition, the idealization of Africa as a point of spiritual and physical return in *Dream on Monkey Mountain* harkens to the historical legacy of Alexander Bedward, who talked about a return to Ethiopia, which would become a key tenet in Rastafari. Empowered by his new title and connection with the mythologized African homeland, Makak begins fulfilling his role as prophet with his friend-turned-disciple and later impersonator Moustique (mosquito). Makak becomes well known for his healing powers when he cures a village of fever. Like Bedward, Makak is both empowered and greatly endangered when he embraces his position as prophet.

After Makak's disciple Moustique is killed by an angry mob for impersonating Makak in order to swindle villagers, the plot returns to "real time" with Makak in his jail cell. Makak escapes the cell after wounding Lestrade and with his fellow prisoners sets off for Africa (actually Monkey Mountain) to claim his kingship. Lestrade pursues the prisoners to the foot of Monkey Mountain, where he experiences a revelation that leads him to accept his black racial identity and become an advocate for Black law, condemning all that is white. At this point Walcott does not explicitly signal that his play has again turned to the realm of dreams. The playwright suggests that Makak's prophecy may be operating in the "real world" of the fictional stage, or it may be another dream that has become indistinguishable from the play's diegetic reality. Caught up in his spiritual conversion and new-found adoration for Makak, Lestrade kills the prisoner Tigre with a spear. Meanwhile, Makak rethinks his back-to-Africa decision and, in a moment of prophetic divination, foresees the violence that will result from the frenzy for power and revenge.

In his Note on Production Walcott emphasizes the importance of the dream concept in his work. He writes, "The play is a dream, one that exists as much in the given minds of its principal characters as in that of its writer, and as such it is illogical, derivative, contradictory. Its source is metaphor and it is best treated as a physical poem with all the subconscious and deliberate borrowings of poetry" (208). Scott Crossley writes that because *Dream on Monkey Mountain* is so difficult to follow, it depends on the "the language of the dream," specifically metaphors, to "illustrate the key concept in [the] play: the reclaiming of blackness in order to forge an independent West Indian identity" (15). William S. Haney also emphasizes genre, calling Walcott's drama a "dream play," and groups it with other twentieth-century works by playwrights August Strindberg, John Synge, and Wole Soyinka.[32] Haney calls the play's main characters "schizophrenic," thus extending the madness beyond Makak to all those who are somehow implicated in the dream that subtends this plot. Haney argues that "Walcott's dream play suggests that a visionary experience is perhaps the most effective way to achieve cultural hybridity, an in-between-ness defined in terms both of an international identity as well as a conceptual void immanent within yet beyond culturally constructed identity. In other words, hybridity is less a state of mind than a state of being beyond conceptual boundaries" (81). Therefore, Haney's concentration on hybridity uses Makak's dream to accomplish a typical line of argument for Walcott's work—a postcolonial reading of what Omotayo Oloruntoba-Oju calls Walcott's "mulatto aesthetics" (12). Similarly, Robert Fox focuses on the mythological aspect of Walcott's drama for a postcolonial reading, arguing that it goes beyond promoting the oppressed to dramatize "the disparities between a consciousness that is creative and metaphoric, and one that is straightforward and imprisoning" (204); Kelly Baker Josephs argues that "dreams and madness . . . create the glue that produces a cohesive Caribbeaness within the play" (1). I consider Makak's dream a meditation on colonialism as do previous scholars, but I choose to concentrate on what the dream can tell us about the nature of prophecy and the paradoxical hermeneutics of nonetheless that subtend the plot of anticolonial and pro-Black revolution.

A frail, destitute man begging to be released on account of madness, Makak at the opening of *Dream on Monkey Mountain* appears like a study in contrast to the deftly defiant Alexander Bedward that Marriott represents in the colonial courtroom scenes. The contrast is illusory, however, when we consider the foundational tenets of each man's argument. Like Marriott's *Bedward*, Walcott's *Dream on Monkey Mountain* exhibits a distinctly late twentieth-century, Afro-Caribbean version of prophetism that brings together anticolonialism with African-derived and Christian themes. For example, Makak's visions include both the angelic white messenger who first gives him the good news of his royal, messianic status and the loa of death in Haitian Vodou, Baron Samedi, who is often syncretized with the Catholic Saint Martin de Porres. In addition, while performing miracles Makak recites Bible verses and prayers while applying herbal remedies common in Jamaican Myal.

Like Bedward, Makak focuses on a millennial future with a necessary orientation toward the ancestral past through the symbolic form of "Africa." In Marriott's *Bedward,* Africa represents both a lost homeland in need of reclaiming and a site of potential salvation for impoverished black Jamaicans. In *Dream on Monkey Mountain,* Walcott uses irony, the ambivalent setting of Monkey Mountain, and the escalating ramifications of Makak's dreams to challenge this romanticized concept of the African motherland. While Walcott's speciousness toward the role of "Africa" and African-derived tropes in the postwar Caribbean theater world is well known thanks to his essay "What the Twilight Says," his drama also criticizes the adoption of both Christian and Western scientific rhetoric. For example, Corporal Lestrade adopts what Achille Mbembe calls a "grammar of animality" (236) for the purposes of racism and colonialism when he conflates Genesis and evolutionary theory in order to call his darker-skinned prisoners animals and savages deserving brutality (*Dream,* 216).

Bedward and Makak are also connected by their prophetic charisma; they both claim that they have been divinely appointed to bring about action on the earth, and they insist that this divine power exists outside of the purview of the state's authority. From the outset of the prologue, Walcott introduces Makak as a study in contrast to the cruelty of those around him. Makak is a Christlike prophet figure; he is an imperially subjugated messiah flanked by two jeering, common criminals, held at the mercy of a vile jailer-turned-judge who explicitly references Roman law (220). Makak sees his prophetic speech acts as manifestations of a higher authority's word. Like Agne Brown in *Changó,* Makak appears to see himself as a translator who has been tasked with mediating divinely given messages to what Manuel Zapata Olivella would call the ekobios, those fighting for the African-descended community's liberation in the New World. Makak, like so many of the mediums, healers, and prophets discussed throughout this book, occupies a precarious position between subject and object in the spiritual chain of command. At being accused of perversion and unlawful behavior, Makak exclaims, "Sirs, I does catch fits. I fall in a frenzy every full-moon night. I does be possessed. And after that, sir, I am not responsible. I responsible only to God who once speak to me in the form of a woman on Monkey Mountain. I am God's warrior" (226). Here the character Makak attempts to repeal himself of legal penalty for his actions by stating that those actions were not his but rather bestowed upon him by God in a state of supernatural "possession" similar to those discussed in chapter 2. Makak then seeks to divest himself of human responsibility by instead claiming his position as a possessed "warrior" of God. He gives God the blame for Makak's human actions.[33]

The term "warrior" also belies the antagonistic potential of Makak's impossible future. Unlike the majority of the vocabulary Makak uses in this scene in his attempts at garnering pity, the phrase "I am God's warrior" rings out like a threat to do battle for the good of a millennial cause. The bellicose tone of the phrase predicts the overtly antagonistic manner in which Makak and Lestrade will later discuss the prophetic prowess of African-derived persons and spirits, and the statement reminds readers of Bedward's millennialism, which is "a form of social mysticism that is deeply politically subversive," even if touted by a self-proclaimed lunatic (Landes, 23). For example, Makak will pray to the ironically white apparition he later sees to

> Help poor crazy Makak, help Makak
> To scatter his enemies, to slaughter those
> That standing around him.
> So, thy hosts shall be scattered,
> And the hyena shall feed on their bones! (229)

In this prayer, which mimics the more exaggeratedly vengeful Psalms in the Hebrew scriptures, we see Makak begin with the seemingly self-deprecating label of "poor crazy Makak" only to contrast that tone with the request to "slaughter" his enemies so that animals will feed on their remains. Makak's formulation of agency here reminds the reader of Patrick Bellegarde-Smith's description of the Vodou possession trance discussed in chapter 2, and his pugilistic rhetoric recalls Agne Brown's missions in *Changó,* the final gory scene in Nalo Hopkinson's *Brown Girl in the Ring,* and Bedward's promise to "crush" the white man.

While Bedward's sentence of lunacy is used as a way to erase his voice from the legal stage and ensure the "impossibility" of his prophetic future, Makak's attempts to "prove" his own madness become the launching place for the "nonetheless" of the dream sequence physically performed on the theatrical stage. In short, his claims to illegitimacy are his key to making physically real what may only exist in the landscape of his mind. After Lestrade says to "let the prisoner make his deposition," Makak begins to speak and "during this speech, the cage [that had been holding him] is raised out of sight," making the act of speaking on his own behalf a liberating gesture for the protagonist (226).

When Makak launches into the story of the dream, he prefaces the act of telling with the future-oriented prophetic tense but immediately switches into the imperative voice, in a way directing his listeners on the stage just as the script of the play directs those who produce and consume it. He says,

> I will tell you my dream. Sirs, make a white mist
> In the mind; make that mist hang like cloth
> From the dress of a woman, on prickles, on branches,
> Make it rise from the earth, like the breath of the dead
> On resurrection morning, and I walking through it
> On my way to the charcoal pit on the mountain.
> Make the web of the spider heavy with diamonds
> And when my hand brush it, let the chain break. (226–27)

As Makak tells the corporal and the other two prisoners to "make a white mist in the mind," he becomes the director of their mental theaters, an authority figure over their thoughts. What Makak orders his witnesses to mentally create is actually a mist, a symbol of confusion and obscurity. In having his audience create a fog of confusion in their own minds, Makak prepares them for the suspension of disbelief all theatergoers agree to participate in at the physical performance. The dream within the dream acts like a play within a play. Walcott emphasizes Makak's mental authority over his jailer by repeating the imperative "make" four times, followed by the seemingly less forceful verb "let." With this phrase "let the chain break," Walcott again plays with the freedom of theatrical representation, a theme he introduces with the raising of the cage at the beginning of the speech.

Unlike Bedward's straightforward path toward self-proclaimed messianism, Makak's conversion narrative, a prime motif of all prophetic careers, overflows with contradictions and establishes the enigmatic nature of his prophetic hermeneutics. Prefiguring his messianic mission, Makak introduces himself as a risen figure who walks "on resurrection morning" and whose hands can break heavy chains. Makak continues his speech by switching into a first-person voice of retrospective reflection:

> I remember, in my mind, the cigale sawing,
> Sawing, sawing wood before the woodcutter,

. . . .
And this old man walking, ugly as sin,
In a confusion of vapour,
Till I feel I was God self, walking through cloud.
In the heaven on my mind. Then I hear this song.
. . . .
As I brush through the branches, shaking the dew,
A man swimming through smoke,
And the bandage of fog unpeeling my eyes,
As I reach to this spot,
I see this woman singing
And my feet grow roots. I could move no more. (227)

In this portion of the narration, we see Makak describe himself in seemingly contradicting ways. He is "ugly as sin" and yet also feels that he is as divine as "God self, walking through cloud," becoming the mystical figure of "a man swimming through smoke." Haney argues that the revelation of seeing himself as God-self makes Makak's experience a mystical one as defined by scholars such as Robert K. C. Forman and William James. I find Haney's argument compelling in this sense, but I feel that by then promoting an idealized concept of hybridity (one popular at the time of his publication), Haney's argument falls short of keeping in mind all the contradictions and complexities of Walcott's drama. These contradictions exemplify the paradoxical authority that Makak manifests through the play. Moments after minimizing himself to those who persecute him, he suggests that they imagine him appearing like God. Similarly paradoxical, the mist acts as both "a confusion of vapour" and a clarifying instrument as "the bandage of fog unpeel[s] [his] eyes." In a 1971 *New York Times* review of the Negro Ensemble Company's staging of *Dream on Monkey Mountain,* Clive Barnes writes, "The acting is coherent and contained, the one sure guidepost in the author's mist-racked world"; Barnes compliments the quality of acting by placing it in contrast to the opacity of the play itself ("Theater: Racial Allegory"). The misty uncertainty of Makak's paradoxical statements prefigures the ultimate confusion of violence in the final scenes. For much of part 2 it is unclear whether characters are in a dream, finding liberation through violence, or simply imagining an alternative construction of reality within the interpretive lens of Makak's untethered prophecy.

Directly under Makak's speech, the stage directions read, "During this, the apparition appears and withdraws" (227). Walcott intends for

Makak's madness to be made manifest on the stage, for what he says happened in his memory to actually occur on the stage. By staging the seemingly impossible, *Dream on Monkey Mountain* is akin to *Bedward,* which also enacts the "nonetheless" of a prophetic past. Only moments after the apparition appears and withdraws, Makak exclaims, "You don't see her? Look, I see her! She standing right there. [*He points at nothing*] Like the moon had climbed down the steps of heaven, and was standing in front of me" (227). Here Walcott, one of Nalo Hopkinson's key inspirations for *Brown Girl in the Ring,* uses visual cues like those layered throughout Hopkinson's novel to indicate how the protagonist's spiritual knowledge challenges the existing visual politics of this society. Hopkinson's Ti-Jeanne proves to be a reliable narrator despite her early uncertainty about the validity of her mythological visions, largely thanks to her grandmother's ability to confirm their validity according to the spiritual paradigm of the novel. In contrast, the majority of *Dream on Monkey Mountain* maintains an epistemological tension between the visual reality of Makak and that of his fellow characters, particularly regarding the apparitional goddess. The corporal responds, "I can see nothing," then asks the judges what they see, to which they respond, "Nothing. Nothing" (228). Because Walcott includes the textual direction for the apparition, even though the other actors do not "see" the "white Goddess" performed by "a dancer" (and end up making fun of Makak for it), the audience is meant to see her (209). Therefore, regardless of Makak's pleas to insanity and lack of corroborating witnesses, the audience is brought into the world according to the protagonist's prophetic lens, and those who "see nothing" become symbols of ignorance and otherness. Though wrapped in mist, the audience is intended to believe in the validity of Makak's dream on the world of the stage and, by extension, his way of seeing the world. We become his disciples whether we like it or not.

By performing the story of Makak's prophetic calling on the stage, Walcott's play actually portrays the elderly charcoal-burner as a prophet and spiritual healer. During the dream sequence the audience watches Makak cure a village of fever through the use of healing charcoals and cure an abscess in a little boy (among other miracles) (249, 258). Like Bedward before him, Makak's rise to prophecy is bestowed on him by a supernatural authority, in this case the apparition, but it is not realized among his own peers until he performs certain miracles. Max Weber explains this particular category of prophetic figures through a religio-social anthropological lens, writing, "It is only under very unusual circumstances that a prophet succeeded in establishing his authority without charismatic authentication, which in practice meant magic" ("The Prophet," 254). Like Makak's followers, Walcott's audience must "see" Makak's powers in order to "believe" them.[34] Even prophets like Bedward and Makak—who primarily seize their spiritual authority through charisma—find themselves needing to prove themselves, needing to prove their powers by performing feats of magic or healing. Each time that Makak's prayer-filled healing rituals are seen as successful, his social and spiritual authority is strengthened (249, 258). The cured villagers see Makak as a healer, and, more importantly, they begin to adopt Makak's beliefs and spread the good news. This means that in both *Bedward* and *Dream on Monkey Mountain* the new hermeneutics of prophecy can only beget a viable social movement so long as the prophet's "vision of a new social order" is consistently reinscribed via public performances (much like the liturgical preaching practices in Zora Neale Hurston's and Toni Morrison's religious materials discussed in chapter 1). This spiritual convention is exemplified when the light-skinned jailer Corporal Lestrade is so deeply affected by becoming a witness to Makak's deposition of prophetic reality that he ultimately experiences a radical conversion. Lestrade turns away from his previous love of the white man's law to the newfound desire for African and Afro-diasporic dominance and vengeance, reflecting his adoption of Makak's "vision for a new social order" (Legesse, 315).

By structuring Makak's prophecy in a physicalized dream, Walcott promotes a hermeneutics of suspicion all while submerging his audience in the physically "revealed truth" of prophecy. This creates a theoretical and interpretive tension because prophecy, by nature of its divine articulation, is supposed to bypass the traditional pursuit of truth that is institutionalized in hermeneutical practices. This dream setup recalls Anthony F. C. Wallace's idea of "mazeway transformation" within prophetism (270). Mazeway resynthesis is a process of prophetic revitalization in which a leader expands his movement by offering followers a new and meaningful cognitive model for making the world intelligible.[35] Wallace's terminology is helpful here because it focuses on the role of collective interpretation in any religious and sociocultural paradigm shift. Robert D. Hamner recognizes the strength of Makak's prophetic spiritual paradigm when he calls Walcott's oeuvre "mythopoetic" because its "motifs, characters, actions, and symbols . . . provide coherent patterns of belief, explanations of a way of life" (35). These patterns engender a hermeneutical method for interpreting and creating meaning within this surreal world. This interpretive method is founded in epistemological questions about the nature of "knowing" reality within any context. Makak prefaces his primary dream sequence with self-doubt and dismay, and the play repeatedly shifts into different possible dream sequences in which characters describe each other and themselves as having lost their minds, as "living over and over a bad dream," or as being "locked in a dream, and treading their own darkness" (281, 305).[36]

Amidst these conflicting messages, the stage directions in *Dream on Monkey Mountain* ask that directors make manifest the supernatural events described in this "psychical poem" (207). These include the apparition's appearance and the miraculous healings that Makak first denies, then proclaims, and then questions again. These contradictions create an ongoing theoretical struggle regarding prophecy's performativity in the play. On the one hand, Makak's prophecies appear performative in the nature of speech acts, but on the other hand, they are also performance-reliant phenomena that must be enacted to be experienced. Walcott manages to introduce suspicion and confusion, all while giving the audience no choice but to participate in the prophetic cosmology despite their doubts. In short, *Dream on Monkey Mountain* presents prophecy as a set of hermeneutical practices.

The irony is as thick as Makak's fog here, because the "dream" is only told and, as a result, enacted because Corporal Lestrade pushes Makak to explain himself, to "make his deposition" in response to having been charged with engaging in "blasphemous, obscene" speech and "describing in a foul, incomprehensible manner . . . a dream which he claims to have experienced, a vile, ambitious, and obscene dream" (224). The emphasis on the "obscene" nature of Makak's speech brings us back to Blanchot's writings: before the dream sequence begins, the prophecy only exists in the realm of that which is incomprehensible and obscene in the social order. The fact that poor old Makak must be contained for blasphemy demonstrates that his prophetic explications represent an impossible future that in its very articulation threatens the stability of the present (Blanchot, 79). Makak's visions are like Bedward's spiritual proclamations: too threatening to the social order to be recognized at all, and yet also necessarily acknowledged so that they can be properly criminalized and contained. In the case of *Dream on Monkey Mountain,* this obscene dream becomes seen and scene as it gets acted out on the stage. It is Corporal Lestrade and the "stage" (from the French *l'estrade*) of colonial law that he represents that force the "scene-ing" of the obscene, compelling Makak to take his stage audience and the larger theatrical audience back into his dream.[37] Makak does not want to manifest his prophetic speech act—he even says that he is mad and his dream need not trouble Lestrade's soul. This is to say that it is the law that provides a new kind of stage for acting out the "nonetheless" of Makak's threatening way of interpreting the world. The nonetheless always operates within the "now-time" of the theater and yet brings about unknown ramifications for the future.

When the action of the play moves to the forest below Monkey Mountain in part 2, Walcott explores the extent to which consistent group participation and, by extension, consent are required for the interpretive methods of prophecy to be successfully actualized. The conversion experiences of Souris and Corporal Lestrade in the latter part of the play demonstrate how this element of prophetic hermeneutics can open the doorway for unforeseen performances of power. Having escaped from the jail with Makak, the two prisoners, Souris and Tigre, follow the elderly man to Monkey Mountain in the hopes of stealing the gold he says is buried there. While Makak waxes poetic about his ability to "prophesy from one crystal of dew" on their way to Monkey Mountain, Tigre becomes impatient with the old man's musings and worries that Makak will wake up from his prophetic fantasy before they can find and steal his money (288). In order to conceal their plans, Tigre attempts to keep Makak in what he sees as a fit of madness with the assumption that in this state, the impoverished prophet will be unlikely to recognize their duplicity. They decide to encourage Makak's fantasy of prophecy by acting like they believe him. Tigre tells Souris, "Let's mix ourselves in this madness. Let's dissolve in his dream" (289). Like theater, prophecy requires both audience and actors to be fully committed to the world of the performance.

This insistence of interrelated participation in the prophetic/theatrical event harkens to the paragraph-long epigraph Walcott provides from Jean-Paul Sartre's controversial introduction to Frantz Fanon's *Les damnés de la terre* (1961), translated into English as *The Wretched of the Earth* by Constance Farrington (1963) and by Richard Philcox (2004).[38] Walcott cites Sartre's prefatory remarks on colonialism at length before parts 1 and 2, suggesting that he is more invested in Sartre's reading of colonialism here than in Fanon's. Sartre's introduction to Fanon's text is often read as an unfortunate misrepresentation of Fanon's ideas, and it is this possible misrepresentation that helps frame *Dream on Monkey Mountain*.[39] Walcott quotes Sartre on the "witchery of . . . Western culture," in which persons betray their brothers and become accomplices to oppression. The epigraph reads: "Let us add, for certain other carefully selected unfortunates, that other witchery of which I have already spoken: Western culture. . . . Two worlds; that makes two bewitchings; they dance all night and at dawn they crowd into the churches to hear Mass; each day the split widens. Our enemy betrays his brothers and becomes our accomplice; his brothers do the same thing" (277). This split existence is well exemplified both in the colonial violence channeled through the light-skinned black character of Corporal Lestrade and in the "brotherly" violence demonstrated by the other two prisoners' attempts to steal from poor Makak. Walcott ends the Sartre epigraph with "The status of 'native' is a nervous condition introduced and maintained by the settler among the colonized people *with their consent*" (277, emphasis in orig.). Just like the collaborative interpretation of prophecy and theater, colonial ideology for Sartre requires the active participation of all those involved. This begs the question, then: When does participation become consent?

It appears that in the world of Walcott's drama, the prophetic mode of interpretation can be fully materialized even if the person choosing to engage with it is skeptical. Like the theatrical event and colonialism according to Sartre, people suspicious of a particular worldview end up enacting that view and in doing so create a setting where it can be actualized. This integral transition from forced to consenting participation recalls the epistemological recalibrations that the spiritually possessed women-turned-mediums in *Changó* and *Louisiana* underwent in order to arrive at a state of "engaged surrender" (see chapter 2).[40] The plot of *Dream on Monkey Mountain* further suggests that the boundaries between consenting to act *as if* one believes in a particular idea and actually believing in that idea are fluid and even slippery. In the forest scene, Souris so convincingly acts as if he has fallen into the "madness" of Makak's alternative reality that within a few lines it is unclear whether he truly does feel spiritually shaken as he begins remembering how he was taught "to be black like coal, and to dream of milk. To love God, and obey the white man" (290). The dissolving of Souris's subjectivity through acting harkens to Constantin Stanislavski's theorization of method acting, in which the actor temporarily loses personal consciousness in the process of "living a part" (13); it echoes as well the possessed medium's loss of self while being "ridden" in a Vodou trance. In an interview with Olivier Stephenson, Walcott says that "possession" is a central theme of his play and Caribbean roots theater in general, saying it "is a primal, powerful, ritualistic experience which comes of dance and religion" (325). Well-versed in European theatrical theory, Walcott was also likely familiar with the work of Stanislavski, including his racist anecdote, which used the "grammar of animality" to explain that to perform the role of the African Othello, the European actor must mimic an animal, becoming "primitive . . . perhaps like a tiger" (Stanislavski, 4).

Patrick Colm Hogan contends that *Dream on Monkey Mountain* examines "the ways in which oppressive ideologies undermine personal identity and even lead to madness" (103), which corresponds well with the postcolonial arguments of Erna Brodber's *Myal* discussed in the previous chapter. In this scene with Souris, however, madness, or the appearance of possession-like madness, acts as a symbol of not only degradation under colonialism but also the journey to reclaiming personal identity outside of oppressive paradigms. Ultimately, Souris refuses to follow his friend's devious plans against Makak and states, "I believe this old man," attesting to his cognitive conversion. Tigre then asks, "What the hell are you talking about?" To which Souris responds, "I believe I am better than I am. He teach me that" (302). Here Souris exhibits the struggle for self-definition as described in Morrison's *Beloved* and Brodber's *Myal*, or what Marley describes in "Redemption Song" as "emancipat[ion] . . . from mental slavery." Souris's newfound claim to belief signals his conversion and repentance as those terms signal a "change of mind," literally a transition into the interpretive mode of Makak's prophecy.[41] Walcott does not clarify the extent to which Souris, who has consented to pretend to believe Makak's anticolonial rhetoric, is capable of consenting to the repentance process that changes his mind to the point of conversion. Souris's conversion to belief in Makak and turning against Tigre preface the even more radical revolution of faith experienced by Corporal Lestrade.

There is no more troubling example of conversion in *Dream on Monkey Mountain* than that performed by Corporal Lestrade. Anthropologist Diane Austin-Broos pulls from the work of Victor Turner to define conversion as a "passage" (1). Lestrade performs his passage on the stage by physically moving from the space of the colonial jail to that of Monkey Mountain. Bearing a physical wound after Makak stabbed him, Corporal Lestrade staggers into the untamed landscape where Makak's prophetic dreams originated. When Lestrade reaches the escaped prisoners in the forest, he approaches while performing a monologue characterized by an erratic stream-of-consciousness filled with imperial imagery and anticolonial revisions. For example, Lestrade utters a Freudian slip revealing newfound recognition of his own racial identity in a culture of white supremacy as he mutters, "Oh I knew this jungle like the black of my hand" (296). Like Blanchot's wandering desert of prophecy, the metaphorical jungle is a familiar place for Lestrade, who, in seeing the blackness of his hand, also opens the door to seeing its connection to the Almighty referenced by Marley, a connection that makes the corporal see his African ancestry as strong and triumphant. The 2003 production by the Harlem School for the Arts made Lestrade's conflation of flesh and landscape explicit by using "actors lying on their backs with their bare legs waving sinuously and slowy in the air . . . to depict the ponderous lazy sway of jungle flora" (B. Weber, "Theater Review"). If we imagine the corporal's conversion experience through the lens of possession in the Vodou tradition elucidated by Benedicty-Kokken, we can see his experience as a passage into repossession of his African heritage through the racialized "material" of his wounded body. Though Lestrade's relative cultural power as a light-skinned representative of the colonial government distinguishes him from the acutely dispossessed Makak and Souris, he still appears to experience a form of self-possession through external spiritual possession. In the 2003 production, Lestrade wades through a field of limbs and during this journey recognizes his own embodied ancestry on his own hand, "'repossessing' the only space that one can ultimately control: the landscape of the body, even if battered, mutilated, disillusioned" (Benedicty-Kokken, 15).

When Lestrade encounters Basil the carpenter—a character dressed as the Vodou loa of death, Baron Samedi, and previously seen in Makak's dream scenes—Basil states, "I am Basil, the carpenter, the charcoal seller. I do not exist. A figment of the imagination, a banana of the mind" (297). Because the audience has to this point only encountered Basil as a character of Makak's dream-theater, the enigmatic figure's sudden appearance to Corporal Lestrade outside of the dream context could mean that the corporal has now fully adopted the prophetic paradigm of his former prisoner. This transition could in turn suggest that the jailer is either going mad or perhaps going into a new kind of sanity, that "nonetheless" reality in which Walcott's audience has already been operating. Basil then adds, "You have one minute to repent. To recant. To renounce" (297). When Corporal Lestrade asks Basil what he should repent, the cabinetmaker (now more explicitly Baron Samedi's "figure of death") answers cryptically, "You know, Lestrade. You know." Austin-Broos, playing on the language of Lewis Rambo, describes the passage of conversion as a "turn from and to," adding, "to be converted is to reidentify, to learn, reorder, and reorient" (1–2). By telling Lestrade that he already possesses the knowledge of his own repentance, Basil makes the corporal's passage of learning—his turning toward a previously invisible, and possibly greater, truth—a turning inward.

The corporal appears to lose his mind in this "turning from and to" process of repentance and conversion, during which he visually recognizes

Makak's anticolonial cosmology in the figure of Basil. As a result of this passage into new belief through possession, Lestrade becomes a fierce convert to the cult of Makak's messianism. While Lestrade appears to experience a form of possession that allows him to repossess formerly rejected aspects of his identity, this encounter with Basil also calls into question the ability to possess one's mind at all. The corporal and Basil engage in a riddle-like dialogue that reminds readers of Ngafúa's interactions with Agne and the logical games that the recently deceased women play with Ella/Louisiana.

> *Corporal:* My mind, my mind. What's happened to my mind?
> *Basil:* It was never yours, Lestrade.
> *Corporal:* Then if it's not mine, then I'm not mad.
> *Basil:* And if you are not mad, then all this is real.
> *Corporal:* Impossible! There is Monkey Mountain. Here is the earth. Banana of the mind . . . ha . . . ha . . . ha . . . (297–98)

Trapped between the options of either accepting his own madness or acknowledging the validity of Makak's "impossible" prophetic nonetheless, Lestrade attempts to orient himself via the landscape. Walcott presents the corporal with a series of false choices, all of which require the former bastion of colonial rule and logic to imagine a world that can only be intelligible through the hermeneutics introduced in Makak's prophetic dreams. Lestrade represents the audience and reader in this moment, because in order to find sense in the dreamscape physically playing out in front of him, he must adopt the interpretive methods fitting the scene. The corporal ultimately performs an apostrophe to the "Africa of [his] mind" and repents for having turned his back on his heritage. Lestrade says he now sees "a new light" and proclaims "the glories of Makak!" (299).

Even though Lestrade's bewilderment during his conversion would suggest that this is a sudden change, the stage directions specify that the speech be performed "flatly, like an accustomed prayer" (299). The familiarity of this devotion suggests that this prophetic script has already existed before Lestrade's radical conversion, much like the events already scripted in the "book" Marley references in "Redemption Song." And yet the "accustomed" nature of Lestrade's recitation also suggests that like the theatrical performance, the prophetic script is constituted through repeated enactments over time. Prophecy, then, is a hermeneutical practice rooted in both text and performance. The collective enactment of Makak's prophecy gains such momentum that it exceeds the elderly man's original authority. The remaining scenes of *Dream on*

Monkey Mountain explore the limits of this prophetic proliferation, creating extreme examples of what Zora Neale Hurston may call "variations on a theme."

In a surprising twist, Makak is unable to see Basil when he is clearly on the stage talking to the corporal. By denying Makak the ability to see and recognize the reality before the corporal and the audience, Walcott shows that the charcoal-burner's prophecy has now taken on a life of its own. Lestrade's anguished shift into the prophetic worldview mirrors Makak's earlier pleas in the jail. Just as Walcott stages the white apparition for the audience but denies Lestrade, Tigre, and Souris the capacity to see her, so do Makak, Tigre, and Souris believe that Lestrade is "talking to nothing" in this moment. Meanwhile, the audience can clearly recognize that the embodied figure of Basil stands on the stage with the corporal (299). Yet again Walcott has his audience operate as converted followers to the prophetic lens of interpretation adopted by his characters, giving the audience no choice but to imagine the world through a new vantage point. This shift in "vision" suggests that in this play, to convert to Makak's prophetic worldview means to adopt a hermeneutical position that, paradoxically, requires the participation of others but also assumes that one person can see prophetic possibilities that others cannot.

Not only does Lestrade's new interpretation of Makak's prophecy exceed its original author, it takes the messages of Black liberation to dangerous and vengeful realms. Foreseeing how his converted will transform his original dreams (another form of prophecy in the play), Makak, like many religious prophets before him, laments, "I have brought a dream to my people and they rejected me," then adds, "Now they must be taught, even tortured, killed. Their skulls will hang from my palaces. I will break up their tribes" (301). These lines inspire images of a vengeful divine ruler similar to the Afro-diasporic god of lightning, Changó, or the biblical God invoked by several Old Testament prophets such as Joshua, who obeys commands from God and "utterly destroyed all that was in [a successfully conquered] city" (Joshua 6:21). And indeed, the corporal kills Tigre when he refuses to convert to the glories of Makak, then arranges the coronation of Makak as king of Africa, along with a ceremony of mass execution of white historical figures ranging from Cecil Rhodes to Abraham Lincoln. Tejumola Olaniyan describes this moment in the text: "The tribes, led by the converted Lestrade, now the chief ideologue of Afrocentric culturalism, are more of praise-singers than effective monitors of their leader. Once in control of power, their preoccupation seems to be with revenge, and this they pursue with a reckless abandon" (107). Olaniyan's reading of the final events points to the critiques of Frantz Fanon's form of anticolonialism as articulated by Julietta Singh: namely that this discourse "did not interrogate thoroughly enough its own masterful engagements" and as a result could fall into the trap of trying to undo "colonial mastery by producing new masterful subjects" (2). According to scholars such as Lewis Gordon and Homi Bhabha, critiques of Fanon may be better understood as criticisms of Sartre's interpretation and framing of *Les damnés de la terre*. The surfeit violence in the final scenes of Walcott's play is certainly a comment on Sartre's preface, which "glorified violence beyond Fanon's words or wishes" and indelibly shaped reception of *Wretched of the Earth* (Bhabha, xxi).

While I contend that *Dream on Monkey Mountain* overwhelmingly concerns itself with Sartre's conception of colonialism rather than Fanon's, I also note that the play bears the "masterful" hallmarks of much early anticolonial discourse, including that of Fanon. It is no coincidence that Makak's coronation—a performative act of sovereignty rooted in legal contestations of mastery—is predicated by Corporal Lestrade's declaration of a new "jungle law" (306) that justifies the destruction of subjectivity for dissidents like Tigre. Singh contends that Fanon (along with Mohandas K. Gandhi) "could not adequately account for the *remainders* of mastery—for those figures of abjection that were reproduced through the liberatory horizons of anticolonial discourse" (30). Tigre's abjectification is not a bug of Lestrade's dialectical interpretation of anticolonial prophecy, but a feature.[42]

The prophecy's entanglement with paradigms of mastery are predicted in the drama's failure to provide substantial representations of its women characters. In *Dream on Monkey Mountain* women function exclusively as either inspirations, objects of desire, or witnesses to the contrastingly complex men around them. By rarely engaging with their lived experiences or fictional stories, Walcott positions women—especially Afro-diasporic women—as the necessary abject figures of the play's masculinist, anticolonial discourse.[43] As is often the case, the treatment of black women (or lack thereof) in a particular anticolonial imaginary foretells the fates of those subjects who, like Tigre, will be deemed unnecessary for the good of the body politic. While the white feminine apparition is often understood to represent Makak's simultaneous idealization and hatred of the racial construction of whiteness, Elaine Savory Fido has explained how the goddess-dancer's ceremonial death later in the drama demonstrates the expendability of feminine characters throughout Walcott's male-centric ouervre and justifies violence against women (114, 117).

In Bill T. Jones's 1994 production of *Dream on Monkey Mountain* at the Guthrie Theater, he replaced the white dancer with a "beam of light," a decision that Tad Simons says occurred after "Maya Angelou convinced [Jones] that ritually sacrificing white women onstage in African-American theatre has been done so often that it is now cliché" (48).[44] In this production designed for a US audience, Jones used the symbolic landscape of Monkey Mountain to physically dominate the stage with visual representations of the racist histories that inspire these unfortunate cycles of mastery and violence. Jones begins the play by staging the mountain with a "white shroud of parachute silk," which physically represents a "snowy mountain peak" and symbolizes not a free homeland of Africa but the dominant "white oppression" that visually frames every scene on the Caribbean island (48). In Jones's production the mountain, described in Walcott's script as volcanic, is revealed to contain within its structure a fiery symbol of racial rage. In the second part of the play, Jones lifts the white silk to reveal "an enormous figure, 18 feet high and 12 feet wide—an outrageously enlarged version of an old Negro coin-bank figure. Its eyes red with rage, its tongue a long white ribbon of smoke, the statue sits Buddha-like in the background, watching over the rest of the play as an inexorable symbol of the ultimate African stereotype—a gigantic representation of all the prejudices, stupidities, dehumanizations and injustices that expatriated African descendants have been forced to endure all over the world during the past 500 years" (48). By dominating the stage with visual cues of white supremacist oppression and explosive Black rage, Jones suggests that the anticolonial dreams of Makak are revolutionary not only because they imagine alternative methods for interpreting the world, but also because they allow for followers to tap into the previously buried emotional valences that underpin liberationist movements within both the play's Caribbean setting and its US site of performance. Jones's set design does not negate the ways in which the play casts women as "both instrumental and sacrificial in the creation of anticolonial masculinities," but it does extend that symbolic abjectification to the theatrical, visual registers of light and landscape (Singh, 33).

The murder of Tigre actualizes Makak's latest prophetic statements about destruction between African-descended groups and provides a counterpoint to the message of Sartre's epigraph. Rather than only criticize the inherent violence between "brothers" in a regime of colonial rule, Walcott also cautions against community bloodshed in the pursuit of liberation. Marley would also warn against disunity and Pan-Africanist strife in his song, "Zimbabwe," which was dedicated to the Bush War in what was then Rhodesia. After the executions of historical figures and even of the white goddess, who revealed Makak's divinity on account of her being "indubitably white," Makak sees himself as a mere puppet of his power-hungry followers and no longer wishes to symbolize the messiah to those around him. Believing his cosmology to be fully corrupted by violence, Makak ends the play as he began, a reluctant and poor dream-prophet who claims to be only a "shadow" not meant to bother the souls of those around him. In the final scenes Makak recognizes the dangerous proliferation of prophetic interpretation, which, when taken up by followers with enough fanaticism, can either corrupt the original message bestowed by the divine authority or expose the violent underpinnings of a seemingly liberating message.

Blanchot's "nonetheless" is integral to reading the drama's final scenes, because by repeatedly staging the prophetic articulations and explications, Walcott suggests that it does not matter if Makak wants to take it all back. The impossible has already been set in motion, even if it seems like time gets restored again at the end. Like a Shakespearean comedy, wherein the curtain closes on a restored paradigm of heteronormativity and social hierarchy, *Dream on Monkey Mountain* leaves its audience with a memory of radical events that threaten the assumptions of productive society. As Souris tells angst-ridden Makak before the scene of mock-juridical executions, "Your dream touch everyone, sir" (304). The corporal, Tigre, Souris, and the wider theatrical audience—that is, those who have become witnesses to Makak's radical collective hermeneutics—have already been changed in some way simply by experiencing the nonetheless. Reality and mental states are not separable, even when Makak wishes them to be. Rather, Walcott shows how the prophetic operates like the theater, collaboratively creating, shifting, and challenging that which we think is "real," or material.

Like Makak at the end of *Dream on Monkey Mountain*, Walcott identifies himself in his 1970 essay "What the Twilight Says" as a prophet who is battling with the repercussions of his charismatic power and has been doomed to sell out his own divine vision as a result of the corrupting possibilities in these new modes of interpretation. In this essay Walcott imagines himself to be a prophet, all while demeaning his acting as such.[45] Like Makak, Walcott muses on what it means to reconcile with one's own prophetic position in real time, not simply once others have accepted that designation.[46] In both self-aggrandizing and self-deprecating terms, Walcott explains that "the self-inflicted role of martyr came naturally, the melodramatic belief that one was message-bearer for the millennium, that the inflamed ego was enacting their will" (4).

Walcott's spiritual figuration was fashioned by the author and his public. Even a cursory search through articles on Walcott demonstrates how he has become a kind of prophet-figure of Caribbean letters.[47] In a February 9, 2004, *New Yorker* profile, Hilton Als writes, "Walcott, the most ardent chronicler of the island's history and landscape and people, sometimes acts as a patron, a kind of John the Baptist of St. Lucia. ('I would be a preacher,/I would write great hymns,' he wrote in the 1973 autobiographical book-length poem 'Another Life')" ("The Islander"). Though this language may seem overwrought, it is difficult to overemphasize the integral role Walcott played for Caribbean literary studies in the United States and United Kingdom. Walcott, whom Als has also called "a terrible person; awful man," has in recent decades received considerable condemnation as well as praise from past students (see "Interview: Hilton Als"; "The Islander"). Overt public regard for Walcott as a mentor, sagacious leader, and pedagogue waned considerably following the scandal at Oxford University in 2009, which involved a public resurfacing of sexual harassment accusations from two of his female students in 1982 and 1995.[48] Though still a contested topic, Walcott's alleged predatory nature with women students has become just one of many open secrets in the academy today. I suggest that Walcott's masculinist literary discourse and his possible abuses of power with young women deserve careful consideration in light of the author's own comments about the dangers of being fashioned into a prophet-figure decades before these scandals surfaced.

In "What the Twilight Says" Walcott appears to suggest that in fulfilling his prophetic role, he comes to see himself as a "Christ" figure and in doing so manages to lose his own soul, just as Makak at first feels empowered and then implicated in violence he no longer believes in. Walcott calls himself a "self-appointed schizoid saint" full of rage that "eroded and demeaned the soul" (32–33). After describing the linguistic (namely English-born) requirements he made of his actors as a "kind of aggression [which] increased an egotism which can pass for genius," Walcott says he "was thus proclaimed a prodigy" for insisting on "a formality which had nothing to do with their lives" (32).[49] Here Walcott suggests that with each label of genius, he is further removed from the community he attempts to serve and that his "mania" and desire to retain artistic power increased above his ability to "help others and treat himself without mercy" (32). Walcott embeds his professional and artistic success within the same structures of literary acclaim that he critiques. In the wake of renewed debates about sexual harassment in literary and academic circles, it is particularly crucial to note how these structures often bestow prominent figures like Walcott with secular versions of the charismatic authority described in Marriott's *Bedward*.[50] Such hierarchical configurations of "genius" and prophet-like powers (particularly when the figures are also meant to unilaterally speak for underrepresented communities) can create environments ripe for abuse.

By the end of "What the Twilight Says," Walcott, like his character Makak, wishes to dispel of his authority in the hopes that doing so will redeem his original theatrical mission. And yet Walcott's earnest (if somewhat narcissistic) tone throughout this essay reveals the truth apparent in *Dream on Monkey Mountain* and Marriott's *Bedward*: that once a prophecy has become powerful in the lives of its followers and its detractors, it no longer matters if the original prophet believes in his prophetic gift or not. Bob Marley also acknowledged his prophetic position in Caribbean culture when he sarcastically referenced Nathaniel's dismissal of Jesus's hometown (John 1:46) in a lyric that replaced "Nazareth" with "Trench Town" ("Trench Town"). Unlike Walcott, Marley was not afforded the time to see how his role would transform over the course of decades; by 1971 his lyrics already reflected the inability to live up to the expectations of those around him. For example, in "Natural Mystic," written before an assassination attempt on Marley but after he devoted himself to the Rastafari religion, Marley takes on an uncharacteristically pessimistic tone, especially within a song often associated with his more uplifting, revolutionary spirituality. The negative connotation of the conjunctive adverb "although" in "Natural Mystic" reminds the reader of Blanchot's "nonetheless," which acknowledges the impossibility of a radically different world while opening the conceptual door to the prophetic future. Marley reflects the practices of Bedward, Makak, and Walcott by simultaneously negating the primacy of his personal authority while prophesying future events in a universal context. In Walcott's play Makak delivers a final monologue during which he imagines future men looking in the direction of his mountain as they say, "Makak lives there. Makak lives where he has always lived, in the dream of his people" (326). He continues to prophesy: "Other men will come other prophets will come, and they will be stoned, and mocked and betrayed, but now this old hermit is going back home, back to the beginning, to the green beginning of this world" (326). Makak acknowledges his own personal obsolescence alongside the inevitable future of his dream and those dreams of future prophets in the Caribbean. While prophets may be misunderstood and forgotten in time, the simultaneously performative and scripted phenomenon of prophecy continues to flow between the beginning and end, past and future. Prophecy, like an artist's creative interpretation of the world, takes on a life of its own as it is received, revised, and reimagined in the minds of those who become its witnesses.

Epilogue
Interpretive Communities

i found god in myself
& i loved her/I loved her fiercely
   —Ntozake Shange, *For Colored Girls Who Have
   Considered Suicide/When the Rainbow Is Enuf*

NTOZAKE SHANGE'S "CHOREOPOEM" *For Colored Girls Who Have Considered Suicide* (first performed 1974) articulates a now-familiar journey from spiritual grief and suffering to self-connection, divine recognition, and "fierce" love. After the "lady in red" utters the lines quoted above, her fellow performers echo the liturgical practices of Zora Neale Hurston's congregations by "bearing up" her performance with their own voices and actions. Shange's stage directions read, "All the ladies repeat to themselves softly the lines 'i found god in myself & i loved her.' It soon becomes a song of joy, started by the lady in blue. The ladies sing first to each other, then gradually to the audience. After the song peaks the ladies enter into a close tight circle" (274). In this moment Shange dramatizes the shared intimacies that emerge from personal encounters with the divine. Shange began writing *For Colored Girls Who Have Considered Suicide* as a poem cycle and later revised it for performance. The choreopoem features a series of poetic monologues that come together to create an ensemble performance piece. Though each "lady" is physically present throughout the performance, *For Colored Girls Who Have Considered Suicide* contains only sparing moments of dialogue between the women. Therefore, Shange's choreopoem becomes an ensemble via its collective choreographies. These choreographies are made manifest on the stage through actors' bodies and printed in the text as stage directions. Shange's script thus calls for one of the foundational moves of a performative textual hermeneutics—attending to bodies as sites of production, mediation, and interpretation within written discourse. The lady in red's revelation of personal divinity mirrors the larger work's transformation from the mode of print to performance and the interpretive maneuvers imbedded within this project's performative textual hermeneutics. Through an interpretive process that involves enunciation and reception, Shange's lady in red discovers a personal god within herself. She then makes that discovery communal by allowing those around her to bodily participate in the revelation through sound and ritualized movements. This moment resonates with the prophetic narratives of Bedward and Makak described in chapter 4; echoes the recognition of shared divinity by Baby Suggs's congregation in the Clearing, as I outlined in chapter 1; and embodies the spiritual connections experienced by Ella/Louisana, Agne, and Ti-Jeanne that are the subject of chapters 2 and 3. In other words, Shange's choreopoem exemplifies the relational process of subjectivity formation, spiritual knowledge production, and meaning-making explored throughout this book.

The lady in red's discovery of a feminine god within herself in *For Colored Girls Who Have Considered Suicide* brings us back around to the Josefina Báez quote that commenced this book. For Báez, "Goddess within is a poet with action," a "performer" who employs "poetic license" (*Comrade, Bliss Ain't Playing*, n.p.). This particular interpretation of spirituality incorporates the elements present in sacred acts of reading: language, performance, and embodied action. In discussing the performance works of Báez and Shange, I return to the concepts of embodiment, performance, and textuality. These concepts are the building blocks for this book's foundational methodology for reading. The performative textual hermeneutics developed throughout this book is the result of my encounters with the spiritual and aesthetic frameworks of Afro-diasporic texts. This project has been motivated by a belief that this interpretive methodology can help contemporary readers respectfully contend with the performative and religious traditions invoked throughout this literary archive. Though I do not suggest that a performative textual hermeneutics can only be valuable in the case of Afro-diasporic literature, I do insist on recognizing the specific contexts by which this method developed. Furthermore, I maintain that the constellation of interpretive practices structuring performative textual hermeneutics may help us to challenge the primacy of Western assumptions regarding the aesthetic and intellectual value of non-European, and specifically Afro-diasporic works.

I opened this epilogue with the final scene of Shange's choreopoem because it physically stages the relational dance between authors, words, mediums, and readers that I trace over and again throughout *The Sacred Act of Reading*. In chapter 1 I detailed how Zora Neale Hurston and

Toni Morrison "translated" their texts across media and genre to elicit particular experiences of religious performance in prose, poetry, drama, and audio. Like Shange's choreopoem, Hurston's and Morrison's stylistic maneuvers illustrate clear authorial awareness of the possibilities and limitations inherent in different artistic formats. Moreover, a comparative reading of their religious materials helped me to enact a performative textual hermeneutics. By using this guiding interpretive methodology, I have illustrated the aesthetic and theoretical significance of orality, visual citations, embodiment, and audience reception in a variety of modern and contemporary Afro-diasporic literature. In chapter 2 I used this methodology of reading and a critical framework rooted in translation studies to understand how mediation and interpretation are inextricably tied to theories of knowledge-formation and subjectivity in the novels of Manuel Zapata Olivella and Erna Brodber. By tracing the stories of two spiritual mediums, chapter 2 vastly expanded the notions of communal knowledge and belonging via embodiment. These novels' plots use spirituality to entangle texts and flesh, deepening the themes introduced in chapter 1. By concentrating on two characters' occupied bodies, I laid the theoretical groundwork for my third chapter's focus on the physical mechanisms underlying abstract ideologies of power. Chapter 3, which analyzed the novels of Erna Brodber and Nalo Hopkinson, shows how interpretations and reinterpretations of discourse (with a focus on written texts) arise through communal practices. These practices further nuance distinctions between texts, bodies, and performance. In chapter 4 I revisited the theme of epistemological uncertainty discussed at length in chapter 2 to show how new interpretations of the self and world can unfold through individual and community interactions, sometimes in chaotic ways. Throughout *The Sacred Act of Reading,* I have focused on literary texts that, whether explicitly connected to actual performances or not, demonstrate how mediation and interpretation occur through an ongoing series of collective, embodied performances. Furthermore, these performances come to inform understandings of an individual's subjectivity in relation to a wider interpretive community. That community may be visible or invisible, physical or metaphysical.

For Josefina Báez the experience of community participation can manifest in the singular *and* the plural. In a 2015 interview with Ana Maurine Lara for *esmiférica,* Báez states,

> Hay una comunidad visible, una comunidad invisible. I talk with them both
> Hay una comunidad elegida, hay otra comunidad impuesta.

Hay otra comunidad heredada, imaginada.
Hay un montón de comunidades. Algunos se entrecruzan.
. . . .
Yo soy mi propia comunidad, también. My best community to tell you the truth.
Me río mucho conmigo misma. Bailo sola, canto, improviso muchas locuras.
Lo que no veo quizás está más presente de lo que veo. ("Into the Invisible," 2015)

There is a visible community, an invisible community. I talk with them both
There is a chosen community, there is another imposed community.
There is another inherited, imagined community.
There is a mass of communities. Some intertwine.
. . . .
I am my own community, too. My best community to tell you the truth.
I laugh with myself. I dance alone, sing, improvise lots of crazy pieces.
That which I can't see is almost more present than what I do. (author's translation)

Though not explicitly spiritual, Báez's commentary echoes the stories of extrahuman communities present throughout the literature in this book. The spiritual fellowships described in the studied texts always incorporate living persons and some combination of the deceased (chapters 1–4), the ancestors (chapters 2 and 3), characters from folk mythology (chapters 3 and 4), and a variety of Christian and African-derived spirits (chapters 1–4).[1] More often than not, living characters first assume that despite sensory evidence they have only imagined these imposed communities until they can accept new methods of knowing. In *Louisiana,* for example, Ella/Louisiana learns to surrender her spirit to the imposed and inherited community of Anna "Mammy" King and Louise "Lowly." To borrow Báez's words, she begins to believe that "that which [she] can't see is almost more present than what [she can]." Ella/Louisiana's continual engagement with the two deceased women allows her to create more spiritual connections with those in New Orleans. As these two groups intertwine, she ultimately embraces a multiplicity of identities within herself.

Báez's one-woman performance pieces as well as her statements during interviews repeatedly emphasize the capacious and various ways in which she conceptualizes her individual identity. Báez presents a fluid and often defiant public persona that is recognizably Afro-diasporic, bilingual, and *Dominicanish* (the title of her 2000 performance text), all while working to confound the common relegation of such authors and artists to geographic and racial categories. In her "secular prayer," *Comrade, Bliss Ain't Playing*, Báez uses spiritual rhetoric like that discussed throughout *The Sacred Act of Reading* to illustrate her multifarious sense of personal subjectivity. In the performance piece, the poet/artist/author plays the parts of medium, prophet, spiritual victim, spiritual healer, and performative preacher. For example, she exclaims,

> I am the chosen one.
> I am the chosen, to polish a letter of the
>
> longest ever and ever sentence.
> A humongous line with a defined period at the
>
> end of its own beginning.
> The mother of all syntaxes starts there.
> There, where it really all started.

Here Báez uses the rhetoric of prophecy and mediumship, calling herself the "chosen one" in order to say that she has been designated by a higher authority to work in the mediating realm of language. Suggesting that she is one of many participants in the collective performance of liturgical syntax, Báez will contribute by polishing "a letter" from an interminable sentence. She defines this "longest ever and ever sentence" through paradox typical of her work and the spiritual cosmologies discussed in this book. Báez says that it is terminal, marked off by a period. However, the grammatical sign of finitude appears back at the sentence's own beginning, creating a sense of infinite continuation. This construction of language as endless via circularity echoes the African-derived religious temporalities that abound in *Bedward, Myal, Louisiana, Changó*, and *Beloved*. She continues to describe this cosmology of an originating syntax in increasingly democratic terms, saying, "Everyone alive and living in this world holds a/letter, not the initial of their name printed and/signed in vital records." In each of these textual iterations of self, Báez invites the audience members (including readers) to consider their own participatory roles in "the gift. The present. Full of past and future." For Báez community requires the recognition of one's own integral subjectivity in ever-expanding circles of articulation and reception.

In each of the literary works included in this book, spiritual power and subsequent sociopolitical power arise via embodied acts of performance and reception like those described and staged by Shange and Báez. Conversely, the authors studied throughout *The Sacred Act of Reading* often depict spiritual encounters far less tender and hopeful than the ones described here. In fact, spiritual and religious phenomena such as spirit possession and prophetic revelation reveal interpretation to be at once capable of both healing and violence, operating through the physical and symbolic registers of subject and community formation. Clearly, religious experiences such as these can allow for socially and politically dispossessed characters (and their audiences) to imagine a world outside of the subjugating political systems marked by colonialism and racism. At the same time, these same spiritual imaginings often warn of a volatile undercurrent that lurks beneath all narratives of power. In particular, *Changó, The Biggest Badass* and *Dream on Monkey Mountain* (works that feature "chosen" mediums and prophets like Báez) illustrate how spiritually inspired quests for social and political justice can result in vengeful violence. In every chapter of this book, I have endeavored to respect the complexity of these literary works by confronting the ethical quandaries and contradictions present in each of these religious stories. From protagonist preachers who become dangerously enraptured with their own cults of personality to the healing ceremonies that require further violations of female bodies to the gory spiritual battles that vanquish foes, the religious characters and events in these texts are, like Báez, never just one thing.

Perhaps the most dangerous and thrilling constellations of spiritual imaginings presented in these texts are those that threaten to upset the New World's predominant epistemologies (exemplified in chapters 2 and 4). Over the course of this book I have shown how Afro-diasporic authors use embodied spiritual events to challenge the methods by which we have learned to determine who and what is truly human and divine. Like all of the characters discussed in this book, the Afro-diasporic women in Shange's *For Colored Girls* must reconcile with the long histories of physical and symbolic subjugation and dehumanization that African-descended communities, and particularly black women, still encounter. Michelle Cliff cites the final line of Shange's choreopoem, "i found god in myself & i loved her/i loved her fiercely," in order to contend that "there is an organic connection between African and Afro-American and Afro-Caribbean ideas and people" (8). Cliff explains that Shange's "statement and what the words represent are intrinsic to the body of African philosophy that Afro-American people have inherited, whether mixed with western philosophy and religion or not, whether they are conscious of their heritage or not" (7–8). Cliff uses the historical and political figures of Nanny of the Maroons, Rosa Parks, and Harriet Tubman to insist that African-derived spiritual beliefs such as "the divinity of Black women, of all life" and "the connection of beings across generations and the mystery inherent in all creation and creative acts," or "what the Yoruba call *áshe, the power to make-things-happen,*" have always been inextricably tied to social and political power in the New World (7, 9). Indeed, the texts studied throughout this project have demonstrated that Afro-diasporic religious practices and philosophies are integral to conceptualizing secular and divine personhoods and collectivities within oppressive societal structures in an array of creative works.

Shange describes her writing process as "a visceral thing," a phrase exemplified by *For Colored Girls Who Have Considered Suicide*'s highly physical content. The choreopoem features lengthy passages devoted to descriptions of sexual trauma and abortion and contains stage directions for dances, children's games, and the final group circle ("Interview with Ntozake Shange," 137). In Shange's poetic performance text, which Sarah Mahurin describes as "a theatre of the physical" (330), the body and spirit are linked, echoing the conceptual connections that I have shown operate in Brodber, Hopkinson, Zapata Olivella, and Morrison's novels. In constructing a new understanding of the body by situating it within both physical and metaphysical registers of knowledge, these authors present alternative epistemologies of the human. Put simply, they construct a new *understanding of the body* as well as a new *body of understanding*. Recouping both bodies is central to a decolonizing process. As De Ferrari writes, "It was not possible for the slave to regain possession of his or her own body without the prior full integration of the black body into the human race at an epistemological level" (5). Paradoxically, it is often through spiritual and bodily experiences of external possession or revelation by which the characters in the texts I study here come to question colonial epistemologies of humanity (and their communities' supposed less-than-human status). These encounters with spiritual forces cause the characters to abandon epistemological certainty, which ultimately allows them to understand themselves as both human *and* spiritual agents inextricably connected to a far more expansive sacred community. In every single text I study throughout this book, the religious and spiritual events that invite characters to reflect on their preexisting methods of interpreting reality also invite that text's readers to pause and consider how their understandings of the world are similarly shaped by embodied performances of literary interpretation.

This project is, above all else, a love letter to reading literature. An especially scholarly love letter, *The Sacred Act of Reading* invokes the academic names, vocabularies, and epistemologies that have become my intellectual home while developing and composing this monograph, but which can only go so far in articulating the value of reading these authors and works. In fact, this academic study of "spirituality, performance, and power in the Afro-diasporic Americas" seeks to demonstrate the limitations of its own genre's epistemological genealogy. This book is but one contribution to a wider interpretive community. Namely, it shows how Afro-diasporic authors have been using concepts such as spirituality to theorize the workings of sociopolitical power and to present alternative formulations of subjectivity and community that operate both within and outside of the parameters of Western discourse.

We can no longer ignore the extent to which our profession is indebted to the intellectual methodologies that aided and abetted the colonialism, targeted inequity, patriarchy, and white supremacy that have shaped this "New World." In response, I situate *The Sacred Act of Reading* within a body of scholarship that seeks to decolonize the academy. I offer it to a community of scholars who are integrating nontraditional, historically marginalized, and even intellectually discriminated-against sources and voices within the specialized framework of academic publications. I have detailed just a few of the ways in which Afro-diasporic authors have long been using tactics I now associate with performative textual hermeneutics to imagine the potential contours of such intellectual decolonization. These authors are asking: How can we think beyond schemas that for centuries have served to establish the humanity of some at the expense of others? How might we learn to think differently within, but more importantly, *beyond* restricted notions of humanity, knowledge, and belonging? In performances and written works, Afro-diasporic individuals have long put voice to the questions that have left so many of us tongue-tied while standing before our students and colleagues.[2]

The Sacred Act of Reading uses the interpretive tools of literary studies and performance to take up Michelle Cliff's call to comparatively read Afro-diasporic arts in the New World, to ponder "the idea of art, the purpose of art, what constitutes a work of art, why art is made, art as an expression of certain theological principles, certain philosophical principles" (16). I hope that this book will serve to honor and build on the robust archives of scholarly, creative, and religious writings by and about Afro-diasporic communities. By approaching these written, literary works by means of a set of hermeneutical practices rooted in religious and performance traditions, *The Sacred Act of Reading* provides several theoretical and methodological avenues for sustained, critical engagement with Afro-diasporic authors and traditions within the academy and beyond. This monograph contributes to the decolonial project. By becoming "all ears" to the spiritual ways of knowing reality presented in these texts, I hope to have emulated the hermeneutics of engaged surrender personified by *Louisiana*'s divinely humbled academic, Ella Townsend. These works have moved and humbled me.

When literature moves us, it uses language to communicate that which exceeds its own linguistic form. I believe that the sacred resides in that movement, revealing itself through the relational dance of interpretation. When reading becomes a sacred act, what was once solitary is divinely shared, even if only for a moment, even if that moment leaves the reader with a familiar ache of loneliness and grief. Every one of the texts in this project stimulates interpretive pain and pleasure as it moves the reader with a spark of truth—the truth of beauty, of cruelty, of suffering, and of healing. Underpinning each of these truths is the recognition of the sacred that manifests in the reader's movements between self and wider world. We are all prophets, mediums, preachers, and healers. Or as Josefina Báez professes, "I am the chosen one./And so are you."

Notes

Introduction

1. Throughout this manuscript, I commonly invoke the prefix "Afro-" to distinguish the African lineage and racialization of authors, communities, and characters. Because the experiences of racial difference and African-derived philosophies and spiritual practices are key to this project, it is important that race and cultural heritage are considered in my analysis. I also capitalize the term *Black* to describe movements of racial identity when crucial to interpretation, as well as when the term is explicitly employed by non-US authors. I have chosen to not capitalize *white* when referring to the racial movements of white supremacy. Following the current trends in scholarship, I use the lower-cased term *black* when describing the racial identity of individual people. When available, I adhere to the terminology of identification employed by the author or works under discussion.

2. It is impossible to entirely disentangle the definitions of politics, society, culture, religion, and spirituality, particularly regarding Black religious practices in the New World. The imbrication of politics and religion in the Afro-diasporic Americas is evidenced in the pivotal role that Candomblé temples play for Brazilian politicians and in François Duvalier's intimidating uses of Vodou images; see Olupona, *African Religions,* 111. For an overview of methods in religious studies, see Hinnells, *Routledge Companion to the Study of Religion.*

3. In *Playing in the Dark,* Toni Morrison contends that in US literature these humanistic values have often been promoted through a representational rejection of "Africanness" in order to "place white masculine authority over racialized others" (45). Alexander Weheliye writes in *Habeas Viscus* that "resistance and agency . . . as explanatory tools . . . have a tendency to blind us, whether through strenuous denials or exalted celebrations of their existence, to the manifold occurrences of freedom in zones of indistinction" (2). This study of power draws heavily on the work of Weheliye as well as from Lisa Lowe's *Intimacies of Four Continents.*

4. For example, Peggy Phelan coins the term "performative writing" in order to posit a method of writing that intends to "enact the affective force of the performance event again" (11). Unlike Phelan's performative writing, which works to textually re-present a performed event, my method of interpreting texts via performance and performativity considers the ways that written works evoke meaning through methods of performance; see Phelan, *Mourning Sex*.

5. See, for example, Hurston, *Tell My Horse, Mules and Men,* and *Sanctified Church*; Harris, "History, Fable and Myth in the Caribbean"; and Ortiz, *Cuban Counterpoint.* Considered the "father" of Afro-Cuban ethnography, Fernando Ortiz's work presents several problems for those working on anthropology and theology today. Michelle Gonzalez writes, "Not only did he initially study Afro-Cuban culture in order to eradicate it, but his hermeneutic as a criminologist hampered his efforts" (*Afro-Cuban Theology,* 127). This led some scholars, including Jorge Castellanos, to call his approach inherently racist; see chapter 7 in *Afro-Cuban Theology.* More recently, Paget Henry's philosophical history of the Caribbean, *Caliban's Reason,* demonstrates the inextricable links between discourse and tradition when tracing the complex patterns of intellectual, religious, and cultural thought in the context of the Afro-diasporic Americas.

6. Unlike Jeannine Murray-Román, who purposefully chose "texts which are marked by a significant distance between performance and literature" for her study of the Fanonian circle in *Performance and Personhood in Caribbean Literature,* I have chosen to engage with texts that theorize meaning-making by establishing fluid boundaries between performance and literature.

7. Anthropological and performance-focused cultural studies by scholars such as Victor Turner, Joseph Roach, and Ngũgĩ wa Thiong'o helped pave the way for performance-focused scholarship in the academy. See Roach, *Cities of the Dead;* Thiong'o, "Notes Towards a Performance Theory of Orature"; and Turner, *Ritual Process.* At the same time, looking beyond the rigid parameters of the visual text in order to discover literary and philosophical meaning has long been a crucial part of Afro-diasporic studies, as exemplified by the works of Houston Baker and Carolyn Cooper. See Cooper, *Noises in the Blood;* and Baker, *Blues, Ideology, and Afro-American Literature.*

8. See Benedicty-Kokken, *Spirit Possession;* De Ferrari, *Vulnerable States;* Aching, *Masking and Power;* and Murray-Román, *Performance and Personhood.* In addition, Katherine Clay Bassard, Tuire Valkeakari, and Kameelah L. Martin have incorporated archival materials, theories, and historical research related to performance in their studies of spirituality and religion in African American literature. See chapter 4, "Transforming the Word, Performing Rememory," in Valkeakari, *Religious Idiom*; Bassard, *Transforming Scriptures* and *Spiritual Interrogations*; and Martin, *Conjuring Moments.*

9. See, for example, J. Butler, *Excitable Speech;* and Derrida, "Signature, Event, Context."

10. Kimberly Benston theorizes this form of ritual participation as *methexis* in African American theatrical experiments; see *Performing Blackness*.

11. There are many available spellings for "Vodou," including "Vodoo," "Vodoun," etc. I use the spelling "Vodou," except when quoting other authors, because this version is used most often by recent religious scholars including Nathaniel Samuel Murrell, Yvonne Daniel, and Patrick Bellegarde-Smith. I am compelled to quote Alessandra Benedicty-Kokken on this note: "To take account of an intellectual history of possession is to note that 'Voodoo,' 'Vaudou,' 'Vodou' are themselves products not only of languages, but of the epistemologies of the scholarly world, which cannot free itself from the compulsion to name." *Spirit Possession*, 2.

12. See Landesman, *Introduction to Epistemology*.

13. Enlightenment philosophies that privilege reason and presume objectivity are also critiqued by postcolonial scholars Aimé Césaire, in *Discourse on Colonialism*, and Édouard Glissant, in *Poetics of Relation*.

14. While the linguistic functions of Legba manifest throughout this book, the specific god (*loa/lwa* in Haitian Vodou or *oricha* in Santería) explicitly appears in chapters 2 and 3. In *Changó, The Biggest Badass*, Legba is referred to as Elegba, and in *Brown Girl in the Ring*, the god is named Legbara. Russell adds, "For the Fon of Benin, Esu/Eshu's corrollary is Legba. Eshu and Legba are often interchangeably used; they serve ostensibly the same function in relation to discourse" (*Legba's Crossing*, 9). Dianne Stewart also presents Legba for theological hermeneutics "that epitomizes the Word of the African Ancestors." *Three Eyes for the Journey*, 227.

15. I appreciate M. Shawn Copeland's definition of practice, which draws from the work of Theodore R. Schatzki. Copeland writes: "Practice is the performance of certain words or actions through which something is achieved. Religious practices are complex integrative practices: linked performances . . . joined by cognitive, prescriptive, and affective structures that seek certain inner dispositions . . . or ends." "African American Religious Experience," 48.

16. See Channette Romero's introduction to *Activism and the American Novel* as an example of how a contemporary literary scholar can reject historical denigrations of "people of color's understandings of the sacred" while still distinguishing between religious and spiritual practices (2). Also see Valkeakari, *Religious Idiom*, 7.

17. While spiritual phenomena in these texts often occur outside the bounds of traditional religious institutions and hierarchies, the vocabulary the authors employ for communicating such experiences of the divine in the physical world still draw heavily from religious discourse. For this reason, *The Sacred Act of Reading* uses the terms "religious" and "spiritual" interchangeably except when it is necessary to clarify distinctions between the spiritual experience and its institutional frameworks. In chapter 3, for example, I carefully distinguish between

the religious terminology of spiritual possession derived from the religions of Haitian Vodou and Jamaican Obeah and the spiritual (but *not* religious) concepts of zombification and sorcery that are popular in Caribbean mythologies but are overwhelmingly discounted by respected practitioners.

18. I choose to capitalize each of these religious traditions throughout this publication except when quoting other authors.

19. Geertz was influenced by his predecessors Max Weber, Emile Durkheim, and Franz Boas, the latter of whose anthropological principle of cultural relevance was crucial to the later religious ethnography of Zora Neale Hurston discussed in chapter 1. Copeland writes that Talal Asad, Anthony Pinn, James Noel, Dianne Stewart Diakité, and Tracey Hucks have all noted that Geertz's definition of religion "has allowed overweening influence of Christianity with its stress on cognitive assent rather than ceremony or ritual or practices." "African American Religious Experience," 46.

20. See Valkeakari, *Religious Idiom*; Ryan, *Spirituality as Ideology*; James Coleman, *Faithful Visions*; and Bassard, *Transforming Scriptures* and *Spiritual Interrogations*.

21. Also see Jennings, *Toni Morrison and the Idea of Africa;* Whitted, *"A God of Justice?"*; and Romero, *Activism and the American Novel*.

22. See Raboteau, *Canaan Land*. For a variety of historical overviews, see West and Glaude's edited volume, *African American Religious Thought*. Georgetown University's creation of the Working Group on Slavery, Memory, and Reconciliation (2015) and their steps toward reparations for Jesuit involvement in the slave trade (2016) attest to the growing acknowledgment of the Catholic Church's monetary investments in the enslavement and oppression of Africans and African-descended people across the New World.

23. Scholar of African religions Jacob Olupona writes, "Africans were pronounced incapable of producing meaningful, sophisticated religious traditions and were said to lack 'true knowledge' of a Supreme God" (*African Religions,* xx).

24. See the appendix to Douglass's *Narrative in the Life of Fredrick Douglass* (86–89). For an in-depth historical analysis of US investments in both Christianity and slavery, see Irons, *Origins of Proslavery Christianity*. Also see T. Johnson, "Reason in African American Theology," 102.

25. Joseph Murphy cautions any readers who encounter colonial European texts about Afro-diasporic—and particularly Afro-Caribbean—religious practices to recognize that their authors perceived such practice not only as disruptions for European masters but also as "a direct threat to these white authorities." *Working the Spirit,* 121.

26. The concomitance of African and Western religious life was enforced by the changing modes of worship in the two Great Awakenings, which allowed black Americans a more recognizable way of participating in Christian theology.

27. Anthropology is a particularly vexed field for Afro-diasporic religious studies because it has been both crucial for documenting certain practices yet

steeped in a lineage of Western discourse that treats African-derived religion as exotic and even primitive. See Murrell, *Afro-Caribbean Religions;* Warner-Lewis, *Central Africa in the Caribbean*; and L. Barrett, *Soul Force.*

28. Thanks largely to Talal Asad's scholarship on the myth of secularization in higher education, there is increasing academic interest in interrogating terms such as "religion" and "spirituality" in literary studies, but this momentum did not generally manifest in theologically informed engagements with Afro-diasporic religions; see Asad, *Formations of the Secular.* This predominance of Christianity, and to a lesser extent Judaism and Islam, in literary criticism reflects the cultural demographics of the US academy and moreover appears to make logical sense considering that, like literary studies, these Abrahamic religions are text-centric. And yet there is no paucity of scholarship on Greek oral traditions, for example.

29. See Olmos and Paravisini-Gebert, *Healing Cultures;* Olmos and Paravisini-Gebert, *Creole Religions of the Caribbean* and *Sacred Possessions*; and Benedicty-Kokken, *Spirit Possession.*

30. See Lincoln and Mamiya, *Black Church;* and Anderson, *Beyond Ontological Blackness* and *Creative Exchange.* For examples of Womanist scholarship, see Douglas, *Black Christ*; and Cannon, *Black Womanist Ethics.* African American theologians, including Dwight Hopkins and George Cummings, similarly performed hermeneutical readings of slave narratives in order to glean a "theological interpretation of their experience" and create ancestral resources for the Black church. *Cut Loose Your Stammering Tongue*, 98.

31. For examples of the various approaches to African-derived religious action, see the African American works by Zora Neale Hurston and Toni Morrison, which are set in the US South and Midwest and evidence the cultural resonances of African traditions that permeate African American culture and literature. On the one hand, as La Vinia Deloise Jennings points out in *Toni Morrison and the Idea of Africa,* Africa "has more than a thousand cultural groups whose traditions and beliefs are tribal and not universal," and so it is crucial to resist the "notion of a monolithic 'African worldview'" when discussing African American (and I would add Afro-diasporic) hemispheric literature (1). At the same time, Jennings cites Gay Wilentz to argue that "a collective concept is not impractical" when discussing Afro-diasporic literature in the Americas because this tradition arose from the historical intermingling of West and Central African cultures and traditions over centuries, resulting in a "worldview alternative taken from many African civilizations" (2); see Wilentz, "African-Based Reading of *Sula.*" Derek Walcott, whose work I consider in chapters 3 and 4, is also widely lauded for his innovative approach to the Western canon, but he too wrote and spoke about his struggles to develop a distinctly "West Indian" theatre that could acknowledge the importance of African traditions in the Caribbean without claiming cultural possession or even a complete understanding of these practices and philosophies. "What the Twilight Says," 8.

1. "You Preached!"

1. For a general history of religion among African Americans and particularly the development of African American Protestantism, see Raboteau's *Canaan Land*.

2. The latter phrase is meant to play on J. L. Austin's sentence regarding performatives: "To *say* something is to *do* something." *How to Do Things with Words*, 12.

3. There is some debate about whether Turner's conception of "ritual," which invokes experiences of communitas, is an inherently conservative phenomenon. Bobby Alexander uses Turner's work to study ritual possession in the African American Pentecostal church, writing that although ritual creates "catharsis," which can diffuse hostility toward the structural status quo, it also "makes possible more direct and egalitarian exchanges (*communitas*)," which are "an implicit criticism" of those structures ("Correcting Misinterpretations," 21). Therefore, for some religious anthropologists catharsis and communitas create opposing relationships toward structure. In this chapter I conceptualize the liturgical rituals in Hurston's and Morrison's work as both maintaining and challenging (and potentially transforming) existing institutional structures through collective performative experiences.

4. No historical information has been found on Rev. C. C. Lovelace, but he may be, like the fictional preachers Hurston creates, an itinerant evangelical preacher, which would mean that he likely delivered this sermon several times in different church congregations. It would be enlightening to know if Hurston managed to hear Lovelace perform this sermon several times, considering how that would appropriately preface her decision to perform it several times as well.

5. No original textual or audio version of Lovelace's sermon is known to exist. Eric Sundquist notes that at the time Hurston recorded it, African American sermons were being included on "race records." "The Drum with the Man Skin," in *Hammers of Creation*, 59.

6. In a letter to James Weldon Johnson from May 8, 1934, Hurston writes, "It just seems that he is unwilling to believe that a Negro preacher could have so much poetry in him. When you and I (who seem to be the only ones even among Negroes who recognize the barbaric poetry in their sermons) know that there are hundreds of preachers who are equaling that sermon weekly. He does not know that merely being a good man is not enough to hold a Negro preacher in an important charge. He must also be an artist. He must be both a poet and an actor of a very high order, and then he must have the voice and figure. He does not realize or is unwilling to admit that the light that shone from *God's Trombone* [sic] was handed to you, as was the sermon to me in *Jonah's Gourd Vine*." Kaplan, *Hurston: Life in Letters*, 302.

7. Unlike Hurston's re-production of Lovelace's sermon in *Jonah's Gourd Vine*, it appears that Jelliffe never recontextualized Hurston's play without giving her coauthor credit.

8. Perhaps one of Hurston's most documented theatrical collaborations was the play *Mule Bone*, which she developed in 1930 with Langston Hughes; like *Sermon in the Valley*, it was also created for Rowena Jelliffe at the Karamu House. Misunderstandings regarding the publication of *Mule Bone* ultimately led to the disintegration of Hurston and Hughes's friendship. The paratextual materials included with the Harper Perennial publication of this play synthesize the existing knowledge about the falling out with introductions by Henry L. Gates and George Houston Bass and excerpts from Robert E. Hemenway's biography of Hurston, *Zora Neale Hurston*; Hughes's autobiography *The Big Sea*; and Arnold Rampersand's biography *Life of Langston Hughes*.

9. The biblical passages quoted here and throughout are taken from David Norton's version of the King James Bible (*The Bible: King James Version with the Apocrypha* [London: Penguin, 2006]). For example, the Lovelace text references Jesus's crucifixion story with Matthew 27:46 and Mark 15:34 (themselves referencing Psalm 22:1), with "My God, my God! Why hast thou forsaken me?"; John 19:30, "It is finished"; and Matthew 27:54, "Surely this is the Son of God."

10. The preacher then references the 53rd chapter of Isaiah as well as the apostle Peter, specifically Peter 1:19–20, to argue that Jesus was fated to be sacrificed for humanity's sins before the beginning of the world.

11. For more on the Church of God in Christ, see Anthea Butler's examination of women's religious and social lives in the African American Pentecostal denomination, *Women in the Church of God in Christ*.

12. I particularly appreciate Eric Sundquist's description of *Jonah's Gourd Vine* as "a palimpsest of autobiographical and cultural rumination that not only fuses her family history to fieldwork and theory but, in fact, self-consciously extends the attack on the boundary between ethnology and narrative that she had begun in *Mules and Men* (1935), which was written before but published after *Jonah's Gourd Vine*." *Hammers of Creation*, 51.

13. Rhythm is not only a crucial aspect of the Sanctified Church, but it also extends to homiletic practices across a range of African American Christian institutions. Dolan Hubbard identifies how African American literature invokes preaching practices through "the use of rhythmical language, role playing, repetition, pauses and stammers." *Sermon and the African American*, 34.

14. Hurston also writes extensively on "bearing up" in "Spirituals and Neo-Spirituals": "Chants and hums are not used indiscriminately as it would appear to a casual listener. They have a definite place and time. They are used to 'bear up' the speaker. As Mama Jane of Second Zion Baptist Church, New Orleans, explained to me: 'What point they come out on, you bear 'em up,'" *Folklore Writings*, 82.

15. Analyzing Hurston's focus on eliciting an oral experience for the white and black readers of her literature is a complex manoeuvre. As Katherine Bassard notes, in the collection of works that became *The Sanctified Church* Hurston discusses a "folk belief" about transferring "virtue" from hearing to sight. Bassard writes, "Hurston's narrative of folk cure poses orality as an antidote to a

subjectivity othered by a racializing specularity" (*Spiritual Interrogations*, 133). In this case, communicating that orality allows Hurston to insist that her readers encounter an alternative sensorial experience that may lead to a recognition of African American subjectivity beyond the limiting parameters that fall under the visual regimes of whiteness. At the same time, the fact that Hurston communicates that orality through *visual* script may again place the African American community under the "racializing specularity" that has long served to diminish Black subjectivity; see chapter 7, "Performing Community," in *Spiritual Interrogations*.

16. Matthew 26:38 reads: "Then saith he unto them, My soul is exceeding sorrowful, even unto death: tarry ye here, and watch with me."

17. The preacher's linguistic complexity here brings to mind James Weldon Johnson's contention that African American folk preachers "were all saturated with the sublime phraseology of the Hebrew prophets and steeped in the idioms of King James English, so when they preached and warmed to their work, they spoke another language, a language far removed from traditional Negro dialect." Qtd. in Sundquist, *Hammers of Creation*, 49.

18. Note that in the anthology and novel versions, Hurston follows up both "monasters" and "oarus" with the "standard" versions in parentheses, indicating that she treats her novel as an opportunity for ethnographic linguistic information.

19. In this discussion of Hurston's sermons, Valkeakari cites the Lovelace sermon as it appears in *Jonah's Gourd Vine* along with a traveling preacher's sermon in the 1935 ethnography *Mules and Men*; see *Religious Idiom*, 35.

20. In *Mules and Men* Hurston's glossary entry on the preacher's breath is almost identical to that in *Jonah's Gourd Vine*, save one line that reads, "The 'hah' is a breathing device, done rhythmically to punctuate the lines" (307).

21. Hurston also writes in "Spirituals and Neo-Spirituals": "It is said of a popular preacher, 'He's got a good straining voice'" (82). Furthermore, in *Mules and Men* she references a preacher who fails to convert his congregation despite his reputation as a man with a good straining voice.

22. See Dubey, "Politics of Genre in *Beloved*," 103–23.

23. This moment also predicts the simultaneous material and physical experiences of colonial indoctrination Ella O'Grady undergoes at the hands of a "schoolteacher" in Erna Brodber's novel *Myal*, which I discuss in chapter 3.

24. Bärbel Höttges claims that Morrison "employs an extended form of orality which openly and simultaneously combines written and oral elements," a practice he states qualifies *Beloved* as a syncretic, specifically African American text. "Written Sounds and Spoken Letters," 15.

25. See Baker-Fletcher, *A Singing Something*.

26. See Genovese, *Roll, Jordan, Roll*; and Higginbotham, *In the Matter of Color*.

27. Dolan Hubbard explains, "Black people came to view white oppression as Egyptian slavery" (*Sermon and the African American*, 3). This hermeneutical

practice is also a tenet of Afro-Christian religions in the Caribbean, including Revival Zion (discussed in chapter 2) and Rastafari (discussed in chapter 4).

28. See Mbiti, *African Religions and Philosophy;* and Young, *Pan-African Theology.*

29. I employ the term *muntu* here as it appears in African American Christian scholarship and appreciate the ways in which it ties into the discussion in the next chapter of Manuel Zapata Olivella's *Changó, The Biggest Badass.*

30. The importance of quiet, rhythmic heartbeats permeates *Beloved,* often as a precursor to moments of sound, such as when Beloved begins singing the song only Sethe's children could know. It should be noted that it is not possible to control and manipulate the heartbeat as easily as it is possible to affect the breath.

31. Carolyn A. Mitchell, who writes a particularly Christian-focused reading of Morrison's text, also compares Baby Suggs to Christ, and says that Baby Suggs's preaching praxis inspires those present to experience "the wildness of the divine," Vincent Harding's "definitive explanation of liberation spirituality." "I Love to Tell the Story," 35.

32. Rubery notes that this began long before it was common practice to have authors narrate recordings.

33. African American voice actress Ruby Dee has recorded audio versions of Hurston's *Mules and Men* and *Their Eyes Were Watching God,* for which she adopts a stylized accent that compliments the dialect Hurston uses in her text. Dee also recorded a version of Morrison's *The Bluest Eye* in 2000.

34. Morrison never narrates in a style that includes syntax or phonetic spellings associated with African American Vernacular English, and she minimally incorporates these elements in her written dialogue. It should be noted that the surprise general audiences have when encountering her narratorial voice may partly result from listeners' generalizations (often grounded in cultural denigrations) about Black speech and literature.

35. One of the well-known aspects of the print version of *Beloved* is its confusing, rapid shifts in narrators and chronological time with no more indication than a break between paragraphs.

36. See Levine, *Black Culture and Black Consciousness,* 26.

2. The Hermeneutics of Spirit Possession

1. In the context in which Patrick Bellegarde-Smith is describing trance, the possessing agent is a deity, or *lwa/loa,* in Vodou's Haitian Kreyol. See also Murrell, *Afro-Caribbean Religions,* 74.

2. For most of the past century, written studies of spirit possession have been the purview of academically trained anthropologists and ethnographers. These scholars' own relationships to their Eurocentric definitions of subjectivity, religion, epistemology, and social experience have naturally inflected the manner in which they discuss unfamiliar phenomena within non-Western geographies and

cultures. While we must not eschew the information provided in these studies, all must be taken with a giant grain of postcolonial salt. I emulate Benedicty-Kokken, Bellegarde-Smith, Erika Bourguignon, Stewart, Paul Johnson, Joseph Murphy, and Murrell by citing an array of studies on spirit possession while carefully resisting the urge to treat a Western lens as an authority. For examples of anthropological studies not referenced in the body of this chapter, see De Heusch, *Why Marry Her?;* and I. M. Lewis, *Ecstatic Religion.*

3. To retrace the scope of these formative tenets in Western philosophy would be beyond the parameters of this project. However, it is worth noting that the topics of internal versus external knowledge and individual subjectivity have been paramount in modern philosophy as it is studied in the English-, French-, Spanish-, and German-speaking academies (those associated with the rise of global imperialism) since the time of Descartes. The writings of and debates between thinkers such as Descartes, John Locke, and David Hume set the stage for ongoing conversations about the individual subject's capacity for epistemological inquiry, which was directly associated with the subject's rights to liberal humanist formulations of freedom. This particular genealogy of philosophical thought often approached the study of our own mental states (and the assumed differences therein with the study of the external world) through rationalist and empiricist modes. These modes of metaphysical philosophy also guided what Lisa Lowe calls the "liberal ways of understanding," which enabled those branches of "European political philosophy" to promote an economy of "affirmation" for certain subjects deemed capable of empiricist and rationalist thought and a coterminous economy of "forgetting" for those subjects (often Afro-diasporic colonial subjects like those studied here) "placed at a distance from 'the human.'" *Intimacies of Four Continents,* 3.

4. Alessandra Benedicty-Kokken notes that these studies on Haiti were informed by earlier writers such as Michel Leiris and Alfred Métraux. *Spirit Possession,* 2.

5. I have included Zapata-Olivella's original text in the body of the chapter to create the sense of constant translational activity for this analysis as well as to give Spanish-language readers the opportunity to check Tittler's choices.

6. The term "cultural translations" became popular in literary studies thanks to the work of Homi Bhabha in *The Location of Culture,* but the concept was also being developed in the realms of ethnography, anthropology, and sociology. See Hanks and Severi, "Translation Worlds," for an overview.

7. Pym adds, "The nineteenth-century development of hermeneutics was closely linked to ways of making sense of the Bible, especially in view of the growing scientific knowledge that contested literal readings of what was supposed to be God's word" (*Exploring Translation Theories,* 99). Clearly translation and interpretation become especially pressing questions regarding spiritual and religious matters.

8. Tittler's approach also speaks to the translational theories of Friedrich Schleiermacher on choosing "foreignizing" translations. Also see the work of French translator Antoine Berman, who advocates for translations that "recogniz[e] and receive the Other as Other." Pym, *Exploring Translation Theories*, 100.

9. For an in-depth look at Tittler's translation of Langston Hughes's "The Negro Speaks of Rivers," see Kutzinski's *Worlds of Langston Hughes*.

10. See Garavito, "En busca de una identidad cultural colombiana" (327); and Tillis, *Manuel Zapata Olivella*. Like Agne Brown, Angela Davis was a professor at an elite university, a leader in the Black Power movement, and an incarcerated activist. Davis was a well-known scholar and activist at University of California at Los Angeles when she was jailed (and later acquitted) for her suspected collaboration with the Soledad Brothers in 1971. *Changó*'s Agne Brown, on the other hand, is not treated as a scholar. Instead, she is considered a "preacher of a new cult" when she is convicted of "procuring and promiscuity," possibly connected to "depraved mysticism" (*Changó*, 317). Vera Kutzinski has noted Agne Brown's resonances with Zora Neale Hurston along with Angela Davis (*Worlds of Langston Hughes*, 51). While Hurston does appear later in the text as a character and Davis does not appear at all, the connection between Agne and Hurston makes sense considering that both studied anthropology and were associated with Columbia University.

11. Unfortunately, Robinson's *Who Translates?* does not consider the traditional African and African-derived spiritual paradigms that characterize the metaphysical world of *Changó*.

12. Zapata Olivella's use of the term "ekobio" also often takes on greater superhuman connotations throughout *Changó* because the deceased ekobios are seen as regular consultants in present life. When translating a letter from Zapata Olivella, Tittler also translates "ekobio" as "warrior" ("Catching the Spirit," 77). According to Mayra Montero, "ekobio" derives from Abakuá origin and is usually associated with "*ñáñigos,* the members of the Secret Abakuá Society . . . founded by Carabalí blacks in the nineteenth-century" Cuba. "Great Bonanza of the Antilles," 198.

13. Because Agne's visitors sometimes claim to embody the messenger-god Ngafúa, Agne is not the only "medium" or translator in this section, although she is the one with the most polyvalent role. In addition, the text creates a parallel between Agne's channeling of Changó and Sojourner Truth's statement that the Christian "Lord spoke through me" (372; el Señor habló por mí, 540). While Agne's character in *Changó*'s plotline is not always at the fore of the novel's final section (particularly in the chapters "The Thunderbolt Makers" and "The Civil War Gave Us Freedom"), her narrative position as the person who listens to and brings together these many historical messages remains consistent throughout.

14. There are numerous instances in the New Testament in which Jesus healed individuals suffering from possession. As Erika Bourguignon notes, "Such

cases of possession were both alterations of consciousness ('madmen') and alterations of physical state (for example: muteness, Matthew 12:22; and crippling, Luke 13:10–13)" (3). It should be noted that the Christian tradition is not limited to the demonic and/or negative view of possession articulated here by Reverend Roberts. Bourguignon writes that amongst twentieth-century Christian churches in the West there exists "the view that a spirit sent by God, or the Holy Ghost, may take over some aspect of the individual's functioning" (4). Erna Brodber's *Louisiana* (discussed later in this chapter) features glossolalia and prophetic utterances, signs that a type of possession trance that Pentacostal and neo-Pentacostal Christian churches (both Protestant and Catholic) call "baptism in the Spirit" is occurring at an individual and/or group level (4).

15. As Michel Foucault explains in the essay "Religious Deviations and Medical Knowledge," determining who and what possesses you demands an articulated system of interior life (50–57). Yet Agne must act as a kind of translator even in the case of her own interior life and story. Specifically, she must find ways to newly articulate the memories of her own childhood told to her by Ngafúa. The experience of mediumship through spirit possession (like the resistant translation) makes it impossible ever to rely on what Brazilian translation theorist Rosemary Arrojo would consider the illusion of stable meanings; see "Asymmetrical Relations of Power."

16. In his historical work on the episteme spirit possession, Paul C. Johnson writes, "Via the labor of the negative 'spirit possession' defined the rational, autonomous, self-possessed individual imagined as the foundation of the modern state, in canonical texts from Hobbes, Jean Bodin, Locke, Charles de Brosses, Hume, Kant, and many others, as those texts constructed the free individual and citizen against the backdrop of colonial horizons and slavery." "Genealogy of 'Spirit Possession,'" 398.

17. For a detailed analysis of the body's materialist role in subject-formation, see the introduction to Elizabeth Grosz's *Volatile Bodies*.

18. The previous publications of *Changó* were by the now-defunct Editorial Oveja Negra press in Bogotá, Colombia, in 1983 and 1985; a third edition published by Rei Andes Ltda. followed in 1992. This edition includes a scholarly introduction and touts itself as an "edición crítica." *Changó*, xi.

19. It is never explained why the editors of the framing letter write "sey" rather than "seh," which appears in the novel's chapter title. Perhaps it is an additional comment on the authorial privileges taken by editors.

20. This phrase "beyond the five senses" brings to mind Jean Strouse's oft-cited praise for the works of Toni Morrison, whose novel *Beloved* is discussed in the previous chapter; see Strouse, "Toni Morrison's Black Magic."

21. See Idowu, *African Traditional Religion*; and Pradel, *African Beliefs in the New World*.

22. In fact, Paul's epistle to the Colossians 1:12–13 in the King James Bible uses the term "translation" to refer to spiritual movement in a prayer of

thanksgiving. The prayer is "giving thanks to the Father, who has qualified you to share in the inheritance of the saints in the light. Who hath delivered us from the power of darkness, and hath translated *us* into the kingdom of his dear Son."

23. In "When Spirits Talk," Jenny Sharpe claims: "Ella's psychic abilities interject supernatural signification into the term *medium,* which alludes to the material used for recording data as well as a person who can communicate with the dead" (91). Sharpe's article considers how material archives in anthropology can communicate unacknowledged histories through affect. I agree that the recording machine becomes a supernatural medium in *Louisiana,* though I concentrate on the interpretive mediumship of Ella herself.

24. Zora Neale Hurston also appears in Zapata Olivella's "Ancestral Combatants" as an ethnographer. Her portrayal in the novel is pointedly negative, suggesting she perceives her fellow African Americans as objectified creatures of study.

25. During the early twentieth century, when this novel is set, there were no defined distinctions between the fields of anthropology and ethnography.

26. To discuss spirit possession and mediumship is to acknowledge that while the events of such phenomena may be material and specific for particular persons, the terms "spirit possession" and "mediumship" were adopted by anthropologists who wanted to group together disparate practices with a few common elements in order to study them; see Barrett and Cohen, "Conceptualizing Spirit Possession."

27. Dianne Stewart also uses the deity Legba to symbolize this hermeneutical strategy. In *Three Eyes for the Journey,* she refers to Legba as Esu.-Elegba, combining two of the god's common monikers.

28. In chapter 3 I explore at greater length the performative hermeneutics of aurality that Brodber invokes in her novels, specifically *Myal.*

29. The Nine-Nights tradition brings together Christian and West African theological elements of animation after death: namely Christological resurrection (the buried are expected to arise on the third night after death) and variations of the West African (especially Yoruban) understandings of interaction between the risen dead and the living, particularly with family. See Mbiti, *African Religions and Philosophy;* Pradel, *African Beliefs in the New World;* and Simpson, "Nine Night Ceremony in Jamaica."

30. Since many African-derived religious theologies in the Caribbean, particularly during times of enslavement, approach the afterlife through a lens of "repatriation," home may symbolize an abstract or physical idealized landscape of liberation, Stewart, *Three Eyes for the Journey,* 33.

31. As Alessandra Benedicty-Kokken points out, "The word 'possession' is not how Voudouyizans in the past generally have designated the experience of receiving another spirit, another subjectivity into their corporeal bodies." *Spirit Possession,* 1.

32. For example, Melville Herskovitz describes spirit possession among Haitians as "a psychological state wherein a displacement of personality occurs when the god 'comes into the head' of the worshipper. The individual thereupon is held to be the deity himself." Qtd. in Barrett and Cohen, "When Minds Migrate," 31.

33. In her 1998 review of *Louisiana,* Evelyn O'Callaghan connects the telepathic conversations throughout *Louisiana* to Brodber's academic interests in psychology and psychiatry, which she studied during a stint at McGill University; see "Cultural Penetration, Arts, and Sciences."

34. The stained glass connects to the metaphor of the spyglass that Ella carries around. Jenny Sharpe links that spyglass with Zora Neale Hurston's "spyglass of anthropology," though Brodber says she did not know about that reference. "Me and My Head-Hurting Fiction," 125.

3. The Spiritual Life of Power

A version of this analysis of *Myal* has appeared as "Sounding Out Spirit Thievery in Erna Brodber's *Myal,*" *Journal of West Indian Literature* 23, no. 1/2 (Nov. 2015): 106–20.

1. Rebecca Romdhani's article on zombifying shame in *Brown Girl in the Ring* cites Brodber's *Myal* as a companion narrative, though she does not explore this connection at length; see "Zombies Go to Toronto."

2. Zora Neale Hurston famously claimed to have met a zombified woman in her ethnography *Tell My Horse* (1938). Other anthropologists known for their work on zombies include Melville Herskovitz, *Life in a Haitian Valley* (1937); Maya Deren, *Divine Horsemen* (1983); and Wade Davis, *Passage of Darkness* (1988).

3. For more on zombies as myth, see Murrell, *Afro-Caribbean Religions,* 82. For more on healing function of African-derived religious practices in the Caribbean, see Stewart, *Three Eyes for the Journey,* 115.

4. I use the term "Myal" in this chapter to refer strictly to religious processes of spiritual healing, while I use "Obeah" to refer to the more expansive religious concept of both spirit-stealing and restoration. "Obeah" is a term used throughout the English-speaking Caribbean to express belief in "the power of spiritually endowed individuals, on behalf of the self or another, to manipulate spiritual forces to procure good or to activate evil or to counter evil" (Eastman and Warner-Lewis, "Forms of African Spirituality," 404). While scholars such as Stewart, Chevannes, Murrell, and Olmos do not agree on the dichotomy between bad Obeah and good Myal, I use Myal to specify healing in light of the way Brodber and Hopkinson deploy the terms in their novels. For more on Obeah, see Olmos and Paravisini-Gebert, *Creole Religions of the Caribbean,* 131.

5. See Herskovitz, *Dahomey,* 243. For more historical information on zombies and legends of white sorcery throughout the Caribbean, see Barrett, "African Religion in the Americas," 190–200; and Warner-Lewis, *Central Africa in the Caribbean,* 196. For those specifically about Jamaica, see Warner-Lewis, "Ancestral Factor in Jamaica's African Religions," 74.

6. Helen Tiffin uses *Myal* to read colonialism and decolonialism in Australia, evidencing the strength of Brodber's colonial message; see "Decolonization

and Audience." Catherine Nelson-McDermott suggests postcolonial critics use *Myal*'s plot as a guide for thinking beyond colonial dialectics and toward noncolonial spaces; see "Myal-ing Criticism."

7. Curdella Forbes says that *Myal* is "the first Anglophone Caribbean novel in which the ancestors as 'living, active dead' and the world of the spirit are not historical descriptors or tropes, but factual reality" ("Redeeming the Word," 7). Tabish Khair compares *Myal* to other religious textual works ("Correct[ing] Images,"), while June Roberts focuses largely on nontextual religious events in the novel as related to Caribbean folk traditions (*Reading Erna Brodber*). Melvin Rahming uses the novel to posit a methodological paradigm that he calls a "critical theory of spirit," which considers spirit and colonialism through consciousness ("Towards a Critical Theory of Spirit").

8. Nelson-McDermott notes that the story of Joseph found in Genesis 37:18–36 also gestures toward Rastafari beliefs that black men are reincarnations of ancient Israelites exiled to the West Indies just as Joseph was exiled to Egypt ("Myal-ing Criticism," 55). This connection is worth noting considering Brodber's membership in the Rastafari Mansion, Twelve Tribes of Israel. O'Callaghan, "Erna Brodber," 73.

9. For a historical and legal reading of "voice" as a complex signifier in debates of property, personhood, and intellectual property rights, see chapter 1 in Stephen Best's *The Fugitive's Properties*.

10. For more on Brodber's reading of Best, see Brodber, "Re-engineering Blackspace," 72.

11. Mass Levi is not directly identified as a practitioner of Obeah, and in fact his form of metaphysical thievery can be aligned with Haitian Vodou. I use the term "Obeah" here because of its Afro-Jamaican connections and Levi's use of a duppy, and to indicate not that his powers were negative but that they were focused on using Anita's spirit rather than her body. For an overview of scholarship delineating Obeah and Myal, see Olmos and Paravisini-Gebert, *Creole Religions*, 155–82.

12. Though Miss Gatha is not explicitly termed a Kumina queen, this association is suggested by the female leadership, the nature of the African drumming, and the novel's location in the southeastern parish of Saint Thomas in Jamaica; see Stewart, *Three Eyes for the Journey*, 130. Martina Urioste-Buschman points out the presence of the female "Mami Wata" deity in Miss Gatha's ceremony; see "Caribbean Allegory of Mami Wata."

13. Michelene Adams uses Anita's story to show how anyone with power can practice colonization; see "The Half Has Never Been Told," 116.

14. For more on the history of Obeah and British colonialism, see Paton, "Obeah Acts."

15. See Murrell, *Afro-Caribbean Religions*, 225–85.

16. It is not clear whether Levi's duppy is his own spiritual essence that he has separated from himself or that of another dead being in his power.

17. Sound (and its counterpart, silence) is also a prominent theme in Brodber's *Louisiana,* which features a recording machine. For two analyses that focus on sound, and particularly music, in the novel, see Pollard, "Writing Bridges of Sound"; and Meriwether, "The Blues Matrix."

18. For one example of Brodber's expansive interests in oral histories, see Brodber, "Oral Sources and a Creation of Social History."

19. The Native Baptist Reverend Musgrave Simpson is also Dan (the dog), who speaks with Willie about spirit thievery. The novel is not completely clear about how this character's dual (and perhaps multiple, considering "the dog") identities relate. For thoughtful discussions on this, see Kortenaar, "Foreign Possessions," 54; and Rahming, "Towards a Critical Theory of Spirit," 305.

20. Maydene associates Ella's demeanor with that displayed by her Afro-Jamaican husband when he was a child.

21. Before seeing the show, Ella had wanted her new husband to "show her how to fill the spaces he had created and give her too, a chance to create" (*Myal,* 82), suggesting that she sees procreation as an opportunity for agency and authorship.

22. Though Ella finally identifies Selwyn as a spirit thief, she has long been performing rituals of spiritual emptying at the hands of the colonial education system; see Adams, "The Half Has Never Been Told," 161.

23. Numerous scholars focus on Hopkinson's use of dialect and extratextual references to construct this Canadian ghetto community with residents of Haitian, Jamaican, Indian, and other origins. For example, see Gregory Rutledge's interview with Hopkinson, "Speaking in Tongues"; Alondra Nelson's interview with Hopkinson, "Making the Impossible Possible"; Ifeoma Nwankwo, "Review of *Brown Girl in the Ring,*" 307; and Monica Coleman, "Serving the Spirits." For sociological information on Afro-Caribbean immigration in 1960s Canada, see Daniel Yon, "Identity and Differences," 491.

24. Extensive botanical knowledge is a tenet of Central African influence in diasporic religions. See Stewart, *Three Eyes for the Journey,* 119; and Murrell, *Afro-Caribbean Religions,* 255. Usually this knowledge is associated with healing rather than harm.

25. For Obeah as "shadow-catching," see Murrell, *Afro-Caribbean Religions,* 255.

26. This "basic" method of zombification aligns with Haitian zombie lore described earlier in this chapter; see Hurston, *Tell My Horse;* Deren, *Divine Horsemen;* Davis, *Passage into Darkness;* and Dayan, *Haiti, History, and the Gods.*

27. The daughter of poet and actor Slade Hopkinson (whose work is featured in one of the epigraphs), Nalo Hopkinson was born in Jamaica and then moved between Jamaica, Trinidad, Guyana, and the United States until settling in Toronto in her adolescence; see Hopkinson's interview with Kellie Magnus, "Nalo Hopkinson: Writing is Believing."

28. Albert Olu Ashaolu also makes this connection for Walcott's *Ti-Jean and His Brothers* in "Allegory in *Ti-Jean and His Brothers.*"

29. Similarly, the Bolom (or unborn fetus) of Walcott's play is represented in *Brown Girl in the Ring* by Ti-Jeanne's ever-wailing infant, who, though alive, is only truly "born" after the trapped soul of Mami Gros-Jeanne's ex-lover is freed from Rudy's calabash and transferred into the baby's body.

30. See Foucault, *"Society Must Be Defended."*

31. For a sustained study of sexual violation and fetishization of white virginity in early twentieth-century zombie narratives, see Lizabeth Paravisini-Gebert, "Women Possessed." For a feminist reading of Hopkinson's work, see Giselle Anatol, "Feminist Reading of Soucouyants."

32. Wade Davis details several complicated procedures for ritually preparing a zombie poison, including one that called for gunpowder and the skin of a white toad (*Passage into Darkness*, 109). By connecting zombification with intravenous drugs that induce "nerve and muscle paralysant," Hopkinson sets up a blunt social commentary on the spirit-thieving effects of narcotics for poor urban populations of color (*Brown Girl*, 211). In addition to critiquing narcotic use, the materiality of the poisonous drug cocktail for zombification in *Brown Girl in the Ring* ensures that any discussion of soul imprisonment also requires consideration of the material body; the soul is then physical and psychological. A queen of a local secret society in Petite Rivière de Nippes in Haiti tells Davis that "there are dozens of powders. They walk in different ways. Some kill slowly, some give pain, others are silent . . . but it is the magic that makes you the master" (*Passage of Darkness*, 110). This "magic," Davis contends throughout his study of zombies, is like all ideological and spiritual systems: always both physical and psychological, material and abstract.

33. Sarah Olutola considers how Hopkinson's focus on Afro-Caribbean populations and cultures in the novel, indicative of the "the privileging of blackness in . . . Afrofuturist" literature, threatens to further dispossess Indigenous peoples by "engaging in the same violent erasure Du Bois decries, but against different bodies." "Blood, Soil, and Zombies," 76.

34. Uttley's campaign invokes Cora Diamond's alternative to vegetarian ethics, which promotes the concept of nonhuman animals as "fellows in mortality" ("Eating Meat," 474). Similarly, the campaign's focus on locating ethical responsibility for animals in their shared, eventual mortality can be productively compared to Anat Pick's theorization of posthumanism in *Creaturely Poetics*.

35. Romdhani connects the concept of service to the tenet of Ashe as explained to her by Vodou priest Ross Heaven; see "Zombies Go to Toronto," 75.

36. Murray-Román is drawing on the writings of Marlene NourbeSe Philip, who is herself discussing Carnival in this moment; see *Performance and Personhood*, 9.

37. James Coleman similarly uses the term "faithful vision" to denote "a belief in sacred, spiritual, and supernatural agency that saves the race and furthers the purposes of individuals who adhere to this agency." *Faithful Visions*, 4.

38. This is an adaptation of Victor Turner's concept of liminality in ritual; see *The Ritual Process*.

39. The phrase "a whole lot of shaking going on" appears to anachronistically reference the song "Whole Lotta Shakin' Goin' On," usually credited to songwriters Dave "Curlee" Williams and James Fay "Roy" Hall. The song was first recorded in 1955 by rhythm and blues singer Big Maybelle and then made popular by Jerry Lee Lewis in 1957. For more on the song's early history, see Tosches, *Unsung Heroes*.

40. Brodber published this chapter of *Myal* as the short story "The Spirit Thief" in *The Faber Book of Contemporary Short Stories*.

41. Described as the "water mother herself," Miss Gatha also represents the Kalunga line, that river in Kongo cosmologies (the geographic area where Kumina originated) between the realms.

4. Reading the Prophetic Stage

1. See West, *Prophesy Deliverance!* and *Keeping Faith*, the latter of which he describes as "an attempt at prophetic criticism" (xi); also see *Black Prophetic Fire*, with Christa Buschendorf.

2. For a particularly political text on prophets in the Caribbean, see Bogues *Black Heretics, Black Prophets*.

3. *Dream on Monkey Mountain* was written for the Trinidad Theatre Workshop and first produced at the Central Library Theatre in Toronto in 1967.

4. For example, the prophetic tradition put forward in Cornel West and Christa Buschendorf's *Black Prophetic Fire* features prominent African Americans such as Frederick Douglass, W. E. B. Du Bois, and Ella Baker. Often these leaders in the US context founded their prophetic discourse in the Christian tradition. A notable exception was Malcolm X, who founded his in the Nation of Islam.

5. In fact, there is a considerable contingency of contemporary religious figures, often women, who prophesy in the ecstatic tradition in the Caribbean. Media discourse on these figures often centers on the implications of spiritual labor for profit and the rise of what is often termed the "prosperity gospel" among Black churches throughout late capitalism.

6. See, for example, "Brainwashing" ([1970] 1973), "Rat Race" (1976), "Revolution" (1974), "Zion Train" (1980), and "African Herbsman" (1973). All of these songs were released with the Wailers, though Marley is considered to be the main lyricist. In 1981 Erna Brodber and John E. Greene published a study of Reggae and Rastafari, *Reggae and Cultural Identity in Jamaica*.

7. Blanchot wrote this during the Algerian War for Independence (1954–62), a conflict he publicly argued against, and penned the "Declaration on the Right to Insubordination in the War in Algeria," also known as "The Manifesto of the 121." While Blanchot does not directly discuss anticolonialism or his increasingly leftist politics here, his Old Testament–focused readings of prophetic speech acts in historical northern Africa invite connections with the growing Pan-African

Negritude movement. See Munro, "Shaping and Reshaping the Caribbean," which integrates these two thinkers' philosophies of prophecy.

8. In *Noises in the Blood* Carolyn Cooper connects this specifically with Jamaica, but I extend it to the broader Caribbean in Walcott's work.

9. A recent presentation on "Redeeming Alexander Bedward" (uploaded to YouTube in April 2016) followed a symbolic march in Kingston by the Jamaica Theological Seminary. The video and march evidence the persistence of Bedward's legacy as the "preacher who tried to fly" but fantastically failed. Interestingly, one of the presenters at this march reads from Veront M. Satchell's 2004 article on Bedward that I quote here ("Early Stirrings of Black Nationalism"). This myth of the flying preacher is likely buttressed by the song "Bedward the Flying Preacher"; see M. Williams, performed by Singers Players, feat. Prince Far I, on *Staggering Heights* (1983). Similarly, the liner notes for the 1954 Smithsonian Folkways recording of Louise Bennett performing the folksong about Bedward, "Dip Dem," describes him as a "religious maniac"; see Clyne, liner notes to *Jamaican Folk Songs Sung by Louise Bennett*.

10. Sylvia Wynter's novel *The Hills of Hebron* (1962), which was originally written as a radio drama for the BBC with the title *Under the Sun*, "fused together" "the whole idea of the legend of Prophet Bedward ... [and] the parallel legend of Prophet Jordan in Guayana"; see Wynter and Scott, "Re-Enchantment of Humanism," 134.

11. Intrigued by the discrepancies between the oral and written histories of Alexander Bedward, Marriott interviewed the small group of still-practicing Bedwardites at the commune Union Camp in 1957. While Marriott made efforts to "sympathize" with the Bedwardites who still venerated their culturally disgraced prophet, his description of the community as paranoid "simple folk" (139) and his complex dramatization of Alexander Bedward suggest that his interest in restaging the prophet's story was neither strictly complimentary nor derogatory. His interest in revisiting the rebellious prophet does speak to the influence of his father, whom Marriott describes as a "passionate nationalist with great pride in Jamaican heritage." *Bedward*, 138.

12. Bedward's conversion story as described by himself to Martha Beckwith in 1929 and by his contemporary and sympathizer A. A. Brooks in *A History of Bedwardism* (a text from which Marriott extensively quotes in his play) charts the archetypal trajectory that Ted Daniels identifies for prophets; see Brooks, *History of Bedwardism*. Bedward is first an adulterous sinner, outsider, and insignificant person who undergoes a crisis [his illness] that leads to a conversion. This realization of a divine calling leads to the subsequent "total and perhaps inexplicable change in [the prophet's] character" (Daniels, "Charters of Righteousness," 6). This typical conversion story for preachers and prophets is exemplified by Bedward's refusal of all "flesh" after receiving his mission from God, including sexual intimacy with his beleaguered wife. Marriott, *Bedward*, 147.

13. According to Satchell, this shift may have also been a conversion, since "prior to his ordination as a minister in the Jamaica Native Baptist Free Church, [Bedward] was a staunch member of the Wesleyan/ Methodist church." "Early Stirrings," 80.

14. Satchell writes that Bedward "must be considered a politico-religious nationalist, a political priest who, in a society marked by racial discrimination, economic oppression, and social and political inequality for the black majority, valiantly challenged white minority rule on behalf of the oppressed" ("Early Stirrings," 77). Ken Post argues, "Bedward's movement was not only a religious one: its doctrines had profound political implications as well. Based . . . on a rural population under economic pressure, it challenged established authority, both ecclesiastical and secular" (*Arise Ye Starvelings,* 7). Roscoe M. Pierson does connect the historical Bedward's fight for racial justice with his charismatic nature but does so in a more secular than religious context; see "Bedward and the Jamaica Native Baptist Church."

15. Marriott does not provide extensive reasoning for why he adapted his research on Bedward into a play rather than a journalistic piece, which was another one of his occupations. He writes, "As a very active member of the continuously busy Caribbean Thespians Dramatic Society . . . I made a successful debut as a playwright that year [*Public Mischief,* 1957]. I then added a Bedward drama to my to-do list" (*Bedward,* 139). Here it appears that Marriott chose to formulate Bedward as a drama because it was convenient given his successful participation in the dramatic society. And yet the script did not first appear in a dramatic society production but was produced in 1960 as the radio drama *The Shepherd,* and (according to Marriott) turned into a theatrical drama after the Jamaica Broadcasting Corporation's producer encouraged the playwright to do so. The theatrical drama premiered at the Ward Theater the same year, also as *The Shepherd,* later to be renamed *Bedward* in the published copy I study here. Though Marriott's choice of genre appears to have resulted from convenience and encouragement, the play *The Shepherd/Bedward* has likely been produced and staged the most of any of his dramas. *The Shepherd/ Bedward* has been performed in 1960 at the Ward Theatre in Kingston, Jamaica; in 1984 at the Little Theatre in Kingston; in 1993 again at the Ward Theatre; and in 2012 at the Karl Hendrickson Auditorium in Kingston. Clearly *Bedward* has had a relatively successful production history in Kingston. It is also clear that the play has not received as much, if any, of the same interest outside of Jamaica.

16. Marriott does have Shakespeare Woods legitimate Bedward's authority through prophesy, which varies from the historical accounts. Satchell explains that at an 1889 convention the Afro-American prophet Harrison "Shakespeare" Woods convened in St. Andrew Parish, he ordained twelve male parishioners (including Bedward) and a number of women to lead his congregation after he returned to the United States, also predicting that there would be one standout leader. "Early Stirrings," 80.

17. Ted Daniels is using Norman Cohn's writings on millennialism here; see Cohn, "Medieval Millenarianism."

18. Patrick E Bryan writes, "The Bedwardian movement was . . . a formal church with a theology defined. Contrary to the supposed Old Testament consciousness . . . there was a very strong 'New Testament' consciousness. Bedwardian theology accepted the Trinity." *The Jamaica People,* 42.

19. Charismatic authority like Bedward's almost always endangers the boundaries set by traditional (coercive) or rational (legal) authority. In the case of colonial Jamaica, traditional authority constitutes social structures of white supremacy and coercive forms of authority are the legal structures that maintain the British regime. For more on Max Weber's descriptions of legitimacy in authority structures, see "The Concept of Legitimate Order," in *Max Weber,* 12.

20. According to historical records, the district medical officer called to testify on Bedward's health claimed that he "was suffering from 'mental intoxication,' more from amentia than dementia. . . . That he spoke without thought like a little child" (Satchell, "Early Stirrings," 88). So we see Marriott's play staging this transition visible in the historical records—the attempt to cast Bedward not as an intentional (e.g., agential) powerful figure who desired to hurt, and was becoming successful at hurting, the colonial government but rather as a lunatic, a buffoon who was only dangerous because he so lacked the personal power to control his own thoughts and actions.

21. In addition to Bedward's constant citation of biblical scripture, Marriott signifies the character's connection to Judeo-Christian prophecy through implicit and explicit biblical allusions. For example, when Shakespeare Woods, the existing pastor of Bedward's church, prophesies about Bedward's rise to power, he riffs on the structure of the beatitudes as found in the Sermon on the Mount in the gospel of Matthew. Even Bedward's reticence to become a religious leader can be read as a gesture toward Old Testament prophet narratives, wherein several prophets, notably Jeremiah, recorded their reluctance and even strong resistance to this divine constraint. Even though Shakespeare Woods does not prophesy Bedward's godliness in Marriott's version, the drama still foreshadows the protagonist's messianic calling by creating connections between Woods and the New Testament zealot John the Baptist, through references to John's biblical declarations, his hermit existence, fasting, and residence in the "woods." After Bedward claims to embody Jesus's second coming, he leads a procession to Kingston, where he and his flock are ultimately trapped by police officers in the Half Way Tree Courthouse and jailed for holding an illegal manifestation. Marriott's stage directions indicate that "some of the women wave palm leaves" during the march, referencing Jesus's entry in Jerusalem (*Bedward,* 191). Parallels between Bedward and Jesus continue in the courtroom scenes, where Bedward responds to linguistic traps with rhetorical evasion, is mocked for his messianic visions, and is sarcastically called "the Lord and Master of August Town" (198).

22. Marriott found that historical documents revealed the validity of Bedward's "claim of race prejudice and fear of his influence" by the colonial legal authorities. *Bedward*, 138.

23. This brings to mind William J. Maxwell's recent monograph, *F.B. Eyes: How J. Edgar Hoover's Ghostreaders Framed African American Literature*, which mines the FBI's renderings of African American Literature while under Hoover's leadership. Maxwell recognizes the ways in which fear of Black political agitation also worked to frame contemporary reception of Black literature.

24. We should not elide the likely class differences between Bedward's agroproletariat audience and those who are likely to attend theatrical performances at the Kingston Ward Theatre.

25. Derrida argues that Antonin Artaud's search for a theatre of immediate and visceral experience in *The Theatre and Its Double* is pointless because theatre is grounded in repetition, or re-presentation. For Derrida, finding a pure presence in theatre would mean the end of theatre; see Derrida, "Theatre of Cruelty"; and Artaud, *Theater and Its Double*.

26. Benjamin is discussing Jewish constructions of time in "Theses on the Philosophy of History."

27. Giorgio Agamben's definition of messianic time arises from his distinctions between eschatological time and messianic time; see *The Time That Remains*. Thank you to Shelby Johnson for pointing me to these messianic theories. Alexander Weheliye critiques Agamben for eliding the histories of colonialism and racialization, particularly as those relate to the construction of "man" throughout his works; see *Habeas Viscus*.

28. Yair Lipschitz is using the ideas of Israeli director Yossi Yzraely, whose dramatic theory draws from Jewish mystical traditions, including those of redemption; see "The Clown's Lost Twin."

29. In addition, Bedward evidences the same affinity that Samuel Murrell notes Revival groups found in Baptist organizational structure and immersion baptism, practices amenable to African traditional customs; see *Afro-Caribbean Religions*, 283.

30. In historical and theological writings on Bedward, he is referred to as a Native Baptist, Revivalist, or Revival Zion preacher. In the play he is simply referred to as a prophet, shepherd, preacher, and messiah. Marriott does not distinguish his particular denomination. Bedward's prophetic vision about the Mona River reveals that his connection to divinity also imbues him with supernatural understanding of the medicinal properties of nature, one of the foundational tenets of Myal, discussed extensively in regards to rituals of healing in chapter 3.

31. The theatrical performances of *Bedward* should not be conflated with ancestral incarnations through spirit possession, for to do so would be to minimize the religious weight of such rituals.

32. As Nasser Dasht Peyma states, Walcott's play "belongs to the twentieth-century genre called 'Dream Plays,'" which Dasht Peyma likens to the work of August Strindberg. *Postcolonial Drama,* 157.

33. This formulation of agency also reminds the reader of Bellegarde-Smith's description of possession trance in Vodou as "handing the keys to your car to a very good friend," which opened chapter 2. Bellegarde-Smith interview by Krista Tippet.

34. Weber argues that even prophets like Bedward and Makak, who clearly seize their spiritual authority through charisma, also find themselves needing to prove themselves through physical feats in order to maintain that authority and the "validity of charisma" ("Nature of Charismatic Authority," 49). Weber cites a variety of historical prophet figures, including medieval Byzantine and nineteenth-century Mormon leaders, writing, "If proof of his charismatic qualification fails him for long, the leader endowed with charisma tends to think his god and his magical or heroic powers have deserted him" (49).

35. While Anthony Wallace's essay here argues for a more universal codification of the mazeway and resynthesis, it should be noted that much of his anthropological fieldwork was focused on indigenous groups in North America, particularly the new religion initiated by a Seneca prophet, Handsome Lake; see "Revitalization Movements."

36. This performance of doubt also echoes the seemingly apologetic introductions to many nineteenth-century slave narratives. Erna Brodber's *Louisiana,* which I discuss in the previous chapter, also draws on this deferential narrative tradition in ways that both perform and satirize how Afro-diasporic authors are expected to negate their own authority to speak to larger audiences, all while still bringing those audiences into the world of the story.

37. Jan Uhrbach also identifies the connection between the name Lestrade and the French word *l'estrade,* saying that the character is "a stage, on and against which the other characters play." "Note on Language and Naming," 579.

38. While Josie Fanon (Frantz Fanon's widow) asked that the Sartre preface be removed from later editions of the text, it is included—with additional framing by Homi Bhabha—in the 2004 edition cited here.

39. Lewis Gordon works to rectify Fanon's legacy by countering Sartre's essentializations and exaggerations in the preface and by pointing out what Gordon sees as poor translational choices; see *What Fanon Said.*

40. For both Agne and Ella/Louisiana, engaged surrender is an ongoing process predicated by disorientation and then inaugurated in agential choice. In contrast, Sartre describes a process in which colonialism first alienates the "native," colonized subject from himself. Then, from that place of forced estrangement, the colonized subject consents (as much as he can be understood to do so) to further alienate himself by participating in sacred rituals like possession. Using classic Marxist reasoning, Sartre explains that "in other words the

colonized protect themselves from colonial alienation by going one step better with religious alienation" (preface to *Wretched of the Earth*, liii). In this situation the colonized consent to being possessed/alienated only in order to escape the alienation they are already experiencing. Unlike Sartre's understanding of colonialism, engaged surrender is the active decision to let go of one's previous understanding of the self—not to escape existing conditions but *in order to participate* in often-opaque, communal formations of spiritual knowledge that can better elucidate, resist, and think beyond those current conditions. Engaged surrender and Sartre's paradigm of consent also differ in terms of their outcomes. Sartre writes that consent-to-being-colonized via religious practices ultimately results in the colonized "having accumulated two alienations, each of which reinforces the other" (liii). It should be noted that Agne's and Ella/Louisiana's experiences of engaged surrender do manifest in what appear as diminutions of individualized control and even subjectivity. These diminutions can seem to those devoted to Western paradigms of individuality like Sartre's "two alienations." And yet in both *Changó* and *Louisiana,* this process of choosing to let go ultimately engenders affirmative formulations of personal identity for the characters via spiritual and relational belonging.

41. In the Septuagint, *metanoia* and *metanoeō* (literally, "a change of mind") often express "repentance" and "repent," and both appear frequently in the New Testament; see Marshall, "Repentance," *Oxford Encyclopedia of the Bible*.

42. From the outset Makak's messianic claims harken to the "master-slave" or "lordship and bondage" dialectic of Hegel because Makak arrives at his new self-consciousness through the white dancer's recognition. Over the course of the play, Makak proclaims increasing dominance for his spiritual knowledge and consciousness of subjectivity. The prophecy threatens the hierarchical "complex of dependence" that, according to Fanon, circumscribes the ontological possibilities for black, colonized subjects (*Black Skin, White Masks,* 216). Moustique notably quotes the publication in which Fanon presents this critique of race via Hegelian mastery, shouting, "black faces, white masks" at the moment he is caught attempting to swindle villagers (*Dream on Monkey Mountain,* 271). Makak, on the other hand, appears largely ambivalent about the narratives of mastery that underpin his prophetic rhetoric until the play's final scenes.

43. Fanon's gender politics are complex. Still, it should be noted that the scarcity of careful consideration for black women's experiences is conspicuous in the anticolonialist works of both Fanon and Walcott. Feminist debates of Fanon's work were particularly prominent in the mid to late 1990s. See, for example, Fuss, *Identification Papers;* and Sharpley-Whiting, *Frantz Fanon*.

44. By having the apparition appear as a beam of light, Jones's production creates visually oriented connections with Brodber's *Louisiana,* which uses the analogy of light through stained glass to describe experiences of divine revelation.

45. The prophetic theme arises when Walcott describes himself and his theatrical collaborators as "new Adams, in a nourishing ignorance which would name

plants and people with a child's belief that the world is his own age." "What the Twilight Says," 6.

46. Paula Burnett identifies the "artist as prophet" that figures largely throughout Walcott's poetry, including "As John to Patmos" (*Another Life*), "The Arkansas Testament," and "The Schooner's Flight." Walcott primarily draws from the Judeo-Christian tradition as he analogies the artist—and arguably himself in the process—to St. John the Divine, Moses, and the Apostle Paul; see Burnett, *Derek Walcott*.

47. For example, after seeing *Ione,* a playgoer wrote in a 1957 letter to the editor of the *Gleaner,* "The poet is a prophet." A 2014 article on Walcott in the [London] *Times* captions Walcott's portrait, "Poet-prophet of his island: Derek Walcott." See "Tracking Derek Walcott's Trek Through the Gleaner (Pt. 1:1950–1960)"; and Noel-Todd, "Poetry of Derek Walcott."

48. See Lyall, "Walcott Withdraws from Poetry Professor Election."

49. Walcott similarly excused his 1982 sexual harassment allegation by saying that his teaching style was "deliberately personal and intense"; see Flood, "Smear Campaign Dogs Walcott." In his profile of Walcott, Als writes that "among his students, Walcott developed a reputation as an electrifying, difficult teacher, a person known for his strong judgments and occasionally off-color remarks" ("The Islander"). It is hard to know where to draw the lines between demanding provocateur and harasser of those with less power.

50. See, for example, Flaherty, "Junot Díaz, Feminism, and Ethnicity"; and Garber, "David Foster Wallace."

Epilogue

1. I distinguish between the deceased and ancestors in order to separate characters such as the ghost Beloved (*Beloved*) and the ghoul Melba (*Brown Girl in the Ring*) from the ancestors who continue to aid those within their extended families on earth. We see ancestors intervening to help Ti-Jeanne in *Brown Girl in the Ring* and Agne in *Changó*. However, the fluidity of these distinctions is apparent in Brodber's novels, where characters such as Ol' African (*Myal*) and Anna and Louise (*Louisiana*) appear to occupy liminal spaces of existence between several categories, including ghosts, spirits, and ancestors.

2. Overwhelmed with sadness and anger, I have watched the rise in racist and anti-Semitic shootings in the last quarter of the 2010s and sought desperately to wrap reason around the barrage of (state-sanctioned and vigilante) discriminatory and murderous public performances for my undergraduate and graduate students. Tragically, as I have revised this book and it goes to press, these performances of physical violation and dehumanization have continued unabated and have in some instances increased.

Works Cited

Adams, Michelene. "'The Half Has Never Been Told': Revisioning West Indian History in *Myal*." *Journal of West Indian Literature* 18, no. 2 (Apr. 2010): 160–86.
Aching, Gerard. *Masking and Power: Carnival and Popular Culture in the Caribbean*. Minneapolis: University of Minnesota Press, 2002.
Agamben, Giorgio. *The Time That Remains: A Commentary on the Letter to the Romans*. Translated by Patricia Dailey. Stanford, CA: Stanford University Press, 2005.
Alexander, Bobby C. "Correcting Misinterpretations of Turner's Theory: An African-American Pentecostal Illustration." *Journal for the Scientific Study of Religion* 30, no. 1 (Mar. 1991): 26–44.
Als, Hilton. "The Islander." *New Yorker*. Feb. 9, 2004.
Als, Hilton, and Emma Brockes. "Interview: Hilton Als." *Guardian*. Feb. 2, 2018.
Althusser, Louis. "Ideology and Ideological State Apparatuses." In *Literary Theory: An Anthology*, edited by Julie Rivkin and Michael Ryan, 2nd ed., 691–702. Malden, MA: Blackwell, 2008.
Anatol, Giselle Liza. "A Feminist Reading of Soucouyants in Nalo Hopkinson's *Brown Girl in the Ring* and *Skin Folk*." *Mosaic* 37, no. 4 (Sept. 2004): 33–50.
Anderson, Victor. *Beyond Ontological Blackness: An Essay on African American Religious and Cultural Criticism*. New York: Continuum, 1995.
———. *Creative Exchange: A Constructive Theology of African American Religious Experience*. Minneapolis: Fortress Press, 2008.
Appiah, Kwame Anthony. *In My Father's House: Africa in the Philosophy of Culture*. New York: Oxford University Press, 1993.
Apter, Emily. *The Translation Zone: A New Comparative Literature*. Princeton, NJ: Princeton University Press, 2006.
Arendt, Hannah. *On Violence*. London: Harcourt, 1970.
Arrojo, Rosemary. "Asymmetrical Relations of Power and the Ethics of Translation." *TEXTconTEXT* 11, no. 1 (1997): 5–24.

Artaud, Antonin. *The Theater and Its Double*. 1938. Translated by Mary Caroline Richards. New York: Grove Press, 1958.

Asad, Talal. *Formations of the Secular: Christianity, Islam, Modernity*. Stanford, CA: Stanford University Press, 2003.

Ashaolu, Albert Olu. "Allegory in *Ti-Jean and His Brothers*." *Journal of Postcolonial Writing* 16, no. 1 (1977): 203–11.

Audible. Reviews of *Beloved*. http://www.audible.com/pd/Fiction/Beloved. Accessed April 22, 2015.

Austin, J. L. *How to Do Things with Words*. Oxford: Oxford University Press, 1975.

Austin-Broos, Diane. "The Anthropology of Conversion: An Introduction." In *The Anthropology of Religious Conversion*, edited by Andrew Buckser and Stephen Glazier, 1–12. Lanham. MD: Rowan and Littlefield, 2003.

Báez, Josefina. *Comrade, Bliss Ain't Playing*. 2008. New York: Ay Ombe Theatre, 2013.

———. *Dominicanish*. New York: Latinarte/Ay Ombe Theatre, 2000.

Báez, Josefina, and Ana-Maurine Lara. "Into the Invisible: A Conversation—Performance Rasanblaj." "Caribbean Rasanblaj," special issue, *e-misférica* 12, no. 1 (2015).

Baker, Houston A. *Blues, Ideology, and Afro-American Literature: A Vernacular Theory*. Chicago: University of Chicago Press, 1987.

Baker-Fletcher, Karen. *A Singing Something: Womanist Reflections on Anna Julia Cooper*. New York: Crossroad, 1994.

Barnes, Clive. "Theater: Racial Allegory." *New York Times*. Mar. 15, 1971.

Barrett, Justin L., and Emma Cohen. "Conceptualizing Spirit Possession: Ethnographic and Experimental Evidence." *Ethos* 36, no. 2 (2008): 246–67.

———. "When Minds Migrate: Conceptualizing Spirit Possession." *Journal of Cognition and Culture* 8 (2008): 23–48.

Barrett, Leonard. "African Religion in the Americas: The 'Islands in Between.'" In *African Religions: A Symposium*. Edited by Newel S. Booth Jr., 183–215. New York: NOK Publishers, 1977.

———. *Soul Force: African Heritage in Afro-American Religion*. London: Heinemann, 1976.

Bass, George H. "Another Bone of Contention: Reclaiming Our Gift of Laughter." 1991. Introduction to *Mule Bone: A Comedy of Negro Life,* by Zora Neale Hurston and Langston Hughes, 1–4. New York: Harper Perennial, 2008.

Bassard, Katherine Clay. *Spiritual Interrogations: Culture, Gender, and Community in Early African American Women's Writing*. Princeton, NJ: Princeton University Press, 1999.

———. *Transforming Scriptures: African American Women Writers and the Bible*. Athens: University of Georgia Press, 2010.

Bassnett, Susan, and André Lefevere. *Translation, History, and Culture*. London: Pinter Publishers, 1990.

Beckwith, Martha Warren. "Some Religious Cults in Jamaica." *American Journal of Psychology* 34, no. 1 (Jan. 1923): 32–45.
Bellegarde-Smith, Patrick. "Living Vodou." Interview by Krista Tippet. *On Being*, Jan. 9, 2014. https://onbeing.org/programs/patrick-bellegarde-smith-living-vodou/.
Benedicty-Kokken, Alessandra. *Spirit Possession in French, Haitian, and Vodou Thought: An Intellectual History.* Lanham, MD: Lexington Books, 2015.
Benítez-Rojo, Antonio. *The Repeating Island: The Caribbean and the Postmodern Perspective.* Durham, NC: Duke University Press, 1996.
Benjamin, Walter. "Theses on the Philosophy of History." 1940. In *Illuminations*, translated by Harry Zohn, 253–64. New York: Schocken, 2007.
———. *Walter Benjamin: Selected Writings.* Vol. 1, *1913–1926*. Edited by Marcus Bullock and Michael W. Jennings. Cambridge, MA: Belknap Press of Harvard University Press, 2004.
Bennett, Louise. "Dip Dem." *Jamaican Folk Songs Sung by Louise Bennett.* Folkways Records, 2004, Smithsonian Folkways Recordings/Folkways Records, 1954.
Benston, Kimberly W. *Performing Blackness: Enactments of African-American Modernism.* London: Routledge, 2000.
Bergthaller, Hannes. "Dis(re)membering History's Revenants: Trauma, Writing, and Simulated Orality in Toni Morrison's *Beloved*." *Connotations: A Journal for Critical Debate* 16, no. 1–3 (2006/2007): 116–36.
Best, Lloyd. "Independent Thought and Caribbean Freedom" *New World Quarterly* 3, no. 4 (Crop Over 1967): 24.
Best, Stephen. *The Fugitive's Properties: Law and the Poetics of Possession.* Chicago: University of Chicago Press, 2004.
Bhabha, Homi K. *The Location of Culture.* London: Routledge, 2004.
Biguenet, John, and Rainer Schulte. Introduction to *The Craft of Translation*, edited by John Biguenet and Rainer Schulte, vii–xvi. Chicago: University of Chicago Press, 1989.
Blanchot, Maurice. *The Book to Come.* 1959. Translated by Charlotte Mandell. Stanford, CA: Stanford University Press, 2003.
Boddy, Janice. "Spirit Possession Revisited: Beyond Instrumentality." *Annual Review of Anthropology* 23 (1994): 407–34.
Bogues, Anthony. *Black Heretics, Black Prophets: Radical Political Intellectuals.* New York: Routledge, 2015.
Borelli, Melissa Blanco. *She Is Cuba: A Genealogy of the Mulata Body.* Oxford: Oxford University Press, 2016.
Bourdieu, Pierre. "On Symbolic Power." 1938. In *Language and Symbolic Power*, edited and introduced by John B. Thompson and translated by Gino Raymond and Matthew Adamson, 163–70. Cambridge: Polity Press, 1991.
Bourguignon, Erika. *Possession.* Prospect Heights, IL: Waveland Press, 1991.

Brecht, Bertolt. *Brecht on Theatre: The Development of an Aesthetic.* 1964. Edited and translated by John Willet. New York: Hill & Wang, 1977.
Bretzke, James T., SJ. *Consecrated Phrases: A Latin Theological Dictionary: Latin Expressions Commonly Found in Theological Writings.* Collegeville, MN: Liturgical Press, 1998.
Britton, Celia. *Edouard Glissant and Postcolonial Theory: Strategies of Language and Resistance.* Charlottesville: University of Virginia Press, 1999.
Brodber, Erna. *Louisiana: A Novel.* Jackson: University of Mississippi Press, 1997.
———. "Me and My Head-Hurting Fiction." *Small Axe: A Caribbean Journal of Criticism* 16, no. 3.39 (Nov. 2012): 119–25.
———. *Myal: A Novel.* London: New Beacon Books, 1989.
———. "Oral Sources and the Creation of a Social History of the Caribbean." *Jamaica Journal* 16 (1983): 2–11.
———. Personal Interview by Anne Margaret Castro. Mar. 18, 2013.
———. Personal Interview by Anne Margaret Castro. July 14, 2013.
———. "Re-engineering Blackspace." Plenary presentation at conference in honor of Rex Nettleford, University of the West Indies, March 1996. *Caribbean Quarterly* 43 no. 1–2 (1997): 70–81.
———. "The Spirit Thief." In *The Faber Book of Contemporary Caribbean Short Stories,* edited by Mervyn Morris, 15–24. London: Faber and Faber, 1990.
Brodber, Erna, and John Edward Greene. *Reggae and Cultural Identity in Jamaica.* St. Augustine, Trinidad and Tobago: Department of Sociology, University of the West Indies, 1981.
Brooks, A. A. *History of Bedwardism or The Jamaica Native Baptist Free Church, Union Camp, Augustown, St. Andrew, Jamaica, B.W.I.* 1917. 2nd ed. Kingston: Gleaner Co., 2005. www.kobek.com/bedwardism.pdf.
Bryan, Patrick. *The Jamaica People, 1880–1902: Race, Class, and Social Control.* Kingston, Jamaica: University of West Indies Press, 2000.
Burton, Richard D. E. *Afro-Creole: Power, Opposition, and Play in the Caribbean.* Ithaca, NY: Cornell University Press, 1997.
Butler, Anthea D. *Women in the Church of God in Christ: Making a Sanctified World.* Chapel Hill: University of North Carolina Press, 2007.
Butler, Judith. *Excitable Speech: A Politics of the Performative.* New York: Routledge, 1997.
———. *Gender Trouble: Feminism and the Subversion of Identity.* New York: Routledge, 2006.
Burnett, Paula. *Derek Walcott: Politics and Poetics.* Gainesville: University Press of Florida, 2000.
Cabrera, Lydia. "Black Arts: African Folk Wisdom and Popular Medicine in Cuba" Translated by Margarite Fernández Olmos. In *Healing Cultures: Art and Religion as Curative Practices in the Caribbean and Its Diaspora,* edited by Margarite Fernández Olmos and Lizabeth Paravisini-Gebert, 29–42. New York: Palgrave, 2001.

Cannon, Katie Geneva. *Black Womanist Ethics*. Atlanta: American Academy of Religion, 1988.
Carlson, Marvin. *Performance: A Critical Introduction*. New York: Routledge, 2013.
Carter, J. Kameron. *Race: A Theological Account*. Oxford: Oxford University Press, 2008.
Castro, Anne Margaret. "Sounding Out Spirit Thievery in Erna Brodber's *Myal*." *Journal of West Indian Literature* 23, no. 1/2 (Nov. 2015): 106–20.
Césaire, Aimé. *Discourse on Colonialism*. 1955. Translated by Joan Pinkham. New York: Monthly Review Press, 2000.
Chevannes, Barry. "Millennialism in the Caribbean." In *The Oxford Handbook of Millennialism*, edited by Catherine Wessinger, 420–34. Oxford: Oxford University Press, 2011.
Cliff, Michelle. "'I Found God in Myself and I Love Her / I Loved Her Fiercely': More Thoughts on the Work of Black Women Artists." *Journal of Feminist Studies in Religion* 2, no. 1 (Spring 1986): 7–39.
Clyne, Ronald. Liner notes to *Jamaican Folk Songs Sung by Louise Bennett*. 1954. LP. Folkways Records, 2004 Smithsonian Folkways Recordings/Folkways Records.
Cohn, Norman. "Medieval Millenarianism: Its Bearing on the Comparative Study of Millenarian Movements." In *Millennial Dreams in Action: Studies in Revolutionary Religious Movements*, edited by Sylvia L. Thrupp, 31–43. New York: Schocken Books, 1970.
Coleman, James. *Faithful Visions: Treatments of the Sacred, Spiritual, and Supernatural in Twentieth-Century African American Fiction*. Baton Rouge: Louisiana State University Press, 2005.
Coleman, Monica A. "Serving the Spirits: The Pan-Caribbean African-Derived Religion in Nalo Hopkinson's *Brown Girl in the Ring*." *Journal of Caribbean Literatures* 6, no. 1 (2009): 1–13.
Collier, Gordon. "Spaceship Creole: Nalo Hopkinson, Canadian-Caribbean Fabulist Fiction, and Linguistic/Cultural Syncretism." In *A Pepper-Pot of Cultures: Aspects of Creolization in the Caribbean*, edited by Gordon Collier and Ulrich Fleischman, 443–58. Amsterdam: Matatu, Journal for African Culture in Society 27–28, 2003.
Cone, James H. *God of the Oppressed*. Ossining, NY: Orbis Books, 1997.
Cooper, Carolyn. *Noises in the Blood: Orality, Gender, and the "Vulgar" Body of Jamaican Popular Culture*. Durham, NC: Duke University Press, 1995.
Copeland, Shawn M. "African American Religious Experience." In *The Oxford Handbook of African American Theology*, edited by Katie G. Cannon and Anthony B. Pinn, 40–67. Oxford: Oxford University Press, 2014.
Crossley, Scott. "Metaphors and the Reclamation of Blackness in Derek Walcott's 'Dream on Monkey Mountain.'" *Journal of Caribbean Literatures* 7, no. 1 (2011): 15–32.

Cummings, George, and Dwight Hopkins, eds. *Cut Loose Your Stammering Tongue: Black Theology in the Slave Narratives*. Maryknoll, NY: Orbis Books, 2002.

Cunard, Nancy, ed. *Negro: An Anthology*. 1934. New York: Negro University Press, 1969.

Daniel, Yvonne. *Dancing Wisdom: Embodied Knowledge in Haitian Vodou, Cuban Yoruba, and Bahain Candomblé*. Champaign: University of Illinois Press. 2005.

Daniels, Ted. "Charters of Righteousness: Politics, Prophets, and the Drama of Conversion." In *War in Heaven/Heaven on Earth: Theories of the Apocalyptic*, edited by Stephen D. O'Leary and Glen S. McGhee, 3–18. London: Routledge, 2014.

Daniels, Walter. *Images of the Preacher in Afro-American Literature*. Washington, DC: University Press of America, 1981.

Dash, J. Michael. "Writing the Body: Edouard Glissant's Poetics of Re-membering." *World Literature Today* 63, no. 4 (Fall 1989): 609–12.

Dasht Peyma, Nasser. *Postcolonial Drama: A Comparative Study of Wole Soyinka, Derek Walcott and Girish Karnad*. New Delhi, India: Rawat Publications, 2009.

Davis, Wade. *Passage of Darkness: The Ethnobiology of the Haitian Zombie*. Chapel Hill: University of North Carolina Press, 1988.

Dayan, Joan. *Haiti, History, and the Gods*. Berkeley: University of California Press, 1998.

De Ferrari, Guillermina. *Vulnerable States: Bodies of Memory in Contemporary Caribbean Fiction*. Charlottesville: University of Virginia Press, 2007.

DeFrantz, Thomas F. *Dancing Revelations: Alvin Ailey's Embodiment of African American Culture*. Oxford: Oxford University Press, 2004.

DeFrantz, Thomas F., and Anita Gonzalez, eds. *Black Performance Theory*. Durham, NC: Duke University Press, 2014.

De Heusch, Luc. *Why Marry Her? Society and Symbolic Structures*. Cambridge: Cambridge University Press, 1981.

Depestre, René. *Change*. Paris: Editions du Seuil, 1971.

Deren, Maya. *Divine Horsemen: The Living Gods of Haiti*. New Paltz, NY: McPherson, 1983.

Derrida, Jacques. "The Theater of Cruelty and the Closure of Representation." *Theater* 9, no. 3 (Nov. 1978): 6–19.

———. "Signature, Event, Context." Translated by Samuel Weber and Jeffrey Mehlman. In *Limited Inc*. Evanston, IL: Northwestern University Press, 1988.

———. *Specters of Marx: The State of the Debt, the Work of Mourning, and the New International*. 1993. Translated by Peggy Kamuf. New York: Routledge, 2006.

Dexter, Noel, Honor Ford-Smith, Louis Marriott, Cecily Waite-Smith, and Sylvia Wynter. *Mixed Company: Three Early Jamaican Plays*, edited and introduced by Yvonne Brewster. London: Oberon Books, 2012.

Diamond, Cora. "Eating Meat and Eating People." *Philosophy* 53, no. 206 (Oct. 1978): 465–79.
Douglas, Kelly Brown. *The Black Christ*. Maryknoll, NY: Orbis Books, 1993.
Douglass, Frederick. *Narrative of the Life of Frederick Douglass, an American Slave*. 1845. South Bend, IN: Infomotions, 2000.
Dubey, Madhu. "The Politics of Genre in *Beloved*." *Novel: A Forum on Fiction* 32, no. 2 (Spring 1999): 103–23.
Du Bois, W. E. B. *Black Reconstruction in America, 1860–1880*. 1935. Foreword by David Levering Lewis. New York: Free Press, 1998.
———. *Du Bois on Religion*. Edited by Phil Zuckerman. Walnut Creek, CA: AltaMira, 2000.
———. *The Souls of Black Folk*. 1903. New York: Dover Thrift, 1995.
Eastman, Rudolph, and Maureen Warner-Lewis. "Forms of African Spirituality in Trinidad and Tobago." In *African Spirituality: Forms, Meanings, and Expressions*, edited by Jacob K. Olupona, 403–15. New York: Crossroad, 2000.
Edwards, Brent Hayes. "The Uses of *Diaspora*." *Social Text* 19.1 (2001): 45–73.
Evans, Stephen C. "Faith and Revelation." In *The Oxford Handbook of Philosophy of Religion*, edited by William J Wainwright, 323–41. Oxford: Oxford University Press, 2007.
Fanon, Frantz. *Black Skin, White Masks*. 1958. Translated by Richard Philcox. New York: Grove Press, 2008.
———. *The Wretched of the Earth*. 1961. Translated by Richard Philcox. Foreword by Homi K. Bhabha. Preface by Jean-Paul Sartre. New York: Grove Press, 2004.
Fido, Elaine Savory. "Value Judgements on Art and the Question of Macho Attitudes: The Case of Derek Walcott." *Journal of Commonwealth Literature*. 21, no. 1 (1986): 109–19.
Flaherty, Colleen. "Junot Díaz, Feminism, and Ethnicity." *Inside Higher Ed*. May 29, 2018. https://www.insidehighered.com/news/2018/05/29/rift-among-scholars-over-treatment-junot-d%C3%ADaz-he-faces-harassment-and-misconduct.
Flood, Allison. "Smear Campaign Dogs Derek Walcott's Bid for Oxford Professor of Poetry." *Guardian*. May 11, 2009. https://www.theguardian.com/books/2009/may/11/smear-walcott-oxford-professor-poetry.
Floyd-Thomas, Stacey, Juan Floyd-Thomas, Carol B. Duncan, Stephen G. Ray Jr., and Lynne Westfield. *Black Church Studies: An Introduction*. Nashville: Abingdon Press, 2007.
Forbes, Curdella. "Redeeming the Word: Religious Experience as Liberation in Erna Brodber's Fiction." *Postcolonial Text* 3, no. 1 (2007): 1–19.
Foucault, Michel. *Discipline and Punish: The Birth of the Prison*. 1977. Translated by Alan Sheridan. New York: Random House, 1995.

———. *The History of Sexuality*. Vol. 1, *An Introduction*. 1978. Translated by Robert Hurley. New York: Random House, 1990.

———. "Religious Deviations and Medical Knowledge." 1962. Translated by Richard Townsend. In *Religion and Culture*, edited by Jeremy Carrette, 50–71. New York: Routledge, 1999.

———. *"Society Must Be Defended": Lectures at the Collège de France, 1975–1976*. Translated by David Macey. New York: Picador, 2003.

Fox, Robert E. "Big Night Music: Derek Walcott's *Dream on Monkey Mountain* and the 'Splendours of Imagination.'" In *Critical Perspectives on Derek Walcott*, edited by Robert D. Hamner, 185–218. Washington, DC: Three Continents Press, 1993.

Fritsch, Matthias. *The Promise of Memory: History and Politics in Marx, Benjamin, and Derrida*. Albany: State University of New York Press, 2006.

Fuss, Diana. *Identification Papers*. New York: Routledge, 1995.

Garavito, Julián. "En busca de una identidad cultural colombiana: *Changó, el gran putas*, de Manuel Zapata Olivella." *Thesaurus* 52, no. 1–3 (1997): 320–29.

Garber, Megan. "David Foster Wallace and the Dangerous Romance of Male Genius." *Atlantic*. May 9, 2018. https://www.theatlantic.com/entertainment/archive/2018/05/the-world-still-spins-around-male-genius/559925/.

Gates, Henry Louis Jr. *The Signifying Monkey: A Theory of African American Literary Criticism*. New York: Oxford University Press, 2014.

———. "A Tragedy of Negro Life." Introduction to *Mule Bone: A Comedy of Negro Life*, by Zora Neale Hurston and Langston Hughes, 5–24. New York: Harper Perennial, 2008.

Geertz, Clifford. *The Interpretation of Cultures*. New York: Basic Books, 2000.

Genovese, Eugene D. *Roll, Jordan, Roll: The World the Slaves Made*. New York: Vintage Books, 1976.

Ghansah, Rachel Kaadzi. "The Radical Vision of Toni Morrison." *New York Times Magazine*. April 8, 2015.

Gibson, Melissa Dana. "Historical Drama." In *The Oxford Encyclopedia of Theatre and Performance*. Vol. 1. Edited by Dennis Kennedy, 592–93. Oxford: Oxford University Press, 2003.

Gilroy, Paul. *The Black Atlantic: Modernity and Double-Consciousness*. Cambridge, MA: Harvard University Press, 1993.

Glissant, Édouard. *Caribbean Discourse: Selected Essays*. Translated by Michael Dash. Charlottesville: University of Virginia Press, 1992.

———. *Monsieur Toussaint: A Play*. 1961. Translated and introduced by Michael Dash. Boulder: Lynn Rienner, 2005.

———. *Poetics of Relation*. 1990. Translated by Betsy Wing. Ann Arbor: University of Michigan Press, 2010.

Gonzalez, Michelle A. *Afro-Cuban Theology: Religion, Race, Culture, and Identity*. Gainesville: University of Florida Press, 2011.

Gordon, Lewis R. *Existence in Black: An Anthology of Black Existential Philosophy.* New York: Routledge, 1997.
——. *What Fanon Said: A Philosophical Introduction to His Life and Thought.* New York: Fordham University Press, 2015.
Grondin, Jean. *Introduction to Philosophical Hermeneutics.* Translated by Joel Weinsheimer. New Haven, CT: Yale University Press, 1994.
Grosz, Elizabeth. *Volatile Bodies: Toward a Corporeal Feminism.* Bloomington: Indiana University Press, 1994.
Gutierrez, Cathy. "The Millennium and Narrative Closure." In *War in Heaven/Heaven on Earth: Theories of the Apocalyptic,* edited by Stephen D. O'Leary and Glen S. McGhee, 47–60. London: Routledge, 2014.
Gyekye, Kwame. "The Relation of *Okra* (Soul) and *Honam* (Body): An Akan Conception." In *African Philosophy: An Anthology,* edited by Emmanuel Chukwudi Eze, 59–66. Malden, MA: Blackwell, 1998.
Hall, Cheryl. "'Beyond the 'Literary Habit': Oral Tradition and Jazz in *Beloved.*" *MELUS* 19, no. 1 (1994): 89–95.
Hall, Stuart. "Cultural Identity and Cinematic Representation." *Framework* 36 (1989): 75–76.
Hamner, Robert D. "Mythological Aspects of Derek Walcott's Drama." *Review of International English Literature (ARIEL)* 8, no. 3 (July 1977): 35–58.
Haney, William S. "Hybridity and Visionary Experience: Derek Walcott's *Dream on Monkey Mountain.*" *Mystics Quarterly* 31, no. 3/4 (2005): 81–108.
Hanks, William F., and Carlo Severi. "Translating Worlds: The Epistemological Space of Translation." *HAU: Journal of Ethnographic Theory* 4, no. 2 (2014): 1–16.
Harris, Wilson. "History, Fable and Myth in the Caribbean and Guianas." *Caribbean Quarterly* 16, no. 2 (1970) 1–32.
Hartman, Saidiya. *Scenes of Subjection: Slavery and Self-Making in the Nineteenth-Century America.* Oxford: Oxford University Press, 1997.
Hemenway, Robert E., and Alice Walker. *Zora Neale Hurston: A Literary Biography.* Urbana: University of Illinois Press, 1980.
Henderson, Mae G. "Toni Morrison's *Beloved*: Re-Membering the Body as Historical Text." In *Comparative American Identities: Race, Sex, and Nationality in the Modern Text,* edited by Hortense J. Spillers, 62–86. New York: Routledge, 1991.
Henry, Paget. *Caliban's Reason: Introducing Afro-Caribbean Philosophy.* New York: Routledge, 2000.
Herskovitz, Melville. *Dahomey: An Ancient West African Kingdom.* Vol 1. New York: J. J. Augustin, 1938.
——. *Life in a Haitian Valley.* 1937. Princeton: Markus Wiener Publications, 2008.
Higginbotham, A. Leon. *In the Matter of Color: Race and the American Legal Process: The Colonial Period.* 4th ed. New York: Oxford University Press, 1980.

Hill, David, and R. N. Whybray. "Prophets." In *The Oxford Companion to the Bible,* edited by Bruce M. Metzger, Michael D. Coogan, and R. N. Whybray. Oxford Biblical Studies Online. http://www.oxfordbiblicalstudies.com/article/opr/t120/e059.

Hinnells, John R., ed. *The Routledge Companion to the Study of Religion.* Abingdon, UK: Routledge, 2005.

Hogan, Patrick Colm. *Colonialism and Cultural Identity: Crises of Tradition in the Anglophone Literatures of India, Africa, and the Caribbean.* Albany: State University of New York Press, 2000.

Holloway, Karla F. C. "The Lyrical Dimensions of Spirituality: Music, Voice, and Language in the Novels of Toni Morrison." In *Embodied Voices: Representing Female Vocality in Western Culture,* edited by Leslie C. Dunn and Nancy A. Jones, 197–211. New York: Cambridge University Press, 1994.

Hopkinson, Nalo. *Brown Girl in the Ring.* New York: Warner Aspect, 1998.

———. "Fantastic Alternatives: Journeys into the Imagination." Interview by Hyacinth M. Simpson. *Journal of West Indian Literature; Bridgetown* 14, no. 1 (Nov. 2005): 96–113.

———. "Making the Impossible Possible: An Interview with Nalo Hopkinson." Interview by Alondra Nelson. *Social Text* 20, no. 3 (2002): 97–113.

———. "Nalo Hopkinson: Writing Is Believing." Interview by Kellie Magnus. *Caribbean Beat* 73 (May/June 2005). caribbean-beat.com.

———. "Speaking in Tongues: An Interview with Science Fiction Writer Nalo Hopkinson." Interview by Gregory E. Nelson. *African American Review* 33, no. 4 (Winter 1999): 589–601.

Höttges, Bärbel. "Written Sounds and Spoken Letters: Orality and Literacy in Toni Morrison's *Beloved.*" *Connotations: A Journal for Critical Debate* 19, no. 1–3 (2009): 147–60.

Hubbard, Dolan. *The Sermon and the African American Literary Imagination.* Columbia: University of Missouri Press, 1996.

Hughes, Andrew, and Edit Gerson-Kiwi. "Solmization." Oxford Music Online: Grove Music Online. Oxford University Press. https://www.oxfordmusiconline.com/grovemusic/view/10.1093/gmo/9781561592630.001.0001/omo-9781561592630-e-0000026154.

Hughes, Langston. *The Big Sea.* 1940. Introduction by Arnold Rampersand. New York: Hill & Wang, 1993.

Humphrey, Paul. *Santería, Vodou, and Resistance in Caribbean Literature: Daughters of the Spirits.* Cambridge: Legenda, 2018.

Hurston, Zora Neale. "Conversions and Visions." 1934. In *The Sanctified Church,* 85–90.

———. Letter to Langston Hughes. Apr. 30, 1929. In *Zora Neale Hurston: A Life in Letters,* collected and edited by Carla Kaplan, 140. New York: Anchor, 2003.

———. *Jonah's Gourd Vine.* 1934. New York: Harper Perennial Modern Classics, 1990.

———. *Mules and Men*. 1935. New York: Harper Perennial Modern Classics, 2008.

———. *The Sanctified Church: The Folklore Writings of Zora Neale Hurston*, edited by Toni Cade Bambara. Berkeley: Turtle Island, 1981.

———. "The Sanctified Church." 1934. In *The Sanctified Church*, 103–8.

———. "Shouting." 1934. In *The Sanctified Church*, 91–94.

———. "Spirituals and Neo-Spirituals." 1934. In *The Sanctified Church*, 79–84.

———. *Tell My Horse: Voodoo and Life in Haiti and Jamaica*. 1938. New York: Harper Perennial Modern Classics, 2009.

———. *Their Eyes Were Watching God* and *Mules and Men*. Narrated by Ruby Dee. New York: Caedmon, 2000. Audio Cassette.

Hurston, Zora Neale, with Rowena Jelliffe. *The Sermon in the Valley*. 1931. In *Zora Neale Hurston: Collected Plays*, edited and introduced by Jean Lee Cole and Charles Mitchell, 193–200. New Brunswick, NJ: Rutgers University Press, 2008.

Hutton, Clinton, and Nathaniel Samuel Murrell. "Rastas' Psychology of Blackness, Resistance, and Somebodiness." In *Chanting Down Babylon: The Rastafari Reader*, edited by Nathaniel Samuel Murrell, William David Spencer, and Adrian Anthony McFarlane, 36–54. Philadelphia: Temple University Press, 1998.

Idowu, E. Bolaji. *African Traditional Religion: A Definition*. London: SCM-Canterbury Press, 1974.

———. *Olódùmarè: God in Yoruba Belief*. London: Longmans, 1962.

Irons, Charles F. *The Origins of Proslavery Christianity: White and Black Evangelicals in Antebellum Virginia*. Chapel Hill: University of North Carolina Press, 2008.

Jakobson, Ramon. "On Linguistic Aspects of Translation." 1959. In *The Translation Studies Reader*, edited by Lawrence Venuti, 138–43. New York: Routledge, 2004.

Jamaica Theological Seminary. *Redeeming Alexander Bedward*. Uploaded Apr. 14, 2016. https://www.youtube.com/watch?v=2QLEKPHF2qE.

Jennings, La Vinia Delois. *Toni Morrison and the Idea of Africa*. Cambridge: Cambridge University Press, 2008.

Jesser, Nancy. "Violence, Home, and Community in Toni Morrison's *Beloved*." *African American Review* 33, no. 2 (Summer 1999): 325–45.

Jiménez, Georgina. "African Transgression." *Latin American Review of Books*, July 1, 2010. http://www.latamrob.com/african-transgression/.

Johnson, Paul Christopher. "An Atlantic Genealogy of 'Spirit Possession.'" *Comparative Studies in History and Society* 53, no. 2: 393–425.

Johnson, Terrence, "Reason in African American Theology." In *The Oxford Handbook of African American Theology*, edited by Katie G. Cannon and Anthony B. Pinn, 96–107. Oxford: Oxford University Press, 2014.

Jonas, Gerald. "Science Fiction." *New York Times*. Apr. 30, 1998. http://movies2.nytimes.com/books/00/04/30/reviews/000430.30scifit.html.

Josephs, Kelly Baker. "Dreams, Delirium, and Decolonisation in Derek Walcott's *Dream on Monkey Mountain*." *Small Axe: A Caribbean Journal of Criticism* 32 (2010): 1–16.

Kaplan, Carla. *Zora Neale Hurston: A Life in Letters*. New York: Anchor, 2003.

Keegan, Daniel. "Performing Prophecy: More Life on the Shakespearean Scene." *Shakespeare Quarterly* 62, no. 3 (Fall 2011): 420–43.

Keizer, Arlene R. "Beloved: Ideologies in Conflict, Improvised Subjects." *African American Review* 33, no. 1 (Spring 1999): 105–23.

Khair, Tabish. "'Correct(ing) Images from the Inside': Reading the Limits of Erna Brodber's *Myal*." *Journal of Commonwealth Literature* 37, no. 1 (2002): 121–32.

Krumholz, Linda. "The Ghosts of Slavery: Historical Recovery in Toni Morrison's *Beloved*." *African American Review* 26, no. 3 (Autumn 1992): 395–408.

Kutzinksi, Vera. "Borders and Bodies: The United States, America, and the Caribbean." *CR: The New Centennial Review* 1, no. 2 (Fall 2001): 55–88.

———. *The Worlds of Langston Hughes: Modernism and Translation in the Americas*. Cornell, NY: Cornell University Press, 2012.

Landers, Jane, and Barry Robinson. *Slaves, Subjects, and Subversives: Blacks in Colonial Latin America*. Albuquerque: University of New Mexico Press, 2006.

Landes, Richard. "Roosters Crow, Owls Hoot: On the Dynamics of Apocalyptic Millennialism." In *War in Heaven/Heaven on Earth: Theories of the Apocalyptic*, edited by Stephen D. O'Leary and Glen S. McGhee, 19–46. London: Routledge, 2014.

Landesman, Charles. *An Introduction to Epistemology*. Cambridge: Blackwell, 1997.

Legesse, Asmarom. "Prophetism, Democharisma, and Social Change." In *Religion in Africa: Experience and Expression*, edited by Thomas D. Blakely, Dennis L. Thompson, and Walter E. A. van Beek, 314–41. London: Heinemann, 1994.

Levander, Caroline Field, and Robert S Levine. *Hemispheric American Studies*. New Brunswick, NJ: Rutgers University Press, 2008.

Levine, Lawrence. *Black Culture and Black Consciousness: Afro-American Folk Thought from Slavery to Freedom*. New York: Oxford University Press, 1997.

Lewis, I. M. *Ecstatic Religion: A Study of Shamanism and Spirit Possession*. 2nd ed. London: Routledge, 1989.

Lewis, Philip E. "The Measure of Translation Effects." In *Difference in Translation*, edited by J. F. Graham, 31–62. Ithaca, NY: Cornell University Press, 1985.

Lincoln, C. Eric, and Lawrence Mamiya. *The Black Church in the African American Experience*. Durham, NC: Duke University Press, 1990.

Lipschitz, Yair. "The Clown's Lost Twin: Messianic Moments in Hanoch Levin's Drama." *Modern Drama* 52, no. 2 (Summer 2013): 232–49.

Long, Charles H. *Significations: Signs, Symbols, and Images in the Interpretation of Religion*. Aurora, CO: Davies Group, 2004.

Lovelace, Earl C. Sermon Delivered 1929. Transcribed by Zora Neale Hurston as "The Sermon." 1929/1934. In *Negro, An Anthology,* edited by Nancy Cunard. New York: Negro University Press, 1969.
Lowe, Lisa. *The Intimacies of Four Continents.* Durham, NC: Duke University Press, 2015.
Luis, William. Introduction to *Changó, The Biggest Badass.* Translated by Jonathan Tittler. Texas Tech University Press, 2010.
Lyall, Sarah. "Walcott Withdraws from Poetry Professor Election." *New York Times.* May 12, 2009. https://www.nytimes.com/2009/05/13/books/13poet.html.
Mahurin, Sarah. "'Speaking Arms' and Dancing Bodies in Ntozake Shange." *African American Review* 46, no. 2/3 (Summer/Fall 2013): 329–43.
Marley, Bob, and The Wailers, "African Herbsman" and "Brainwashing." *African Herbsman,* Trojan Records, 1973.
———. "Natural Mystic." *Exodus,* Island Records, 1977.
———. "Revolution." *Natty Dread,* Island Records, 1974.
———. "Redemption Song" and "Zion Train." *Uprising,* Island Records, 1980.
———. "Trenchtown." *Confrontation,* Island Records, 1983.
———. "Zimbabwe." *Survival,* Island Records, 1979.
Marriott, Louis. *Bedward, A Play in Two Acts.* In *Mixed Company: Three Early Jamaican Plays,* edited by Yvonne Brewster, 133–208. London: Oberon Books, 2012.
Marshall, Christopher D. "Repentance." In *The Oxford Encyclopedia of the Bible and Theology.* Oxford Biblical Studies Online. http://www.oxfordbiblicalstudies.com/article/opr/t467/e195.
Martin, Kameelah L. *Conjuring Moments in African American Literature: Women, Spirit Work, and Other Such Hoodoo.* New York: Palgrave Macmillan, 2012.
Marx, Karl. "Wage Labor and Capital." In *Literary Theory: An Anthology.* Edited by Julie Rivkin and Michael Ryan, 2nd ed., 659–65. Malden, MA: Blackwell, 2008.
Matory, J. Lorand. *Black Atlantic Religion: Tradition, Transnationalism, and Matriarchy in the Afro-Brazilian Candomblé.* Princeton, NJ: Princeton University Press, 2005.
Maxwell, William J. *F.B. Eyes: How J. Edgar Hoover's Ghostreaders Framed African American Literature.* Princeton, NJ: Princeton University Press, 2015.
Mbembe, Achille. *On the Postcolony.* Introduced and translated by A. M. Berrett, Janet Roitman, Murray Last, and Steven Randall. Berkeley: University of California Press, 2001.
Mbiti, John. *African Religions and Philosophy.* 2nd ed. Garborone, Botswana: Heinemann, 1990.
Meriwether, Rae Ann. "The Blues Matrix: Cultural Discourses and Community in Erna Brodber's *Louisiana.*" *Small Axe: A Caribbean Journal of Criticism* 16, no. 3.39 (Nov. 2012): 103–18.

Métraux, Alfred. *Voodoo in Haiti*. Translated by Hugo Charteris. New York: Schocken, 1972.

Michlitsch, Gretchen J. "Breastfeeding Mother Rescues City: Nalo Hopkinson's Ti-Jeanne as Superhero." *FEMSPEC* 6, no. 1 (June 2005): 18–43.

Miller, Kei. *Augustown*. London: Weidenfeld and Nicolson, 2016.

Mills, Charles W. *Blackness Visible: Essays on Philosophy and Race*. Ithaca, NY: Cornell University Press, 1998.

Mitchell, Carolyn A. "'I Love to Tell the Story': Biblical Revisions in *Beloved*." *Religion and Literature* 23, no. 3 (Autumn 1991): 27–42.

Mitchell, Henry H. *Black Preaching: The Recovery of a Power Art*. Nashville: Abingdon Press, 1990.

Montero, Mayra. "The Great Bonanza of the Antilles." In *Healing Cultures: Art and Religion as Curative Practices in the Caribbean and Its Diaspora*, edited by Margarite Fernández Olmos and Lizabeth Paravisini-Gebert, 195–202. New York: Palgrave, 2001.

Montilus, Guérin C. "Vodun and Social Transformation in the African Diasporic Experience: The Concept of Personhood in Haitian Vodun Religion." In *Haitian Vodou: Spirit, Myth, and Reality*, edited by Patrick Bellegarde-Smith and Claudine Michel, 1–7. Bloomington: Indiana University Press, 2006.

Mori, Aoi. *Toni Morrison and Womanist Discourse*. New York: Peter Lang, 1991.

Morini, Massimiliano. *Tudor Translation in Theory and Practice*. Farnham, UK: Ashgate Publishing, 2006.

Morrison, Toni. *Beloved*. New York: Plume, 1988.

———. *Beloved*. Narrated by Toni Morrison. Random House Audio, 2007.

———. *The Bluest Eye*. Narrated by Ruby Dee. Unabridged ed. Random House Audio, 2000. CD.

———. *Playing in the Dark: Whiteness and the Literary Imagination*. Cambridge: Harvard University Press, 1992.

———. "Rootedness: The Ancestor as Foundation." In *Black Women Writers (1950–1980): A Critical Evaluation*, edited by Mari Evans, 339–45. Garden City, NY: Anchor/Doubleday, 1984.

———. "'Talking to Myself': An Interview with Toni Morrison." Conducted and introduced by Matthew Rubery. *Audiobook History* (blog), June 28, 2013. https://audiobookhistory.wordpress.com/2013/07/29/talking-to-myself-an-interview-with-toni-morrison/.

Mountford, Roxanne. *The Gendered Pulpit: Preaching in American Protestant Spaces*. Carbondale: Southern Illinois University Press, 2003.

Munro, Martin. "Shaping and Reshaping the Caribbean: The Work of Aimé Césaire and René Depestre." PhD diss., University of Aberdeen, 2000. MHRA Texts and Dissertations 50.

Murphy, Gretchen. *Shadowing the White Man's Burden: U.S. Imperialism and the Problem of the Color Line*. New York: New York University Press, 2010.

Murphy, Joseph M. *Working the Spirit: Ceremonies of the African Diaspora.* Boston: Beacon Press, 1994.
Murray-Román, Jeannine. *Performance and Personhood in Caribbean Literature: From Alexis to the Digital Age.* Charlottesville: University of Virginia Press, 2016.
Murrell, Nathaniel Samuel. *Afro-Caribbean Religions: An Introduction to Their Historical, Cultural, and Sacred Traditions.* Philadelphia: Temple University Press, 2009.
Nelson-McDermott, Catherine. "Myal-ing Criticism: Beyond Colonizing Dialectics." *Review of International English Literature* 24, no. 4 (Oct. 1993): 53–97.
Noel-Todd, Jeremy. "The Poetry of Derek Walcott, 1948–2013." *Sunday Times.* May 4, 2014. https://www.thetimes.co.uk/article/the-poetry-of-derek-walcott-1948-2013-selected-by-glyn-maxwell-7bq6k8hmdh9.
Nwankwo, Ifeoma. *Black Cosmopolitanism: Racial Consciousness and Transnational Identity in the Nineteenth-Century Americas.* Charlottesville: University of Virginia Press, 2016.
———. "Review of *Brown Girl in the Ring.*" *FEMSPEC* 4, no. 2 (2003): 307.
Obama, Barack. "Remarks by the President in Eulogy for the Honorable Reverend Clementa Pinckney." June 26, 2015. https://obamawhitehouse.archives.gov/the-press-office/2015/06/26/remarks-president-eulogy-honorable-reverend-clementa-pinckney.
O'Callaghan, Evelyn. "Cultural Penetration, Arts, and Sciences: A Review of Erna Brodber's *Louisiana.*" *Journal of West Indian Literature* 7, no. 2 (April 1998): 70–80.
———. "Erna Brodber." *Fifty Caribbean Writers: A Bio-Bibliographical Critical Sourcebook,* edited by Daryl Cumber Dance, 71–82. New York: Greenwood, 1986.
———. "Play It Back a Next Way: Teaching Brodber Teaching Us." *Small Axe: A Caribbean Journal of Criticism* 39 (2012): 59–71.
O'Leary, Stephen D., and Glen S. McGhee. *War in Heaven/Heaven on Earth: Theories of the Apocalyptic.* London: Routledge, 2014.
Olaniyan, Tejumola. *Scars of Conquest, Masks of Resistance: The Invention of Cultural Identities in African, African-American, and Caribbean Drama.* Oxford: Oxford University Press, 1995.
Olaveson, Tim. "Collective Effervescence and Communitas: Processual Models of Ritual and Society in Emile Durkheim and Victor Turner." *Dialectical Anthropology* 26, no. 2 (June 2001): 89–124.
Olmos, Margarite Fernández, and Lizabeth Paravisini-Gebert. *Creole Religions of the Caribbean: An Introduction from Vodou and Santería to Obeah and Espiritismo.* 2nd ed. New York: NYU Press, 2011.
———, eds. *Healing Cultures: Art and Religion as Curative Practices in the Caribbean and Its Diaspora.* New York: Palgrave, 2001.

———, eds. *Sacred Possessions: Vodou, Santería, Obeah and the Caribbean*. New Brunswick, NJ: Rutgers University Press, 1997.

Olupona, Jacob K. *African Religions: A Very Short Introduction*. Oxford: Oxford University Press, 2014.

Olutola, Sarah. "Blood Soil and Zombies: Afrofuturist Collaboration and (Re)-Appropriation in Nalo Hopkinson's *Brown Girl in the Ring*." *Journal of Science Fiction* 2, no. 2 (Jan. 2018): 64–81.

Omotayo, Oloruntoba-Oju. "The Redness of Blackness: Revisiting Derek Walcott's Mulatto Aesthetics." *Caribbean Quarterly* 52, no. 1 (March 2007): 12–25.

Orpana, Simon. "The Law and Its Illicit Desires: Transversing Free Market Claustrophobia and the Zombie Imaginary in *Dredd 3-D*." *Review of Education, Pedagogy, and Cultural Studies* 36, no. 4 (Sept. 2014): 298–319.

Orpana, Simon, and Evan Mauro. "First as Tragedy, Then as Ford: Performing the Biopolitical Image in the Age of Austerity, from the G20 to Toronto City Hall." *TOPIA: Canadian Journal of Cultural Studies* 30–31 (2014): 271–89.

Ortiz, Fernando. *Cuban Counterpoint: Tobacco and Sugar*. 1940. Translated by Harriet de Onís. Durham, NC: Duke University Press, 1995.

Paravisini-Gebert, Lizabeth. "Women Possessed: Eroticism and Exoticism in the Representation of Woman as Zombie." In *Sacred Possessions: Vodou, Santería, Obeah, and the Caribbean*, edited by Margarita Fernández Olmos and Lizabeth Paravisini-Gebert, 37–58. New Brunswick, NJ: Rutgers University Press, 1997.

Paris, Carl. "Reading 'Spirit' and the Dancing Body in the Choreography of Ronald K. Brown and Reggie Wilson." In *Black Performance Theory*, edited by Thomas F. DeFrantz and Anita Gonzalez, 99–114. Durham, NC: Duke University Press, 2014.

Parker, Andrew, Eve Kosofsky Sedgwick, and the English Institute. *Performativity and Performance*. New York: Routledge, 1995.

Paton, Diana. "Obeah Acts: Producing and Policing the Boundaries of Religion in the Caribbean." *Small Axe: A Caribbean Journal of Criticism* 28 (Mar. 2009): 1–18.

Patterson, Orlando. *Slavery and Social Death: A Comparative Study*. Cambridge, MA: Harvard University Press, 1982.

Phelan, Peggy. *Mourning Sex: Performing Public Memories*. New York: Routledge, 1997.

Pick, Anat. *Creaturely Poetics: Animality and Vulnerability in Literature and Film*. New York: Columbia University Press, 2011.

Pickering, Kenneth. *Key Concepts in Drama and Performance*. New York: Palgrave MacMillan, 2010.

Pierson, Roscoe M. "Alexander Bedward and the Jamaica Native Baptist Church." In *Black Apostles: Afro-American Clergy Confront the Twentieth Century*, edited by Randall K. Burnett and Richard Newman, 1–10. Boston: G. K. Hall, 1978.

Pinn, Anthony B. *Varieties of African American Religious Experience: Toward a Comparative Black Theology*. Minneapolis: Fortress Press, 2017.

Pollard, Velma. "Writing Bridges of Sound: *Praise Song for the Widow* and *Louisiana.*" *Caribbean Quarterly* 55, no. 1 (Mar. 2009): 33–41.
Post, Ken. *Arise Ye Starvelings: The Jamaica Labour Rebellion of 1938 and Its Aftermath.* The Hague: Institute of Social Studies, Martinus Nijhoff, 1978.
Pradel, Lucie. *African Beliefs in the New World: Popular Literary Traditions of the Caribbean.* Translated by Catherine Bernard. Trenton, NJ: Africa World Press, 2000.
Puri, Shalini. "'An Other' Realism: Erna Brodber's *Myal.*" *Ariel* 24, no. 3 (1998): 95–115.
Pym, Anthony. *Exploring Translation Theories.* 2nd ed. New York: Routledge, 2014.
Raboteau, Albert J. *Canaan Land: A Religious History of African Americans.* Oxford: Oxford University Press, 2001.
Rahming, Melvin B. "Towards a Critical Theory of Spirit: The Insistent Demands of Erna Brodber's 'Myal.'" In *Changing Currents: Transnational Caribbean Literary and Cultural Criticism,* edited by Emily Williams and Melvin B. Rahming, 305–20. Trenton, NJ: Africa World Press, 2006.
Rainbow, Bernarr, and Charles Edward McGuire. "Tonic Sol-Fa." Oxford Music Online: Grove Music Online. https://www.oxfordmusiconline.com/grovemusic/view/10.1093/gmo/9781561592630.001.0001/omo-9781561592630-e-0000028124.
Ramin, Zohreh, and Monireh Arvin. "Derek Walcott's *Dream on Monkey Mountain:* A Multifaceted Phantasmagorical Narrative." *Journal of Teaching and Research* 8, no. 6 (Nov. 2017): 1161–69.
Rampersand, Arnold. *The Life of Langston Hughes.* 2 vols. Oxford: Oxford University Press, 1986.
Rankine, Claudia. *Citizen: An American Lyric.* New York: Greywolf Press, 2014.
Rappaport, Roy A. *Ecology, Meaning, and Religion.* Berkeley: North Atlantic Books. 1979.
Redmond, Shana L. *Anthem: Social Movements and the Sound of Solidarity in the African Diaspora.* New York: NYU Press, 2014.
Reed, Roxanne R. "The Restorative Power of Sound: A Case for Communal Catharsis in Toni Morrison's *Beloved.*" *Journal of Feminist Studies in Religion* 23, no. 1 (Spring 2007): 55–71.
Reid, Michelle. "Nalo Hopkinson." In *Fifty Key Figures in Science Fiction,* edited by Mark Bould, Andrew M. Butler, Adam Roberts, and Sherryl Vint, 106–11. New York: Routledge Taylor and Francis, 2009.
Roach, Joseph R. *Cities of the Dead: Circum-Atlantic Performance.* New York: Columbia University Press, 1996.
———. "Introduction [to Hermeneutics and Phenomenology]." In *Critical Theory and Performance,* edited by Janelle G. Reinelt and Joseph Roach, 353–55. Ann Arbor: University of Michigan Press, 1992.
———. *It.* Ann Arbor: University of Michigan Press, 2007.

Roberts, June. *Reading Erna Brodber: Uniting the Black Diaspora Through Folk Culture and Religion.* Westport, CT: Praeger, 2006.
Robinson, Douglas. *Who Translates? Translator Subjectivities Beyond Reason.* Albany: State University of New York Press, 2001.
Romdhani, Rebecca. "Zombies Go to Toronto: Zombifying Shame in Nalo Hopkinson's *Brown Girl in the Ring.*" *Research in African Literatures* 46, no. 4 (2015): 72–89.
Romero, Channette. *Activism and the American Novel: Religion and Resistance in Fiction by Women of Color.* Charlottesville: University of Virginia Press, 2014.
Rowe, Marcia. "Different Approach as 'Bedward' Return." *Gleaner.* Nov. 28, 2011. jamaica-gleaner.com.
Russell, Heather. *Legba's Crossing: Narratology in the African Atlantic.* Athens: University of Georgia Press, 2009.
"Rutgers-Camden Spanish Professor Translates Prize-Winning Latin American Novel." Press release. Apr. 7, 2010. https://news.rutgers.edu/newsrelease/rutgers%E2%80%93camden-spanish-professor-translates-prize-winning-latin-american-novel/2010040#.WuR83ZPwOQ.
Ryan, Judylyn S. *Spirituality as Ideology in Black Women's Film and Literature.* Athens: University of Georgia Press, 2005.
Satchell, Veront M. "Early Stirrings of Black Nationalism in Colonial Jamaica: Alexander Bedward of the Jamaica Native Baptist Free Church, 1889–1921." *Journal of Caribbean History* 38, no. 1 (2004): 75–106.
Saussure, Ferdinand de. *Course in General Linguistics.* 1916. LaSalle, IL: Open Court, 1998.
Schechner, Richard. *Performance Studies: An Introduction.* 3rd ed. New York: Routledge, 2013.
Searle, John R. *Speech Acts: An Essay in the Philosophy of Language.* London: Cambridge University Press, 1970.
Shange, Ntozake. *For Colored Girls Who Have Considered Suicide/When the Rainbow Is Enuf.* 1974. In *Totem Voices,* edited by Paul C. Harrison, 223–75. New York: Grove Press, 1989.
———. "An Interview with Ntozake Shange." Interview by Henry Blackwell. *Black American Literature Forum* 13, no. 4 (1979): 134–38. doi:10.2307/3041478.
Sharpe, Jenny. "When Spirits Talk: Reading Erna Brodber's *Louisiana* for Affect." *Small Axe: A Caribbean Journal of Criticism* 16, no. 3.39 (Nov. 2012): 90–102.
Sharpley-Whiting, Denean T. *Frantz Fanon: Conflicts and Feminisms.* Lanham, MD: Rowman & Littlefield, 1997.
Sheller, Mimi. *Consuming the Caribbean: From Arawaks to Zombies.* London: Routledge, 2003.
Simons, Tad. "Bill T. Jones Sets Walcott's Mountain in Motion." *American Theatre* 11, no. 5–6. (May 1994): 48.
Simpson, George Eaton. "The Nine Night Ceremony in Jamaica." *Journal of American Folklore* 70, no. 278 (1957): 329–35.

Singh, Julietta. *Unthinking Mastery: Dehumanism and Decolonial Entanglements*. Durham, NC: Duke University Press, 2017.
Smith, Valerie. *Self-Discovery and Authority in Afro-American Narrative*. Cambridge, MA: Harvard University Press, 1987.
Southern, Eileen. *The Music of Black Americans: A History*. New York: Norton, 1997.
Spenser, Jon Michael. *Sacred Symphony: The Chanted Sermon of the Black Preacher*. New York: Greenwood Press, 1987.
Spillers, Hortense. "Fabrics of History: Essays on the Black Sermon." PhD diss., Brandeis University, Waltham, MA, 1974. ProQuest Dissertations Publishing.
———. "'Mama's Baby, Papa's Maybe': An American Grammar Book." In *Black, White, and in Color: Essays on American Literature and Culture*, 203–29. Chicago: University of Chicago Press, 2003.
———. "Moving On Down the Line: Variations on the African American Sermon." In *Black, White and In Color*, 251–76.
Spivak, Gayatri Chakravorty. *In Other Worlds: Essays in Cultural Politics*. London: Routledge, 1987.
Stanislavski, Constantin. *An Actor Prepares*. 1936. New York: Routledge, 1989.
Stewart, Dianne M. *Three Eyes for the Journey: African Dimensions of the Jamaican Religious Experience*. New York: Oxford University Press, 2005.
Stoller, Paul. *Embodying Colonial Memories: Spirit Possession, Power, and the Hauka in West Africa*. New York: Routledge, 1995.
Strouse, Jean. "Toni Morrison's Black Magic." *Newsweek*. March 30, 1981, 52–57.
Sundquist, Eric J. *The Hammers of Creation: Folk Culture in Modern African-American Fiction*. Athens: University of Georgia Press, 1992.
Taylor, Diana. *The Archive and the Repertoire: Performing Cultural Memory in the Americas*. Durham, NC: Duke University Press, 2003.
Taylor, Patrick. *The Encyclopedia of Caribbean Religions*. 2 vols. Champagne: University of Illinois Press, 2015.
Ten Kortenaar, Neil. "Foreign Possessions: Erna Brodber's *Myal:* The Medium and Her Message." *Ariel* 30, no. 4 (Oct. 1990): 51–74.
Thiong'o, Ngũgĩ Wa. "Notes Towards a Performance Theory of Orature." *Performance Research* 12, no. 3 (2007): 4–7.
Thomas, Marion A. "Reflections on the Sanctified Church as Portrayed by Zora Neale Hurston." *Black American Literature Forum* 25, no. 1 (1991): 35–41.
Thompson, Robert Farris. "Recapturing Heaven's Glamour: Afro-Caribbean Festivalizing Arts." In *Caribbean Festival Arts: Each and Every Bit of Difference*, edited by John W. Nunley and Judith Bettelheim, 16–29. Seattle: University of Washington Press, 1988.
Thurman, Howard. *Deep River* and *The Negro Spiritual Speaks of Life and Death*. 1945. Richmond, VA: Friends United, 1975.

Tiffin, Helen. "Cold Hearts and (Foreign) Tongues: Recitation and Reclamation of the Female Body in the Works of Erna Brodber and Jamaica Kincaid." *Callaloo* 16, no. 4 (1993): 909–21.

———. "Decolonization and Audience: Erna Brodber's *Myal* and Jamaica Kincaid's *A Small Place*." *SPAN* 30 (1990): 27–38.

Tillis, Antonio. "*Changó, El Gran Putas:* A Postmodern Historiographic Metafictional Text." *Afro-Hispanic Review* 21, no. 1/2 (2002): 171–78.

———. *Manuel Zapata Olivella and the "Darkening" of Latin American Literature*. Columbia: University of Missouri Press, 2005.

Tittler, Jonathan. "Catching the Spirit: *Changó, El Gran Putas* in English Translation." *Afro-Hispanic Review* 21, no. 1/2 (2002): 107.

———. "*Changó, el gran putas* de Manuel Zapata Olivella en traducción: Movimiento lateral y pensamiento lateral." In *"Chambacú, la historia la escribes tú": Ensayos sobre cultura afrocolombiana*, edited by Lucía Ortiz, 183–96. Madrid, Spain: Iberoamericana, 2007.

———. Letter to Manuel Zapata Olivella. Sept. 11, 1995. Manuel Zapata Olivella Collection, Vanderbilt University, Nashville.

Tosches, Nick. *Unsung Heroes of Rock 'n' Roll: The Birth of Rock in the Wild Years Before Elvis*. New York: Da Capo Press, 1999.

"Tracking Derek Walcott's Trek through the Gleaner (Pt. 1: 1950–1960)." dig Jamaica: Digital Information on the Gleaner. Mar. 21, 2017. http://digjamaica.com/m/blog/tracking-derek-walcotts-trek-through-the-gleaner/.

Turner, Victor, with Roger D. Abrahams and Alfred Harris. *The Ritual Process: Structure and Anti-Structure*. Chicago: Aldine Publishing, 2011.

Uhrbach, Jan R. "A Note on Language and Naming in *Dream on Monkey Mountain*." *Callaloo* 29 (Autumn 1986): 578–82.

Urioste-Buschman, Martina. "The Caribbean Allegory of Mami Wata: A Decolonial Reading of Gendered 'Plantation Memories' within Contemporary Jamaican Fiction." In *Essays: Exploring the Global Caribbean*, edited by Susan Roberson, 2–19. Newcastle, UK: Cambridge Scholars, 2013.

Valkeakari, Tuire. *Religious Idiom and the African American Novel, 1952–1998*. Gainesville: University of Florida Press, 2007.

Venuti, Lawrence, ed. *The Translation Studies Reader*. New York: Routledge, 2004.

———. *The Translator's Invisibility: A History of Translation*. London: Routledge, 2008.

Walcott, Derek. *Dream on Monkey Mountain and Other Plays*. New York: Farrar, Straus, and Giroux, 1970.

———. *Ti-Jeanne and His Brothers*. In *Dream on Monkey Mountain and Other Plays*, 81–166.

———. "What the Twilight Says." In *Dream on Monkey Mountain and Other Plays*, 3–40.

———. Interview by Olivier Stephenson. In *Visions and Voices: Conversations with Fourteen Caribbean Playwrights*, edited by Olivier Stephenson. London: Peepal Press, 2013.
Wall, Cheryl. "Mules and Men and Women: Zora Neale Hurston's Strategies of Narration and Visions of Female Empowerment." *Black American Literature Forum* 23, no. 4 (Winter 1989): 661–80.
Wallace, Anthony F. C. "Revitalization Movements." *American Anthropologist* 58, no. 2 (April 1956): 264–81.
Warner-Lewis, Maureen. "The Ancestral Factor in Jamaica's African Religions." In *African Creative Expressions of the Divine*, edited by Kortright Davis and Elias Farajaje Jones, 63–80. Washington, DC: Howard University School of Divinity, 1991.
———. *Central Africa in the Caribbean: Transcending Time, Transforming Culture*. Barbados: University of West Indies Press, 2003.
Watson, Roxanne. "The Native Baptist Church's Political Role in Jamaica: Alexander Bedward's Trial for Sedition." *Journal of Caribbean History* 42, no. 2 (2008): 231–54.
Watson, Sonja Stephenson. "*Changó, El Gran Putas*: Contemporary Afro-Hispanic Historical Novel." *Afro-Hispanic Review* 25, no. 1 (2006): 67–85.
Weber, Bruce. "Theater Review: An Old Man Fights for His Kingly Tribal Dream." *New York Times*. Oct. 14, 2003.
Weber, Max. "The Concept of Legitimate Order." 1947. Translated by A. R. Henderson and Talcott Parsons. In *Max Weber: On Charisma and Institution Building*, edited by S. N. Eisenstadt, 11–17. Chicago: University of Chicago Press, 1968.
———. "The Nature of Charismatic Authority and Its Routinization." 1947. Translated by A. R. Henderson and Talcott Parsons. In *Max Weber: On Charisma and Institution Building*, 48–69.
———. "The Prophet." 1922. Translated by Ephraim Fischoff. In *Max Weber: On Charisma and Institution Building*, 253–67.
———. "The Pure Types of Legitimate Authority." 1947. Translated by A. R. Henderson and Talcott Parsons. In *Max Weber: On Charisma and Institution Building*, 46–47.
Weems, Renita J. "African American Women and the Bible." In *Stony the Road We Trod: African American Biblical Interpretation*, edited by Cain Hope Felder, 61. Minneapolis: Fortress Press, 1991.
Weheliye, Alexander. *Habeas Viscus: Racializing Assemblages, Biopolitics, and Black Feminist Theories of the Human*. Durham, NC: Duke University Press, 2014.
Wessinger, Catherine, ed. *The Oxford Handbook of Millennialism*. Oxford: Oxford University Press, 2011.
West, Cornel. *Keeping Faith: Philosophy and Race in America*. New York: Routledge, 1994.

———. *Prophesy Deliverance!* Louisville: Westminster John Knox Press, 2002.
———. "Reviving a Grand Tradition of 'Black Prophetic Fire.'" Interview by Scott Simon. *Weekend Edition Saturday,* NPR. https://www.npr.org/2014/11/01/360452483/reviving-a-grand-tradition-of-black-prophetic-fire.
West, Cornel, and Christa Buschendorf. *Black Prophetic Fire.* Boston: Beacon Press, 2014.
West, Cornel, and Eddie S. Glaude, eds. *African American Religious Thought: An Anthology.* Louisville: Westminster John Knox Press, 2003.
Whitted, Qiana. *"A God of Justice?": The Problem of Evil in Twentieth-Century Black Literature.* Charlottesville: University of Virginia Press, 2009.
Wilentz, Gay. "An African-Based Reading of *Sula.*" In *Approaches to Teaching the Novels of Toni Morrison,* edited by Nellie Y. McKay and Kathryn Earle, 128–29. New York: MLA, 1997.
Williams, Delores. *Sisters in the Wilderness: The Challenge of Womanist God-Talk.* Maryknoll, NY: Orbis Books, 1994.
Williams, Michael (composer). "Bedward the Flying Preacher." Singers & Players, featuring Prince Far I. *Staggering Heights,* Sound Boy Records, 1983.
Wood, Sarah. "'Serving the Spirits': Emergent Identities in Nalo Hopkinson's *Brown Girl in the Ring.*" *Extrapolation* 46, no. 3 (Fall 2005): 315–26.
Worthen, W. B. "Introduction: Drama, Theater, and Culture." In *The Wadsworth Anthology of Drama.* 6th ed., edited by W. B. Worthen, 1–10. Boston: Wadsworth Cengage Learning, 2011.
Wynter, Sylvia. "No Humans Involved: An Open Letter to My Colleagues." Knowledge on Trial, special edition of *Forum N.H.I. Knowledge for the 21st Century* 1, no. 1 (Fall 1994): 42–73.
———. "The Re-Enchantment of Humanism: An Interview with Sylvia Wynter." Interview by David Scott. *Small Axe: A Caribbean Journal of Criticism* 8 (September 2000): 119–207.
———. "Unsettling the Coloniality of Being/Power/Truth/Freedom: Towards the Human, After Man, Its Overrepresentation—An Argument." *CR: The New Centennial Review* 3, no. 3 (Fall 2003): 257–337.
Yon, Daniel. "Identity and Differences in the Caribbean Diaspora: Case Study from Metropolitan Toronto." In *The Reordering of Culture: Latin America, the Caribbean, and Canada in the Hood,* edited by Alvina Ruprecht, 479–98. Montreal: McGill-Queen's University Press, 1995.
Young, Josiah III. *A Pan-African Theology.* Trenton, NJ: Africa World Press, 1992.
Zahan, Dominique. *The Religion, Spirituality, and Thought of Traditional Africa.* Chicago: University of Chicago Press, 1979.
Zapata Olivella, Manuel. *Changó, el gran putas.* Bogotá, Colombia: Editorial Oveja Negro, 1983.
———. *Changó, The Biggest Badass.* Translated by Jonathan Tittler. Lubbock: Texas Tech University Press, 2010.

———. Letter to Dorita Piquero de Nouhaud. Feb. 19, 1985. Manuel Zapata Olivella Collection, Vanderbilt University, Nashville.
———. Letter to Jean-Luc Pidoux Payot. Mar. 28, 1985. Manuel Zapata Olivella Collection, Vanderbilt University, Nashville.
Zauditu-Selassie, K. *African Spiritual Traditions in the Novels of Toni Morrison.* Gainesville: University of Florida Press, 2009.
Zimmerman, Jens. *Hermeneutics: A Very Short Introduction.* Oxford: Oxford University Press, 2015.
Žižek, Slavoj. *The Sublime Object of Ideology.* London: Verso, 1989.

Index

Aching, Gerard, 7, 122–24, 131–32
acting, 6, 16, 24, 29, 33, 35–36, 39, 51, 54, 164, 175–76, 179–80, 182, 188, 191, 206n6
Africa, 16, 50, 68–69, 73–75, 166, 170, 186, 218n7; beliefs and practices brought over from, 4, 6, 9–10, 12–13, 15–17, 23, 26–27, 31–32, 42, 44, 50–51, 53, 59, 64–65, 69, 89, 103–5, 108–9, 116, 140–41, 148–49, 153–54, 156–58, 164–68, 171–72, 194–96, 201n1, 205n31, 213n30, 216n24; Ethiopia, 170; Ghana, 64; literature of, 59; Rhodesia, 187; symbolism of, 170, 172, 180–84, 186. *See also* tribes
African American Vernacular English, 37, 55, 209n34. *See also* dialect
African Diaspora, 15–17; as Middle Passage, 16, 26
African Methodist Episcopal (AME) Church, 45
Agamben, Giorgio, 165–66, 222n27
agency, 3, 7, 20, 50, 52, 61–62, 65, 67, 74, 77, 82, 85, 95–96, 98–99, 102–3, 138–40, 147, 157, 159–60, 162, 163, 168, 173
Als, Hilton, 188
Althusser, Louis, 106, 109, 142
Americas, 2–4, 6, 11–13, 15–18, 26, 64, 80, 99, 116, 118, 132, 152; Afrodiasporic, 3–6, 11, 15–18, 31, 103, 148, 156, 198; Black, 11, 201n1; as New World, 3, 6, 12, 14, 16, 31, 125, 149–50, 156, 172, 196–98; North, 17, 70, 72, 119; South, 14
ancestors, 50, 74, 76, 83, 139–40, 194, 215n7, 225n1; as Divine Community, 117, 137, 168; hermeneutics and, 9, 17, 89, 95, 97–98; and performance style, 59; possession and, 83, 91, 145, 222n31; realms, 63, 88, 100, 145; temporality and, 88, 166–68, 172; in translation and mediation, 75–76, 80
Anderson, Osborn Perry, 75, 98–99
Anderson, Victor, 14, 43
Angelou, Maya, 186
Anglican/Episcopal Church, 95–96
anthropology, 5, 13, 74, 83, 86, 157, 204n27, 211n10, 213n23, 213n25
anticolonialism: discourse, 185; spiritual movements, 108, 171, 181, 183, 185–86
apocalypse, 151, 157, 159–60, 165, 168. *See also* eschatology
Appiah, Kwame Anthony, 13
Arendt, Hannah, 142
Artaud, Antonin, 222n25
áshe, 197, 217n35
Audible.com, 53–55
audience: academic, 73, 84, 89; audiobook listener as, 54, 56; community and, 21, 56; English-speaking, 71–73, 81; hermeneutics and, 149, 152–53, 167, 169, 174, 176, 178–79, 182–84, 187, 196; human bodies as, 144; knowledge of, 122, 152, 159, 165; as legitimating force, 162–63, 176–77, 184; participation of, 3, 8, 20, 33–35, 44–45, 53, 56, 63–64, 81, 84, 138–39, 191, 195; race and nationality of, 36, 61, 67, 84, 89, 91, 186; reader as, 1, 8, 54, 56, 154; reception of, 5, 53, 162, 193; theatrical, 156, 162–64, 167, 169, 176–79, 182–84, 187, 196; transformation of, 42, 49. *See also* congregation

audiobooks, 3, 8, 14, 18, 24, 26, 45–46, 48, 52, 62
Augustine of Hippo (Aurelius Augustinius), 97
Augustown (Miller), 154, 160
Austin, J. L., 7, 40, 206n2
authority, 12, 14, 16, 18, 23, 25, 27, 32, 44, 46, 48–49, 51–52, 63–64, 149, 153–54, 156–57, 159–61, 163, 168, 172, 174–75, 177, 183, 187–89, 195; methods of establishing and maintaining, 20, 32–33, 35, 47, 117, 152, 157–59, 160, 168, 176–77
authorship, 29, 67, 74

Babylon, 151
Báez, Josefina, 1–2, 18, 21, 192–96, 199
Baker-Fletcher, Karen, 48
Balandier, George, 67
Bantú, 50, 69, 74–75. *See also* Africa; tribes
Baptists, 30, 32, 45, 89, 166, 222n29; Native Baptist, 155–56, 165, 168, 216n19, 220nn13–14, 222n30; Second Zion, 43, 207n14; services, 28, 31, 41, 63. *See also* Christianity
Baptist War of 1831, 12
Baron Samedi, 172, 182–84
Barnett, Leonard, 14
Bassard, Katherine Clay, 11, 27, 48, 61, 207n15
BBC (British Broadcasting Company), 154, 219n10
Bedward: A Play in Two Acts (Marriott), 148–50, 152–54, 156–74, 176–78, 189, 192, 195, 220nn15–16, 221nn20–21, 222nn30–31
Bedwardism, 152, 154–56, 158, 165, 168, 219n12
belonging, 74, 81–83, 100, 103, 121, 137–40, 193, 198, 224n40
Beloved (Morrison), 3, 8, 18, 24, 26, 34, 44–62, 64–65, 84, 103, 139, 181, 195, 209n30
"Beloved, Beloved, Now We Are the Sons of God," 34, 36
Bellegarde-Smith, Patrick, 66–67, 173
Benedicty-Kokken, Alessandra, 4, 6, 67, 77, 80, 182, 203n11, 213n31
Benítez-Rojo, Antonio, 8, 91
Benjamin, Walter: "Philosophy of History," 165, 222n26; "The Task of the Translator," 66, 75, 81, 88, 165

Bennett, Louise (Miss Lou), 120, 219n9
Bergthaller, Hannes, 48
Best, Lloyd, 106, 108–9
Best, Stephen, 114, 215n9
Bhabha, Homi, 111, 185, 201n6
Bible, 40, 46–47, 97, 106, 148–49, 162, 172, 207n9, 210n7, 212n22; Colossians, 212n22; I Corinthians, 163; Exodus, 49; Genesis, 105, 113, 172, 215n8; Isaiah, 30, 53, 207n10; Jeremiah, 221n21; John, 30, 34, 189, 207n9; Joshua, 184; Luke, 212n14; Mark, 30, 207n9; Matthew, 30, 37, 166, 207n9, 208n16, 212n14, 221n21; Peter, 30, 207n10; Psalms, 173, 207n9; 2 Timothy, 106, 162; Zechariah, 30
biopolitics, 119, 124–25, 131, 133; and biopower, 116, 124, 127, 130; and race, 129–31, 133
biotechnology, 116, 122–25, 130
Black Church, 23–24, 26
Black Church Studies: An Introduction (Floyd-Thomas, et al.), 24, 30, 58, 148
Blanchot, Maurice, 150, 152, 156, 159–60, 164, 168, 178, 181, 187, 189, 218n7
Boas, Franz, 26, 88
Boddy, Janice, 67, 92, 95
bodies: agency and, 9, 60, 62, 82, 133; caring for and healing, 60–62, 64–65, 143; community and, 49, 58, 63–64, 82, 95–97, 103, 136, 138; discourse and, 6, 9, 39, 47, 73, 75–76, 79–82, 101, 108–10, 123, 138, 191, 193; economies and, 116, 118–19, 121, 123–25, 130, 133–34, 141; epistemology and, 9, 14, 79, 197; injured, 45, 47, 52, 102–3, 110–11, 115, 181–82, 138, 140, 143; as metaphysical, 61, 80, 128; mortality and, 123, 132–33, 136; occupied, 19, 67, 79, 102, 193; as place, 77, 97, 182, 197; power over, 20, 40, 44, 47, 49, 116–19, 124–26, 128–32, 135–36, 138, 141; relationship to mind, soul, and spirit, 50–51, 64–65, 67, 82, 108–9, 113, 115, 117, 126–28, 133, 137, 143, 158, 197; as signs, 19, 102, 113, 115, 132, 135, 143; during spiritual and religious events, 27, 35, 42–44, 51–53, 58, 63, 66–67, 77, 79–80, 94–96, 127, 143–45; within structures of racism and colonialism, 47, 49, 59, 61, 64–65, 80,

105, 113–14, 125–26, 130, 132, 134; subjectivity and, 14, 63, 79, 82, 96, 101, 197, 145; theological understandings of, 50, 58–59, 64–65; women's, 19, 103, 115, 126, 132, 143, 196. *See also* flesh; hands; heart; mouth; skin
Borelli, Mellisa Blanco, 9
Bourguignon, Erika, 78, 211n14
Brathwaite, Kamau, 154
Brazil, 116, 210n2
breath, 23, 33, 35, 45, 56, 58, 144, 174; and "ha," 40–42, 51; rhythmic, 18, 36; textual markers of, 35, 38, 41–42, 47
Brecht, Bertolt, 8
Brewster, Yvonne, 164
British Broadcasting Corporation (BBC), 154, 219n10
British empire, 16, 105–7, 111, 113, 135, 159–60, 221n19
Britton, Celia, 85
Brodber, Erna, 3–4, 14, 19–20, 47, 63, 68, 83–91, 96–97, 100–114, 116, 120, 129, 135, 140, 142–46, 150, 162, 181, 193, 197, 214n33, 215n8
Brown Girl in the Ring (Hopkinson), 3, 19–20, 51, 90, 97, 101–4, 115–42, 146–47, 149, 170, 173, 176, 203n14, 216n23, 217n29, 217n32, 225n1
Brown, Henry "Box," 12
Butler, Judith, x, 7

Cabrera, Lydia, 75
Canada, 3, 130–31; Afro-Caribbeans in, 216n23; The Burn, 115, 117, 124, 128–32, 134–35, 139–42; Toronto, 115, 118, 124, 127, 129–31, 133, 135, 216n27, 218n3
Candomblé, 73, 80, 201n2
Cannon, Katie Geneva, 14
capitalism, 2, 20, 102, 115, 117–19, 124, 129–32, 140, 142; late, 20, 102, 218n5
capitulation, 3, 19, 83, 95, 98
Carlson, Marvin, 9
Caribbean, 13–14, 17, 104–5, 125, 131, 150, 153, 165, 168, 170–72, 186, 189; Afro-Caribbean people and practices, 10, 31, 67, 84, 103–6, 108, 115, 127, 130, 141, 144, 150, 156, 158, 168, 171, 196; culture, 119, 122, 124, 154, 189; discourse, 13–14, 67, 77, 85–86, 91, 103, 106, 111, 146, 149, 154–55,

164–65, 171–72, 180, 188; Francophone, 77; religion in, 13–14, 67, 84, 103–5, 111, 116, 120, 122, 140–42, 144, 148, 150, 153–54, 156, 158, 166, 168, 171, 180; southern, 77; West Indies, 94, 154, 171, 205, 215n8
Castro, Anne Margaret, 86, 104, 106
catharsis, 25–26, 30, 33–34, 37, 45, 50, 62, 206n3
Césaire, Aimé, 135, 203n13
Changó, el gran putas (*Changó, the Biggest Badass;* Zapata Olivella), 3, 19, 66–85, 87, 90–91, 94–95, 98–100, 102, 110, 140, 143, 170, 172, 180, 184, 195–96, 203n14, 209n29, 211n10, 211nn12–13, 212n18
charisma, 20, 25, 149, 154, 156–61, 169, 172, 176–77, 187, 189, 221n19, 223n34
Church of God in Christ, 30
Christianity: Afro-diasporic, 11–12, 14, 16, 23–25, 27–28, 30–38, 40–48, 50–51, 63, 68, 76, 88–90, 97, 105, 108, 141, 148–49, 151–52, 154–59, 163, 165–68, 171–72, 204n26, 209n27, 211n13, 213n29, 221n21, 225n46; Anglican/Episcopal Church, 95–96; beliefs and practices, 12, 44, 49–51, 53, 57–58, 68, 70, 76–77, 88, 97, 105, 108, 141, 143, 148–52, 157–58, 165, 166–68, 171–72, 194, 204n19, 212n14; Black Church, 23–24, 26; Catholic, 12, 68, 172, 204n22; Church of God in Christ, 30; early, 148, 157, 163; Euro-American, 9, 12, 14, 44, 46, 50, 70, 76–77, 97, 108, 111, 157, 172, 179, 204n26; hermeneutics and, 70, 76, 97, 205n28; Methodists, 111, 220n13; Protestant, 11–12, 14–15, 18, 23–35, 37–38, 41–43, 45, 57, 63, 80, 89, 95–96, 108, 111, 151, 155–56, 165–68. *See also* Baptists; Bible; Pentecostalism; Sanctified Church
citation, 5, 9, 37, 120–21, 193
Citizen: An American Lyric (Rankine), 102
Classical Theater of Harlem, 169, 182
Cliff, Michelle, 196, 198
Coleman, James, 11, 217n37
collaboration: authorial and directorial, 28–29, 31; embodied, 18, 24, 44, 52, 63; interpretive, 54–55, 169, 180, 187; liturgical, 27, 31–35, 42, 44, 52, 53, 63; sonic, 107

254 Index

Colombia, 3, 212n18; Afro-Colombians in, 67
colonialism, 3, 9, 12–13, 16, 73, 85, 107, 116, 118, 129, 135, 150–51, 153, 171–72, 178–83, 185–86, 196, 198; allegories of, 102, 105, 107–8, 112, 114–15, 118, 122, 135, 146, 151, 166, 171, 214n6, 215n7; authorities of, 151, 153, 156–57, 159, 161–62, 166, 168, 178, 182–83; education, 106, 111–14, 208n23, 221n19; epistemology and, 17, 73, 85, 91, 111, 183, 197–98; ideology and discourse of, 4, 17, 107, 111–14, 125, 129, 132, 142, 151, 153, 160–62, 164, 171–72, 179–80, 183, 185, 198, 204n25, 210nn2–3; Sartre on, 179–80, 185, 223n40; subjectivity and, 73, 85, 91, 102, 111–13, 132, 159–60, 171, 180–81, 185–86, 210n3, 212n16, 223n40
Comrade, Bliss Ain't Playing (Báez), 1–2, 18, 21, 192, 195, 199
community, 11, 16–17, 19, 24–25, 30, 34, 42, 44–45, 49–52, 55–56, 58, 60–61, 63–68, 74–75, 80, 82, 86, 89, 95–96, 98, 100–101, 103–7, 113–14, 117, 121, 124, 127, 134–35, 137–40, 142–43, 145–46, 158, 168, 172, 186, 188, 193–98; Divine Community, 89, 117, 168
congregation, 24, 27, 30–32, 34–35, 40–43, 47, 51–52, 55–56, 58, 62, 64, 142, 144, 158, 166, 191–92; as flock, 30, 32–34, 41, 43, 158, 161. *See also* audience
conjure, 84, 97, 105–6, 113–14, 117, 122, 127, 133
consent, 83, 86, 91, 129, 180–81, 223n40
conversion, 3, 170, 174, 177, 179, 181–83, 219–20nn12–13
Cooper, Carolyn, 120, 151, 154, 219n8
cosmologies, 9, 14, 21, 26, 51, 84, 116, 169, 178, 183, 187, 195, 218n41
creatures, 118, 131–35; animals, 67, 90, 105, 118, 121–22, 124–26, 134, 139, 141, 143, 170, 172–73, 180, 216n19, 217n34; human, 131; nonhuman, 135
crucifixion, 30, 32, 34
Cuba, 211n12; Afro-Cuban religion, 74, 202n5; Spanish of, 67

Daily Gleaner, 157, 161, 164–65, 167
dance, 4, 7, 9, 26, 46, 50, 53, 58, 62, 64, 120–21, 135, 137–40, 176, 180, 185, 194
Daniel, Yvonne, 53
Dash, Michael, 109, 133
Davis, Angela, 73, 211n10
Davis, Wade, 128, 217n32
Dayan, Joan (Colin), 102, 115
death, 33, 37, 43, 49, 51, 65, 80, 82, 88, 90, 92, 99, 117, 124, 127, 133, 137, 139–41, 143, 145, 151, 158, 172, 182, 185, 213n29; the deceased, 50, 53, 76, 80, 83, 87–90, 93–94, 99–100, 123, 128, 139–41, 143, 161, 166–67, 183, 194, 211n12, 213n29, 225n1; existence after, 51, 88, 90, 104, 111, 117, 140–41, 161, 168, 215n7; mortality, 116, 133, 136–37, 141; murder, 65, 75, 117, 119, 124, 130–31, 139–40, 143, 151, 170, 184, 186, 189; psychological, 93–95; spirits of the dead, 71, 74, 89, 117. *See also* ancestors
decolonization: affective, 136; mental, 151; of scholarship, 197–98; spiritual, 9
Dee, Ruby, 209n33
De Ferrari, Guillermina, 6, 80, 125, 132, 136, 197
DeFrantz, Thomas, 9, 138
dehumanization, 12, 129, 133–34, 186, 196, 225n2
Depestre, René, 135
Deren, Maya, 77, 90
Derrida, Jacques, 7–9, 167, 202n9, 222n25
devil, 113, 121–22, 125, 136
dialect, 35, 37–39, 41, 47. *See also* African American Vernacular English
diaspora, 17, 99. *See also* African Diaspora
dispossession, 98, 102, 104, 114, 116, 118–19, 125, 127–28, 130, 132, 135, 140, 146, 149, 154, 157, 182, 196
Dominicanish (Báez), 194
Douglas, Kelly Brown, 14
Douglass, Frederick, 12
Dream on Monkey Mountain (Walcott), 3, 20, 90, 123, 148–50, 152–53, 168–89, 196, 224n42
dreams, 117, 148, 153, 155, 168–84, 186–87, 189; theatrical representations of, 153, 169–71, 173–79, 182–83, 187, 223n32

drugs, 117, 123, 125, 128, 132, 136, 139, 217n32
drums, 26, 42, 144
Du Bois, W. E. B., 23–24, 47, 129, 131, 135, 217n33, 218n4
duppy, 108, 110–11, 117–18, 124–26, 128–29, 136, 139–41, 145, 215n11, 215n16
Durkheim, Emile, 25
dystopia, 104, 117, 125, 130

eating, 97, 121–22, 125, 128, 135, 139, 217n34
Ebeling, Gerhard, 10
ekobio, 74–76, 98–99, 172, 211n12
epigraphs, 81, 119–21, 124–25, 137, 139, 147, 169, 179–80, 186
epistemology, 9, 13–15, 17, 91–93, 150, 164, 177, 180, 196–98, 203n11; spiritual, 4–5, 9, 13–14, 17, 102–4, 108; subjectivity and, 81, 83, 93, 96, 100, 103, 210n3; and uncertainty, 19, 21, 81, 83, 85–87, 102, 176, 193. *See also* knowledge
eschatology, 154, 156, 158–59, 222n27. *See also* apocalypse
ethnography, 8, 18, 26, 28–31, 36, 39, 63, 88–89, 93, 121, 140, 202n5, 204n19, 208n19, 209n2, 210n6, 213nn24–25
Europe: colonialism of, 12, 16, 73, 118, 129, 132; epistemologies of, 73, 164
European Enlightenment, 4, 9, 14, 50, 87, 108

Fanon, Frantz, 179, 185, 202n6, 223nn38–39, 224nn42–43
flesh, 10, 19, 34, 50, 53, 57–62, 68, 79–81, 83, 95–96, 101, 104, 108, 114–19, 123, 125–26, 129–33, 136–37, 140–41, 182, 193
folklore, 84, 103, 115, 117, 119–22, 207n15, 215n7; performances, 102, 104, 119, 121–23, 219n9; preacher, 23, 208n17
For Colored Girls Who Have Considered Suicide/When the Rainbow Is Enuf (Shange), 21, 191–92, 196–97
Foucault, Michel, 4, 133; *Discipline and Punish*, 118, 128–29; *Society Must Be Defended*, 124, 130; *History of Sexuality*, 125; "Religious Deviations and Medical Knowledge," 212n15, 217n30
freedom, 4, 64, 75, 100, 136, 141, 150–51, 163, 174, 210n3, 212n16; as emancipation, 49, 151, 155; as manumission, 12, 45, 52. *See also* liberation

Garvey, Marcus, 155, 159
Gates, Henry Louis, 10
Geertz, Clifford, 11, 204n19
gender, 7, 27, 33, 46–48, 51, 59, 65, 74–75, 80–82, 90, 93, 103–4, 108, 115, 120, 122, 126–27, 130, 143–45, 185–86, 188, 192, 196, 224n43; and sexuality, 104, 108, 123, 126–27, 131, 144, 188–89, 197
genre, 1–2, 6, 8, 15, 18, 20, 26–28, 35, 57, 63, 81–82, 87, 117, 122, 152–54, 156, 160, 164, 169, 171, 191, 197–98
ghost, 65, 92, 108, 117, 169, 225n1
ghoul, 138, 225n1
Gibson, Melissa Dana, 162, 164
Gilpin Players, 28–29, 32, 38
Glissant, Édouard, 4, 85, 109–11, 133, 164–65; *Caribbean Discourse*, 86, 146; *Monsieur Toussaint*, 156; *Poetics of Relation*, 91–92, 101, 110, 112, 164
glossaries, 37, 42, 69–70, 208n20
God, 1–2, 12, 33–34, 41–42, 46, 49, 51, 76–77, 96–97, 106, 134–35, 143, 147, 156, 159, 163, 172–73, 175, 180, 184; as god, 77, 191–92, 196
Goddess/goddess, 1–2, 140, 176, 185, 187, 192
God Help the Child (Morrison), 54
gods, 10, 31, 42, 68, 73–74, 94, 127, 137, 139–41, 184; Changó/Shango, 68, 73, 75–77, 82, 98, 140, 184; Elegba/Esu/Eshu/Legba/Legbara, 10, 74, 79–82, 117, 127–28, 137, 140–41, 203n14, 213n27; Osain, 140–41. *See also* loas; orichas
Gordon, Lewis, 185, 223n39
grace: and charisma, 157; through imagination, 44, 49–51, 53, 56, 58, 95
Greek chorus, 33, 64
grief, 30, 53, 136–37, 167, 191, 199
Guadeloupe, 116
Guinea Land, 127, 139, 170
Guthrie Theater, 186

Haiti, 116; Kreyol, 67; San Domingo Revolution in, 12; scholarship on, 67; Vodou in, 69, 77, 90, 172, 203n14, 215n11; zombie lore in, 117, 128, 217n32
Hall, Cheryl, 48
Hall, Stuart, 99
hands, 59–62, 113–14, 132–33, 145, 150, 174, 181–82
Haney, William, 171, 175
Harlem School for the Arts, 169, 182
Harpers Ferry, 98
Hartman, Saidiya, 132
healing, 19–20, 23, 25, 101, 103–4, 109, 115–17, 135, 137, 140–41, 143–44, 147, 149, 155, 157, 165, 170, 176–78, 195–96, 199, 211n14, 214n4
hearts, 18, 45, 50, 65; as beating, 23, 51–52, 62, 64, 209n30; of Jesus, 33, 95–96; as metaphor, 52, 62, 65, 141; transplant of, 117–19, 124, 130–31, 134–35, 139, 141–42
Hegel, G. W. F., 164–65, 224n42
Hemenway, Robert E., 28–29
Henry, Paget, 7, 202n5
hermeneutics, 5, 10; African and Afro-diasporic religious, 10, 13, 24, 26, 76, 88–89, 97, 166, 203n14; ancestrally oriented, 89, 95, 205n30; anti-establishment, 20, 151, 153, 166, 171, 179, 183, 187, 198; Christian, 5, 46, 11, 70, 88, 97, 166, 208n27, 210n7; of closure, 160; collectivity and, 21, 54–56, 58, 63, 81, 84, 101, 149, 177, 184, 187; engaged surrender in, 84, 86, 97, 199; of nonetheless, 153, 169, 171; of opacity, 19, 72, 85, 91–93; performance and, 2–3, 5–9, 12–13, 18–21, 24–27, 30, 45–47, 63, 67–68, 89, 93, 95, 102–5, 110, 114, 147, 149, 151, 153, 166, 169, 183, 191–98; subjectivity and, 68, 77–79, 81, 83, 93, 101, 197; of suspicion, 177–78; of uncertainty, 68, 70–71, 73, 77–78, 81, 83, 85, 87, 169, 174. *See also* performative textual hermeneutics
Hermes, 10
Herskovits, Melville, 6, 31, 90, 213n32
heterophony (Southern), 44
Hinds, Robert, 155
Holy Ghost, 156, 158–59, 163, 212n14
Hoodoo, 105
Hopkinson, Nalo, 3, 14, 19–20, 51, 97, 101–4, 115–16, 119–35, 137, 139–42, 147, 173, 176, 193, 197, 216n23, 216n27, 217nn32–33
Hopkinson, Slade, 120, 147, 216n27
Hubbard, Dolan, 25, 207n13
Hughes, Langston, 28–29, 32, 36, 41, 207n8
humanity, 4, 12, 50, 81–82, 131–33, 135, 140, 197–98
Humphrey, Paul, 11
Hurston, Zora Neale, 3–4, 6–7, 14, 18–19, 23–32, 34–44, 46–48, 51–52, 62–65, 67, 88–89, 103, 121, 149, 163, 177, 184, 191–93, 206–7nn3–8, 207nn14–15, 208nn18–21, 211n10, 213n24, 214n34, 214n2

ideology: African and Afro-diasporic theologies and, 3, 12, 142, 184; Althusser on, 106, 109, 111–12, 142; capitalist, 20, 118, 123, 134–35; colonial, 106–7, 111–13, 129, 160, 180; embodiment of, 6, 19–20, 101, 103, 105, 109, 111–16, 123, 129, 132, 134–36, 142, 146, 149, 193, 217n32; race and, 3, 12, 132, 134, 146, 149; sound and, 106–7, 111, 113, 142, 146; state apparatus, 106, 111, 113; subjectivity, 112–13, 131, 181
Idowu, E. Bolaji, 140–41
"If We Must Die" (McKay), 72–73, 81
imagination, 8, 10, 30, 46, 49–51, 53, 55–56, 58, 65, 95, 107, 135–36, 146, 149, 154, 174, 182, 190, 194; community, 16, 194
improvisation, 25, 31, 44, 138–39, 194. *See also* performance
individualism, 4, 50, 67, 79, 95, 100–101, 145
interpellation, 7–8, 58, 61, 111, 113, 142. *See also* ideology; subjectivity
Islam, 16, 69, 205n28; Nation of, 218n4

Jab-Jab, 122–23, 137, 139
jail, 82, 153, 160, 168, 170–74, 177, 179, 181–82, 184, 211n10
Jakobson, Ramon, 69
Jamaica, 3, 12, 20, 68, 83–84, 87–88, 90, 94, 97, 104–17, 149–51, 154–68, 216n27, 220n15; Afro- and black Jamaicans in, 68, 83, 88, 107–8, 113, 154–55,

168, 172; August Town, 154–55, 164; Creole of, 120, 216n23; culture of, 4, 111, 120, 161; Grove Town, 104, 106, 113–14, 143–44, 146; histories of, 12, 87, 105, 155, 159; Kingston, 154–55, 160, 219n9, 220n15, 221n21, 222n24; Mona River, 155, 166, 222n30; religion and spirituality in, 12, 89, 108, 111, 117, 151, 155–59, 161–68, 172, 204, 215n11; St. Mary Parish, 90; Trench Town, 189; Union Camp, 155, 159, 219n11
Jelliffe, Rowena, 29–30, 32, 35, 38, 41, 206nn7–8
Jennings, La Vinia Delois, 26, 50, 53, 60, 205n31
Jerry, Bongo, 155
Jesser, Nancy, 45, 49, 64
Jesus, 30, 32–34, 37, 39–42, 44, 46–47, 52, 95, 115, 143, 155, 159, 163, 166, 189, 207nn9–10, 211n14, 221n21; as Christ, 30, 34, 49–50, 95–96, 143, 159, 163, 172, 188, 209n31
John the Baptist, 188, 221n21
Johnson, James Weldon, 206n6, 208n17
Johnson, Paul Christopher, 73, 77, 79, 85, 89, 212n16
Jonah's Gourd Vine (Hurston), 28–30, 34–38, 40–44
Jones, Bill T., 186, 224n44
Judaism, 16, 105, 165, 167, 221, 205n28, 222n26, 222n28, 225n46
justice, 76, 148, 150, 162, 196, 220n14

knowledge, 5, 12, 197–98; community, 19, 44, 51, 67, 100–101, 145, 193; embodied, 2, 9, 27, 44, 51, 53, 79–80, 93, 109, 111, 115, 129, 139, 142, 145, 197; literacy and, 46–48; as meaning-making, 2–3, 7–8, 10, 13–14, 17–18, 55, 71, 73, 77, 119, 138, 192; power and, 5, 12, 123, 125–27, 129, 152, 176; production of, 69–70, 73, 92, 97; spiritual, 8, 53, 67, 74, 80, 85, 88, 91, 94–95, 98, 116–17, 129, 143, 145, 176, 182, 192, 197; subjectivity and, 19, 67, 91–96, 100, 182, 193; ways of knowing, 6, 13, 18, 80, 87–88, 92–97, 108, 110, 177, 194, 198–99; wisdom, 59, 67, 75, 111. *See also* epistemology
Kongo Cosmogram, 58

Kumina, 9, 11, 13–14, 108, 120, 144–45, 215n12, 218n441
Kutzinski, Vera, 88, 211nn9–10

Legba. *See* gods: Elegba
loas, 117, 139, 141, 172, 182. *See also* gods; orichas
labor, 19, 40, 52, 56, 72, 99, 109, 111, 117–19, 130, 132, 135, 142; enslaved, 12, 16, 52, 118; interpretation as, 19, 56, 72, 99, 109, 111; power, 118–19; time, 130–31
Lawal, Babatunde, 65
Lee, Jarena, 12
Lewis, Phillip E., 72
liberation, 12, 45, 49, 64, 75, 80, 98, 100, 103, 108, 116, 126, 137, 141, 151, 156, 158, 169, 172, 175, 184–86. *See also* freedom
Lincoln, Eric, 14, 24–25
liturgy, 18, 24, 27, 30–36, 38, 40–45, 51–53, 55–56, 58, 61–64, 67, 147, 177, 191, 195
Lomax, Alan, 39
Long, Charles H., 13
love, 28, 45, 49–50, 52, 58–62, 64–65, 103, 106, 109–10, 120, 122, 136–37, 157, 161, 177, 180, 191, 196–97
Lovelace, Earl C., 28–30, 32, 35–36, 43–44, 49, 206nn4–5, 207n9, 208n19
Louisiana (Brodber), 3, 19, 68, 83–98, 100–103, 170, 180, 194–95, 199, 214n33, 216n17, 223n36
Lowe, Lisa, 4, 201n3, 210n3
Luis, William, 68
lwa. *See* loas

madness, 79, 93, 117, 128, 155–56, 160–62, 168, 171, 173, 176, 178–83
magic, 145, 149, 177, 217n32, 223n34
Malcolm X, 75, 218n4
Mamiya, Lawrence, 14, 24–25
Marley, Bob (Nesta Robert), 150–51, 154, 163, 181, 183, 186, 189, 218n6; "Natural Mystic," 189; "Redemption Song," 150–51, 163, 181, 183; "Trench Town," 189; "Zimbabwe," 186
Marriott, Louis, 3, 14, 20, 147, 149–50, 152–54, 156–62, 164–68, 171–72, 189, 219n11, 220nn15–16, 221nn21–22
Martinique, 85, 116

Marx, Karl, 118–19, 130
masks, 148, 104, 121–23, 131–32, 224, 140; carnival, 6; masking, 20, 119, 121–23, 127, 131–34
Matory, J. Lorand, 17
Mbiti, John, 13, 166
mediumship, 21, 66–68, 73–101; bodily experiences during, 66–67, 73–74, 77, 79–82, 90, 94–97, 101; capitulation, 3, 19, 83, 95, 98; community and, 66–68, 74–75, 80, 82, 86, 88–89, 95–96, 98–101; engaged surrender, 19, 68, 82–84, 86, 91, 97–100, 102, 180, 199, 223n40; gender and, 80–82, 93
messianism, 20, 30, 49, 64, 98, 149, 151–53, 156, 158–60, 164–65, 167–68, 170, 172, 174, 183, 221n21, 222n27, 224n42; as failed, 151–52, 155–56, 159, 164, 219n9; and millennialism, 151–52, 155–56, 158–61, 164, 172–73, 188
Methodists, 111, 220n13
Métraux, Alfred, 128
Michlitsch, Gretchen, 136
miracles, 160, 172, 176
Mitchell, Henry, 24–25
Montero, Mayra, 74, 211n12
Morant Bay Rebellion, 159
Morrison, Toni, 3–4, 8, 14, 18–19, 23–27, 34, 44–51, 53–64, 67, 84, 95, 103, 107, 177, 181, 193, 197, 201n3, 209n34
mouth, 7, 52, 60–61, 65, 127, 132–33; teeth, 37, 39, 123, 132–33, 147; tongue, 39, 52, 76, 113, 186
Mules and Men (Hurston), 39, 46–47, 207n12, 208nn20–21
muntu, 50, 58, 69, 75, 82, 99, 209n29
Murphy, Joseph, 17, 80, 94, 142, 204n25
Murray-Román, Jeannine, 7, 138–40, 202n6
Murrell, Nathaniel Samuel, 14, 77, 81, 90, 149, 155, 166, 203n11, 205n27, 222n29
music, 84, 115, 142–44, 150; reading and, 54–56, 107–9, 112, 120; singing, 30–32, 34, 39, 41, 43–44, 56, 64, 88, 90, 92, 94, 107, 109–10, 138, 144, 150–51, 158, 161, 163, 175, 191, 194, 209n30, 218n39, 219n9; solfa-ing/solmization, 47, 109–10, 144; spirituals and spiritual-making, 31, 34, 36–38, 42, 44, 62, 94. *See also* sound

Myal, 9, 11, 14, 73, 108, 116, 120, 137, 141, 143, 145, 165–66, 168, 172; afterlife in, 141; as healing, 104, 116, 143, 172, 214n4, 222n30; as political, 166, 168
Myal (Brodber), 3, 19–20, 47, 81, 90, 101–17, 120, 122, 126–29, 132, 135, 137, 140–47, 149–50, 162, 170, 181, 195, 214–15nn6–7, 216n21
mythology, 10, 68, 116–17, 119, 169, 171, 176–77, 194; Africa as, 170, 172; Bedward as popular, 154, 161, 219n9; Hamitic, 49; historical narrative as, 164; zombie as, 103, 117, 119, 130, 204n17

National Public Radio (NPR), 67, 148
Negro: An Anthology (Cunard), 28–29, 35–36, 38, 40–41, 56, 208n18
Negro Ensemble Company, 175
New York Times, 29, 116, 175; magazine, 54
New Yorker, 188
Ngafúa, 75–79, 183
Nine-Nights, 89–90, 213n29
"nonetheless," 152–53, 156, 164, 168–69, 171, 173, 176, 179, 182–83, 187, 189
NPR (National Public Radio), 67, 148
Nwankwo, Ifeoma, 120, 129

Obama, Barack, 23
Obeah, 14, 104, 108, 117–18, 120, 125, 129, 132, 133, 137, 214n4, 215n11
O'Callaghan, Evelyn, 96, 107, 214n33, 215n8
Olaniyan, Tejumola, 184
Olmos, Margarite Fernández, 14, 117, 142, 144
Olupona, Jacob, 12, 166–67, 201n2, 204n23
"Onward Christian Soldiers," 158
opacity, 19, 63, 72, 84–86, 91–93, 95, 98, 100, 175
orichas, 67, 80–81. *See also* gods; loas
Orisha, 77
Orpana, Simon, 130
Ortíz, Fernando, 6, 202n5
Osmosis, 112, 115, 143

pain, 52, 80, 94, 100, 102, 125, 136–37, 145, 199
Panama, 155

Index 259

paratext, 70, 73, 86–87, 207n8. *See also* epigraphs; glossaries
Paravisini-Gebert, Lizabeth, 14, 117, 126, 142, 144
Paul, Apostle, 163, 165, 212n22
Pentecostalism, 63; African American and Black, 31, 151, 206n3; Holiness-Pentecostal, 30, 45
performance: African American, 31, 44, 48; Afro-diasporic, 31, 42, 53; archives and repertoire of, 6, 24, 120, 197–99; audiences of, 8–9, 33, 53–56, 61, 84, 125, 153, 163, 174, 179, 186; audiobooks and, 45, 53–57, 84; bodies and, 9, 14–15, 19, 34–35, 38–41, 43–45, 52–53, 62–63, 104, 114, 121, 138, 147, 178, 191–92, 195, 197; Caribbean, 31, 119–20, 154; codes and practices of, 8, 41, 64; collaboration in, 33, 44, 52–54, 56, 61–62, 84, 138, 163, 191, 195; community and, 17, 61, 63, 195, 198; cultural, 27, 31, 93, 111; definitions of, 6, 9, 36; as enacting or doing, 2, 7, 9, 26, 35, 52, 61, 64, 111, 149, 153, 156, 163, 166, 172, 177–78; hermeneutics and, 2–3, 5, 7, 17, 27, 46, 54, 56, 103, 116, 147, 149, 151, 153, 169, 183, 198; knowledge and methods of knowing in, 2, 14, 17, 53, 94, 115, 139; literary representations of, 6–8, 14–15, 18–21, 24, 27, 34–36, 38–39, 41, 45, 57, 89, 104, 107, 119–21, 144, 146, 169, 191, 193, 197, 202n7; oral, 18, 36, 45, 53–55, 63, 84, 106, 111–13, 164; power and, 19, 32, 40, 43, 52, 64, 103, 106–7, 142, 149, 162, 177, 195; reading and, 1–2, 6, 8, 46, 53–57, 63, 84, 110–12, 142, 144, 149, 192; relationship between textuality and, 1–2, 8, 15, 34, 36, 46, 107, 110, 120, 146–47, 151, 169, 183, 192–93; religious events as, 17, 24, 27, 30, 32, 34–35, 38–39, 41–44, 48, 62–64, 95, 152, 149, 164, 172, 177, 193, 203n15; repetition and, 7, 9, 153, 156, 163–64, 183; subjectivity, 14, 94, 113–14, 142, 194–95; theatrical, 114, 148, 153, 164, 174, 176, 179, 183, 186; transformation and, 7, 19, 30, 94, 112, 180; visual, 116, 120–21, 125, 138, 146; writing as, 29, 202n4. *See also* acting; dance; performance studies; speech; theater

performance studies, 2, 4, 6–7
performatic (Taylor), 6
performative textual hermeneutics, 2, 5–6, 8–10, 12–13, 18–21, 24–27, 30, 45, 47, 63, 67–68, 89, 103–5, 110, 114, 149, 153, 191–93, 198, 202n4
performativity, 5–7, 18, 21, 25–27, 31, 37, 40, 42–43, 45, 52–53, 55, 62–64, 103–5, 112, 114, 119, 142, 149, 178, 185, 192–93, 195, 206nn2–3
Pinn, Anthony, 14
pitch, 37, 45, 55–56, 58–59, 61, 109. *See also* music; performance; speech
Plato, 10
politics, 2–4, 11, 15–17, 20, 23, 49, 75, 84, 104, 106, 116, 122–25, 128–30, 132–35, 141, 148–49, 151–53, 155–58, 160, 162, 167–68, 176, 185, 196–97
possession, 3, 7, 9, 12, 14, 19–20, 31, 42, 66–67, 73, 76–90, 92, 94–95, 97–98, 100, 102–6, 108, 120, 127–28, 139, 142, 144–45, 147, 149, 168, 172–73, 180–83, 196–97, 209n2, 211–12nn14–16, 213n26, 223n40; and re-possession, 104, 106, 135, 142–44, 182–83; spirit, 9, 14, 67, 73, 77, 79, 81–85, 89–90, 92, 95, 104–5, 120, 147, 196; subjectivity and, 68, 76–86, 93, 94–95, 97–98, 100–102, 180, 183, 193; trance, 66–67, 73, 76–78, 90, 95, 139, 145, 173, 180, 212n14; as Vodou, 66–67, 73, 77, 80, 90, 173, 180, 182, 203n11, 204n17, 213nn31–32
prayer, 1, 8, 27–28, 32, 36–37, 42, 48, 57, 172–73, 177, 183, 195, 212n22
preaching, 3, 14, 18, 24–25, 27–28, 30, 33–53, 55–65, 147, 163, 166, 177, 209n31; calling, 42, 45–46, 50, 52–53, 57–58, 65; gender and, 47–48, 51, 59; homiletics, 24–25, 35, 45, 51–52, 57, 63, 149, 165, 207n13; liturgical, 24, 27, 32–36, 38, 40–45, 52–53, 55, 58, 61–64
prophecy, 14, 20, 76, 94, 98, 100, 147–56, 157–63, 165–81, 183–87, 189–90, 195, 221n21, 224n42; hermeneutics and, 149, 151–53, 157, 160, 166, 168–69, 171, 174–75, 177–81, 183–87, 190; impossibility and, 152–54, 156, 159, 162, 164–65, 173, 176, 178, 183, 187; messianic or millenialist, 149, 151–56, 158–61, 164–65, 167–70, 172–74,

prophecy (continued)
  183, 187–88; possession and, 149, 168, 172–73, 180–83; power and, 149–54, 156–64, 168, 170, 172, 174–77, 179, 182–84, 187–89; proliferation of, 147, 153, 184, 187
Prosser, Gabriel, 12
proverb, 119, 121, 124–25, 137
Pukumina, 89
Puri, Shalini, 104, 108
Pym, Anthony, 69–70, 89, 97, 210n7

racism, 3, 12, 16, 39, 47, 49, 58–61, 64–65, 67, 74, 76–78, 80, 99, 106, 114–16, 123, 126, 129–34, 149, 172, 151, 153–54, 180–81, 186, 196–98, 225n2. *See also* white supremacy
rage, 125, 170, 186, 188
Rappaport, Roy, 26, 64
Rastafari/Rastafarianism, 11, 14, 150–52, 154–55, 168, 170, 189, 209n27, 215n8, 218n6
recitation, 6, 112–13, 142, 144, 183
recording: machine, 83, 88, 92–93, 95–97, 213n23; oral histories, 83, 86, 90; practices, 39, 54, 78, 84
Reed, Roxanne, 47, 60
Relation (Glissant), 85, 110, 112–14, 143–44
religions, 11–14, 16, 84, 203nn15–17, 204n19; African, 44, 68, 141, 149, 165–67, 196; African American and Black, 14, 23–27, 31–32, 35–37, 42–44, 55, 57, 61–64; Afro-diasporic, 2, 9, 11–14, 16–17, 23–27, 31–32, 35–37, 42, 53, 57, 61–64, 68–69, 73, 84, 89–90, 103–5, 108, 116–17, 141–42, 144–45, 148, 151–52, 154–55, 158–59, 165–68, 195, 197–98, 204n23; Caribbean, 84, 89, 103, 105, 108, 116–17, 120, 141–42, 144–45, 150–52, 154–55, 156, 158–59, 166–68, 180, 189; politics and, 2–4, 11–12, 15, 17, 23, 74–75, 77, 148–58, 167–68, 173, 196–98, 201n2; Western and Euro-American, 12, 44, 49–50, 76, 108, 205n44. *See also* spirituality and specific religions
repetition, 7, 33–34, 38, 48, 59, 121, 153, 156, 162–64, 168, 183, 187, 191, 207n13, 222n25

re-presentation, 18, 28–29, 32, 156, 162–63, 202n4
Revival Churches, 120, 154, 159, 165–66; Revival Zion, 11, 14, 80, 108, 165, 167, 209n27, 222n30
repentance, 181–83, 224n41
resurrection, 49, 76, 80, 82, 88, 90, 95–96, 100, 141, 174, 213n29
rhythm, 1, 18, 31, 36–37, 42–43, 48, 51, 54, 56–57, 59–60, 120, 144, 147, 207n13, 208n20, 209n30
ring games, 20, 51, 104, 119, 121, 135, 137–39; Bluebird Bluebird, 138; Brown Girl in the Ring, 138; Punchinella, 138
ring shout, 50–51, 53
ritual: African and Afro-diasporic, 2, 6, 11, 26–27, 31, 42, 46, 53, 57, 90, 97, 102–3, 108, 142, 149, 154; the body and, 6, 14, 27, 31, 53, 57–58, 61–62, 77, 80, 108, 111–13, 123, 125, 127, 137, 143–45, 192; devotional, 89–90; healing, 103, 135, 143–46, 177, 149, 222n30; hermeneutics and, 5, 17, 26–27, 41, 46, 89, 97, 146–47; ideology and, 103, 111, 113, 142; knowledge and methods of knowing, 2, 4, 13, 67, 80, 90, 108, 113, 116, 125, 127, 143; participation in, 8, 25, 27, 32, 43, 61, 139, 142, 192, 203n10, 223n40; performance and, 5–7, 17, 31, 35, 56, 103, 111–13, 120, 123, 135, 139, 142, 147, 154, 180, 186; performativity and, 26, 35, 43–44, 62, 103, 177, 206n3; possession, 3, 67, 77, 90, 97, 103, 127, 222n31; preaching and, 3, 25–27, 31–32, 35, 42–44, 57, 62; reading and, 5, 8, 10, 56–58, 111–13, 146; subjectivity and, 77, 86, 113, 145; theologies and, 13–14, 53, 103, 108; of zombification, 20, 103, 125, 127, 137
Roach, Joseph, 5, 148
Roberts, June, 108, 215n7
Robinson, Douglas, 73, 76
Romero, Chanette, 11, 140
Roots: The Saga of an American Family (Haley), 66
Rubery, Matthew, 53–56
Russell, Heather, 10, 74, 80, 82, 164–65, 203n14
Ryan, Judylyn S., 11

Index   261

sacrifice, 52, 95, 101; to anticolonial project, 186; of Jesus, 30, 33–34, 207n10
Saints of God in Christ, 30
Sanctified Church, 11, 18, 27–35, 37–38, 42, 45; African possession in, 31, 42; bearing up in, 30–33, 35, 41, 191, 207n14; shouting in, 26, 31, 42–43
Sanctified Church, The (Hurston), 28, 207n15; "The Sanctified Church," 31–32, 42; "Shouting," 42–43; "Spirituals and Neo-Spirituals," 23, 31, 44, 64, 207n14, 208n21
Santería, 67, 73, 80–81, 203n14
Sartre, Jean-Paul, 133, 179–80, 185–86, 223nn38–40
Satchell, Veront, 155, 219, 220nn13–14, 220n16
Schechner, Richard, 5, 7, 10, 163
Schleiermacher, Friedrich, 70, 211n8
science: class, 112; fiction, 116, 119–20, 122, 124; methods and tenets of Western, 9, 83, 87–88, 90, 92–93, 116, 133, 172, 210n7; social, 4, 13, 83–84, 89, 91–92
Sermon in the Valley, The (Hurston), 3, 7, 24, 28–30, 32–36, 38, 41, 43–44
sermons, 7, 18, 23–44, 46–47, 49–50, 52–53, 55–59, 61–65, 95, 103, 149, 157–58, 166, 206nn4–6, 221n21; intoned, 55–56
Selassie, Rastafari Haile, I, 151, 153
serving the spirits, 129, 137, 139–40, 142
Shakespeare, William, 120, 187; *Hamlet*, 166; *Othello*, 180
Shange, Ntozake, 21, 191–93, 195–97
Sheller, Mimi, 131
Simpson, Hyacinth, 120, 122
Singh, Julietta, 185–86
skin, 118, 125–26, 132–33, 138, 140, 143; scars, 45, 52, 140
slavery, 3, 16, 45, 47–50, 52, 58–59, 102, 104–7, 114, 118, 132, 150–51, 164, 197; mental, 151, 181; Middle Passage, 16, 26; narratives of, 44, 86–87; religion and, 48–49, 105, 148, 204n22, 208n27; zombies and, 102, 104, 126
sociology, 4, 13–14, 92–93, 104, 111, 157
soul, 37, 64, 69–70, 78, 105, 108–9, 113–14, 117–18, 125–29, 131–32, 136–37, 141–42, 144, 161, 169, 178, 187–88, 208n16, 217n32

sound, 5, 9, 20, 34, 36–40, 42, 47–48, 54, 57, 59–61, 76, 89, 103–7, 111–13, 115, 122, 135, 142–46, 162, 192, 209n30, 216n17; aurality, 36, 38–39, 47, 51, 55–57, 107, 109, 144, 163; listening, 6, 28, 39, 45–46, 53–61, 64, 84, 88, 93–94, 143–46, 151, 156, 162, 174; materiality of, 20, 104–5, 107, 109–10, 143–45; and mind, 106, 160, 162; oral exposé, 109, 146; orality, 6, 38, 45, 48, 60, 107, 109, 111–13, 115–16, 120–21, 146, 148, 154, 161, 193, 205n28, 207n15, 208n24; as spirit, 105–6, 113–14, 127, 146. *See also* music; voice
sovereignty, 7, 16, 132, 185
speech, 7, 53–55, 76, 155, 174–75; acts, 25, 35, 77, 152, 162–63, 170, 172, 178, 218n7; enunciation, 111, 146–47, 149, 192; performative, 26, 40; preaching and, 37, 41–42; prophetic, 149–50, 152–53, 160–63, 170, 172, 178, 168, 218n7; recitation, 6, 112–13, 142, 144, 183. *See also* performativity
Spillers, Hortense, 25, 55, 101, 133–34
spirituality: the body and, 2, 9–10, 11, 13–15, 19, 27, 49–51, 53, 55–56, 60, 65, 80, 101, 103, 108, 115, 119, 128, 135, 144–45, 193, 196–97; community and, 17, 21, 44–46, 49, 53, 65, 74–75, 89, 95–96, 99–100, 103, 105, 121, 137, 139–42, 144, 146, 194, 197, 199; economics and, 19, 117–18, 142; epistemology and, 4–5, 9, 13, 87–88, 93, 102, 180, 197; healing and, 20, 104, 116, 135, 143, 176, 196; hermeneutics and, 2–3, 5, 7–10, 13–14, 19, 21, 46, 56, 63, 68, 89, 102, 146, 149, 177, 197, 199; literature and, 2–5, 7–8, 10–11, 14, 19, 21, 63, 68, 89, 169, 188, 192, 198; knowledge and methods of knowing, 7–9, 13, 27, 67, 80, 87–88, 90, 98, 116, 127, 143, 176–77, 192, 199; as material and physical, 2–3, 7, 10, 15, 19, 21, 51, 53, 60, 67–68, 80, 105, 112–17, 136, 142, 145–47, 158; mediation or mediumship and, 21, 73–74; performance and, 2, 5, 7–10, 19, 21, 31, 43, 46, 55–56, 89, 102–3, 144, 198; possible transcendence in, 49, 65; power and, 2–4, 12, 14, 18, 19, 24–25, 27, 43–44, 52, 63, 68, 86, 98, 104, 106–8,

spirituality (*continued*)
118, 128, 142, 150, 158, 162, 168, 172, 176–78, 188–89, 195–96, 198; reading and, 5, 8–10, 14, 55–56, 63, 192; science fiction and, 116, 124, 133; subjectivity and, 3, 7, 12, 17, 20, 51, 67, 77, 81, 93, 97, 100–101, 170, 180, 182, 192, 195; translation and, 19, 74, 88, 99; violence and, 58, 60, 103, 110, 115, 117, 119, 128, 135, 144, 196. *See also* religions

spirit thievery, 20, 47, 104–8, 111, 116, 129, 144. *See also* zombification

St. Lucia, 3, 188

stained glass, 86, 95–97, 214n34, 224n44

Stanislavski, Constantine, 180

Stewart, Dianne, 13–14, 89, 108, 137, 140, 145, 165, 203n14, 213n27, 213n30, 215n12, 216n24

subjectivity, 19, 50, 51, 63–64, 67–68, 76–83, 86, 93, 95, 98, 100–103, 113, 162, 168, 172–75, 180–81, 185, 188, 192–93, 195, 198, 209n2, 210n3; personhood, 17, 50, 79–80, 114, 140, 197; racial identity and, 17, 49, 158, 170–71, 181, 194, 201n1, 208n15

Sundquist, Eric J., 29, 38–39, 48, 206n5, 207n12, 208n17

syntax, 1, 55, 57, 144, 195, 209n34

Tar Baby (Morrison), 54

Taylor, Diana, 6

time, 3, 6, 15, 37, 57, 60, 68–69, 71, 74, 83, 85, 99, 150–51; African and Afro-diasporic notions of, 59, 69, 88–89, 153, 156, 164–69, 195; biological, 130–33; dramatic time, 9, 153, 156, 165, 170, 179, 183, 187; future, 11, 50, 69, 117, 119, 152–53, 156, 162, 165–67, 169, 172–74, 178–79, 189–90; labor, 130–31; messianic, 20, 165, 222n27; narrative structures of, 59, 71, 78, 84, 87–88, 107, 160, 167; now-time, 165, 179; past, 57, 69, 88, 90, 94, 97–99, 140, 156, 160, 165–68, 172, 176, 190, 195; present, 64, 69, 99–100, 142, 152, 160–61, 164–65, 167–68, 178, 195; prophetic, 20, 98, 152–53, 156, 158, 161, 164, 167–69, 174, 176, 178, 183, 187, 189–90; waiting, 96–98; Western notions of, 71, 90, 164, 166–67

theater: African American and Black Church as, 24–25; conventions of, 8, 10, 20, 28, 35–36, 64, 152–53, 156, 162, 164–65, 167–71, 174–76, 178–80, 186–88; historical, 20, 162, 164; legal, 161–62, 170–71, 173, 179, 187, 221n21; minstrelsy, 114–15; reviews of, 164, 167, 169, 175, 182, 186; stage directions, 32–34, 41, 174–76, 178, 183, 191, 197, 221n21. *See also* performance; *specific plays*

theology, 4, 9, 11, 13–14, 24, 30, 33, 44, 47–51, 53, 56, 58–60, 63, 70, 97, 103, 108–9, 140, 144, 148, 157–58, 164, 198; African American or Black Christian, 14, 24, 30–31, 33, 44, 49–50, 59; African and Afro-diasporic, 4, 9, 13–14, 24, 30–31, 33, 44, 49–50, 53, 59, 103, 108–9, 140–41, 144, 158, 164; Bedwardian, 158, 221n18; the body and, 14, 50–51, 58–60, 108–9; Christian, 14, 24, 30–31, 33, 44, 47–50, 58–59, 70, 97, 108, 148, 157; Womanist, 48, 49

Thigpen, Lynn, 54

Thompson, Robert Farris, 127

Ti-Jean and His Brothers (Walcott), 119, 121–22, 125, 136

Tittler, Jonathan, 19, 71–76, 81–82, 85, 91, 98, 210n5, 211nn8–9, 211n12

transcendence, 44, 49, 51, 64–65, 100, 136–37, 146

transformation, 2, 7, 19–20, 26–27, 29, 35, 39, 42, 45, 48, 55–56, 69, 74, 80, 86, 94, 97, 99–100, 105, 107, 112, 132, 137, 139, 141–42, 145, 177, 184, 189, 192

translation, 10, 19, 48, 63, 66, 68–78, 81–84, 88–89, 91, 99, 149, 164, 179, 193–94, 210n5; back-translation, 73, 81; cultural, 69, 84, 88–89, 91; as death, 88–89, 100; across genre and modality, 18, 193; intersemiotic, 69, 109; resistant, 71–72, 75, 84–85, 91

trauma, 11, 17, 94, 103, 119, 138, 140, 197

tribes, 184; African, 50, 68–69, 104; Akan, 64; Congo, 42, 68, 69; Dahomey, 104; twelve of Israel, 215; Yoruba, 10, 14, 68–69, 127, 140–41, 197, 213n29

trickster, 119, 121–22, 139, 154; Elegba as, 81; narrative, 117, 122

Trinidad, 216n27; Creole of, 120; folktales of, 119; Theatre Workshop, 218n3
Turner, Victor, 25, 181, 206n3, 218n38

United Kingdom, 188. *See also* British empire
United States, 3, 11–12, 73, 75, 83–85, 89–90, 92, 104, 155, 216n27, 220n16; audiences in, 61, 67, 84, 87, 100, 186, 188; Brooklyn, 95; Chicago, 83, 89; Cincinnati, 45; Cleveland, 28–29; empire, 107; Florida, 18, 28, 39; Harlem, 82, 169, 182; Louisiana, 83–84, 90–93, 194; midwestern, 205n31; New Orleans, 84, 97, 194, 207n14; religion in, 14, 23–25, 31–32, 44–45, 48–49, 55, 61, 69, 80, 151, 204n26, 218n4; scholarship in, 11, 26, 91, 165, 205n28; southern, 37, 39, 89, 92, 205n31; violence towards African Americans in, 49, 59–60, 76, 87, 114, 126, 130

Valkeakari, Tuire, 7, 11, 39, 45, 48, 51, 208n19
Venuti, Lawrence, 71, 91
violation, 20, 102, 108, 114–17, 125–27, 130, 138, 140, 143–45, 196, 217n31, 225n2
violence, 9, 11, 12, 60–61, 103, 115–16, 119, 124–25, 127, 133–34, 140, 143, 145, 160, 170, 173, 175, 180, 184–86; domestic, 65, 139; as physical, mental, and spiritual, 103, 108, 110, 112, 115, 135, 151, 170, 187–88, 196
vision: agency and, 125, 128–29, 131–32, 138–40; blindness, 128; community and, 137–38, 193; invisibility, 89, 124, 127–28, 131–32, 193; knowledge and, 94, 96–98, 110, 123, 127, 129, 137, 176, 184; performance and, 5, 104, 116, 120–21, 123, 128, 135, 138, 146, 153, 174, 176, 183, 186, 193; power and, 20, 47, 104, 116–17, 119, 123–25, 127–32, 134, 138–40, 147, 176–77, 186; prophecy and, 20, 122, 148–49, 152, 155–56, 158, 161–63, 165, 169–70, 172, 177–78, 182–84, 187, 222n30; regimes of, 123–28, 130–32, 134, 138, 208n15; relationship between sound and, 34, 36, 38–39, 66, 109–10, 120, 207n15; spiritual, 94, 117–18, 122–23, 127–29, 135, 137, 139–40, 148–49, 155, 162–63, 165, 172, 175–76, 182–83, 217
Vodou, 9, 11, 12, 14, 53, 66–67, 69, 73, 77, 80–81, 90, 105, 141, 173, 180, 182, 203n11; loas in, 81, 172, 182; mythology of, 103, 117, 130, 201n2
voice, 20, 42–43, 45, 51, 54–56, 58, 75–76, 78, 85, 87–89, 92–94, 97, 100, 104–7, 110–15, 143, 145–46, 162, 173–74, 191
vulnerability, 9, 40, 44, 51, 101, 125, 133, 136, 138, 143, 146

Walcott, Derek, 3, 14, 20, 119–23, 125, 136, 141, 147, 149–54, 168–72, 174–89, 205n31, 224–25nn45–46, 225n49
Walker, David, 12
Wall, Cheryl, 36
Wallace, Anthony F. C., 177, 223n35
Warner-Lewis, Maureen, 14, 214n5
Weber, Max, 157–58, 176, 204n19, 221n19, 223n34
Weems, Renita, 48
Weheliye, Alexander, 4, 82, 133–34, 201n3, 222n27
West, Cornel, 148, 218n1, 218n4
"What the Twilight Says" (Walcott), 172, 187–89, 205n31
"White Man's Burden" (Kipling), 111
white supremacy, 4, 12, 49, 134, 151, 164, 181, 198, 201n1; White Wolf, 99. *See also* colonialism; racism
Whitted, Qiana, 11
Wilentz, Gay, 205n31
Williams, Delores, 48
Woodard, Alfre, 54
Woods, Harrison, "Shakespeare," 155, 220n16, 221n21
Works Project Administration (WPA), 83, 88, 94
"Wounds of Jesus, The" (Lovelace and Hurston), 24, 26, 28–30, 34–40, 43–44, 46, 51–52, 56
Wynter, Sylvia, 81–82, 129, 131, 133–34, 219n10

Zahan, Dominique, 167
Zauditu-Selassie, K., 50, 59
Zapata Olivella, Manuel, 3–4, 14, 19, 50, 63, 67–77, 81–82, 85, 87–88,

Zapata Olivella, Manuel (*continued*) 98–99, 103, 140, 172, 193, 197, 210n5, 211n12

Žižek, Slavoj, 131

zombie, 101–4, 111, 115–19, 121, 125, 127–33, 135, 140, 144–45, 214n2; as disembodied docile body, 118, 126, 128–29; and economies, 116, 118–19, 121, 133; as flesh object, 117–18, 126, 129, 132; imaginary, 130

zombification, 12, 14, 19–20, 102–7, 115, 117–19, 121, 125–29, 135, 138, 145–46, 204n17, 216n26, 217n32. *See also* spirit thievery

Recent books in the series
New World Studies

The Sacred Act of Reading: Spirituality, Performance, and Power in Afro-Diasporic Literature
Anne Margaret Castro

Caribbean Jewish Crossings: Literary History and Creative Practice
Sarah Phillips Casteel and Heidi Kaufman, editors

Mapping Hispaniola: Third Space in Dominican and Haitian Literature
Megan Jeanette Myers

Mourning El Dorado: Literature and Extractivism in the Contemporary American Tropics
Charlotte Rogers

Edwidge Danticat: The Haitian Diasporic Imaginary
Nadège T. Clitandre

Idle Talk, Deadly Talk: The Uses of Gossip in Caribbean Literature
Ana Rodríguez Navas

Crossing the Line: Early Creole Novels and Anglophone Caribbean Culture in the Age of Emancipation
Candace Ward

Staging Creolization: Women's Theater and Performance from the French Caribbean
Emily Sahakian

American Imperialism's Undead: The Occupation of Haiti and the Rise of Caribbean Anticolonialism
Raphael Dalleo

A Cultural History of Underdevelopment: Latin America in the U.S. Imagination
John Patrick Leary

The Spectre of Races: Latin American Anthropology and Literature between the Wars
Anke Birkenmaier

www.ingramcontent.com/pod-product-compliance
Lightning Source LLC
Chambersburg PA
CBHW021350300426
44114CB00012B/1153